The First European Description of Japan, 1585

In 1585, at the height of Jesuit missionary activity in Japan, which was begun by Francis Xavier in 1549, Luis Frois, a long-time missionary in Japan, drafted the earliest systematic comparison of Western and Japanese cultures. This book constitutes the first critical English-language edition of the 1585 work, the original of which was discovered in the Royal Academy of History in Madrid after the Second World War. The book provides a translation of the text, which is not a continuous narrative, but rather more than 600 distichs or brief couplets on subjects such as gender, child rearing, religion, medicine, eating, horses, writing, ships and seafaring, architecture, and music and drama. In addition, the book includes a substantive introduction and other editorial material to explain the background and also to make comparisons with present-day Japanese life. Overall, the book represents an important primary source for understanding a particularly challenging period of history and its connection to contemporary Europe and Japan.

Luis Frois S.J. was a long-time Jesuit missionary in Japan in the later years of the sixteenth century.

Daniel T. Reff is an anthropologist and Professor in the Department of Comparative Studies in the Humanities, The Ohio State University, USA.

Richard K. Danford is an Associate Professor of Spanish and Portuguese and Vice-President for Diversity and Inclusion at Marietta College, Ohio, USA.

Robin D. Gill is a translator, author and editor, Key Biscayne, Florida, USA.

Japan Anthropology Workshop Series

A Japanese View of Nature
The world of living things by
Kinji Imanishi
Translated by *Pamela J Asquith,*
Heita Kawakatsu, Shusuke Yagi and
Hiroyuki Takasaki
Edited and introduced by *Pamela J Asquith*

Japan's Changing Generations
Are young people creating a new society?
Edited by *Gordon Mathews* and
Bruce White

The Care of the Elderly in Japan
Yongmei Wu

Community Volunteers in Japan
Everyday stories of social change
Lynne Y. Nakano

**Nature, Ritual and Society in Japan's
Ryukyu Islands**
Arne Røkkum

Psychotherapy and Religion in Japan
The japanese introspection practice
of naikan
Chikako Ozawa-de Silva

Dismantling the East-West Dichotomy
Essays in honour of jan van bremen
Edited by *Joy Hendry* and
Heung Wah Wong

**Pilgrimages and Spiritual Quests
in Japan**
Edited by *Maria Rodriguez del Alisal,*
Peter Ackermann and *Dolores Martinez*

The Culture of Copying in Japan
Critical and historical perspectives
Edited by *Rupert Cox*

Primary School in Japan
Self, individuality and learning in
elementary education
Peter Cave

**Globalisation and Japanese
Organisational Culture**
An ethnography of a Japanese Corporation
in France
Mitchell W. Sedgwick

Japanese Tourism and Travel Culture
Edited by *Sylvie Guichard-Anguis* and
Okpyo Moon

Making Japanese Heritage
Edited by *Christoph Brumann* and
Robert A. Cox

**Japanese Women, Class and the
Tea Ceremony**
The voices of tea practitioners in
northern Japan
Kaeko Chiba

The First European Description of Japan, 1585

A critical English-language edition of
Striking Contrasts in the Customs of Europe and Japan by Luis Frois, S.J.

Translated from the Portuguese original and
edited and annotated by
**Richard K. Danford, Robin D. Gill, and
Daniel T. Reff**

With a critical introduction by
Daniel T. Reff

Routledge
Taylor & Francis Group

LONDON AND NEW YORK

First published 2014
by Routledge
2 Park Square, Milton Park, Abingdon, Oxon, OX14 4RN

and by Routledge
711 Third Avenue, New York, NY 10017

Routledge is an imprint of the Taylor & Francis Group, an informa business

British Library Cataloguing in Publication Data
A catalogue record for this book is available from the British Library

Library of Congress Cataloging-in-Publication Data
Fróis, Luís, -1597.
[Tratado em que se contêm muito susinta- e abreviadamente algumas contradições e diferenças de custumes entre a gente de Europa e esta província de Japão. English]
The first European description of Japan, 1585: a critical English-language edition of striking contrasts in the customs of Europe and Japan by Luis Frois, S.J. / translated from the Portuguese original and edited and annotated by Richard K. Danford, Robin D. Gill, and Daniel T. Reff; with a critical introduction by Daniel T. Reff.
pages cm. —(Japan anthropology workshop series; 25)
Includes bibliographical references and index.
1. Japan—Civilization—1568–1600—Early works to 1800. 2. Japan—Social life and customs—1185–1600—Early works to 1800. 3. Japan—Description and travel—Early works to 1800. 4. Europe—Civilization—16th century—Early works to 1800. 5. Europe—Social life and customs—16th century—Early works to 1800. I. Danford, Richard K., 1964- , editor, translator. II. Gill, Robin, 1951- , editor, translator. III. Reff, Daniel T., 1949- , editor, translator. IV. Title.
DS822.2.F6613 2014
952'.024—dc23
2013034113

ISBN: 978-0-415-72757-0 (hbk)
ISBN: 978-1-315-85214-0 (ebk)

Typeset in Times New Roman PS
by diacriTech, Chennai

Table of contents

Figures and maps

Preface

Joy Hendry

I am delighted to introduce this new book to our series. It is quite unlike anything we have done before, and has many exciting features. It does start out as a translation, and we had one before, but this one is from Portuguese to English, rather than from Japanese to English. As it happens, we are quite late in the game for it has already been a popular book in its Japanese language translation, and has appeared in German, Chinese, French, Spanish, and modern Portuguese as well. It is, as the title would suggest, an early account of Japan, penned in a comparative fashion by a Jesuit missionary from Portugal, but this book is not just a translation of the original text; it comes with a great deal of value added by its three highly qualified editors, and makes a special contribution to the Japan Anthropology Workshop series for several reasons.

First, the original text represents a kind of early forerunner to the anthropological studies that we usually publish in the series. Written in couplets comparing Japan and Europe, the style may be very different, but the observations are based on first-hand experience gathered during a long stay, in this case of more than twenty years, and with a deep knowledge of the language, and the ways of thinking and behaviour of the people. It thus builds on a root understanding common with the anthropology of today. It also has an amazingly anachronistic ability to consider the Japanese as equally "civilized", if not more so, than Europeans, and thus achieves an even approach still being sought by some anthropologists.

Secondly, the couplets themselves are presented with an immediate historical context, explaining both the reasons why certain aspects of the comparisons were chosen from a sixteenth-century European perspective, as well as how Japanese customs have changed since that time. Our editors comprise a team of scholars with different skills: Danford to translate from Portuguese into English; Gill, who like Frois, lived in Japan for some twenty-odd years, adding a contemporary commentary based on a similarly deep experience, though separated by more than four centuries; and Reff, who supplies the scholarship on the Jesuits of "early modern Europe".

Daniel Reff has also written a very helpful introduction to the "tratado" or main body of the text, which assesses the aim of Frois's writing, probably meant to help newly-arrived Jesuit missionaries to settle in. His superior, Valignano, was determined to convince Europeans that Japanese were "civilized" enough to become clergy themselves, and thus take over judicial control of the Church in Japan. He realised that neither Spain nor Portugal would ever be in a position to successfully invade Japan (and China) and overpower the indigenous elite, so learning the language and local customs was essential. He also took four Japanese teenagers to Rome, partly to convince them that Europeans were not barbarians either, but still he asked his missionaries to live like Japanese in Japan.

In his introduction to the text, Frois wrote:

> Many of their customs are so distant, foreign, and far removed from our own that it is difficult to believe that one can find such stark contrasts in customs among people who are so civilized, have such lively genius, and are as naturally intelligent as these [Japanese].

This book demonstrates that some of these stark contrasts have been amazingly persistent on both sides of the world despite a growing knowledge about each other's ways. Would that a few more of the Europeans who set out to study around the world could be as accepting of such continuing difference as a couple of priests committed to conversion in the sixteenth century!

Acknowledgments

Over the years, a number of people read drafts, fielded questions, or otherwise helped with the realization of this book. We especially want to thank Nina Berman, Serena Connolly, Liza Dalby, Frank Dutra, Nancy Ettlinger, Prudence Gill, Hanna Gotz, Joy Hendry, Natsumi Hirota, Suzanne Inamura, Eric Johnson, Karen Kupperman, Sarah Kernan, Donald Larsen, Mary McCarthy, Sabine McCormack, Catarina Marot Mendez, Wamae Muriuki, Hirochika Nakamaki, Shelley Fenno Quinn, Kristina Troost, Tenki-san, and Julia Watson.

We also appreciate the support of the College of Arts and Humanities at The Ohio State University and the National Endowment for the Humanities (Daniel Reff), Marietta College (Richard Danford), and the Grapetree Productions Fellowship (Robin D. Gill).

Thanks also to Jeff La Frenierre for compiling our maps.

Critical introduction

The *Tratado*, the Jesuits, and the governance of souls

Daniel T. Reff

Introduction

Nobody seems to want to go to prison and yet it has provided a surprising number of people with the opportunity and some might say inspiration for some of the most moving literature that the world has ever known. Consider the *Travels of Marco Polo*, which was committed to paper in 1298, while Polo was in a Genoese prison. The *Travels* encouraged generations of Europeans to dream of far-away lands abounding in fabulous riches that were strange and exotic—where men might have long tails and heads like dogs.[1] Although Polo wrote at considerable length of China (Cathay), what particularly fired the imaginations of Europeans were his brief comments about an island to the east of China called Cipangu. According to Polo it was inhabited by a good-looking people with fair complexions and good manners who were awash in gold, fine pearls, and precious stones.[2]

Little more was heard of Cipangu until 1549, when Francis Xavier initiated a sustained Jesuit commentary on what was now referred to as *Japão*.[3] The Japan that Portuguese sailors and Jesuits "discovered" in the 1540s was a society in the throes of profound changes, including a rapidly expanding and highly mobile population, increased urbanism and trade, and political instability, evidenced by frequent wars between aspiring members of a feudal warrior class, the *bushi* or samurai. In Japan, as in Europe, a religious elite wielded

1 Syed Manzurul Islam, *The Ethics of Travel, From Marco Polo to Kafka* (Manchester: Manchester University Press, 1996), 120, 143; Geraldine Heng, *Empire of Magic* (New York: Columbia University Press, 2003).

2 *The Travels of Marco Polo* (New York: The Orion Press, 1958), 281, 262–266.

3 Two of Xavier's letters from 1549 can be found in a two-volume compendium of Jesuit correspondence first published in 1598 and recently re-published in a facsimile edition by José Manuel Garcia, *Cartas que os Padres e Irmãos da Companhia de Iesus Escreuerão dos Reynos de Iapão & China aos da Mesma Companhia da India & Europa, des do Anno de 1549 Até o de 1580*. 2 Vols. (Maia: Castoliva Editora, 1997), I, 7–16; Donald F. Lach, *Asia in the Making of Europe*, Volume I, Book 2 (University of Chicago Press, 1965), 651–729.

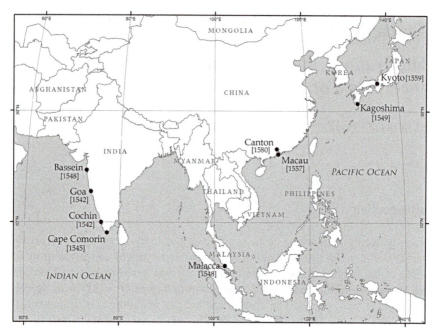

Map 1. Jesuit Missionary Activity in Asia to 1585

considerable power, including fielding armies of Buddhist monks who sought to protect and expand the interests of particular temples and sects.[4]

When Portuguese traders and the Jesuits happened on the south coast of Japan,[5] both were embraced by a small number of Japanese lords or *daimyo* who sought to use Christianity and Western goods, including firearms, to advance their political interests. Between 1549 and 1585, a relatively small number of Jesuit missionaries,[6] beginning with Francis Xavier, used this window of opportunity to establish some 200 churches with upwards of 150,000 Japanese converts, principally on the southern-most island of Kyûshû.[7]

---

4 Neil McMulin, *Buddhism and the State in Sixteenth-Century Japan* (Princeton: Princeton University Press, 1984); William W. Farris, *Japan's Medieval Population: Famine, Fertility, and Warfare in a Transformative Age* (Honolulu: University of Hawai'i Press, 2006).

5 Japanese sources indicate the first Europeans to reach Japan were Portuguese merchants who were "cast ashore" in 1541. Shin'ichi Tani, "East Asia and Europe." In *Namban Art, A Loan Exhibition from Japanese Collections*. International Exhibitions Foundation., eds. Shin'ichi Tania and Sugase Tadashi13–18 (New York: International Exhibitions Foundation, 1973), 13.

6 As late as 1577 there were only eighteen Jesuits in all of Japan. The number jumped to fifty-five in 1579, and eighty-two in 1583. *Cartas . . . de Iapáo & China*, I,432, II, 89.

7 See Ross, *A Vision Betrayed*; J.F. Moran, *The Japanese and the Jesuits* (London: Routledge, 1993); Donald F. Lach, *Asia in the Making of Europe*, Volume I, Book 2 (University of Chicago Press, 1965), 651–706. C.R. Boxer, *The Christian Century in Japan 1549–1650* (Berkeley: University of California Press, 1951); George Elison, *Deus Destroyed: The Image of Christianity in Early Modern Japan* (Cambridge: Harvard University Press, 1973); Josef F. Schütte, *Valignano's Mission*

In 1585, at the very height of Jesuit success, a twenty-year veteran of the Jesuit mission to Japan, Luis Frois (1532–1597), drafted the earliest systematic comparison of Western and Asian cultures.[8] Frois' comparative study apparently was not conceived as a book to be published. The manuscript, which is thirty-three folios, with text front and back, was written in Portuguese and has no title *per se*. Just below "Jesus [and] Mary"—a dedication at the top of the first page—the first line of the manuscript reads tratado em que se contem muito susinta e abreviadamente algumas contradisões e diferenças de custumes antre a gente de Europa e esta provincia de Japaõ (see Figure 1). The same line in English reads: treatise containing in very succinct and abbreviated form some contrasts and differences in the customs of the people of Europe and this province of Japan. The bottom half of the title page and page two of the Tratado list fourteen chapters on subjects as varied as gender, child rearing, religion, medicine, eating, horses, writing, ships and seafaring, architecture, and music and drama. Interestingly, whereas most Jesuit missionary texts from the period are dramatic narratives (i.e. epistles/letters, histories, dialogues) intended for the public as well as a Jesuit audience, the *Tratado* is a catalogue of over 600 numbered distichs or brief couplets, again divided among fourteen chapters. The following distich is from Chapter 9 (Figure 2), which is titled "Physicians, Medicines and Mode of Healing:"

11. Among us, abscesses are treated using intense heat; the Japanese would rather die than use our harsh surgical methods.

Here Frois sought to convey to fellow Europeans (implied by "us" and "our") how the Japanese perceived Western medical practices as harsh or invasive. Similarly, in the following distich from Chapter 2, which is entitled "Women, Their Persons and Dress," Frois rather dispassionately described the Japanese attitude toward female chastity:

1. In Europe a young woman's supreme honor and treasure is her chastity and the inviolate cloister of her purity; women in Japan pay no mind to virginal purity, nor does a loss of virginity deprive them of honor or matrimony.

As detailed below, we believe Frois and his Jesuit superior, Alessandro Valignano, drafted the *Tratado* as a pedagogical tool to explain Japanese customs to European Jesuits recently arrived in Japan. Quite unlike Marco Polo or other would-be ethnologists (e.g. Mandeville, Isidore of Seville, Pliny, Herodotus),

Principles for Japan, 1573–1582, Parts I and II (St. Louis: The Institute of Jesuit Sources, 1980, 1985); Jacques Proust, *Europe Through the Prism of Japan* (Notre Dame: Notre Dame Press, 2002); Dauril Alden, *The Making of an Enterprise, The Society of Jesus in Portugal, Its Empire, and Beyond 1540–1750* (Stanford: Stanford University Press, 1996); Samuel H. Moffett, *A History of Christianity In Asia, Volume II, 1500–1900* (Maryknoll, N.Y.: Orbis Books, 2005), 68–105; Ana Fernandes Pinto, "Bibliography of Luso-Japanese Studies." *Bulletin of Portuguese/Japanese Studies* 3(2001):129–152.
8 For a discussion of early commentators on Japan see See Rui Manuel Loureiro, "Jesuit Textual Strategies in Japan Between 1549 and 1582." *Bulletin of Portuguese/Japanese Studies* (2004) 8:39–631; Lach, *Asia in the Making*, I, Bk 2, 651–689.

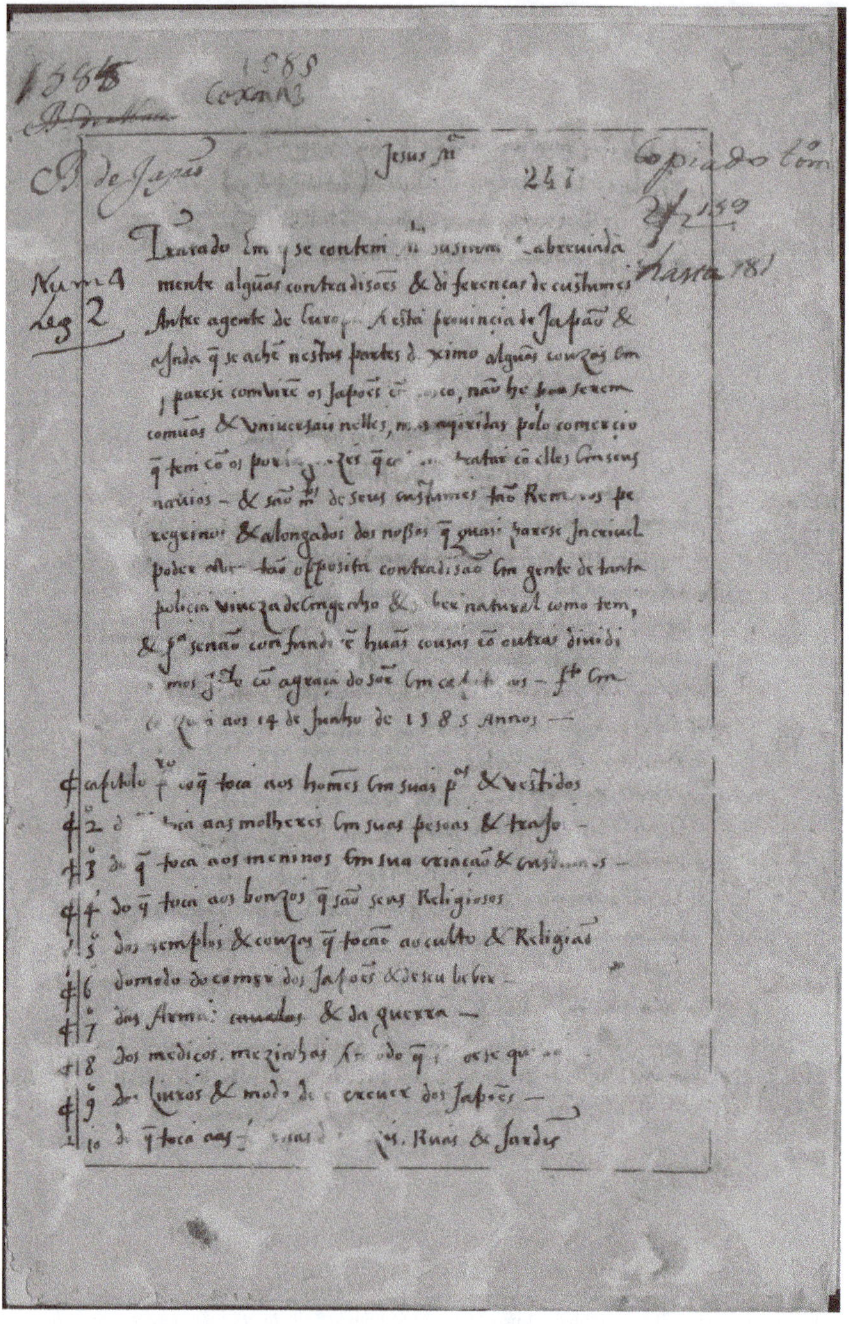

Figure 1. Photocopy of Title Page of Tratado

267

capitolo nono Das Doenças Medicos
& mezinhas —

1. ¶ Antre nos Alpores – dor de pedra – polagra & peste he cousa sogeite
, das estas Doenças em Japão são Raras –

2. ¶ nos vzamos d sangrias – os Japões de botoes de fugo cõ eruas

3. ¶ os homes ... antre nos se custumaõ ordinariamete sagrar nos braços
os Japões cõ sanbinagas – ou c.ª jaca na testa – saos canales cõ lanceta

4. ¶ nos vzamos de cristeis ou sixir ... elles p.ª nenhũ cazo vzaõ deste Remedio
Antre nos Receitão os Medicos f.ª os boticas –
Medicos de Japão mandaõ os mezinhas de sua caza

6. ¶ os n. Bos Medicos tumaõ o pulso a homes Amolheres p.ª no braço de depois no siquerdo
... poes aos homes p.ª no esquerdo & aas molheres p.ª no derceito –

¶ s noßos medicos vē os ourines p.ª terē mais noticia da sua midade
os Ja ... es por nenhũ cazo as vem —

8. ¶ A carne ... a dos de Curo p.ª p.ª ser dilicada vai sarando m̃ de vagar
A dos Japões p.ª ser Robusta de graues feridas gebraduras postemas &
o ... stres saraõ m̃ milhor & mais depresa —

9. ¶ Antre nos se coze os feridas – os Japões llrfpoẽ hũ pouco de papel axulado

10. ¶ toda agura ... fazemos cõ panos – faze os Japões cõ papeis –

11. ¶ Antre nos queimaõ se as ... & mas cõ fugo –
os Japões antre... ... seraõ q̃ vzaõ dos noßos Remedios asperos da suxugre

12. ¶ Aos noßos doentes se he sustio trabalhage co elles p.ª q̃ comaõ por força –
os Japões otem por cruega & seo... sente tem fo.ª o deixauõ asi morer

13. ¶ os Noßos doentes estaõ em catres ou leitos cõ lensoes colchoes & tranuesseiros
os Japões sobre hũa esteira no chão cõ hũa maquera de pau ... seu queimaõ Cm Riba

14. ¶ Em Curopa se tem os galinhas & frangãos por mezinha p.ª os doentes
os Japões tē ßt por pesonha ... mandaõ lhr lanpexe & Rataõ salgado

... nos tiramos os dentes cõ bot.... al...as ... co bigo de papagayo &
os Japões cõ escopro de ma ... te ou cõ aro... &... atuda no dente ou c....
troxes de ferreiro —

including contemporary and fellow Jesuit, José de Acosta,[9] Frois based his comparative study almost entirely on first-hand observation. Moreover, rather that relegate Japanese difference, excepting perhaps Buddhism, to *Homo monstrum* or the work of the devil, Frois attributed it to rationally-based choice.[10] As suggested, this understanding that civilized and European were *not* necessarily the same thing undoubtedly sprang in significant part from Frois' many years study-ing the Japanese language and his more than twenty years residence in Japan.[11] Paradoxically, Frois' generosity—the many instances where he states or implies that Japanese customs were on a par or even superior to European practices—remains problematic, inasmuch as it is Frois, the European (not the Japanese), who judges, makes distinctions, categorizes, and pronounces.[12] Moreover, for all his respect, neither Frois nor his fellow Jesuits recanted their "mission from god," even when it led—as it often did—to the razing and burning of temples and the upending of many thousands of Japanese lives.[13]

Luis Frois: jesuit missionary and author

The *Tratado* was discovered after World War II by Josef Franz Schütte, S.J., in the *Real Academia de la Historia*, in Madrid, Spain.[14] In 1955, Sophia University published a German-language edition of the manuscript, edited and translated by Schütte.[15] The edition also contains a transcription of the original Portuguese, which has been used by scholars to generate editions in Japanese, Chinese, French, Spanish, and modern Portuguese. Somewhat surprisingly, this is the first critical, English-language edition of the *Tratado*.

Although the *Tratado* is not signed and lacks other direct evidence of author-ship, scholars universally have followed Schütte in attributing the manuscript to

9 Acosta's *Natural and Moral History of the Indies* (1590) was based largely on what others had observed and reported, and quite unlike Frois, Acosta emphasized satanic deception as much as reason or free will when reflecting on the customs of Amerindians such as the Mexica or Inca.

10 For the medieval traditions of travel writing and the earliest forms of ethnology, see Margaret Hogden, *Early Anthropology in the Sixteenth and Seventeenth Centuries* (Philadelphia: University of Pennsylvania Press, 1964); Islam, *The Ethics of Travel; Heng, Empire of Magic*; Stephen Greenblatt, *Marvelous Possessions The Wonder of the New World* (Chicago: University Of Chicago Press, 1991).

11 Thus Frois' rhetoric amounted to more than a "theoretical curiosity." Greenblatt, *Marvelous Possessions*, 45–46.

12 Heng, *Empire of Magic*, 250–51. For a discussion of the contingencies that governed Jesuit missionary perceptions and representations of "others" see Daniel T. Reff, "Critical Introduction." In *History of the Triumphs of Our Holy Faith Amongst the Most Fierce and Barbarous Peoples of the New World*, by Andrès Pérez de Ribas, 11–46, eds. D.T. Reff, M. Ahern, and R. Danford (Tucson: University of Arizona Press, 1999).

13 To give but one example, the *anua* for the year 1582 recounts how the Jesuits' long-time friend and recent convert, the *daimyo* Ōtomo Yoshishige, invaded nearby Chikuzen, destroying Buddhist temples and the homes of three thousand Buddhist monks. *Cartas . . . de Iapáo & China*, II, 25.

14 *Real Acadêmia de la História* (Jesuitas 11–10–3/21), Madrid, Spain.

15 Josef Franz Schütte, S.J., *Kulturgensäte Europa-Japan (1585)* (Tokyo: Sophia University, 1955).

Luis Frois.[16] There are striking, substantive similarities between the *Tratado* and a table of contents for an otherwise missing Part I of Frois' *Historia de Japam*,[17] which was written around the same time as the *Tratado*. Moreover, Frois was perhaps the only Jesuit who had the knowledge of Japanese language and culture that is evident in the *Tratado*.[18] This knowledge, and Frois' substantial respect for Japanese customs, is apparent in the letters Frois wrote during the years preceding the drafting of the *Tratado*.[19]

Frois was born in Lisbon in 1532 and was given the name Polycarp at birth. Not much is known about Frois, although it is apparent that he was born into a mercantile or otherwise affluent family that could provide him with a quality education. In practical terms this meant learning to read and write in Portuguese and Latin.[20] This education made possible at age thirteen Frois' employment as an apprentice scribe in the Royal Secretariat in Lisbon. Although by 1545 rag paper and the printing press had ushered in a communication revolution, the functioning of government and society, more generally, still hinged on scribes who drew up all manner of decrees, contracts, legal decisions, exams, licenses, etc. Scribes essentially operationalized the wishes of the rich and powerful; they were accordingly respected and well paid.

During Frois' childhood, his city of birth, Lisbon, was the hub of Portugal's far-flung empire—an empire secured financially in 1498 when Vasco de Gama stunned the Western world by reaching India and establishing a sea route to Far Eastern

---

16 Englebert Jorißen, "Exotic and 'Strange' Images of Japan in European Texts of the Early 17th Century." *Bulletin of Portuguese Japanese Studies* 4 (2002): 37–61; *Das Japanbild im "Traktat" (1585) des Luis Frois* (Munchen: Aschendorffsche Verlagsbuchhandlung Gmbh & Co., 1998).

17 Frois' history was not published until the twentieth century, and by then, Part I of the monumental work had been lost. The extant table of contents for the missing volume has chapter titles that are very similar to those in the *Tratado*. See Luís, Fróis, S.J. *Historia de Japam*, ed. Jose Wicki, S.J. 5 vols. (Lisbon: Biblioteca Nacional de Lisboa, 1976[1597]), 11–12.

18 Were it not for the fact that João Rodrigues only had been in Japan a relatively short time, one might suspect him to be the author of the *Tratado*. Rodrigues "the interpreter" would go on to demonstrate a marvelous knack for languages and a profound understanding of Japanese culture. He authored *Arte da Lingoa de Japam* (1604) and a later (1620) abridged edition (*Arte Breve da Lingoa Iapoa*). He was no doubt also the chief contributor to the anonymous ("compiled by some fathers and brothers…") *Vocabulario da Lingoa de Iapam* (1603). Toward the end of his life, Rodrigues authored a history of the Church in Japan. See Michael Cooper, ed. and trans., *This Island of Japon*. Tokyo: Kodansha International Limited.

19 Several dozen of Frois' letters can be found in *Cartas . . . de Iapão & China*. See also Joseph Wicki, S.J.,ed., *Documenta Indica IV (1557–1560)* (Rome: Monumenta Historica Soc. Iesu., 1956), 269–305, 643–694; For a list of Frois' letters see *Cartas . . . de Iapão & China*, I, 30–31; G. Schurhammer and E.A. Voretzsch, *Die Geschichte Japans (1549–1578) von P. Luis Frois, S.J.* (Leipzig: Verlag der Asia Major, 1926), xxviii–xxiii. For an English-language example of one of Frois' letters from 1565, see Peter C. Mancall, ed., *Travel Narratives from the Age of Discovery, An Anthology* (Oxford: Oxford University Press, 2006), 156–165.

20 While Latin remained the official language of the Church, during the thirteenth century the Portuguese crown made Portuguese the exclusive language of secular government. A.R. Disney, *A History of Portugal and the Portuguese Empire* (Cambridge" Cambridge University Press, 2009), 95.

markets.[21] For the next sixty years or so Portugal enjoyed a near-monopoly on the importation of pepper and other expensive spices.[22] Frois as a child would have watched ships from Asia, Africa and America arrive in Lisbon harbor—unloading slaves, precious spices, gold, and all manner of exotic plants and animals.[23] (In 1515, King Manuel I staged a fight between an elephant and a rhinoceros for the amusement of the queen!)[24] And then there were the parades of new found peoples from places such as Africa, Brazil, and India.

In 1540, King John III of Portugal invited a new religious order, the Society of Jesus, to Lisbon. The Jesuits (Francis Xavier and Simon Rodriguez) began a mission at All-Saints Hospital and quickly won popular acclaim for their work with the city's poor and infirm.[25] The young Polycarp apparently was among those impressed by the black robes, for Frois rather suddenly—at age sixteen—abandoned his career as a scribe and entered the Society of Jesus, taking as his new first name, Luis. Within a month, during the spring of 1548, Frois left home forever, sailing from Lisbon down the west coast of Africa, around the horn of Africa, and then on to India.[26]

Frois undertook a two-year novitiate in Goa at the recently-founded Jesuit College of Saint Paul. Goa already had a reputation as a colonial paradise, seemingly celebrated by Camões in his 1572 epic poem *Os Luisadas*.[27] Frois, however, was destined for the priesthood and followed his novitiate with a "tertiary" year, during which he essentially demonstrated he had internalized a Jesuit identity. The

21 Luís Adão de Fonseca. *Vasco de Gama; o homem, a viagem, a Epoca* (Lisbon: Comissáo de Coordenacáo da Regiáo Alentejo, 1997); Damiáo de. Góis, *Lisbon in the Renaissance* [Urbis Olisiponis Descriptio], trans. Jeffrey S. Ruth (Ithaca, N.Y.: Ithaca Press, 1996[1554]).

22 Vitorino M. Godinho, *Os Descobrimentos E A Economia Mundial.* 2 Vols. (Lisbon: Editora Arcádia, 1965), 173–262.

23 José Sebastião da Silva Dias, *Os descobrimentos e a problematica cultural do século XVI* (Coimbra: University of Coimbra, 1973), 6.

24 After the fight, which never really materialized as the elephant fled, King Manuel sent the rhinoceros to Rome as a gift for Pope Leo X; the rhino died en route but descriptions of it found their way to Dürer, who turned them into his perhaps most famous engraving. Felipe Veiera de Castro, *The Pepper Wreck* (College Station: Texas A&M Press, 2005), 11; David Johnston, trans., *The Boat Plays by Gil Vicente* (1997), 8.

25 See Damião de Góis, *Lisbon in the Renaissance*, 265–26; Nigel Griffin, "Italy, Portugal, and the Early Years of the Society of Jesus." In *Portuguese, Brazilian, and African Studies*, eds. T.F. Earle and Nigel Griffin, pp. 133–149 (Warminster, England: Aris & Phillips, 1995).

26 The trials and tribulations of the long voyage to India are powerfully conveyed by Georg Schurhammer, S. J., *Francis Xavier, His Life and Times*, 4 Vols. (Rome: Jesuit Historical Institute, 1977), II, and Jonathan Spence, *The Memory Palace of Matteo Ricci* (New York: Viking Penguin, 1984), 76–80.

27 Van Linschoten, the Dutch accountant for the archbishop of Goa, Fonseca, noted that many merchants and colonists in Goa had up to thirty slaves who attended to *every* need of their mostly Portuguese masters. Arun Saldanha, "The Itineraries of Geography: Jan Huygen van Linschoten's *Itinerario* and Dutch Expeditions to the Indian Ocean, 1594–1602." *Annals of the Association of American Geographers*:101(2011):149–178, 163. For another contemporary account of Goa, see Guido Gualtieri, *Relationi della venuta de gli ambasciatori Giaponesi a Roma, sino alla partita di Lisbona* (Venetia: Appresso I Gioliti, 1586), 16–20; Antonio da Silva Rego, *História das Missoes do Padroado português do Oriente, vol. 1, India, 1500–1542* (Lisbon: Agencia Geral das Colonias divisao de Publicacoes e Biblioteca, 1949).

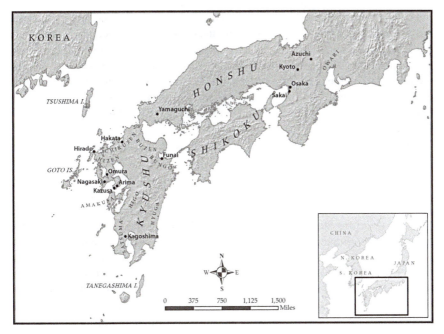

KOREA

TSUSHIMA I.

H O N S H U

Azuchi
Kyoto
Osaka
Sakai
OWARI

Yamaguchi

Hakata
Hirado
CHIKUZEN
BUZEN
Funai
BINGO
S H I K O K U

GOTO IS.
Omura
Nagasaki
Arima
Kazusa
AMAKUSA
HIGO
K Y U S H U
HYUGA

Kagoshima

TANEGASHIMA I.

N
W   E
S

0   375   750   1,125   1,500
                            Miles

CHINA
N. KOREA   JAPAN
S. KOREA

Map 2. Jesuits in Japan, 1585

heart and soul of this identity is the "Spiritual Exercises" of Ignatius of Loyola. The Exercises involve a stepwise progression of prayer and reflection, during which the Jesuit engages God in a "devout conversation"—a conversation that ideally endures with regular infusions of grace, helping the individual Jesuit realize and perfect his vocation.[28] In 1551, the main vocation of the Jesuits was missionary work—attending to the corporal and spiritual needs of European Catholics and the innumerable gentiles lately "discovered" in Goa and other parts of Asia.[29]

Having completed his novitiate and tertiary year, Frois left Goa in 1554 and travelled to Malacca. Here he worked for three years before returning to Goa in 1557 to complete his studies as a scholastic.[30] Because of his talents as a writer,[31] Frois was tapped to serve as assistant to the Jesuit Provincial of India, who entrusted Frois with the annual report for India and other correspondence with

---

28 John W. O'Malley, *The First Jesuits* (Cambridge: Harvard University Press, 1993), 37–50.
29 By the time Frois wrote the *Tratado*, the Jesuit order was essentially redefining itself as a teaching rather than missionary order.
30 When individuals enter the Jesuit order they undergo training for either the priesthood (spiritual coadjutors) or as "brothers" (temporal coadjutors). Scholastics are those pursuing the first "track," which can lead to yet more academic training and the highest rank of the Jesuit order, the "professed." See O'Malley, *The First Jesuits*, 345–347.
31 A catalogue drawn up in 1559 by Frois' Jesuit superior, P. G. da Siveira, describes Frois as "of slight build, humane spirit, well-intentioned, and naturally discreet. In time he will benefit by becoming a coadjutor having taken three vows." Joseph Wicki, S.J., *Documenta Indica IV (1557–1560)* (Rome: Monumenta Historica Soc. Iesu, 1956), 472.

the Church and the Society of Jesus in Portugal and Rome.[32] During these early years—in 1553, to be precise—Frois had the opportunity to meet Francis Xavier, the Basque Jesuit who landed at Kagoshima in August, 1549, initiating the Jesuit mission to Japan. While the Jesuits took satisfaction in winning souls from among the poor, dark-skinned peoples of Goa, the Japanese and Chinese had white skin and were as civilized as Europeans![33] Or so Francis Xavier wrote in his stirring letters, which Frois undoubtedly read before they were bundled with other letters from Asia and shipped from Goa to Europe.

Frois was ordained a priest in 1561 and apparently petitioned to be sent to Japan,[34] for late in 1562, at age thirty, he left Goa and sailed first to Macao and then on to the southern-most Japanese island of Kyûshû. Here during the previous decade, the Jesuits and Portuguese traders—with their access to guns and silk—had been embraced by the powerful *daimyo* of Bungo, Õtomo Yoshishige. With the *daimyo's* blessing, Fathers Torre and Vilela and several Jesuit brothers followed up on Francis Xavier's initial success and baptized perhaps a thousand or so Japanese, mostly in and around the town of Funai. Several hundred additional converts were made during brief visits to various parts of the island such as Satsuma, Yokoseura, Hakata, and Hirado.[35] Jesuit success in Funai among Õtomo's subjects was enhanced in 1557 when a former merchant and surgeon turned Jesuit, Luis de Almeida, used his personal fortune to open a hospital and foundling home for needy Japanese.[36]

Frois spent his first two years in Kyûshû (1563–1564) in Takashima and the port town of Hirado, where he continued his study of Japanese and attended to a small Japanese-Christian community as well as Portuguese merchants and sailors who visited the port on a regular basis.[37] Once his proficiency in Japanese was established, late in 1564 Frois was sent to the main island of Honshu and the capital city of Kyoto, to work with Father Gaspar Vilela. Earlier the Jesuits had

---

32 See, for example, Frois' lengthy letters for 1559 and 1560 in Wicki, *Documenta Indica IV*, 269–305, 643–694.

33 *Cartas . . . de Iapão & China*, I, 22. The Jesuits' racist attitude toward people of color, who were cast as inherently inferior to whites and thus suitable as slaves, is made explicit in colloquy #5 of *De Missione Legatorum Iaponensium ad Romanam Curia* (Macao, 1590), which was largely authored by Valignano. See also Schütte, *Valignano's Mission Principles*, I, PI, 130–131; Alonso de Sandoval, *Treatise on Slavery, Selections from De instauranda Aethiopum salute*, ed. and trans. Nicole von Germeten (Indianapolis: Hackett Publishing, 2008).

34 The Goa mission was plagued by poor leadership and declining morale during the decade Frois spent in the city. Apparently many Jesuits besides Frois wanted out of Goa, as the Jesuit Father General, Lainez, found it necessary in 1560 to require that they remain at their posts. Donald F. Lach, *Asia in the Making of Europe, Volume I, Book 1* (University of Chicago Press, 1965), 252–253.

35 Jurgis Elisonas, "Christianity and the Daimyo," In *The Cambridge History of Japan, Volume 4, Early Modern Japan*, ed. John W. Hall, 301–372 (Cambridge: Cambridge University Press, 1991), 318–320.

36 In the anua of 1579 it was noted that there were scarcely 2,000 Christians in all of Bungo and the vast majority were the poor and sick who came to be cured at de Almeida's hospital. *Cartas . . . de Iapão & China* I, 436,

37 Ibid., 145–151.

used their friendship with the *daimyo* of Bungo, Ōtomo, to secure an audience with the shogun, who allowed Vilela in 1560 to begin missionary work in and around the capital city. By the time Frois arrived in Kyoto, Vilela and a remarkable Japanese assistant named Lourenço had won over a number of prominent *daimyo* and their samurai supporters. However, no sooner did Frois arrive in the capital, during the summer of 1565, when the shogun was assassinated and fighting raged between competing *daimyo*, which forced Frois and Vilela to flee Kyoto. Frois moved to Sakai where he worked for the next four years, devoting part of his time to preparing Japanese-language editions of the catechism, lives of the saints, sermons, and other texts for mission converts.

In 1568, the ever-changing political landscape of Japan witnessed the political maturation of Oda Nobunaga (1534–1582). Nobunaga was a minor warlord from Owari Province who spent a decade out-smarting and out-muscling fellow clansman and neighboring warlords. In the fall of 1568, Nobunaga triumphantly marched into Kyoto, where he installed a new shogun, who was in turn embraced by the emperor. Both the shogun and emperor were beholding to Nobunaga, but not so the Buddhist monks of the powerful Tendai sect who resided near Kyoto on Mt. Hiei. In part to counter the monks' influence,[38] Nobunaga allowed the Jesuits to return to Kyoto. The following year (1569), Frois was the first Jesuit to take up residence in the city, which had a population of close to 100,000.[39] Like Lisbon, Kyoto was home to the Imperial court. For centuries, it had been Japan's economic, political, and cultural center.

It had been seven years since Frois arrived in Japan and clearly he had mastered Japanese. Nobunaga was a difficult man to impress but apparently got on well with Frois,[40] whom he granted permission to proselytize within his domain. Frois and a handful of fellow Jesuits, notably Organtino Gneechi-Soldo, enjoyed considerable success in the region about Kyoto over the next eight years or until 1577, when civil strife, coincident with a challenge to Nobunaga's rule, once again forced Frois and his Jesuit colleagues to flee central Japan and take refuge to the south, in the province of Bungo. It was while serving as the local superior of the Bungo mission that Frois received word that the Jesuit "father visitor," Alessandro Valignano, had arrived in Japan to conduct an inspection of the mission. As visitor, Valignano enjoyed the authority of the Father General of the Society, meaning that he could make whatever changes he felt necessary, regardless of the views of the local Jesuit superior, Francisco Cabral.

Valignano knew or soon learned of Frois' impressive grasp of the Japanese language and culture and made Frois his assistant and translator. For the next three

---

38 In 1571 Nobunaga's patience seemingly ran out and he laid siege to Mt. Hiei, attacking and destroying the monastery of Enryaku-ji and killing several thousand men, women and children.

39 Elisonas, "Christianity and the Daimyo," 63, 75–76.

40 In letters reproduced in a Jesuit volume from 1575, Frois mentions long conversations he had with Nobunaga and how the Japanese ruler personally escorted him around Gifu and Azuchi castles. *Cartas que los padres y hermanos de la Compañia de Iesus que andan en los Reynos de Iapon escriuieron alos dela misma Compañia* (Alcala: En casa de Iuan Iñiguez de Lequerica, 1575), 287–294.

years (1579–1582) Frois travelled to various parts of Japan, helping Valignano assess Jesuit operations. At the end of Valignano's inspection in 1583, at age fifty-one, Frois was entrusted by Jesuit superiors to write a history of the Jesuit mission enterprise. Much of Frois' subsequent career as a Jesuit (Frois died in 1597) was spent writing this multi-volume work, which covered the entire history of the Jesuit experience in Japan until 1593.[41] As noted, an extant prologue and table of contents for Frois' *Historia* is strikingly similar to the *Tratado*.[42] The title page of the *Tratado* bears a date of June, 1585, indicating that it was written at roughly the same time as Part I of Frois' *Historia*.

The cultural-historical context of the *Tratado*: A Jesuit mission in peril

While it seems certain that Frois wrote the *Tratado*, apparently basing it on Part I of his history (or *vice versa*), nowhere does he make explicit why he drafted the text and for whom it was intended. Because most distichs in the *Tratado* reference Europe in terms of "we," "us," and "ours," the text obviously was written for a European, rather than a Japanese audience. Because the *Tratado* contains Japanese terms that are not translated, it would further seem that the text was intended for European Jesuits, presumably those recently arrived in Japan who were expected to learn Japanese. Along these lines, the title page of the *Tratado* indicates that it was drafted in Canzusa (Kazusa), which was in the province of Arima on the southern end of the Shimabara peninsula. Kazusa was home to a Jesuit college for novices and scholastics and was also where Frois resided while serving as *socius* or assistant to the Jesuit vice-provincial Gaspar Coelho.[43]

The *Tratado's* central focus—Japanese customs, particularly among elites, and how they differed from European behaviors and beliefs—was a major preoccupation of Frois' immediate superior and the highest ranking Jesuit in Asia, the father visitor Alessandro Valignano.[44] When Valignano arrived in Japan in 1579,

---

41 Frois was assigned this task after Claudio Acquaviva, the fifth father general of the Jesuit order (1581–1615), instructed Jesuit provinces around the world to select a member to compile letters and other documents and write a history of each Jesuit province. Frois' primary responsibility of writing his *Historia* was interrupted on occasion by stints as *socius* or secretary/assistant to the Jesuit vice provincial in Japan as well as the father visitor, Valignano. Also, from 1592–1595 Frois was in Macao as Valignano's assistant.

42 Not only does the table of contents for the lost book parallel the chapters of the *Tratado*, but the latter begins with a dedication to "Jesus [&] Mary," which is how Frois also began at least some of his letters. See, for instance, *Cartas . . . de Iapáo & China*, I, 416.

43 Schütte, *Kulturgegensätze*, 94–95; Lach, *Asia in the Making*, I,2, 686–687; J.F.Moran, *The Japanese and the Jesuits, Alessandro Valignano in Sixteenth-Century Japan* (London and New York: Routledge, 1993), 153.

44 In his *Summary of Japan*, written in 1582–83, Valignano repeats many of the contrasts that show up in the *Tratado*. *Sumario de Las Cosas de Japon (1583), Adiciones del Sumario de Japon (1592)*, ed. José Luis Alvarez-Taladriz (Tokyo: Sophia University, 1954). See also Valignano's *Historia del Principio y Progresso de la Compañia de Jesus en las Indias Orientales*, ed. Josef Wicki, S.J. (Rome: Jesuit Historical Institute, 1944), 136–162. One can well imagine that the contrasts were suggested or elaborated on by Frois while serving as Valignano's "guide." This possibility is further suggested by the first paragraph from the title page of the *Tratado*, which rhetorically, at least,

having spent the previous five years in India and Macao, he quickly realized that the reports he had been receiving from Japan exaggerated Jesuit success.[45] Although the Jesuits could boast upwards of 150,000 Japanese baptisms, a good number of *daimyo* had embraced Christianity to gain access to Chinese as well as European trade goods, including guns. Prior to the 1540s and the arrival of the Portuguese, Japanese pirates[46] had plundered settlements along the coast of China, prompting the Chinese to forbid all trade with Japan—this despite Chinese interest in Japanese silver and the latter's desire for Chinese silk.[47] Portuguese merchants, who traveled in state-of-the-art ships (see chapter 12) and essentially were required by the Portuguese Crown to facilitate the work of the Jesuits, seized the opportunity to act as middle-men in a reinvigorated trade between Japan and China and all of Asia and beyond.[48] Japanese elites quickly realized that befriending a Jesuit could open doors to Chinese silk and weapons. Indeed, to fund their mission enterprise in Japan, the Jesuits invested large sums of their own money in Chinese silk, which was delivered to Japanese ports by Portuguese merchants.[49]

Valignano became rightly suspicious of the motives of not only the *daimyo*, but of Japanese commoners, who were in the habit of following the example of their rulers. Arguably, neither *daimyo* nor commoners had sufficient knowledge of Christianity, which had been explained by fellow Japanese trained in the basics by the Jesuits.[50] Both segments of Japanese society were likely to abandon Christianity (and the Jesuits) at the first sign of significant opposition. And there was ample trouble in the form of Buddhist monks who at first tolerated, but subsequently opposed the Jesuits.[51] Unlike the New World, where the Jesuits

speaks of more than one author (i.e. "In order to avoid confusing certain matters with others, *we* [emphasis ours] divide this work…"). See also Schütte, *Valignano's Mission Principles*, I, Pt. I, 285–289.

45 See Valignano's letter to Father General in Rome, in Moran, *Japanese and the Jesuits*, 35. See also Schütte, *Valignano's Mission Principles*, I, Pt. I, 270–271; M. Antoni Ücerler, S.J., "Alessandro Valignano: man, missionary, and writer." In *Asian Travel in the Renaissance*, ed. Daniel Carey (London: Blackwell Publishing, 2004), 12–42.

46 As Elisonas points out, while the Japanese were blamed for this piracy, most of the pirates were actually Chinese. Jurgis Elisonas, "The inseparable trinity: Japan's relations with China and Korea," In *The Cambridge History of Japan, Volume 4, Early Modern Japan*, ed. John W. Hall, 235–301 (Cambridge: Cambridge University Press, 1991), 250.

47 Before China prohibited trade with Japan, Chinese fleets with upwards of two hundred ships put into Japanese ports each May, trading silk for silver. Yoshitomo Okamoto, *The Namban Art of Japan* (New York: Weatherhill, 1972), 12.

48 L.M. Cullen, *A History of Japan, 1582–1914* (Cambridge: Cambridge University Press, 2003), 18–62.

49 This mercantile involvement was in clear violation of Church rules, but it was defended by Valignano on the grounds that there was simply no other source of revenue to support the Japan mission.

50 Prior to circa 1574, there were relatively few Jesuits in Japan and only a few such as Frois and Vilela knew Japanese. The Jesuits on the whole relied heavily on Japanese assistants called *irmao* and *dojuku*, who often lived in or near Jesuit residences and did much of the actual preaching and work of converting fellow Japanese. See Ross, *Vision Betrayed*, 49–51.

51 Arguably the monks' opposition to the Jesuits was precipitated by the violent destruction of Buddhist temples by prominent *daimyo* (e.g. Omura Sumitada in Bungo in 1563) who converted to Christianity.

followed in the wake of introduced diseases that undermined native religions,[52] Japan suffered no demographic and cultural collapse coincident with the arrival of Europeans.[53] Buddhism and Shinto remained alive and well in Japan, even if the abbots of some Buddhist temples alienated their followers by embroiling themselves in power struggles with Japanese nobles.[54] In this regard, powerful *daimyo* such as Nobunaga and Hideyoshi, both of whom embraced or tolerated the Jesuits, never rejected or opposed Buddhism *per se*. Their problem was with particular Buddhists (i.e. Tendai of Mount Hiei, Shingon of Negoro, monks of Osaka) who fielded armies and otherwise opposed Nobunaga's and Hideyoshi's hegemony.[55]

Valignano worried about not only the Japanese, but his fellow Jesuits, many of whom looked down on the Japanese, who everyone acknowledged, beginning with Francis Xavier, were an incredibly proud people.[56] Contrary to Valignano's own orders, which had been conveyed over the years from India and Macao, Jesuit superiors, particularly Francisco Cabral, the resident superior of the Japan mission, had made little effort to train European Jesuits in the Japanese language. Still more disturbing, Valignano discovered that Cabral and his assistants had systematically discriminated against those Japanese who had aspired to the priesthood or who had sought admission to the Jesuit order; the Japanese were relegated to a class of assistants or *dojuku*, rather than receiving training as scholastics.[57]

In point of fact, the Jesuit mission enterprise in Japan was a proverbial "house of cards" that might collapse at any moment. Valignano astutely realized[58] that if the Jesuits and Christianity were to have a future in Japan, it was imperative that the Jesuits embrace Japanese customs as well as the Japanese language, and in the process learn to compete with Buddhist monks, who often were masters of both old and new traditions such as calligraphy, poetry, and *chanoyu* or the "way of tea."[59] Importantly, Valignano realized that his fellow Jesuits would have to embrace not only Japanese language and culture, but his soon-to-be-revealed plan to train Japanese converts for the priesthood. No European power, including Habsburg

52 Daniel T. Reff, *Disease, Depopulation, and Culture Change in Northwestern New Spain, 1518–1764* (Salt Lake City: University of Utah Press); *Plagues, Priests, and Demons* (Cambridge: Cambridge University Press, 2005).
53 The Japanese had a long history of exposure to Old World diseases (and thus acquired resistance to) maladies that devastated Amerindians. Ann Bowman Janetta, *The Vaccinators, Smallpox, Medical Knowledge, and the "Opening" of Japan* (Stanford: Stanford University Press, 2007). See also Linda Newson, *Conquest and Pestilence in the Early Spanish Philippines* (Honolulu: University of Hawai'i Press, 2009), 17–18.
54 McMulin, *Buddhism and the State in Sixteenth-Century Japan*.
55 Ibid. See also Moran, *The Japanese and the Jesuits*, 70; Murdoch, *History of Japan*, II, P.I, 164.
56 Michael Cooper, *They Came to Japan, An Anthology of European Reports on Japan, 1543–1640* (Ann Arbor: University of Michigan Press, 1999[1965]), 42.
57 Schütte, *Valignano's Mission Principles*, I, Pt 1, 251–260; Ross, *A Vision Betrayed*.
58 Ross, *Vision Betrayed*, 59, points out that this realization arose after Valignano visited the Honshu missions founded by Vilela and Frois and run by Organtino, all of whom had acquired an intimate knowledge of Japanese language and culture.
59 The "way of tea" took definitive shape in the sixteenth century. Dennis Hirota, *Wind in the Pines, Classic Writings of the Way of Tea as a Buddhist Path* (Fremont, California: Asian Humanities Press, 1995).

Spain, had the men and resources to invade Japan and introduce European juridical authority and institutions (e.g. *audiencia*, inquisition, universities, cathedrals), which would greatly facilitate the conversion of the Japanese to Christianity. This was of course what happened in colonial Mexico and Peru. It was further apparent, particularly given the challenge of the Reformation back in Europe, that there would never be enough European priests to convert, never mind staff a Catholic Church in Japan. Confronted with these realities, Valignano concluded that the only hope for Japan was a Church staffed by the Japanese themselves. In one of his characteristically blunt letters to superiors, Valignano wrote:

> Japan is not a place which can be controlled by foreigners, for the Japanese are neither so weak nor so stupid a race as to permit this, and the King of Spain neither had nor ever could have any power or jurisdiction here. Therefore, there is no alternative to relying on training the natives in the way they should go and subsequently leaving them to manage the churches themselves."[60]

A Catholic Church staffed by non-Europeans was unheard of at the time, owing to the long-held belief that only Europeans could be entrusted with the mysteries and sacraments of the Roman Catholic Church. Although Jesuit correspondence published in Europe cast the Japanese as civilized, the Jesuits also reported that the Japanese had traditions of infanticide, suicide, and pederasty. In part, to assuage any European doubts about the wholesomeness of the Japanese, Valignano sent four Jesuit-educated Japanese teenagers to Europe as envoys to Rome in 1582. The teenagers arrived in Lisbon in 1584 and over the course of twenty months visited some seventy towns and cities where they were received by Catholic elites, including the regent of Portugal, the King of Spain, the doges of Venice and Genoa, and two popes (Pope Gregory died and was replaced by Sixtus during the legates long stay in Rome).

The four young Japanese converts were ostensibly actors in a conversion drama orchestrated by the Jesuits to impress Europe's Catholic elite and to secure their support of the Jesuit enterprise in Japan.[61] The drama as such featured a Japanese "other" who was paradoxically civilized yet antipodean (a central theme of the *Tratado*), who was rendered fully civilized or un-problematically so as a result of conversion to Christianity. This drama was staged by repeatedly having the Japanese appear in native dress and by having the Japanese perform their "curious" Japanese customs (e.g. tea ceremony) alongside what were understood as more advanced, European behaviors. For example, the Jesuits had the Japanese dress in kimonos and give public demonstrations of eating with chopsticks. Often on the same day the Japanese would attend Mass, and while in Rome, the opera, appropriately attired in European clothing and dutifully exhibiting the

---

60 Ross, *A Vision Betrayed*, 72. See also J.M. Kitagawa, *Religion in Japanese History* (New York: Columbia University Press, 1966).

61 Because the Japanese considered Europeans barbarians, Valignano also wanted to impress the four young Japanese with the wealth, power, and grandeur of the Catholic Church and Europe's ruling families. *Cartas . . . de Iapão & China*, II, 89.

appropriate respect for and understanding of European ritual (e.g. removing hats, genuflecting).[62]

The *Tratado* and the education of European Jesuits

The visit to Europe by the Japanese teenagers was still two years in the future when Valignano, in 1580, convened a momentous meeting of the Jesuit order in Bungo, Japan. At the meeting the father visitor unveiled his new programs to train Japanese converts for the priesthood and to train European Jesuits to behave in accordance with Japanese language and culture.[63] We believe Frois drafted the *Tratado* at the behest of Valignano as a teaching tool, to clarify for European Jesuits fundamental differences in Western and Japanese cultures. Again, what is significant is Frois' explicit recognition that one need not think and behave as a European to be civilized. Thus in the title page of the *Tratado*, he essentially warns his reader not to be surprised that "...one can find such stark contrasts in customs among [us and] people who are so civilized, have such lively genius, and are as naturally intelligent as these [Japanese]."

Certainly the substance of the *Tratado* is consistent with Valignano's plan to train European Jesuits to behave as Japanese. As noted, Frois drafted over six hundred distichs that deal with a wide variety of customs, ranging from sleeping to gift giving. The *Tratado* at the same time reveals a particular concern with behaviors and beliefs that were critical to Jesuit success in Japan. Chapters one through three, for instance, focus on gender and child-rearing practices. Several generations before the Jesuits arrived in Japan, the nation's unity, which had been maintained by the Emperor and his military commander, the shogun, was shattered when hundreds of once-cooperative nobles and "knights" (samurai) as well as militant abbots began putting their own interests above those of the Emperor and the handful of clans that had ruled Japan for centuries. The very lives of European Jesuits—never mind whether they could proselytize—depended on the Jesuits comprehending the complex gender roles of the nobility and the samurai class, and how these roles were inculcated in Japanese children.

---

62 Frois devoted a whole section of his *Historia* to a detailed account of the ambassadors' trip to Europe. See J.A. Abranches Pinto, Yoshitomo Okamoto, and Henri Bernard, S.J., eds. *La Premiere Ambassade du Japon en Europe. Monumenta Nipponica Monographs 6*. (Tokyo: Sophia University, 1942). See also: Guido Gualtieri, *Relationi della venuta de gli ambasciatori Giaponesi a Roma*; Luis de Guzman, *Historia de las Misiones de la Compañía de Jesus en La India Oriental, en la China y Japon desde 1540 hasta 1600* (Bilbao: El Mensajero del Corazon de Jesus, 1891[1601]), 422–458; Judith C. Brown, "Courtiers and Christians: The First Japanese Emissaries to Europe." *Renaissance Quarterly* 47 (1994): 872–906; Michael Cooper, *The Japanese Mission to Europe, 1582–1590* (Kent UK: Global Oriental, 2005), 169–170; Christina H. Lee, "The Perception of the Japanese in Early Modern Spain: Not Quite 'The Best People Yet Discovered," *eHumanista* 11(2008):345–381. One or more of the Japanese teenagers purportedly kept diaries of their trip to Europe, which Valignano re-worked into the thirty-four dialogues that make up *De Missione Legatorum Iaponen*, trans. Duarte de Sande (Macao 1590).
63 Schütte, *Valignano's Mission Principles*, I, Pt. II.

Because the samurai, nobility, and Buddhist elite enjoyed particular privileges (e.g. distinctive clothing, weapons, riding a horse) and often were supporters of the "arts," Frois also has chapters on subjects as different as horses, letters and writing, and drama and music. A chapter with seemingly less obvious import, chapter six, focuses on Japanese customs with regard to eating and drinking, including *chanoyu* or the "way of tea." The eating habits of Europeans (e.g. use of hands, emphasis on meat) deeply offended the Japanese and early on became a serious stumbling block in terms of Japanese respect for Europeans and by extension, Christianity. The Japanese, in fact, considered Europeans "slobs" (*sucios*).[64] One of Valignano's first mandates was that European Jesuits eat in the manner of the Japanese (e.g. chopsticks, small bite-size portions, rice instead of bread, less meat). Valignano also mandated that Jesuit residences—built in the Japanese fashion (thus Frois' Chapter 11 on architecture)—include a reception room where guests would be served tea by a *chanoyusha*, that is, somebody trained in tea etiquette.[65] During the sixteenth century rather distinct Japanese traditions of consuming tea—one followed by Zen monks and the other by *literati* and nobles who shared poetry and their collections of Chinese art objects—merged to form *chanoyu*. The "way of tea" as defined by Sen Rikyu (1522–1591), which was embraced by Japanese warlords, combined the ritualized, contemplative sharing of tea with an engagement with art. Now, however, the art objects, particularly the tea service, were valued not because they were necessarily Chinese or expensive, but because they conveyed in their simplicity and rusticity transcendent truths (e.g. "chill," "withered," "lean") that long had been celebrated by *renga* poets and appreciated by reclusive hermits and wandering monks. As Hirota has pointed out, *chanoyu* was all about the "…dissolution of the habitual, mundane frames of reference within which the things of the world are identified and gauged."[66]

Frois' literary model, relativism, and comparisons

At the time Frois wrote, the term "tratado" or treatise was used to refer to a work that was explicitly pedagogical and didactic rather than argumentative in the Scholastic or modern sense of the term (i.e. a work that poses a question and then pursues it systematically, realizing a conclusion).[67] As noted, the *Tratado* is not an argument *per se* about whether, for example, the Japanese were civilized. At the very outset of the *Tratado* (i.e. title page), Frois asserts this as a

---

64 Valignano, *Sumario de Las Cosas de Japon*, 242; see also Schütte, *Valignano's Mission Principles*, 1 Pt. II, 242–243.

65 This offering of tea to a guest in a receiving room is different from the more formal "tea ceremony," which usually entailed several men sharing tea ("ritually" prepared and served by the host) in a room or primitively-styled hut, set in a garden. The earliest definitive study of *chanoyu* remains Juan Rodriguez's *Arte del Cha*, ed. J.L. Alvarez-Taladriz. *Monumenta Nipponica Monographs* 14 (Tokyo: Sophia University, [1620]1954).

66 *Wind in the Pines*, 44.

67 Antônio Houaiss, Mauro de Salles Villar, and Francisco Manoel de Mello Franco, eds., *Dicionário Houaiss da língua portuguesa* (Rio de Janiero: Objetiva, 2001), 2756–7.

"fact." Working with this given, the *Tratado* describes some of the differences between European and Japanese customs. The *Tratado* as such, particularly Frois' use of the distich, was entirely consistent with Valignano's plan to engender a Jesuit understanding of Japanese customs or "frames of reference." In this regard, Frois presumably drafted the *Tratado* with the idea that his couplets would serve as a point of departure for more nuanced discussion of Japanese behaviors and beliefs. This presumption seems warranted in light of Frois' use of qualifiers such as "generally" or "for the most part." Moreover, Frois devoted much of the prologue to his *Historia* to a discussion of how comparing customs was potentially misleading. Consider, for example, Frois' discussion of the handkerchief and Japanese use of what today we call tissues or Kleenex:

> Told that the Japanese blow their nose but once per handkerchief, the European reader will find it odd if not ludicrous. It is like being told that the kings of Malabar eat just once from the same plate. They eat on banana leaves, so when the meal is over they throw them away. Thus, when it is said that once a handkerchief has been spit in or blown upon, the Japanese throw it away without washing it, the following must be explained: the Japanese go about with many thin, handkerchief-like, folded papers in their pocket [bosom], instead of a handkerchief. As this paper is very cheap, for a very small outlay [of money], they can use as much as they please.[68]

The use of the distich as a point of departure was entirely consistent with the scholastic method, which often entailed posing a question to which there were discordant answers, supported by strong evidence. Contrasts that entailed contradiction[69] functioned as a "hermeneutic irritant," engendering insight, including the realization that two different things can be true at the same time (e.g. two societies with very different customs can both be civilized).[70]

One of the most influential examples of the pedagogical use of distichs is *The Distichs of Cato*, which was the most popular textbook on Latin and ethics during the Middle Ages.[71] *Cato* was still prized during the sixteenth century (Erasmus, among others, published an edition) and very likely figured in Frois' education and that of fellow Jesuits.[72] The *Disticha* Catonis ordinarily was read to students by school

---

68 *Historia de Japam*, Vol. I.

69 The thought-provoking use of contradiction is also characteristic of popular texts such as the *Libro de buen amor* (1330) and Chaucer's *The Canterbury Tales* (1380) (e.g. "The Wife of Bath" tale that articulates but then demolishes the case for gender equality).

70 Constance Brittain Bouchard, *Every Valley Shall Be Exalted, The Discourse of Opposites in Twelfth-Century Opposites* (Ithaca: Cornell University Press, 2003); Catherine Brown, *Contrary Things, Exegesis, Dialectic, and the Poetics of Didacticism* (Stanford: Stanford University Press, 1998).

71 Ronald E. Pepin, *An English Translation of Auctores Octo, a Medieval Reader* (Lewiston, N.Y.: Edwin Mellen Press, 1999); "The Distichs of Cato, A Famous Medieval Textbook," trans. Wayland Johnson Chase. *The University of Wisconsin Studies in the Social Sciences and History*, Number 7 (1922).

72 Richard Hazelton, "Chaucer and Cato." *Speculum*: 35 (1960): 357–380; Mário Martins, "Os 'Di- sticos de Catão' na base da formação a o universita ria." *Revista Portuguesa de Filosofia* 24, Issue 1 (1968): 103–113.

masters who used the couplets as the starting point for a discussion of Latin grammar as well as matters of virtue and morality. In the prose introduction to the *Disticha Catonis*, "Cato" outlined his purpose, which paralleled Valignano's and Frois' concern with making sure that young Jesuits from Europe behaved properly in Japan:

> When I noticed how very many men go seriously astray on the path of morals, I decided that their judgment should be aided and advised, especially so that they might live gloriously and attain honor. Now, Dearest Son, I shall teach you how to form good morals for your mind....[73]

Whatever Frois' literary model, or models, his distichs generally are neutral or explicitly respectful of Japanese customs. For instance, most of Frois' contrasts in Chapter 2, which focuses on women, steer clear of value judgments:

> 56. When wearing a head covering, women in Europe cover their faces all the more when speaking with someone; Japanese women must remove their scarf, for it is discourteous to speak with it on.

Of course, Frois was a product of his times, and not unlike modern ethnographers and ethnologists,[74] he at times fashioned contrasts that implied that Japanese customs were less than rational. In chapter 2, for instance, Frois implicitly belittled Japanese names:

> 47. Among us, women's names are taken from the saints; the names of Japanese women are: kettle, crane, turtle, sandal, tea, bamboo.[75]

Worse yet—from the perspective of cultural relativism—are Frois' chapters on Buddhism and Buddhist monks (Chapters 4 and 5). Frois casts Buddhist monks as charlatans or money-grubbing pedophiles, ignoring the widespread abuses of his own Catholic Church, which was torn apart during Frois' own lifetime. It should be noted that Frois' "sins" in these two chapters cannot be attributed to ignorance, as Frois spent considerable time conversing with Buddhist monks. Indeed, Frois and fellow Jesuit Organtino Gnecchi-Soldo were tutored for a year by a former Buddhist monk.[76] Because he was a Jesuit "on a mission from God," Frois apparently was unwilling to entertain the possibility that Buddhism represented a reasonable alternative to Christianity.[77] Moreover,

---

73 Pepin, *An English Translation of Auctores Octo*, 9. Note that while Frois may have drawn inspiration from Cato, Serena Connolly (personal communication) has noted a number of significant differences between the *Tratado* and Cato: for instance, the *Tratado* is not in verse and the text comprises observations or simple statements rather than gnomic reflections. Also, Cato does not regularly contrast one group in the first line with another in the second.

74 James Clifford and George Marcus, eds. *Writing Culture, The Poetics and Politics of Ethnography* (Berkeley: University of California Press, 1986).

75 As we point out in our distich commentary, Frois could have mentioned popular Japanese names for women such as snow or chrysanthemum.

76 Schütte, *Valignano's Mission Principles*, I, Pt.2, 109.

77 See Sabine MacCormack, *Religion in the Andes* (Princeton: Princeton University Press, 1991), 240.

if, as suggested, Frois wrote for a young, European-Jesuit audience—an audience that would face ample challenges as missionaries in Japan—then one can well imagine Frois and Valignano not wanting to further try their faith by inviting meaningful comparisons between religions.[78]

While the *Tratado* does not always reflect the ideals of modern ethnology (i.e. cultural relativism; systematic, "objective" comparison) it comes surprisingly close, shedding valuable light on sixteenth century Europe and Japan. The reader will note in this regard that Frois chose to contrast Japanese with European, rather than Portuguese customs.[79] Reading the *Tratado*, it becomes apparent from Frois' distichs on subjects such as food, architecture, drama, and religion that "Europe" for Frois meant Mediterranean Europe, namely Portugal, Spain, southern France, and Italy. This thoroughly Catholic part of Europe[80] supplied the vast majority of Jesuits sent to Japan, particularly after 1570. For instance, the largest contingent of Jesuits sent to Japan was recruited by Valignano and sailed from Lisbon in 1574. Valignano brought with him seven Italians and over thirty *conversos* (!) that he had recruited from Jesuit colleges and houses in Spain.[81]

Frois probably also spoke of European, as opposed to Portuguese customs because in 1548, when he left Europe, the idea of national identities was just emerging.[82] The nation states we know today (e.g. Portugal, Spain, France, Italy) were in their infancy. People often were distinguished by regional dialects and customs, which coalesced in Europe's larger cities.[83] Lisbon, in particular, was as cosmopolitan as any city in Europe and home to large numbers of merchants, craftsmen, artists, and adventurers[84] from northern as well as southern Europe. Bankers from Italy and Germany, for instance, flocked to Lisbon, where they invested heavily in Portuguese ships that set sail for Africa, the Far East, and Brazil.[85] Portuguese scholars as well as

---

78 Such dangers are explored in Shusaku Endo's novel *Silence*.

79 The concept of "Europe" was first used by the ancient Greeks as a referent for the Greek archipelago, and in contradistinction to the other side of the Mediterranean (meaning Africa and the Middle East). Merry E. Wiesner-Hanks, *Women and Gender in Early Modern Europe* (Cambridge: Cambridge University Press, 2008), 9.

80 Frois seemingly retained notions of a medieval Europe, united by Christianity (Christendom); he ignored the fact that Europe has always evidenced conflict and division. Egar Morin, *Penser L'Europe* (Paris: Gallimard, 1990).

81 Portuguese superiors in Lisbon were shocked at Valignano and his "recruiting class," but they could do little to oppose Valignano, given the latter's support from the Father General of the Society. Ross, *A Vision Betrayed*, 36–40.

82 Ignatius Loyola also consciously strove to make the Jesuits an "international order," even if the Jesuits themselves struggled with incipient nationalism. It is interesting to note in this regard that the *anuas* for Japan often distinguished Italians. See for example *Cartas . . . de Iapáo & China*, I, 152, 444, 454.

83 Portuguese openness to ideas emanating from outside Portugal, particularly northern Europe, diminished appreciably after ca. 1550, when conservative forces in Portugal, including the Jesuits and the Inquisition, ushered in an era of censorship and hostility toward Erasmian humanism. Disney, *A History of Portugal*, 190–192.

84 Van Lincschoten is a good example of such an adventurer. Saldanha, "The Itineraries of Geography: Jan Huygen van Linschoten's *Itinerario*."

85 Pedro Dias, *The Manueline: Portuguese Art During the Great Discoveries* (Lisbon: Programa de Incremento do Turismo Cultural, 2002), 18–19.

the sons of Portuguese nobility often studied outside Portugal, in France, Italy, and Spain.[86] The Portuguese art scene likewise was crowded with Flemish painters, some of whom settled in Lisbon and adopted Portuguese names (e.g. Francisco Henriques). The dominant influence on Portuguese literature in 1550 emanated from "Italy,"[87] and correspondingly, printing houses in Venice supplied most of the books read in Portugal (and Spain).[88] The Portuguese queen invariably was Castilian, and Castilians were prominent among Portugal's elite, so much so that Gil Vicente wrote close to half his theatrical works in Castilian.

Thus, while the notion of Europe or European remain to this day contested, it is understandable that Frois spoke of European rather than Portuguese customs.

The *Tratado* and the governance of souls

The *Tratado* and Valignano's twin initiatives of embracing Japanese customs and creating a Japanese clergy can be seen as significant departures from European colonialism in as much as they seem to imply a respect for and even the empowerment of a Japanese other.[89] In this regard, scholars long have acknowledged the impressive ethnographic and linguistic literature produced by Jesuit missionaries during the sixteenth and seventeenth centuries. Jesuit grammars and *artes* of non-Western languages such as Japanese, Guaraní, or Cahita continue to be valued by linguists.[90] Similarly, anthropologists, literary scholars, and historians have marveled at the "proto-ethnographies" of non-Western peoples compiled by the likes of Blas Valera, Pérez de Ribas, Paul LeJeune, or Mateo Ricci.[91] Significantly, the Jesuits "walked the talk" of cultural relativism, for instance, supplying their Guaraní neophytes in Paraguay with firearms so they could resist Luso-Brazilian slave raiders ("Paulistas").[92] In northern Mexico, the black robes often blocked Spanish miners from exploiting Indian labor. And in Japan, as we have seen, the Jesuits led by Valignano made plans to

86 Frank Pierce, ed., *Luís De Camões, Os Lusiadas* (Oxford: Clarendon Press, 1973), xvi–xvii.
87 Joaquim de Carvalho, *Estudos sobre a Cultura Portuguesa do século XVI*, Volume II (Coimbra: University of Coimbra, 1948), 7.
88 Andrew Pettegree, *The Book in the Renaissance* (New Haven: Yale University Press, 2010), 66, 114, 260–261.
89 See Ross, *A Vision Betrayed*, for perhaps the most forceful discussion of Valignano's "progressive" vision and cultural relativism with respect to Japan and China (although Ross seems unduly forgiving of Valignano's attitudes toward people of color).
90 As recently as June, 2011, the Mi'kmaq of Nova Scotia asked the Jesuits for help preserving their language.
91 See for example, Sabine Hyland, *Gods of the Andes: An Early Jesuit Account of Incan Religion and Andean Christianity* (University Park: Penn State Press, 2011). Jesuit cultural relativism took various "textual" forms, including Mateo Ricci's *mappamondo* that placed China near the center and the Holy Land in a western quadrant. See Jensen, *Manufacturing Confucianism*, 37.
92 Beatriz Helena Dominguez, *Tão Longe, Tão Perto* (Rio de Janiero: Editora Museu da Republica, 2007), 41–71; Nicholas P. Cushner, *Why Have You Come Here* (New York: Oxford University Press, 2006); Daniel T. Reff, "The Jesuit Mission Frontier in Comparative Perspective, The Reductions of the Rio de la Plata and the Missions of Northwestern New Spain, 1588–1700." *In Contested Ground*, eds. Thomas Sheridan and Donna Guy (Tucson: University of Arizona Press, 1998), 16–32.

create a Catholic Church that was staffed from the top down (bishops, clerics, and religious) by the Japanese themselves.[93]

The Jesuits' "progressive" missions and texts often have been explained in terms of the Jesuit embrace of Renaissance Humanism and Thomism, which predisposed the Jesuits to see potentially virtuous pagans where others saw irredeemable savages.[94] Jesuits were indeed thoroughly convinced (it was at the heart of their own religious election) that God's grace was ubiquitous. Jesuits disembarking in Japan, China, or the Americas expected to find societies with serious flaws because these societies never had benefited from revealed truth (i.e. Gospels) and the sacraments. But the same Jesuits understood that God never would have abandoned his creation. Through the simple application of reason to the majesty of creation (as per Thomas Aquinas), many Indians or Asians were likely to arrive at some knowledge of and reverence for the one, true God.[95] Jesuits, in fact, were open to the possibility that pagans got quite a few things right, so to speak.[96]

While it is true that the Society of Jesus was nourished by a revival of Thomism and the flowering of humanism, the half-century prior to 1540 also was an age of discovery that provided unprecedented European access to distant worlds that abounded in fabulous riches. The riches were difficult to secure, however, in the absence of European juridical control. As Valignano himself pointed out, neither Spain nor Portugal ever were in a position to successfully invade Japan and China and overpower the indigenous elite, installing European institutions and authority. It was much easier to transplant European juridical control (e.g. the *audiencia*, the *presidio*, bishoprics) in the New World, where the arrival of Europeans was coincident with epidemics that devastated the Indian population, killing countless elders and thus undermining indigenous authority.[97] As noted, the arrival of Europeans in China and Japan did not precipitate a population collapse resulting from the introduction of infectious diseases.[98]

In Asia as well as frontier areas of Latin America, the inextricable Christian imperatives of commodity and spiritual conversion[99] required an "indirect" means

93 From 1581–1610, ninety-eight Japanese were admitted to the Jesuit order. Isabela Pina, "Cultural Adaptation and the Assimilation of Natives." *Bulletin of Portuguese Japanese Studies* 2 (2001): 59–76, 68.

94 O'Malley, *The First Jesuits*, 1993. See also James T. Moore, *Indian and Jesuit* (Chicago: Loyola University Press, 1982); Sangkeun Kim, *Strange Names of God, The Missionary Translation of the Divine Name and the Chinese Responses to Matteo Ricci's Shangti in Late Ming China, 1583–1644* (New York: Peter Lang, 2004), 33–70.

95 Blaise Pascal, *The Mind on Fire*, ed. J.M Houston (Vancouver: Regent College, 2003), 245–246. Jensen, *Manufacturing Confucianism*, 33. For a recent Jesuit expression of this view of grace, see Agbonkhianmeghe E. Orobator, *Theology Brewed in an Africa Pot* (New York: Maryknoll, 2008), 52–65, 130–137.

96 In both America and Asia, the Jesuits found indigenous traditions worth celebrating. See Hyland, *Gods of the Andes*; Jensen, *Manufacturing Confucianism*, 54–59; Ines G. Zupanov, *Disputed Mission* (Oxford: Oxford University Press, 1999), 3–4.

97 Reff, *Plagues, Priests, and Demons*, 174–206.

98 Thus, one of Frois' briefest chapters (9) deals with disease.

99 Greenblatt, *Marvelous Possessions*, 71.

of gaining access to and control of the indigenous population. Arguably, the Jesuit mission met this requirement by operationalizing what Foucault has referred to as "governmentality." In a series of lectures toward the end of his life, Foucault observed that, beginning in the sixteenth century, the exercise of power in Europe increasingly came to be based on disciplinary rather than juridical authority.[100] Whereas polities during the Middle Ages were maintained by threat of force,[101] increasingly during the early modern period they came to rely on a complex arrangement of various "technologies of the self," which simultaneously championed freedom, all the while "free" human beings were busy disciplining themselves in accordance with socially-constructed truths about their identities. The sixteenth century witnessed the publication of books that mapped out in great detail "appropriate" beliefs, practice, and identities: *The Perfect Wife* (1585), *The Book of the Courtier* (c. 1521), *The Education of a Christian Woman* (1523), *The Prince* (1505), *On Civility in Boys* (1530). What Greenblatt[102] has termed "Renaissance self-fashioning" was effected through a host of new and old disciplines (e.g. the theater) that provided Europeans from all walks of life with the opportunity to model their social performance after the roles delimited in texts, sermons, on stage, or in the visual arts.[103]

Interestingly, it is around the middle of the sixteenth century, when Foucault notes there is a huge outpouring of reflection and publication on the government of oneself, of one's soul, of children, and of the state,[104] that the Society of Jesus was founded by Ignatius Loyola. The new religious order alientated many contemporaries (i.e. Mendicants, secular clergy) precisely because it broke with the juridical or cenobitic model of religious life[105] and flaunted what was a new technology of the self that balanced religious freedom with Christian zeal. The Jesuits ignored "purity of blood," admitting *conversos*; they wore no distinctive garb; they were not permanently assigned to religious houses; they did not recite the divine office as a community; Jesuit superiors were obeyed, but not in defiance of one's conscience. All this "freedom" was held in check by what Foucault termed techniques of disciplinary power such as yearly performance of the Spiritual Exercises (a well-defined

100 Nancy Ettlinger, "Governmentality as Epistemology." *Annals of the Association of American Geographers*, 101(3) 2011: 537–560, provides an excellent synthesis of Foucault's ideas, which were articulated over years and in various lectures; Michel Foucault, "Governmentality." In *The Foucault Effect, Studies in Governmentality*, eds. Graham Burchell, Colin Gordon, and Peter Miller, (Chicago: University of Chicago Press, 1991), 87–107; *Security, Territory, Population* (London: Macmillan, 2007); *The Birth of Biopolitics: Lectures at the College de France, 1978–1979* (London: Palgrave, 2008). See also Nikolas Rose, *Governing the Soul, The Shaping of the Private Self* (London: Routledge, 1989); Terry Eagleton, *The Idea of Culture* (London: Blackwell, 2000), 26.
101 For example, the Duke of Savoy forbade the sons of the nobility from leaving his domain to be educated without his permission.
102 Stephen Greenblatt, *Renaissance Self-Fashioning: From More to Shakespeare* (Chicago: University of Chicago Press, 1980).
103 Larry F. Norman, "The Theatrical Baroque." In *The Theatrical Baroque*, ed. Larry Norman (Chicago: University of Chicago Press, 2001), 1–13.
104 Foucault, *Security, Territory, Population*, 88.
105 Giorgio Agamben, *The Highest Poverty* (Stanford: Stanford University Press, 2013), 45–47.

religious retreat involving a general confession), regular letter writing between Jesuits, and the circulation and consumption[106] of a public discourse (e.g. the *anuas* or "Jesuit Relations") that celebrated the Jesuit "way of proceeding."

Although the Jesuits frightened many traditional Catholics (not to mention contemporary "heretics" or Protestants), the order very quickly gained the favor of the Portuguese and Spanish Crowns and the Papacy, particularly because of its successful mission enterprises in Asia and subsequently America. As Bernard Cohn,[107] among others, has pointed out, successful colonial ventures presuppose "cultural technologies of rule" that classify and naturalize indigenous subjects. In this regard, the Jesuits mastered indigenous languages and drafted impressive "proto-ethnographies" of indigenous peoples not because they were intent on celebrating difference or desired reciprocal understanding, but because systematically mapping difference facilitated the Jesuits' unidirectional program for directed culture change.[108] Knowledge of indigenous languages and customs was a prerequisite of operating within societies where the Jesuits were juridically powerless.[109]

Significantly, with knowledge of otherness the Jesuits proceeded to develop seminaries, boarding schools, and confraternities to transform (using, for example, Japanese and Latin editions of Western/Christian texts[110]) "good pagans" into true Christians. To quote one of Valignano's assistants, Duarte de Sande, "...it is necessary to enter with theirs to come out with ours."[111] Writing to Valignano from China in 1583, Mateo Ricci reported "...we have become Chinese so that we may gain the Chinese for Christ."[112]

---

106 For instance, it was common practice for Jesuit novices to conclude dinner with readings from Jesuit missionary letters and published volumes of the same, or to stage theatrical re-enactments of the heroic battles of pioneer Jesuit missionaries and saints such as Francis Xavier. See Joseph de Guibert, *The Jesuits: Their Spiritual Doctrine and Pratice; A Historical Study* (Chicago: Loyola University Press 1964), 217; Liam M. Brockey, *Journey to the East, The Jesuit Mission to China, 1579–1724* (Cambridge: Belknap Press, 2007), 207–208.

107 *Colonialism and Its Forms of Knowledge* (Princeton: Princeton University Press, 1996).

108 Although Foucault and others have cast the modern state of the late eighteenth and nineteenth centuries as the earliest expression of "bio-power" (societies that are conceived and managed on the basis of censuses and statistically-defined social realities), the Jesuit mission enterprise from the preceding centuries entailed very sophisticated "catalogues" of population and property that were part and parcel of the Jesuit "state" or mission. See Daniel T. Reff, *Disease, Depopulation, and Culture Change in Northwestern New Spain, 1518–1764* (Salt Lake City: University of Utah Press, 1991), 181–193.

109 Ana Fernandes Pinto, "Japanese Elites As Seen By Jesuit Missionaries." In *Bulletin of Portuguese Japanese Studies* 1(2001): 29–43, 30; See also Pérez de Ribas, *History of the Triumphs of Our Holy Faith*, 101.

110 Murdoch, *A History of Japan*, II. P. I, 119; Hubert Cieslik, "The Training of a Japanese Clergy in Seventeenth Century." In *Studies of Japanese Culture*, ed. J. Roggendorf, 41–78 (Tokyo: Sophia University, 1963); Proust, *Europe Through the Prism of Japan*, 9–10; Francesco C. Cesareo, "Quest for Identity: The Ideals of Jesuit Education in the Sixteenth Century." In *The Jesuit Tradition in Education and Missions, A 450-Year Perspective*, ed. Christopher Chapple (Scranton: University of Scranton Press, 1993), 17–34.

111 Quoted in Brockey, *Journey to the East*, 44.

112 Jensen, *Manufacturing Confucianism*, 42.

The Jesuit mission to Japan, including Valignano's liberal re-structuring of the enterprise appears entirely consistent with Foucault's characterization of "governmentality.[113] In Japan, as elsewhere, the Jesuits produced detailed studies of the Japanese language as well as an extensive "ethnographic" literature, including Frois' systematic comparison of European and Japanese customs. As suggested, the *Tratado* apparently was drafted to help explain Japanese customs to European Jesuits, with the further idea that this understanding would make it easier to embrace *certain* customs. Note, however, that neither Frois nor Valignano (nor anybody else at the time) anticipated the modern anthropological understanding of culture as an integrated system of behaviors and beliefs—this despite the *Tratado's* systematic survey of customs (e.g., chapters on gender, architecture, plays, writing, warfare, etc.). Like Montaigne, Valignano and Frois may have suspected or intuited that customs were interrelated[114]—that a society's cuisine or architecture might be integrally related to its religious beliefs and practices. Nevertheless, neither Valignano nor Frois seemed concerned that European Jesuits who "lived like the Japanese" (i.e. following many of their customs) might become "destabilized," assimilating if not valuing, for instance, Buddhist and Shinto values and beliefs.[115] In keeping with Jesuit first principles as articulated by Loyola,[116] Valignano and Frois believed that European as well as Japanese Jesuits were "formed" and steeled in a significant way (an essential identity) by the operation of the Holy Spirit and the embrace of a fundamental set of Christian/Jesuit beliefs and practices.[117] This understanding was entirely in keeping with the Jesuit "way of proceeding," which assumed that a Jesuit who remained connected to god and fellow Jesuits was free to follow their conscience and be adaptable with respect to externals (e.g., wear whatever is appropriate; pray when possible; help the poor or befriend a king).

Although the Jesuits principally were concerned with re-making their converts, they nevertheless went further than many of their European contemporaries in understanding and respecting difference. As Foucault pointed out, "governmentality"—regimes of diffuse power where people essentially

---

113 Surprisingly, Foucault never acknowledged the applicability of his concept of governmentality to colonial contexts.

114 In his essay on customs (ca. 1572), Montaigne observed "It is very doubtful whether there can be such evident profit in changing an accepted law, of whatever sort it may be, as there is harm in disturbing it; inasmuch as government is like a structure of different parts joined together in such a relation that it is impossible to budge one without the whole body feeling it." Michel de Montaigne, *Essays*, tran. J. M. Cohen (London: Penguin, 1958), 79.

115 Destabilized in the sense of being not only troubled by notions of cultural superiority, but willing to embrace alternative practices. Larry Wolff, "Discovering Cultural Perspective, The Intellectual History of Anthropological Thought in the Age of Enlightenment." In *The Anthropology of the Enlightenment*, eds. Larry Wolf and Marco Cipolloni, 3–33 (Stanford: Stanford University Press, 2007), 7–10.

116 See O'Malley, *The First Jesuits*, 37–38.

117 See Valignano's *Il cerimoniale per I missionary del Giappone*, ed. J.F. Schütte, S.J. (Rome: Edizioni Di Storia e Lettteratura., 1946), 25–26; Chikeo Irie Mulhern, "Cinderella and the Jesuits." *Monumenta Nipponica* 34 (1979): 409–447.

discipline themselves—nevertheless entails a freedom to explore and embrace alternative behaviors and beliefs. Arguably, European Jesuits such as Frois, Organtino, and Rodrigues, who may have initially "performed" Japanese customs to access potential converts, discovered that the "performances" were satisfying and rewarding. In Japan and the Americas, the Jesuits did, in fact, accommodate indigenous traditions.[118] However, it must be kept in mind that the Jesuits never questioned their "mission from God," which was fundamentally about altering Japanese identity—even when it meant destroying Japanese lives[119] If Valignano wanted fellow Jesuits to embrace Japanese customs, it was because he perceived this embrace of *certain* customs as largely inconsequential from the perspective of one's fundamental identity and "soul."[120] Correspondingly, Valignano was willing to create a Catholic Church staffed by the Japanese, but only on the condition that the Japanese, beginning in childhood, were "formed" with an essentially Western/Christian worldview, imparted by the study of Latin and the consumption of a select (e.g. no Erasmus or Lucretius), Humanist canon that came to include works as diverse as the lives of the saints, Aesop, and Cinderella, all of which were edited and translated into Japanese.[121] Again, these expressions of governmentality held the promise of rebellion—"there is no power without potential refusal or revolt"[122]—as Japanese trained by the Jesuits could, upon assuming positions of power as priests, "fall back" on whatever Japanese traditions they may have secretly cherished or rediscovered in later life. An excellent example of such rebellion is Fukan Fabian (1565–1621). Fabian was a Japanese convert to Christianity who received training as a Jesuit "scholastic" and was destined for ordination as a priest. Rather late in his life (1608), Fabian apostatized, subsequently authoring *Ha Daiusu* (1620), a sophisticated theological critique of Christianity as the one true faith.[123]

In the case of Japan, we can only speculate about what might have been, had Valignano's plans for a Catholic Church been fully realized. Two years after Frois

---

118 Ikuo Higashibaba, *Christianity in Early Modern Japan* (Leiden: Brill, 2001), 161–165.

119 In Chapter V of his *History of Japan*, II, P. I, historian James Murdoch missed no opportunity, seemingly, to critique the Jesuits. Murdoch's critique, nevertheless, appears sound inasmuch as the Jesuits themselves expressed delight in the merciless destruction of those who opposed them. See, for instance, *Cartas . . . de Iapáo & China*, I, 439v.

120 Jensen, *Manufacturing Confucianism*, 39, may err in this regard, in suggesting that Jesuits who pursued Valignano's accommodation strategy "reinvented themselves, in effect abandoning their identity as European priests..."

121 Elison, *Deus Destroyed*, 65–69; Chikeo Irie Mulhern, "Cinderella and the Jesuits." *Monumenta Nipponica* 34 (1979): 409–447.

122 Michel Foucault, "What is Critique?" In *The Politics of Truth*, ed. S. Lotringer, trans. L. Hochroth and C. Porter (Los Angeles: Semiotext(e), 1984), 41–95. (Originally published in the Foucault Reader, ed. P. Rabinow, Pantheon, 1984).

123 As Schrimpf has recently pointed out, Fabian's anti-Christian critique bespeaks a well-reasoned religious pluralism rather than a simple bashing of Christianity and the Jesuits, owing to Fabian's disappointment at not being ordained. Monika Schrimpf, "The Pro- and Anti- Christian Writings of Fukan Fabian (1565–1621)." *Japanese Religions*: 33 (2008): 35–55.

drafted the *Tratado* the Jesuit enterprise in Japan started to unravel. Japanese *daimyo*, particularly the most powerful of these elites, seemingly became frightened by the Jesuits or what they represented. For reasons that are still debated by scholars,[124] Japan's most powerful *daimyo*, Toyotomi Hideyoshi, became convinced in 1587 that the Jesuits posed a threat to his power and authority. Hideyoshi issued an order of expulsion, which while largely symbolic (only three Jesuits actually left Japan), marked the beginning of a tense decade that culminated in 1597 in the very public persecution of twenty Japanese Christians and six Franciscan friars. (The Franciscan order had come to Japan in 1593, over Jesuit objections.[125]) Bickering and competition between the Catholic orders contributed further to fears among Japanese elites and led in 1614 to a new round of persecutions, expulsions, and the widespread destruction of Christian churches. Those Christians who survived went into hiding until 1637–38, when they joined a peasant uprising (the Shimbara rebellion) that was promptly crushed. Henceforth the Tokugawa regime effectively closed Japan to Christian missionaries and what remained of the Catholic Church went underground.[126] As an aside, today less than 1 percent of all Japanese consider themselves Christian; the overwhelming majority identify with Shinto and Buddhism[127]

Preparation of an English-Language edition of the *Tratado*

It was in recognition of the importance of the *Tratado*, both as a primary source for early modern Europe and Japan and an encounter text—reflecting the many forces that governed European perceptions and representations of others—that we undertook the preparation of an English-language edition of the *Tratado*. In preparing an English translation we have relied on Schütte's transcription as well as a microfilm copy of the Portuguese original obtained from the *Real Academia* in Madrid. We have indicated in footnotes instances where we disagree with Schütte's rendering of the Portuguese original, which is not altogether legible in places, owing to minor damage the manuscript sustained during the centuries prior to its discovery.[128] Because the *Tratado* is

124 Ross, *A Vision Betrayed*, 76–77; Mary Elizabeth Berry, *Hideyoshi* (Cambridge: Harvard University Press, 1982); M. Stephen Steichen, *The Christian Daimyos, A Century of Religious and Political History in Japan (1540–1650)* (Tokyo: Rikkyo Gakuin Press, 1909), 128–137; J.S.A. Elisonas, "The Evangelic Furnace: Japan's First Encounter with the West." In *Sources of Japanese Traditions, Second Edition, Volume Two: 1600 to 2000*, eds. Wm. T. de Bary, T.C. Gluck, and A.E. Tiedemann, 143–185 (New York: Columbia University Press, 2001).

125 Pedro Lage Reis Correia, "Alessandro Valignano Attitudes Towards Jesuit and Franciscan Concepts of Evangelization in Japan (1587–1597)." *Bulletin of Portuguese Japanese Studies* 2 (2001), 79–108.

126 For the complexities of this period see Reiner H, Hesselink, *Prisoners from Nambu* (Honolulu: University of Hawai'i Press, 2002); Berry, *Hideyoshi*; Boxer, *The Christian Century*; Ellison, *Deus Destroyed*.

127 Hirochika Nakamachi, *Japanese Religions At Home and Abroad* (London Routledge, 2003), 13.

128 The *Tratado* has a good number of sizeable worm-holes.

in the form of over six-hundred brief couplets, rather than a narrative,[129] our biggest challenge with respect to translation has been insuring lexical accuracy. Special attention has been given to the translation of Portuguese and Japanese terms whose meanings have changed significantly over the past four-hundred years. We generally have left un-translated Portuguese or Japanese terms with meanings specific to the sixteenth century. These cultural or temporally-bound terms are italicized and are discussed in footnotes. The reader will note that we especially have relied on Houaiss' encyclopedic dictionary of the Portuguese language.[130]

It is perhaps the human condition to live out our lives unsure of the changes taking place all around us. Today, for example, we speak of "globalization," but are at a loss to define adequately what may be a new historical epoch. Frois offered no reflection on how the societies and customs he compared might have been in flux (except perhaps when he used qualifiers such as "for the most part" or "generally"). And yet, it is difficult to imagine a period in the history of either Japan or Europe that was as dynamic as Frois' lifetime (1532–1597). In Japan, the demise of the Muromachi shogunate in the late 1400s ushered in a century of warfare that intensified with the arrival of the Jesuits and Portuguese traders. Indeed, during what scholars have designated the Azuchi (ca. 1568–82) and Momoyama periods (ca. 1582–1600), which coincided with the "reigns" of Oda Nobunaga and Toyotomi Hideyoshi, respectively, the scale of violence seemingly reached unprecedented heights.[131] And yet paradoxically, the Azuchi and Momoyama periods were a time of cultural fluorescence, as seen in the elaboration of the tea ceremony, the appearance of Kabuki, or the stunning perfection of various "material" arts (e.g. ceramics, lacquer, screen painting, castle architecture).[132] As Masahide[133] has pointed out, Japan during the Azuchi-Momoyama period also experienced a religious reformation of sorts, as it is during this period that the Pure Land tradition of Buddhism, earlier elaborated by Shinran (1173–1263), spread rapidly. The appeal of Shin Buddhism stemmed not only from its concern with the salvation of all people (rather

---

129 For a discussion of the challenges associated with translating a Jesuit narrative, see the critical introduction to *History of the Triumphs of Our Holy Faith Amongst the Most Barbarous and Fierce Peoples of the New World*, trans. Daniel T. Reff, Maureen Ahern, and Richard K. Danford (Tucson: University of Arizona Press, 1999[1645]).

130 Antônio Houaiss, Mauro de Salles Villar, and Francisco Manoel de Mello Franco, eds., *Dicionário Houaiss da língua portuguesa* (Rio de Janiero: Objetiva, 2001).

131 Both rulers embraced firearms and fielded armies of tens-of-thousands of soldiers who fought in battles or destroyed whole towns, resulting in casualties that numbered in the thousands.

132 See for instance Money L. Hickman, ed., *Japan's Golden Age, Momoyama* (New Haven: Yale University Press, 1996); Patricia A. Graham, *Faith and Power in Japanese Buddhist Art, 1600–2005* (Honolulu: University of Hawai'i Press, 2007); Susan Hanley, *Everyday Things in Premodern Japan* (Berkeley: University of California Press, 1997).

133 Bitō Masahide, "Thought and Religion, 1550–1700," trans. Kate W. Nakai. In *The Cambridge History of Japan, Volume 4, Early Modern Japan*, ed. J.W. Hall, 373–424 (Cambridge: Cambridge University Press, 1991), 378–87.

than a select, mostly aristocratic few), but its doctrine that salvation required no esoteric or scholarly knowledge or practices, but a "simple" faith in Amida Buddha.[134]

Only in recent decades have we fully appreciated that all cultures are dynamic and contested. We should not be surprised that Frois spoke of customs as if they were static and invariable. Although one would think that Frois had a much better understanding of his own European culture, it might not have been apparent in 1548, when Frois left Europe for good, that Erasmus and Luther irrevocably had shaken the foundations of Christendom. During Frois' lifetime Europe also was changed forever by the discovery of whole new worlds on the other side of the planet. The sixteenth century likewise witnessed a communication revolution in the forms of the printed book and broadside. Today we also look back and recognize the nation state, polyphonic music, opera, the rise of the bourgeoisie, and a host of other new societal forms and expressions.[135]

As noted, the *Tratado* consists of over six-hundred distichs, divided by Frois into fourteen chapters. Our translation of each of Frois' distichs is followed by a brief commentary in which we clarify—with the benefit of hindsight— the contingencies (e.g., literary, theological, political, historical, cultural) that seemingly governed Frois' representation of Japanese and European customs. Often in our commentaries we point out how Frois' distichs are partial truths that actually pertained to a particular segment of European or Japanese society (i.e. elites), or to a particular time (e.g. summer, new year's) or place (e.g. a shrine or tea house). Our work of contextualization was helped significantly by Akio Okada's enormously popular Japanese-language edition of the *Tratado*.[136] Similarly, we often turned to Marques' *Daily life in Portugal in the Late Middle Ages* for an understanding of the European customs referenced by Frois.

Although the sixteenth century in Japan and Europe witnessed unprecedented change, Japanese and European cuisine, architecture, drama, and aesthetics—to name but a few arenas—are still to this day governed by distinct and enduring principles. Accordingly, we have drawn on the comments of perceptive Europeans who wrote about Japan subsequent to Frois, particularly Engelbert Kaempher (1690), Sir Rutherford Alcock (1863), Isabella Bird (1880), Edward Morse (1886), Alice Bacon (1893), Eliza Scidmore (1897), and Basil Chamberlin (1902). Like Frois, these Europeans spent many months or years in Japan and sometimes offered

---

134 Dennis Hirota, *Asura's Harp, Engagement with Language as Buddhist Path* (Heidelberg: Universitätsverlag Winter, 2006), 3–13.

135 While his focus is England, Thomas offers a sweeping overview of the profound changes that impacted Europe as a whole during this period. Keith Thomas, *The Ends of Life* (Oxford: Oxford University Press, 2009).

136 Okada's edition has gone through at least a dozen printings in Japan since it was first published in 1965. Akio Okada, trans. and ed., *Yoroppa-Bunka to Nihon-Bunka* [European Culture and Japanese Culture] (Tokyo: Iwanami Shoten, 1965).

"thick" descriptions of Japanese customs.[137] Along these lines, readers of our edition may be surprised (pleasantly, we hope) that our edition incorporates observations about present-day Japanese customs. Because most readers of our edition are likely to be Westerners, they will know that Europeans (for the most part) no longer beat their wives, eat with their hands, or attend hangings for entertainment. These same readers are *not likely to know* that the Japanese (for the most part) no longer eat dog, carry their children on their backs, or commit ritual suicide. We thought it important to reflect on present-day Japan, if only to preclude stereotypes of a timeless or tradition-bound Japan.

In general, our goal has been to convey the cultural-historical context of the *Tratado* and the dynamic and contested reality of Japanese and European cultures. The *Tratado* is a fascinating text because it reflects how humans know and constitute themselves both in relation to and distinct from others. We have tried to draw the reader's attention to how this comparative "project," which is an essential part of the human condition, can entail a narrow or ethnocentric logic. The *Tratado* suggests that cultures are amenable to formulaic statements. Arguably this type of thinking, which once heralded the birth of anthropology as a discipline, survives today in popular stereotypes of the Japanese, or in the case of the Japanese, of Westerners. In translating and commenting on Frois' text, we have sought to emphasize how identities are sometimes rooted in empirical generalizations (e.g. Europeans do tend to be physically larger than the Japanese) but more often in contested social constructions. Being a man or woman, or modes of expressing or feeling pain, are, in fact, quite variable.

The very breadth of Frois' *Tratado*, which encompasses topics as diverse as architecture, gender, shipbuilding, and childrearing, poses a challenge in terms of providing appropriate contextual information to appreciate Frois' individual comparisons. To meet this challenge, the project has engaged an interdisciplinary group of scholars. Although each of us has handled multiple tasks, we each brought particular skills and knowledge to the text. Richard Danford was ultimately responsible for our translation from Portuguese into English; Robin D. Gill, who, like Frois, lived in Japan for over twenty years, supplied commentary and insight into the Japanese language, culture, and history; and Daniel Reff provided insight into the Jesuits and early modern Europe.

---

137 Sir Rutherford Alcock, *The Capital of the Tycoon, A Narrative of a Three Years' Residence in Japan* (London: Longman, Green, and Roberts, 1863); Alice Mabel. Bacon, *A Japanese Interior* (Boston: Houghton, Mifflin & Company, 1893); *Japanese Girls and Women* (London: Kegan Paul, 2001[1892]); Isabella L. Bird, *Unbeaten Tracks in Japan* (Boston: Beacon Press, 1987[1880]); *Korea & Her Neighbours*. 2 Vols. (London: John Murray, 1898); Basil H. Chamberlain, *Things Japanese, Being Notes on Various Subjects Connected with Japan*. Fourth edition (London: John Murray, 1902); Engelbert Kaempher, *The History of Japan, Together With a Description of the Kingdom of Siam, 1690–92*. 3 Vols. (Glasgow: James MacLehose and Sons, 1906[1690–92]).

Jesus [&] Mary

Treatise containing in very succinct and abbreviated form some contrasts and differences in the customs of the people of Europe and this province of Japan. Although in the region of Ximo[1] there are some things that appear to coincide between us and the Japanese, this is not because they are common and universal, but because they were acquired [by the Japanese] from the Portuguese who come here in their ships to trade. Many of their customs are so distant, foreign, and far removed from our own that it is difficult to believe that one can find such stark contrasts in customs among [us and] people who are so civilized, have such lively genius, and are as naturally intelligent as these [Japanese]. In order to avoid confusing certain matters with others, we divide this work into chapters. Completed with the grace of Our Lord in Canzusa [Kazusa], June 14, 1585.

1 "Ximo" here refers to the west coast region of Kyushu. See *Cartas que os Padres e Irmãos da Companhia de Iesus Escreuerão dos Reynos de Iapão & China aos da Mesma Companhia da India & Europa, des do Anno de 1549 Até o de 1580.* 2 Vols. Facsimile edition by José Manuel Garcia (Maia: Castoliva Editora, 1997), I, 460v. By 1585, the Japanese of Nagasaki (a major port of call for Portuguese ships), in particular, had begun emulating the Portuguese in fashion and other customs. Yoshitomo Okamoto, *The Namban Art of Japan* (New York: Weatherhill, 1972), 68–78.

Chapter 11 Horses and related Dogus[2]
Chapter 12 Ships, Seafaring and related Dogus
Chapter 13 Drama, Farces, Dancing, Singing, and Musical Instruments
Chapter 14 Miscellanea

2 *Dogus* = tool, equipment, implement, apparatus. Frois may have used this Japanese term in these
   two chapter titles because he was particularly struck by the distinctiveness of Japanese equestrian
   and sailing "gear" (e.g. saddles, reins, anchors, ropes, sails).

1 Concerning men, their persons, and their clothing

1. Europeans for the most part are tall and well built; the Japanese for the most part are not as tall or robust as we are.

In both Japan and Europe men generally enjoyed more rights and privileges than women.[3] Japanese men of the samurai class, in particular, wielded enormous power, so it is not surprising that Frois devoted this first chapter to men, particularly elites.

During the sixteenth century Europeans entertained ancient theories that physical attributes were somehow significant correlates or actual determinants of one's character and identity. Frois, to his credit, did not apparently put much stock in physiognomy, as he begins this chapter with a handful of distichs that focus on physical attributes (e.g. stature, eyes, nose, skin, hair). More to his credit, he makes no essentialist claims about the Japanese based on the shape of the eye, the size of the nose, hair color, or other physical traits.[4] However, this very first distich is revealing in that it shows how bias figures in nearly any comparative project, if only because language is inescapably value-laden. Frois clearly sought to be accurate; note his use not once, but twice, of the qualifier "for the most part." However, to say that Europeans are "well built" is as much a value judgment as an apparent reference to the robust European body-type. In 1585, life expectancy at birth in Japan was higher than in Europe;[5] this continues to be true today. Clearly from the perspective of longevity, the Japanese were and are "well built."

2. Europeans consider large eyes beautiful; the Japanese think they are horrendous and consider beautiful eyes those that are narrow in the inner corner of the eye [i.e., eyes that are almond-shaped rather than round].

The Japanese until fairly recently considered round eyes beastly; Europeans were said to have eyes like dogs. Japanese consumption of Western popular culture–everything from Mickey Mouse and John Wayne to the Beatles and Bono– has contributed to a Japanese desire for large, round eyes. Indeed, some Japanese have had surgery to double their eyelids, making their eyes appear larger. A glance at Japanese comic books or Pokémon characters (eyes filling half the face to the

---

3 Of course, class and wealth also mattered and thus male peasants exercised less power than wealthy and upper-class women in both Europe and Japan. See for example, Anne Walthall, "The Life Cycle of Farm Women," in *Recreating Japanese Women, 1600–1945*, ed. Gail Lee Bernstein, 42–70 (Berkeley: University of California Press, 1991), 43.

4 Bronwen Wilson, *The World in Venice* (Toronto: University of Toronto Press, 2005), 205.

5 William E. Deal, *Handbook to Life in Medieval and Early Modern Japan* (Oxford: Oxford University Press, 2006), 358.

exclusion of other features) is further suggestive of recent Japanese acceptance of "big is beautiful."

3. We don't think it strange to have white eyes; the Japanese consider it monstrous and it is rare among them.

A Japanese boy who has done something wrong will get a scolding or *omedama chodai*, literally "a gift of eyeballs." Westerners, by contrast, register displeasure with a frown, compressing the eyes. Okada[6] notes that eyes with light irises have larger sclera and these large white surfaces shine coldly and sharply. Apparently this feeling is shared by other Japanese, for "to look coldly upon" or frown upon someone in Japanese is to "stare with white eyes" (*shirome-de niramu*).

4. Europeans have long and occasionally aquiline noses; the Japanese have short noses with small nostrils.

This contrast should have had the same qualification (for the most part) as distich 1. Historically, some upper class Japanese had high-bridged noses, apparently reflecting their centuries-old ties to Mongolian immigrants, whose noses were every bit as "aristocratic" as those found on ancient Roman sculpture. Although nostrils are less value-laden than bridges, they also are linked to class difference in Japan. A typical drawing of a beastly peasant or a *busu* (an "ugly" as opposed to a "beauty") shows big black nostrils where there should be a nose. Japanese from Frois' time to ours have depicted Caucasians with enormous bird-like beaks (or mountain goblin beaks, from the Japanese perspective), which more often than not have been equated with rapacity.

5. Europeans generally have full beards; the Japanese usually have sparse, scraggly beards.

Full beards were indeed the rage in sixteenth-century Europe.[7] Frois' Jesuit contemporary, Rodrigues, suggested that the Japanese beard was so sparse that one might more appropriately say they don't have them. Rodrigues at the same time implied that the Japanese were much freer than Europeans with respect to how they wore their beards, "... and in this they are imitated out here in the East by the Portuguese, Spaniards and Moors, who have abandoned the traditional Portuguese style."[8] By the early seventeenth century, coincident with the expulsion and persecution of Europeans, few Japanese had beards and the samurai in particular were entirely smooth-shaven.

6. Europeans take pride and honor in their beards; the Japanese take pride in a little tuft of hair that is bound at the back of their heads.

European men invested considerable time in their beards, which were not only shaped in various ways, but waxed, curled, perfumed, starched, stiffened, dyed,

6 Akio Okada, trans. and ed., *Yoroppa-Bunka to Nihon-Bunka* [European Culture and Japanese Culture] (Tokyo: Iwanami Shoten, 1965), 16.
7 Allan D. Peterkin, *One Thousand Beards, A Cultural History of Facial Hair* (Vancouver: Arsenal Pulp Press, 2001), 29–32.
8 Michael Cooper, *They Came to Japan, An Anthology of European Reports on Japan, 1543–1640* Rev. ed. (Ann Arbor: University of Michigan Press, 1995), 37.

and powdered.[9] Men even swore by their beards and criminals such as "fornicators" were punished by having their beards publicly removed with a sharp axe.[10]

At the time Frois wrote Japanese hair fashion was about to change, with more and more samurai switching from a Chinese-inspired, half-loop ponytail (*queue*), bound at the back of a shaved forehead (as per Frois), to a topknot folded forward, which stood up freely like a brush and usually was cut short and controlled with wax.[11] This *chonmage* or "bobbed-bent" style became common during the Tokugawa era (1603–1867). On TV "Easterns" or *chambara*,[12] which remain popular in Japan, there is often a dramatic moment when the sword wielding villain's *chonmage* is cut off by the "good guy" or victor. Despite an obvious psycho-cultural investment in the top knot, in less than a generation after Perry opened Japan to the West (1854), Japanese men abandoned the top knot in favor of western hair fashion.

7. Among us, men always keep their hair groomed and consider it an affront to have it removed; the Japanese remove their hair with tweezers, enduring pain and tears in the process.

Although European men wore their hair relatively short (i.e. off the shoulders) during much of the sixteenth century, they still made sure it was carefully arranged. Elites often had the heads of their vassals and slaves shorn to symbolize their subordination.[13] The Japanese *queue* and top knot were accentuated by shaving the front of the head, which apparently also entailed removing hair with a tweezers.

8. Among us there are many men and women who have freckles; the Japanese, while fair[-skinned], rarely have freckles.

Europeans initially considered the Japanese "white" or, as Frois here phrased it, fair. Perhaps because the Japanese were, and are, especially anxious about marks on the skin (folklore attributes it to vengeful female ghosts), Japanese women and noblemen traditionally have taken great care to keep their skin soft and white. Even today it is common to see Japanese farmers wearing not only a hat, but underneath it a towel that drapes down both sides of the face. The idea that the Japanese have

---

9 Peterkin, *One Thousand Beards*, 32.

10 Linda Schiebinger, *Nature's Body* (Boston: Beacon Press, 1993), 120–25; Allan Peterkin, *One Thousand Beards*, 29.

11 Japanese screen art or *biombos* suggest that the *chonmage* was indeed a seventeenth-century development. See João Paulo Oliveira e Costa, *Da Cruz de Cristo ao Sol Nascente, Um Encontro do Passado e do Presente* (Lisbon: Instituto dos Arquivos Nacionais/Torre do Tombo, 1998), 22–23, 30.

12 These Japanese analogs to the American "Western" are typically set during the Tokugawa era and feature a patient "good-guy" who is trying to lead a quiet life as a small-town doctor, judge, or travelling blind man. The reluctant hero invariably is compelled to take up his sword against the forces of evil (often corrupt authority figures). Like the hero of the American "Western" who wields his six-gun with breath-taking skill, the *chambara* hero deftly uses his sword to vanquish his unsuspecting and arrogant enemies, winning the gratitude of peasants, townspeople, and, not infrequently, a fair maiden.

13 Schiebinger, *Nature's Body*, 121.

yellow skin dates to the late nineteenth century. This notion was popularized in the United States during World War II, when American films and propaganda went to extremes to dehumanize the Japanese, who often were pictured and spoken of as "little yellow-bellies."[14]

9. Among us it is rare for a man or woman to be pock-marked; among the Japanese it is very common and many lose their sight from the pox.

By 1585, smallpox largely was a disease of childhood in both Europe and Japan.[15] It is not clear why the Japanese would have suffered more than Europeans from blindness and pock-marks, common complications of *Variola major* (the more serious form of the disease). Because the smallpox virus is variable, it is possible that Japan experienced a particularly virulent outbreak of the disease in the 1530s or 1540s, a generation or so before Frois arrived in Japan.

10. Among us it is considered unclean and uncivilized to have long fingernails; Japanese men, as well as noblewomen, wear some [of their] nails like talons.

European elites may not have cultivated long, shovel-like pinky-nails, as among the Mandarin Chinese and Japanese, but they were well manicured nevertheless. To otherwise have the hands of a laborer was incompatible with gentility.[16] Long fingernails were not nearly as common among the Japanese as Frois implies. Most Japanese depicted in *ukiyo-e* prints,[17] for instance, have nails cut so short that the meat of the finger-tip is clearly visible. It was mostly priests, nobles and merchants (the last were despised by the samurai, but wealthy enough to do no manual labor) who boasted long fingernails, particularly on one or both pinkies.

11. Among us, facial scars are considered a deformity; the Japanese are proud of their scars, and because the wounds are poorly treated, the scars look even more deformed.

Fencing was part of the curriculum in many secondary schools in Europe and students often stoically received and then proudly displayed facial "smites." Nevertheless, it would be hard to find a nation more *macho* than sixteenth-century Japan. This "toughest dudes around" attitude continued throughout the Tokugawa period (1603–1868) and is one reason why Japan never was colonized by the West. Today, one still finds scars at work in popular culture; Japanese sitcoms and comic books frequently show a scarred *yakuza* or *chinpira* (a *yakuza* underling) intimidating people (usually in the subway).

---

14 John W. Dower, *War Without Mercy, Race and Power in the Pacific War* (New York: Pantheon Books, 1986).

15 Ann Jannetta, *The Vaccinators: Smallpox, Medical Knowledge, and the "Opening" of Japan* (Stanford: Stanford University Press, 2007), 19; William McNeill, *Plagues and Peoples* (New York: Anchor Books, 1976), 124, 202; Linda A. Newsom, *Conquest and Pestilence* (Honolulu: University of Hawai'i Press, 2009), 17.

16 Keith Thomas, *The Ends of Life* (London: Oxford University Press, 2009), 83, 107.

17 *Ukiyo-e* prints were mass-produced and relatively inexpensive woodblock prints that were popular among Japan's urban class, particularly in Edo (Tokyo) during the second half of the seventeenth century. The prints often depict "city life," particularly the entertainment district with its courtesans, actors, and sumo wrestlers.

Men's clothing

1a. We dress the same throughout the four seasons of the year; the Japanese change their dress three times a year: natsu katabira, aki-awase, fuyu kimono.

This is the first and only time in the *Tratado* that Frois sub-sectioned a chapter, numbering his distichs anew. To avoid confusion, we have given the distichs in this subsection, which continues to the end of the chapter, a letter designation (e.g. 1a, 2a, ... 63a). Although Frois implies that the entire subsection concerns clothing, at least a third of the distichs focus on accessories that were a significant part of elite male identity, such as swords and fans (the latter in the Japanese case). Another third pertain to behavior: distichs about spitting, for instance, or sitting or standing in the presence of servants, or removing one's hat or shoes as a matter of courtesy. Frois in this regard seemingly understood that identity was mostly learned and performed and yet in mysterious ways still tied to one's God-given body and soul.[18]

Today we still acknowledge that "clothes make the man [or woman]." During Frois' day clothing was held to have even greater power; what you wore not only conveyed your identity (e.g. noble, servant, prostitute, executioner), but seemingly had the power to transform an individual.[19] Sumptuary laws, which attempted to restrict elite access to particular fabrics, jewels, furs, and other luxury items, still were in effect in many parts of Europe during Frois' lifetime.

In this first distich, Frois is reflecting on seasonal changes, correctly noting that Europeans generally shed or donned additional layers of clothing (i.e. a coat or mantle),[20] whereas the Japanese changed the dress itself. Although today many non-Japanese use "kimono" to refer to all robe-like clothing, Frois understood that the Japanese used specific terms. The *natsu* or "summer" *katabira* is an unlined, gauze-thin robe or gown, ideally suited for sultry weather. As noted in the following chapter (#2, #7), the *natsu-katabira* also could serve as a head covering. Today the closest thing is the *yukata*, which is worn at home, at certain festivals, or at hot-springs resorts.

The *aki-awase* or "autumn combo" is a more substantial two-layered robe that can properly be called a kimono. It was "officially" worn for about nine days in mid-October (the Japanese observed certain formal dates for changing dress), perhaps partly to air it out before it was stuffed with cotton (or flock silk in the case of nobles), thereby converting it into a *fuyu-kimono* or winter kimono. At the start of "summer," on what was called "clothes-change" day (*koromogae*), this stuffing was removed, converting the winter kimono into a *hatsu-awase*, or "first combo." Frois simplifies by jumping straight to the inner layer, the *katabira*.

18 Stephen Greenblatt, *Renaissance Self-Fashioning, From More to Shakespeare* (Chicago: University of Chicago Press, 1980).

19 Ann Rosalind Jones and Peter Stallybrass, *Renaissance Clothing and the Materials of Memory* (Cambridge: Cambridge University Press, 2000).

20 "Basic attire" for Portuguese peasants was a knee-length tunic and trousers of coarse wool or cotton, and shoes; a hooded-mantle and a simple cap or *sombrero* were worn outdoors, depending on the weather. Marques, *Daily Life in Portugal*, 73, 92.

2a. Among us, to wear clothing made from printed fabrics would be considered foolishness and nonsense; among the Japanese everyone except the bonzes and old men with shaven pates wear clothing made from printed fabrics.

Europeans with money certainly wore brocades and silks with printed designs. However, wool was the principal material for clothing in Europe and was typically rendered attractive and expensive by dying.[21] (Cochineal from the Americas made it possible to produce cloth dyed in breath-taking shades of red.) When Frois speaks of "us," however, perhaps he was thinking mostly of Jesuits, who consciously wore cassocks made of simple black cloth.[22]

Frois' Jesuit contemporary, Rodrigues, noted that some Japanese kimonos were handsomely decorated with floral and striped patterns, solid colors, and often featured gold designs intermingled among crimson and violet flowers.[23] Men's attire in fifteenth-century Europe could also be colorful, as evident from Botticelli's painting "Adoration of the Magi," which features the artist and members of the Medici family in brilliant togas and other colorful attire.[24] Perhaps by 1585, as Frois suggests, Europe had embarked on what J.C. Flugel[25] has called "the great masculine renunciation" or graying of male fashion. During the Tokugawa era in Japan (1603–1868), strict sartorial laws were enacted that paralleled trends in Europe.

In the 1960s and 1970s, most Japanese were appalled at the revival of color in Western menswear. Such fashion was dismissed as a product of excessive individualism. Through all of this, only the young Japanese construction worker and the truck driver remained true to their pre-modern Japanese roots. Today you can still find them wearing purple and orange trousers and "wild" hairdos. (University students in Japan also tend to dress informally or colorfully; once out of school, however, they very rapidly make the transition to colorless adulthood.)

3a. Among us a new look in clothing is created nearly every year; in Japan styles are always the same, without ever changing.

European elites were indeed fashion conscious and apparently quick to embrace new styles, even if it meant securing a new sword to match the latest fashions.[26] Actually, Japanese dress was constantly changing, but in different ways from European fashion. There was less variety in the overall forms but as much or more change in the color and designs inside and out. What were subtle yet significant changes in clothing went unobserved by Frois and other Europeans.

---

21 Ibid., 92.
22 Although under Valignano the Jesuits emulated the Japanese in many of their customs, the Jesuits abandoned silk kimonos as early as 1570 because such dress was at odds with their vow of poverty. Josef Franz Schütte, *Valignano's Mission Principles for Japan 1573–1582*. Volume I, Part II, trans. J. Coyne (St. Louis: Institute for Jesuit Sources, 1985), 43–44.
23 Cooper, *They Came to Japan*, 205–206.
24 Joanna Woods-Marsden, *Renaissance Self-Portraiture: The Visual Construction of Identity and the Social Status of the Artist* (New Haven: Yale University Press, 1988), 49–51.
25 J.C. Flugel, *The Psychology of Clothes* (London: The Hogarth Press, 1950), 110–111.
26 Capwell, *The Noble Art of the Sword*, 34, points out that an Italian sword in the Wallace Collection that dates to ca. 1540 has a bulbous pommel that apparently was designed to complement the "puffed-and-slashed clothing" of the period.

Today the Japanese consider themselves–for better or worse–particularly prone to fads or "booms," as they call them. In the hey-day of Japan-as-Number-One, when newspapers referred to Europe as a museum, Japanese intellectuals went so far as to call the West a tradition-bound "stock culture" incapable of coping with the new. The Japanese not only reversed the hoary stereotype of the sleepy changeless East and the active protean West, but, as befits a stereotype, they made it intrinsic to civilization.

4a. Among us it is customary to wear a coat over our doublets and shirts; the Japanese wear a very lightweight, open-fronted sambenito made of a printed fabric over their thin robe or kimono.

A doublet was a snug fitting and often padded jacket (to enhance the chest) worn over a shirt, and under an overcoat or mantle when outdoors. Doublets could be made of rich textiles and decorated with embroidery or fur.[27] Frois labored in this contrast to describe what is apparently the Japanese *haori* (literally "wing weave"). The *haori* might be said to resemble an open-fronted *sambenito*, which is a smock worn by penitents in Europe. The *haori* is lightweight, and while it ties in front, it remains slightly open.

5a. Our sleeves are narrow and extend to the palm of the hand; those of the Japanese are wide, and in the case of men, women, and the bonzes, they reach only halfway down the arm.

As Frois notes below (9a), European clothing was generally tight-fitting, a pattern that Marques attributes to the new armor that was worn in the late Middle Ages (the armor necessitated tight-fitting undergarments).[28] Wide sleeves were a long-established tradition in Japan; short sleeves apparently only became fashionable during Japan's century-long warring period that preceded the arrival of Europeans in the 1540s. For most of Japanese history, sleeves extended to near or even past the wrist, although men may never have worn their sleeves quite so long as women.

6a. Our breeches or underwear have an opening in the front; those of the Japanese have an opening on either side and a small loin cloth or front knot [missing text].[29]

Breeches that fastened around the leg just below or above the knee were popular in Europe during Frois' lifetime. The Japanese had something similar called *momohiki* (literally, "thigh-pullers"), which apparently were worn for formal occasions. High-level administrators wore another type of formal trousers (*hakama*). Whether *momohiki* or *hakama*, Japanese bifurcated clothing did not fasten in the front, but rather on the sides, where the flaps or panels are tied together. Unfastened, the part above the crotch opens up completely.

27 Marques, *Daily Life in Portugal*, 59–61.
28 Ibid., 37.
29 ... *nas ylhargas e hum tanga[nho] ou arsáo de sela de* [?]. A knot of some kind is suggested by Frois' mention of a "saddle pommel."

For the most part, commoner or noble, the Japanese man was comfortable in his loincloth, which, to quote Rodgriques,[30] was "merely a sash, silk for the nobles and linen for ordinary people." The loincloth often was the only thing worn in summer, and this was true even as late as the early Meiji period (1868–1912). Nevertheless, the Japanese felt a need to prove themselves to be a "civilized" people to a West that ignorantly (especially considering its own Greco-Roman tradition) equated clothing with culture, and this resulted in a crackdown by Japanese authorities on the loincloth as an outdoor garment. By the time Japan proved itself "civilized" by defeating Russia in 1905, the Japanese themselves did not care to see loincloths in public. Today loincloths are only worn by men performing ablutions on Shinto religious retreats or on pilgrimages.

7a. Our pants and imperial breeches are made of silk with gold worked in; while other clothing may be of silk, Japanese underpants are always made of coarse or ordinary cotton.[31]

Decorated Japanese screens or *byôbus* from the sixteenth century depict Portuguese merchants wearing ankle-length, billowing pants or pantaloons in various colors and rich fabrics.[32] Although the Jesuits admired the Japanese embrace of simplicity, they more frequently celebrated the material wealth and presumed progress of Christian Europe, as evidenced by significant investments of gold in baroque architecture and, in this instance, pantaloons. The Japanese did not wear trousers much, but when they did, they wore trousers of hemp and cotton because they were stronger and cooler than silk (again, summers are very hot and humid in much of Japan). *Nuno*, which is the Japanese term for ordinary cotton, is relatively cheap and was/is used for sundry purposes, including head-bands and house-cleaning.

8a. Among us, no item of men's clothing is suited for use by women; the Japanese kimono and thin robe are suited for men and women alike.

Up until the ninth century, when the Germans introduced breeches, European clothing tended to be unisex and followed Roman precedents (i.e. togas and tunics).[33] Although both Japanese men and women may wear kimono or *katabira*, they do not wear them in quite the same way. Belts, for instance, are tied in different places (high for women and low for men) and some colors are gender specific.

9a. Our clothing is fitted, narrow, and tight on the body; Japanese clothing is so loose-fitting that people rapidly and without embarrassment disrobe from the waist up.

Most restrictive Western attire is poorly suited to muggy weather. During the summer most Japanese (excepting nobles, who often wore fine white cotton under gowns) wore a lightweight robe or kimono, which both men and women often would remove above the waist while indoors, or conversely, tuck up under their

---

30 Cooper, *They Came to Japan*, 206.
31 The terms used by Frois for these materials are *canga* (apparently from the Chinese word *yang*, meaning coarse fabric of cotton) and *nuno*. Josef Franz Schütte, S.J., *Kulturgensate Europa-Japan (1585)* (Tokyo: Sophia University, 1955), 102, f.2.
32 Okamoto, *The Namban Art of Japan*, 25, 38; Oliveira e Costa, *Da Cruz de Cristo*, 20, 34, 56.
33 Marques, *Daily Life in Portugal*, 39–41.

belt when on the road. Prior to the opening of Japan to Western influence in the mid-nineteenth century, such innocent nudity was quite common, even in cities. Writing in 1562, the Jesuit de Almeida noted that the relative ease with which the Japanese could disrobe made it easy to scourge oneself![34]

As an aside, not all Japanese fashion is loose and comfortable; far from it. When one of us (Gill) appeared on Japanese late-night television, he was cinched up in a kimono as stiff as a straightjacket. Formality, in the East or West, can be excruciating.

10a. Because of our buttons and lacings, we cannot easily keep our hands close to our bodies; since Japanese men and women are not thus restricted, they always leave their sleeves hanging empty and pull their hands in close to their bodies, especially in winter.

With minimal heating (see Chapter 5 on houses) and no wool to speak of, the Japanese understandably conserved body heat by withdrawing into their kimonos. Frois' Jesuit contemporary, Rodrigues, noted that this withdrawal also was useful in hot weather, as "... people can insert their hands inside with the greatest of ease and wipe away body sweat with a handkerchief."[35] However, to do so in the presence of nobles, one's master, or on formal occasions was a grave discourtesy and impertinence. Today on television "Easterns," loose-dangling sleeves are a mark of the gambler and other social misfits.

11a. We wear our best clothing on the outside and our lesser clothing underneath; the Japanese wear their best underneath and their lesser clothing on top.

It is not known if this inside-outside reversal began in Japan because the best dress was preserved for one's intimates, because of sartorial regulations, or simply out of fear of envy (or maybe being noticed by the tax collector). Today it is usually explained in terms of a subtle Japanese aesthetic preference.

12a. With us, the outside of a garment must be better than the lining; among the Japanese gentry, their dobukus whenever possible have linings that are better than the exterior of the garment.

Dobuku is a Japanese term that transliterates as "torso-wear." Frois apparently had in mind *dobuku* with linings of silk. Like Japanese trousers, *dobuku* originated in China and usually were sleeveless. This torso-wear evolved during the Tokugawa era into the silk *haori*, which usually had sleeves and was always lined. For two and a half centuries, wealthy merchants and townsmen vied with one another for the most ornate lining for their plain black *haori*. There is aesthetic pleasure in this inside-outism: the plain black outside of the *hoari* makes the inside seem magical, like the once hidden contents of a geode.

13a. We wear vests made from animal hides with their fur on the inside; Japanese vests have the fur on the outside.

Europeans, including the Portuguese, were wild about fur linings and clothing accents, despite sumptuary laws that tried, unsuccessfully, to curb public affection

---

34 James Murdoch, *A History of Japan*. 3 Vols. (New York: Ungar Publishing, 1964), II, P. I, 80, f.5.
35 Cooper, *They Came to Japan*, 206.

for furs.[36] In light of 12a above, as well as Japan's Buddhist heritage, which frowned on killing animals, it is doubly surprising that the Japanese wore fur vests with the fur showing. Today fur vests are rare and are seen primarily on elderly women out for their New Year's shrine visit or young ladies celebrating adulthood and their twentieth birthday.

14a. Among us a man cuts his hair or shaves his head to alleviate suffering[37]; the Japanese shave their heads out of grief or sorrow or because they have fallen from their master's grace.

Both Europeans and the Japanese shaved their heads to alleviate suffering from lice. Frois is nevertheless correct in emphasizing how the Japanese shaved their heads as an act of grieving. Correspondingly, those in mourning largely ignored their personal grooming for months and did not clean their houses either. Even today, men of means let themselves go for a year after their father dies. However, perhaps the most common reason for shaving one's head (as opposed to having one's topknot cut) signified a do-or-die determination. Better to shave off one's hair–literally "round one's head" (*atama-o marumeru*)–to show contrition and determination to make a fresh start, than cut off a finger in the style of the courtesan or *yakuza*. The Japanese also shaved their heads to signal retirement from the world.

15a. Among us one shaves his beard when he wants to enter a religious order; the Japanese cut off the tuft of hair on the back of their head as a sign that they have left behind the concerns of the material world.

As noted, Europeans equated beards and hair in general with power and virility. Accordingly, individuals who surrendered themselves to God shaved their beards, signaling "contempt for the world." Shaving one's beard made less sense in the Far East, where many men have little beard to speak of. Shaving off one's topknot to signal a profound life change made more sense for the Japanese, who, like other Asians, ordinarily have a full head of hair. Like head-shaving, cutting off one's topknot could symbolize "burning the bridge" and setting off on an endeavor that was likely to get one killed. Even the Japanese language seems to reflect this behavior, for to make up one's mind once and for all is most commonly expressed by the double-verb *omoi-kitte*, or "think-cut." Today, such haircuts are commonly the final and most dramatic part of an always tearful ceremony undertaken by retiring sumo wrestlers. Frois here failed to mention that Japanese samurai, when taken prisoner, also have their topknot removed (see 6a).

As an aside, the Japanese relationship to hair is fascinating for its ambiguity. One word for hair, *kami*, is homophonic with "god(s)" while another, *ke*, is homophonic with "filth/pollution." Being on top of the body (kami also means "upper"), hair is pure. However, an abundance of hair was associated with Japan's own "primitives," the Ainu, and later the "barbarian" West. Moreover, hair was associated with desire, although not as clearly as in Korean (Japanese's only cognate language).

---

36 Marques, *Daily Life in Portugal*, 52–53.
37 *Dores*.

16a. We fold our robes right over left; the Japanese do it left over right.

Wrapping the edge of one's garment right-over-left is called "left gusset" (*sajin*) and was used by the Chinese as a derogatory term for "barbarians," including their early medieval kin, the Japanese. In 719 C.E. the Japanese officially switched to left-over-right (*ujin*). Eight-hundred years later they called Western visitors like Frois and Rodrigues "left-gussets." Then as now, the left has sinister connotations in Japanese as in Western languages. In the West today, men's shirts, jackets and coats button left over right, and the cover over the fly on men's trousers also is open on the right. Likewise, the 'proper' way for a man to wear a belt on his pants is so that it crosses left to right across the midriff and through the buckle. Women's wear, in contrast, is assembled so that it crosses right to left.

17a. Our shirts[38] have ruffs and are closed in the front; Japanese katabiras have no collars and are open in the front.

Ruffled or pleated collars were all the rage in sixteenth century Europe. The ruff actually was separate from the shirt and was easily removed and washed, thus protecting the neck of the more expensive doublet from getting soiled.

This is yet another open and closed contrast deriving largely from the different climate of Europe and Japan. Today Western clothing is the norm in Japan. Shirts worn by white-collar workers are called *wai-shyatsu*, from "white shirt," although they need not be white any more than our "blankets" (from the French 'blanc' or white).

18a. We store our clothing by folding it with the outside in and the inside out; the Japanese fold theirs with the inside out and the outside in.

Today it would seem that most people in the West (at least those who fold clothes) do so in the "Japanese" style. As is true for many things, the Japanese, for their part, still maintain two styles. They put away *wafuku* ("gentle-dress" or Japanese clothing) in the Japanese style and *yofuku* ("ocean-dress" or Western clothing) in the Medieval/Renaissance/Western style.

19a. Our handkerchiefs are made of very fine cloth, embroidered or with fringes, etc.; some Japanese handkerchiefs are made of something similar to heavy tow cloth[39] and others are made of paper.

According to Marques,[40] Europeans rediscovered the handkerchief (the Romans were fond of them) during the Renaissance and only during the sixteenth century was it used outside Italy to dry perspiration or blow one's nose. Japanese rags or paper used for wiping brows, drying hands, and such were probably as beautiful in their way as the ornate European handkerchiefs mentioned by Frois. Today many visitors to Japan quickly come to appreciate their naturally colored handmade paper and the simple prints on Japanese *tenugui* (a handkerchief used to wipe sweat, rolled up as a sweat-band, or tied as a wrapped cap). As noted in the critical introduction, in Frois' time the Japanese used disposable tissues for

---

38 We have translated *camisas* as shirts to reflect current English usage, although shirts during the sixteenth century often were belted and could extend well below the waist, even to the knee.

39 *Liteiro.*

40 *Daily Life in Portugal*, 91.

blowing noses, and these were collected and recycled. (Even today one can find plentiful boxes of tissues and even bare rolls of toilet paper on desks in offices).

20a. We show courtesy by removing our hats; the Japanese show it by removing their shoes.

Note the parallel with servants mentioned in 29a, below. There is a slight incommensurability in Frois' contrast, as Europeans usually tipped and sometimes removed their hats to acknowledge equals. In the Japanese case, this courtesy is shown by a slight bow. The removal of shoes was more a matter of signaling respect and class status. Thus, the pariah class (*eta*) in Japan was not permitted to wear footwear in anyone's presence, ostensibly because it would be inappropriate for their "animal" (*yotsu* or four-footed) identity, and logically because they were the inferiors of all and had to remain physically lower. Today, no one in Japan removes footwear to show respect.

21a. We use a double-edged sword; the Japanese use a cutlass[41] that has only a single cutting edge.

As the sixteenth century unfolded, Europe's elite increasing came from among the ranks of the well-educated, particularly in rhetoric and law. Still, Europe remained a sufficiently violent place (see Chapter 14) and the society as a whole clung to the medieval idea that elites enjoyed their power and privilege because they were protectors and defenders of the less fortunate. Thus in Europe, and perhaps more so Japan, swords were a big part of elite identity. While European swords were quite variable, many elites wore a straight, narrow-bladed, double-edged rapier such as the Spanish *espada ropera*. European swords were designed mostly for stabbing or thrusting. The Japanese samurai did little of the latter; his razor-sharp cutlass was designed for slashing and removing body parts, especially heads![42] (see 28a and Chapter 7).

22a. Our scabbards are made of leather or velvet[43]; the Japanese use lacquered wood, except their nobles, whose scabbards are covered with gold or silver.

The lacquered wood usually was *magnolia hypoleuca* (black rather than the vermillion that often was used for plates), which protected the blade equally as well as, or better than leather or felt. Elsewhere Frois noted that the thickness of the gilt on Japanese scabbards depended on an individual's wealth.

23a. Our swords have chapes, hilts and pommels; Japanese swords have none of these things.

The chape is a metal fitting at the bottom of the scabbard, which further protects the tip of the blade as well as the sword bearer. European swords usually had a well-shaped handle (hilt) with an often decorative butt end (pommel). Because Japanese scabbards were usually of wood they had no need for a chape, and while Japanese swords obviously had a handle, it was a rather simple affair. Frois might also have mentioned that European swords had a

41 *Traçado*
42 Tobias Capwell, *The Noble Art of the Sword* (London: The Wallace Collection, 2012), 28–82; Thomas, *The Ends of Life*, 44–78; Dobrée, *Japanese Sword Blades*.
43 *Veludo*. Note that Frois speaks of felt (*feltro*) in distich 26a.

hand guard, which, in its simplest form–a cross-bar–stopped an opponent's sword blade from sliding down into the hand. Japanese swords often had a simple washer-like device for a "hand guard."

24a. Our swords are tested on lumber or animals; the Japanese insist upon testing their swords on human corpses.

Like Damascus steel, the best Japanese swords were tempered[44] and then tested on human flesh; "a first class blade sometimes cut through three corpses with one blow, although seven is on record."[45] This testing continued long after the Jesuits expressed dismay at the custom. Executed criminals, whose bodies were sometimes sewn together and re-used, were the principal source material for blade testing. Using corpses is one thing, but criminals and evil people in authority, including one Shogun, took to testing swords on any poor-looking passerby. *Suji-kire*, or "crossroads-cutting," is still a favorite theme of Japanese television "Easterns."

Lest the Japanese seem particularly inhumane, criminals who were convicted of especially heinous crimes were quartered in modern Europe and tens of thousands of witches and other "evil-doers" were burned or otherwise dispatched with spectacle. Paradoxically, while Europeans showed few qualms about ritual killing, they did pause–more than the Japanese, it seems–when it came to injuring a lifeless body. Perhaps Europeans feared offending God by complicating His work at the time of resurrection. Grave-robbing was a serious crime in Europe.

25a. Our cutlasses or scimitars are worn with the convex side downward; the Japanese wear theirs with the convex side up and the concave side down.

As Frois himself points out, Europeans favored straight, double-edged swords. The cutlass or scimitar, which was made famous (and frightening) by the Ottoman Turks who laid siege to Vienna in 1529, were sometimes reproduced by European swordsmiths as a "costume accessory."[46] The Japanese wore their cutlasses in scabbards fastened more or less horizontally or thrust through the belt diagonally, but still far closer to horizontal than vertical. For this contrast to make sense, we must assume European swords likewise hung somewhat off the vertical. As Frois later discusses in Chapter 7 on weapons and warfare (#4, #7–#11), the Japanese wore two swords (and a dagger); the larger was worn in the traditional bow up way (like a smile) and the smaller sword was worn with the bow down (like a frown). Because ends tend to hang down, scabbards holding a smile-like position had to have proper fasteners. In retrospect, Frois' exaggeration turns out to be a prediction, as Tokugawa period artwork shows that within a hundred years, both Japanese swords were worn like a frown. This method better holds a scabbard casually stuck through a belt.

---

44 Actually it is the cutting edge that is made of tempered steel; behind the edge is soft steel that is wrapped in hard steel, making the sword incredibly sharp and resilient. Coats, "Arms & Armor," 263.

45 Cooper, *They Came to Japan*, 167.

46 See for instance, Capwell, *The Noble Art of the Sword*, 77.

26a. We wear felt caps, capes,[47] *and hats in the rain; the Japanese, both rich and poor, wear hats and very long capes all made of straw.*

The Japanese do not have nor need a rain hat *per se*. Their traveling or working "hat" and "umbrella" are homophones (*kasa*). Because the *kasa* is umbrella-shaped, it provides excellent protection from both rain and sunlight. Moreover, because it does not cling to the head, but is instead supported by a harness, it provides ventilation and is perfectly suited to a muggy climate. In 1585, the Japanese apparently were in the process of "inventing" a raincoat, creating capes of straw that were layered like a thatched roof.[48] A century after Frois, Kaempfer speculated that the Japanese had learned the use of it, together with the name, from the Portuguese.[49] He further described a "large cloak ... made of double varnish'd oil'd paper, and withal so very large and wide, that it covers and shelters at once man, horse and baggage." At first, *kappa* meant any kind of cape, but during the Meiji era (1868–1912) *manto* (mantle) came to mean a cape or shawl and *kappa* came to mean only a raincoat.

27a. We regard strolling as great recreation, as well as very healthful and calming; the Japanese do not go strolling at all, and they are amazed and view our strolling as a hardship and penance.

During the nineteenth century America's first Ambassador to Japan, Townsend Harris, was told that prisons were not punishment for the Japanese because they did not feel a need to walk about in the first place (see also Chapter 14, #11). Both the Japanese and Chinese purportedly found the idea of "a constitutional" ludicrous. To relax and think, they sat still. The Portuguese evidently did not succeed in spreading the practice of walking in the Western sense, since the term for "a walk," which is *sanpou* or "scattered-steps," rarely was used until the Meiji era.

There are several caveats to Frois' contrast of "we who walk" and "they who do not." First, the Japanese may well have led the civilized world in two types of walking: pilgrimages and stylized pageantry. Japanese of all classes took advantage of their excellent roads and would walk from shrine to shrine, from temple to temple, covering distances of hundreds and even thousands of miles. As is apparent from the later Haiku of poets such as Basho, these pilgrimages were the occasion for

47 *Beden.* Not only is "*bedém*" a Moorish tunic; it can also be a rain-cape or a tunic made of rushes. Frois' use of the term, which is Arabic in origin, makes it clear that in Europe such capes were not made of rushes. This raises the interesting question of whether the Portuguese experience in Japan eventually led to a broadening in the semantics associated with this term. No similar term is used in Spanish.

48 In yet another twist to the raincoat story, it has been suggested that a group of Japanese who visited Mexico in 1610 introduced the raincoat of grass to the Indians of West Mexico! Zelia Nuttall, "The Earliest Historical Relations Between Mexico and Japan." *University of California Publications in American Archaeology and Ethnology* 4:1–47 (Berkeley: University of California Press, 1906–07), 47.

49 Englebert Kaempher, *The History of Japan, Together With a Description of the Kingdom of Siam, 1690–92.* 3 Vols. (Glasgow: James MacLehose and Sons, 1906[1690–92]), I, 400.

all manner of reflection on life.[50] The Japanese may not have walked much, but when they did, they walked like it was nobody's business. Mention should also be made of *neri-aruki* or "polished walking." There were many varieties of this walk-as-dance, ranging from the rapid and tiny up-and-down toe movements used by most Shinto float (*dashi*) carriers, which still can be seen today in Japan, to the slow-motion deliberate wobbling and rotating of each foot in turn by courtesans on parade on high *geta* clogs. Finally, during the Tokugawa period poor poets were said to engage in "aimless walking" (*sozoro-aruki*) through the so-called "pleasure quarters" of Edo, poking fun at people.

28a. Our swords and most valuable possessions are beautifully adorned; their precious belongings have no grandeur or adornment.

Europe's elite prized well-balanced swords with blades, pommels, hilts, and hand guards that often were engraved or featured complex designs, high-lighted with gold and silver and sometimes jewels. The peak of perfection in Japanese sword manufacturing, which was characterized by simple-looking yet incredibly sharp and resilient blades, was reached in the fourteenth century. By Frois' time, the secrets of the old masters were so completely lost that no one has since been able to duplicate the quality of Japanese blades from the four-teenth century.[51] It is no wonder, therefore, that the Japanese valued old, "plain-looking" swords.[52] However, the best and most revered swords were not really "plain," as Dobrée points out; the blades often had exquisite wavy markings like wood grain. Some swordsmiths apparently also signed their blades, albeit on the hidden tang of the blade, and occasionally embellished their blades with inscriptions or images.[53]

29a. We consider it rude if a servant does not remain standing once his master is seated; they consider it poor etiquette if the servant does not take a seat when his master does.

Japan shared the extreme up-and-down consciousness of much of Southeast Asia and Pacific island cultures, where a superior had to be literally higher than others at all times. To fold a wife's clothing on top of a husband's would disrespect him; to use a book as a pillow would disrespect the author.

30a. We use black for mourning; the Japanese use white.

The equation, black = mourning has not always held true in the West. Aristocratic women in Roman antiquity wore white for mourning, as did European queens during the Middle Ages and the early modern period. In Portugal, black was adopted for mourning only decades before Frois' birth.[54]

---

50 See Maria Rodriguez del Alisal, Peter Ackerman, and Dolores P. Martinez, eds., *Pilgrimages and spiritual quests in Japan* (London: Routledge, 2007).

51 Dobrée, *Japanese Sword Blades*, 11.

52 According to Okada, *Yoroppa-Bunka to Nihon-Bunka*, 27, the Japanese did, in fact, embellish with gold and silver certain swords that were used for ritual purposes.

53 Catharina Blomberg, *The Heart of the Warrior* (Sandgate, UK: Japan Library, 1994), 55; Coats, "Arms & Armor," 263.

54 Marques, *Daily Life in Portugal*, 92.

With respect to Japan, the association of white with mourning apparently originated in China. The association, however, was not as absolute as Frois implies, because in one of his letters Frois noted that the bonzes wore fine black upper garments to funerals. Today, partly as a result of Western influence, black is more common than white at Japanese funerals. In neighboring Korea, white is still *the* color of bereavement (and worn all the time by the elderly as if to say "I'm ready to go!").

31a. When we walk, we lift up the front of our clothing so it does not get soiled; the Japanese lift up the back of their clothing, so much so that their entire north[55] is exposed.

Japanese men typically lifted and then tucked the hem of their kimonos into their obi belt such that their behinds, and more often, their loin-cloths, were exposed. The Japanese even have a term for this "tucking up" (*shiri-karage*). It is possible that men showed more than their rear-ends, for loin-cloths were loosened in the humid summer and might be washed and tied to a bamboo pole to dry while walking. Japanese women, kept "the north" covered, "tucking up" instead in the front (and less radically, to be sure).

32a. Among us, pages and nobles accompanying their master should never reveal even so much as a toe; when travelling down the street with their master, the Japanese roll their breeches up clear to the groin.

If Europeans found their inferiors' nudity insulting and professed to be disgusted by it, the Japanese rather enjoyed it. This attitude lasted well into the Edo era (1603–1868), when Issa wrote haiku of cold winter moonlight congealing on the rumps of butt-proud footmen. In Japan, a lord would be proud of, rather than embarrassed by the magnificent *gluteus maxima* of his charges.

33a. We spit at any time; the Japanese normally swallow their sputum.

In his influential work, "On Good Manners," Erasmus (d. 1536) did not take issue with spitting, but rather advised fellow Europeans to "Turn away when spitting to avoid spitting or spraying someone else."[56] Today, it is Japanese men who seem to spit too freely for the taste of most Westerners. Interestingly, neither Frois nor other Europeans mention that one bodily function that is considered a privilege of the male sex, and which aroused by far the most international controversy, at least judging from the countless letters to the editor on this topic published in English-language newspapers in Japan. We are referring here to *tachi-shoben* or "standing-urination." Japanese men were once infamous for doing this practically anywhere and at any time, and eighteenth-century short poems called *senryu* (similar to haiku) tell of wise guys who peed on signs that forbid urination in public.

34a. We wield our swords with one hand; since Japanese swords are so heavy, all of them are wielded with both hands.

As noted, the civilian swords worn by European elites were mostly a thin, straight-bladed thrusting weapon. Although Frois attributes the Japanese use of two hands to their heavy swords, two hands holding, grasping, or cupping an

---

55 *Todo o norte desquberto.* Far be it for Frois to make a direct reference to the *derriere.*
56 Erika Rummel ed., *The Erasmus Reader* (Toronto: University of Toronto Press, 1990), 105.

object seem to sanctify it and its function. Polite drinking (a mark not just of formality but also of sincerity) was done with two hands, as was all giving and receiving of gifts. As is true of many things, this attitude and practice apparently was introduced from China during Japanese antiquity.

35a. We wear leather shoes and, [in the case of] our nobles, [shoes made of] felt; Japanese of all classes wear sandals made of rice straw.

Europeans did not want for shoes made of calfskin, goatskin, deerskin, sheep-skin, and unsoled cloth or felt, which were worn indoors.[57] Unlike shoes from the Middle Ages, which were ridiculously pointed, those of the sixteenth century tended to have rounded toes.

The humidity in Japan is high during a good part of the year and especially in summer. Therefore, in addition to being costly because of a lack of cattle hides, shoes made of felt or leather would have given many Japanese athlete's foot. Made from rice straw or not, the fine weave of the *zori*, worn by the wealthy, and the crude macramé weave of the *waraji*, worn by the poor, both kept the feet cool and relatively dry. Today this footwear is seldom worn except by elderly ladies and visiting foreigners. Japanese men say they don't wear sandals for fear of having their feet crushed on the subway, while women, by contrast, do not hesitate to wear toeless shoes. Those sandals that are found in Japan today are mostly hideous plastic *surippa* (slippers). The footwear situation proves beyond a doubt that the Japanese have become vulnerable to fashion trends, particularly from the West.

36a. We in Europe would think it insane for a noble to remove his shoes before presenting himself before a prince; the Japanese consider it poor etiquette not to remove one's shoes before presenting oneself before another, regardless of rank.

You have to believe European feet stunk a lot,[58] given their bathing habits (or lack thereof). With regular bathing and cooler and better ventilated footwear, presumably Japanese feet stunk a lot less (even if the same feet were more easily soiled).

37a. We enter our homes with our shoes on; in Japan this is rude and shoes should be left at the door.

Shoes do not mix with finely woven *tatami*; these straw mats are easily scuffed and soak up dirt. However, leaving one's shoes outside did have its drawbacks. The Jesuits were quick to realize that they could not go anywhere without *komono* (literally "little-people"), child servants responsible for keeping track of their shoes. The problem was not that shoes were stolen, but that they got lost amid hundreds of other shoes at public places. Even today, finding one's shoes at a public function can be like trying to find your car in an airport parking lot. Today, the Japanese generally trade in their shoes for slippers at the office, and both home and office have a special rack or container with slippers for guests. But all is not well, for unlike the open-heeled traditional *geta* or *zori*, the Western shoe, which the modern Japanese seem to be stuck with, does not easily shake off. The sole

---

57 Marques, *Daily Life in Portugal*, 45, 50, 67.
58 Mary Dobson, *Tudor Odours* (New York: Oxford University Press, 1997).

exception to the shoes-off-at-the-door rule is when someone dies; those removing the deceased from the house do not remove their footwear.

38a. In order to wash our face and hands, we roll up our sleeves only as far as the wrist; for the same purpose the Japanese strip down from the waist up.

Stripping to the waist was both easy to do (see 9a above) and hygienic, inasmuch as it exposed more of the body for washing. Ease of dressing and undressing apparently was one reason the Japanese engaged in bathing as often as they did.

39a. We show obeisance by placing a knee on the floor; the Japanese prostrate themselves with their legs, arms and head virtually flat to the ground.

"One knee for my lord, two knees for The Lord" is an apt way of conveying European obeisance. Neither Frois nor his equally observant contemporary, Rodrigues, noted the wordless auditory element of Japanese obeisance. The Englishman Saris was the first European to mention these noises, which seem to say "I am tense and awed! I am tense and awed!" Alcock, writing in the mid-nineteenth century, was the first to do the subject justice:

> ... suddenly, on some signal apparently, there is a general and long-prolonged sibilated sound impossible to describe, something between a 'hiss'and a long-drawn 'hish-t.' ... It was immediately after one of these rustlings of the breeze of reverence vibrating through the lips of a thousand sibilating courtiers, that I received the signal to advance to the entrance of the council chamber. I have never seen or heard anything like it, or, indeed, in the least resembling this strange but impressive way of bespeaking reverence.[59]

Today, the Japanese still occasionally suck air and make strange noises in the presence of superiors. However, they no longer prostrate themselves (that custom was given up in the mid-nineteenth century).

40a. We wear angular or rounded hats made of cloth; the Japanese wear silk hats, some of which are pointed and others shaped like bags.

Round hats of fine cloth or velvet and sombrero-like-hats with narrow brims do seem characteristic of sixteenth century Mediterranean Europe. Japanese portraiture from the sixteenth century includes figures with what might be described as "pointed" and "baggy" hats,[60] but the reality might not have been so simple. Japan's most beloved poet, Matsuo Basho (1644–1694), is usually shown wearing a hat shaped like a cake about two layers high.[61]

41a. Among us, patched clothing is considered extremely vulgar; in Japan, princes think very highly of a kimono or dobuku made entirely of patchwork.

The sixteenth-century Japanese were hardly into grunge. Tea masters and poets were nevertheless wild about patchwork, mostly made of old brocade and other fine materials. Some nobles emulated the "art crowd's" taste for patchwork.

---

59 Sir Rutherford Alcock, *The Capital of the Tycoon, A Narrative of a Three Years' Residence in Japan* (London: Longman, Green, and Roberts, 1863), I, 394.

60 See Money L. Hickman, ed., *Japan's Golden Age, Momoyama* (New Haven: Yale University Press, 1996), 70, 85

61 See the book cover to the Penguin edition (1966) of Basho's *The Narrow Road to the Deep North*, which features a reproduction of a portrait of Basho in the Itsuo Museum in Ikeda City, Osaka.

The rage apparently became an aesthetic tradition that was not confined to fine materials. Two hundred years after Frois, Issa celebrated what is probably a poor poet's dress (his own garb): a kimono of paper or *kamiko* that was a collage of *hanko*, i.e., reusable paper from old books, calendars, paintings, manuscripts, etc.

42a. In Europe, all our cloth is cut with scissors; in Japan everything is cut with a knife.

It is not that the Japanese did not have scissors, but they preferred to cut cloth with a particular knife called a *monotachi* or *monotachi-gatana*, literally "thing-cut-off-sword." Apparently if a single blade is sharp enough, there is no need for two. Conversely, scissors may have developed further in Europe in order to allow tailors and seamstresses to make "fine cuts," button holes, "pinking," and such—functions that were unnecessary for the production of Japanese clothing.

43a. In Europe it would be considered effeminate for a man to carry and use a fan; in Japan a man always carries a fan in his belt and he would otherwise be considered base and wretched.

If you ever have been stared at by a barracuda fanning its fins you can imagine that a samurai with a fan could look menacing, even if the fan itself rarely was used as a lethal weapon (as in Japanese TV "Easterns"). The Dutch physician Philipp Franz von Siebold, who lived in Japan for six years between 1823 and 1829, nicely captured some of the fan's uses:

> Among the men, the fan serves a great variety of purposes: visiters [sic] received the dainties offered them upon it; and the beggar, imploring charity, holds out his fan for the alms his prayers may have obtained. The fan serves the dandy in lieu of the whalebone switch; the pedagogue instead of a ferule for the offending schoolboy's knuckles; and, not to enumerate its many other uses, a fan, presented upon a peculiar kind of salver to the high-born criminal, is said to be the form of announcing his death-doom, his head being struck off the moment he stretches it towards this emblem of his fate.[62]

Fans are still common in Japan and are distributed free for use in folk dances (*bon*) that are held throughout Japan during the summer, although today little children and elderly women dominate the "fan dancing."

44a. Among us, lords and princes are preceded by [retainers carrying] torches of wax; in Japan they use bundles of old, dried lengths of bamboo, or bundles of straw.

Quality candles and torches of beeswax were important to Europeans, especially religious men like Frois (Catholicism, then as now, involved considerable sacrifices of candles as part of religious ritual). The common Japanese term for torch is *taimatsu* or "pine-light," reflecting the fact that pine resin was the principal combustible used to "light the way" for nobility. Ideally, the resin was applied to straw and bound up within a bamboo (*yadake*) framework.

---

62 Phillip Franz Von Siebold, *Manners and Customs of the Japanese in the Nineteenth Century* (Rutland, Vermont: Charles E. Tuttle Company, 1973[1841]), 25–26.

45a. In Europe baring even one's foot before a fire to get warm would be considered strange; in Japan anyone standing before the fire to get warm unabashedly bares his entire backside.

The Zen abbot, Sengai, painted himself with his testicles in plain view, and punning on their euphemistic name, "golden gems," wrote an accompanying poem about breaking out the gold for the entire world to share! (*kintama-o uchi-akete ...*). This lack of shame with respect to revealing one's private parts in a non-sexual context survived the long feudal era to shock the nineteenth-century West. Conversely, the nineteenth-century Japanese were equally shocked by the *décolletage* of Western women, not to mention corsets and other devices that emphasized the "female figure." The Japanese also took umbrage with nudes in painting exhibitions, because they had no similar tradition of showcasing the naked body. Thus, while they could look at pornography in private with little if any of the guilt attached to it by Westerners, the idea of displaying the human figure as a beautiful ideal was so far from their mind that they could only see this Western art as vulgar or "low-culture."

46a. We consider it effeminate for a noble to look in the mirror; Japanese nobles ordinarily all get dressed in front of a mirror.

The mirror had negative and positive connotations for Europeans as a function of how much time one spent looking into it: a brief glance could reveal virtue and remind the viewer of the transient nature of life, while prolonged scrutiny bespoke one or more of the "seven deadly sins."[63] As Frois' comment implies, women in Europe were perceived as being particularly prone to vanity. Of course, it is ridiculous to believe that European men, particularly nobles, did not prune themselves before venturing out to "perform" in public, as per Castiglione or Machiavelli. Correspondingly, Okada has pointed out that *Hagakure*, the classic manual for the samurai revival of the Edo era (1603–1868), advises warriors to use a mirror to make certain that they are properly dressed and groomed. In Shinto, the mirror is revered as a gift from the gods for our spiritual edification; in Buddhism, it was identified with the redeeming light of the moon. Its use by either sex was not thought to be narcissistic, but reflective, in the best meaning of the word (i.e., as an instrument of self-knowledge, purity, or cleansing). Philosophy apart, however, Japanese men spent so much time grooming that the presence of a mirror was hardly surprising.

47a. Among us, to wear clothing made of paper would be considered a joke or madness; in Japan, bonzes and many nobles dress in paper [kimonos] with silk fronts and sleeves.

As noted above (see 41a), paper kimonos were becoming high fashion in Frois' time, particularly those made of fancy paper, which had a fine, lacquered finish made of persimmon sap. During the seventeenth century, paper robes called *kamiko* came to be associated with poets and prostitutes, who could not afford silk. Like many homeless in America today, the Japanese understood that many

63 Woods-Marsden, *Renaissance Self-Portraiture*, 31.

layers of paper make good insulation in the winter, particularly in Japan where those months are the driest part of the year. During the eighteenth century only the elderly were allowed to use paper kimonos.

48a. What we consider a dressing robe for wearing around the house, the Japanese wear [in public], with sleeveless dobukus over their katabiras.[64]

Here Frois seems to be suggesting that the Japanese wear their light robes outside whereas Europeans do not. The *dobuku* vest, which during the seventeenth century became the sleeveless *haori*, was *de rigeur* in Japan during Frois time for men who would be called professionals: magistrates, doctors and tea-masters.[65] These professionals generally worked indoors.

49a. We wash clothes by scrubbing them by hand; in Japan clothing is washed by stomping on it with the feet.

Okada has taken issue with Frois and argues that the Japanese generally washed clothes by hand and less frequently did so using their feet. As it happens, some people in the West also used their feet: Thomas Hood wrote a poem in 1815 about women in Edinburgh who used their feet. While not stomping, pounding new silken cloth with sticks to soften it (called *kinuta* or "clothes-board") is perhaps the most common human sound found in haiku (no matter where a poet hears it, he thinks of mother). It may well be that *kinuta* was once the preferred Japanese method of cleaning all laundry, as was the case in Korea.

50a. We carry handkerchiefs and tissues in our sleeves or pockets; the Japanese tuck theirs into their breasts, and the higher up, the dandier.[66]

The broad sash worn by the Japanese turned the entire garment above the waist into an enormous pocket, and the contents were by no means limited to tissue. Okada cites two Tokugawa-era sources (one Japanese and one Russian) who marveled at the way Japanese men turned their kimonos into "warehouses," filled at times with "cakes from receptions" and sundry other items that would put a contemporary woman's purse to shame. While sleeves apparently were fairly short, i.e., narrow, at the time the *Tratado* was written, in earlier centuries they sometimes held more than the body of the kimono.

51a. We use pockets[67]*; the Japanese use a purse hung from their belt.*

Europe at this time was in the midst of transitioning from an external purse to an internal pocket; the first such pockets were often purses worn within one's clothing that were accessed by reaching through a slit or open side seam.

Purses worn by Japanese of both sexes were made of leather, cotton, and occasionally wood. While the sleeves served for coins and other little trinkets, the dangling body purses mentioned above served to carry paper, books, and more specialized items: nosegays, writing equipment, medicine, tobacco, fire-making

---

64 See 1-1a, 1-4a, 1-8a, 1-12a, and 1-13a above.

65 Okada, *Yoroppa-Bunka to Nihon-Bunka*, 33.

66 *Primor*. Elsewhere (see footnote 17 above) we have translated this term as stylish. Here we elected to go with "dandier" as it seems more consistent with Frois' thoroughly male-gendered perspective.

67 *Aljibeiras*.

kits, and so forth. The purse string usually was wrapped around the obi, or sash, rather than being tied to it. To prevent them from slipping off, a counter-weight was tied to the end of the purse string. This counterweight, or *netsuke*, forms the main body of perhaps the finest Japanese miniature sculptures. It kept the purses from falling not so much by its weight as by the fact that, small or not, it was big enough to catch on the upper or lower edge of the belt (depending on which way it was wrapped). Unlike most pockets, the dangling container has the advantage of not spilling its contents when one sits or lies down.

52a. In Europe purses are used to carry money; in Japan the purses of nobles and soldiers are used to carry scents, medicines and flint.

Japanese men, especially nobles, were very big on scent. The *Tale of Genji* tells of nobles who roamed about all night visiting women and leaving behind a scent trail that was still detectable a day later. A generation after Frois wrote, tobacco appears to have been the main scent left by all men, gentry or peasant.

53a. Among us people bathe at home, well hidden from the eyes of others; in Japan, men, women, and bonzes use public baths or bathe at night by their doorstep.

During the late Middle Ages, "licentious behavior" and the plague largely ended a European tradition of public bathing begun by the Romans.[68] In Japan, public baths were everywhere and often run by Buddhist temples. Some claim the practice of collective bathing started with laity who were recruited to clean Buddhist sculptures (getting wet and "blessed" in the process). Be that as it may, bathing caught on and by the Edo period (1603–1868) the Japanese enjoyed bathing and were not embarrassed to do so by their doorsteps or in public baths.

Considering the amount of bathing and showering that Europeans and Americans do today, one could say that this is one instance in which the West has emulated Japan, rather than the other way around. But alas, public baths seem headed for extinction in Japan as well; today most Japanese homes have their own baths and public baths are found mostly in rural areas. This is lamentable in light of Alcock's (1863) perceptive comment that the bathhouse in Japan was "what the baths were to the Romans, and what the cafe is to the Frenchman–the grand lounge."

54a. When it rains we wear boots or ordinary shoes; the Japanese go barefoot or wear wooden clogs[69] and walk with a staff.

The wooden clogs mentioned here apparently were a wooden *geta* elevated by two six-inch stilts called *ashida*. This footwear was worn during Frois' time primarily during the summer, when monsoon rains inundated towns and villages. The cane staff obviously provided additional stability for navigating mud and

---

68 Paris in 1292 (with a population of seventy thousand) had twenty-six public bathhouses. François De Bonneville, *The Book of the Bath* (New York: Rizzoli International Publications, 1998[1997]), 34. Today perhaps only the Finns can be said to enjoy public bathing. Garrett G. Fagan, *Bathing in Public in the Roman World* (Ann Arbor: University of Michigan Press, 1999), 1–2.

69 *Chapis.*

standing water. Up to the mid-twentieth century this footwear continued to be worn as rain, or rather, mud gear by men working in the so-called "water trades" (men working in bars and cheap inns, possibly because these tended to be in muddy areas). During the Tokugawa era, wooden *geta* were worn by prostitutes in parades. They used no staffs and walked in slow motion, taking advantage of the length of the stilts, slowly rotating each foot.

55a. We make our shoes of strong, thick leather; in Japan the tabi *are made of glove leather.*

As noted, Europeans who could afford good shoes had access to various types of footwear, including outdoor shoes of well-oiled zebra hide or calfskin, not to mention more expensive shoes and boots of deerskin, sheepskin, or polished goat-skin.[70] This contrast, however, is perhaps misleading, as *tabi* (literally "leg-bags") are more like socks or slippers than shoes. Perhaps Frois was misled by the fact that tabi at the time often were made of goatskin (soon to be replaced by cotton). *Tabi* divided the first and second toe and were worn with sandals or *geta*. If the soles of the *tabi* were clean, they also could be worn indoors. Today, most Japanese carpenters still wear *tabi* that have thin corrugated rubber soles. Unlike American construction workers who worry about things falling on their feet (thus their heavy boots), the Japanese worry about falling from beams. Since we are on the subject of footwear, many Japanese today wear socks that have individual "compartments" for all ten toes. The cotton variety keep the spaces between the toes cool and healthy in summer, while the wool variety (*gun-soku* or military-socks) are great in winter (although they are despised by young people). Doctors often prescribe the latter to combat athlete's foot (or "water-worm," as the Japanese call it).

56a. Our gloves are folded back at the wrist; Japanese gloves sometimes extend as high as the elbow.

Because Japanese "gloves" worn by both sexes are fingerless (see Chapter 2 #25), they might better be called palm-gloves. At first glance, they resemble Western archery arm-guards, but the back of the arm is covered as well as, if not better than, the front. The Japanese also had (and Buddhist priests still wear) bamboo mesh tubes on the forearms to keep the sweaty skin from rubbing on the inside of the sleeve.

57a. Among us, only a crazy man would wear clothing with unfinished edges; the Japanese wear their fur dobukus *the way the hides were cut from the deer.*

The Japanese side of this distich fits the tendency of Japanese handicrafts to preserve natural textures and shapes. This is equally true for architecture, food, utensils, and clothing. Thus, the natural grain of wood was preferred to paint (see Chapter 11, #7); unglazed pottery was used for formal occasions (Chapter 6, #30), and clothing was worn as it was woven, in the best form (rectangular) to show off the material rather than the human body underneath.

70 Marques, *Daily Life in Portugal*, 45.

58a. Our shoes, boots and slippers have soles that are separate [from the uppers]; Japanese tabi have no separate sole and are made of one continuous piece of leather.

Tabi are a lot like moccasins and, as noted above (see 55a) they functioned as a "thick sock" when worn with *geta* or *zori.*

59a. In Europe it would be ridiculous to wear shoes with half the foot sticking out; in Japan this is considered most stylish[71] and only bonzes, women and the elderly wear shoes that fit the entire foot.

This idea of the hanging heel as stylish persists to this day with respect to traditional Japanese footwear. Note that it is not the case that the foot does not fit into the shoe. The Japanese shoes are all open and generally wide enough for any foot; the length of the sole is just too short in the back. Foreigners, who complain that the Japanese *zori*, *geta* or *surippa* (a semi-traditional slipper) are far too small, often receive a lecture on the correct and stylish way to wear traditional Japanese footwear. It is interesting that there was a stylish way to wear shoes. Perhaps it might be compared to Europeans generally having correct ways to wear hats. It also is economical: an entire population (men and women) utilized but one, or two, medium-size *geta* or zori.

It is hard to say how this tradition started. Ancient Japanese footwear generally had gripping pegs. In Frois' time, thongs that could be gripped between the first two toes were common. Either way, people with large or small feet could wear medium-size footwear. Note that if traditional Japanese shoes are one-size, their socks or *tabi* come in as many sizes as European shoes, for they must fit just right, as they do not stretch like Western socks.

60a. We walk with our entire foot touching the ground; the Japanese walk on only the front part of the foot, which is placed on the short shoe.

For the reason of style noted immediately above (see 59a), the Japanese had to either exercise their arches (walking on the front of their feet) or soil the heels of their *tabi*. They chose the former. It is no wonder the Japanese did not walk for relaxation (see 27a above).

61a. At no time of the year, be it summer or winter, do we wear clothing so thin as to reveal the body; in Japan summer clothing is so thin that almost everything can be seen.

Inexpensive summer linen was so thin that *haikai* (proto-*haiku*) joke about poor women not being able to ford waist-high rivers. Be that as it may, the West (including the purveyors of Western fashion in Japan who are blind to traditional wisdom) still has a lot to learn from Japan when it comes to hot-weather fabrics. Traditional Japanese sheets soak up and evaporate sweat extremely quickly, and *jinbei* (a Bermuda-length shorts suit) boast a cotton and hemp fabric that is far, far cooler than our seersucker.

71 *Primor.*

62a. The hem on our long coats and robes extends all the way to the floor on all sides; in Japan, on both men's and women's katabiras and kimonos, the front hem is a hand's span higher than it is on the back.

Fellow missionary Rodrigues,[72] who wrote some twenty years after Frois, contradicted the latter, noting that women's robes were floor-length and were worn over a white petticoat. Either there was a change in fashion during the two intervening decades or each Jesuit described different classes of women or robes. A full- or floor-length hem was difficult to keep clean, but apparently this was not a concern for Europeans, particularly those who had servants to wash and repair clothing.

63a. We never stitch or mend[73] black clothing with white thread; the Japanese see no problem in sewing black clothing with white thread.

The Japanese sometimes retained, as decoration, thread that was used for fitting a *kimono*.[74] This fits the same general pattern of contrast noted in 57a above, and we might add the Japanese theatrical tendency to show prop changes or a puppeteer. Sometimes it is beautiful to reveal rather than conceal things.

72 João Rodrigues, *This Island of Japon*, trans. and ed. Michael Cooper (Tokyo: Kodansha International Limited, 1973[ca. 1620]).
73 Part of the text is missing here, but what is missing begins with the letter 'r,' most likely (given the context) *remendar*, or repair.
74 Okada, *Yoroppa-Bunka to Nihon-Bunka*, 38.

2 Women, their persons and customs

1. In Europe a young woman's supreme honor and treasure is her chastity and the inviolate cloister of her purity; women in Japan pay no mind to virginal purity nor does a loss of virginity deprive them of honor or matrimony.

During the sixteenth century European women continued to struggle as they had for centuries with societal norms that cast them in a subordinate role relative to men. Although women did "men's work" (e.g. butcher, fisher, merchant, renter, moneylender, sovereign), and did it well,[1] this reality was systematically obscured and women by and large were denied access to education, opportunity, and power. The situation *might* have been better for Japanese women; it is hard to say, given that literature and the historical record are ambiguous. While Shinto's most beloved *kami* was a woman–(the Sun Goddess, Amaterasu–) and the Pure Land schools of Buddhism proclaimed women capable of salvation, Shinto, Buddhism, and Confucianism more frequently spoke of women as "imperfect" (respectively: sources of pollution; spiritually "obstructed;" a potential threat to familial harmony) and best suited to supporting roles.

As this first distich and the twenty-seven that follow suggest, Europeans treated women's bodies as a fetish. This fetishization is often reflected in Frois' surprise that Japanese women's clothing revealed as much as it did. Beginning with distich twenty-nine, Frois' focus is more on behavior and rights and responsibilities. Again, the tone of the distichs is one of surprise that Japanese women enjoyed inheritance of property, relative freedom of movement, etc.

While Frois' distichs in this chapter necessarily provide a partial picture of the lives of women in Japan as well as Europe, they tend to support recent scholarship that has emphasized the significant changes in gender roles in Japan, particularly since the Meiji Period (1868–1912). The Japan that Frois experienced was a nation of mostly farm households and small businesses (i.e., artisans and merchants) where men and women worked together at home, sharing many rights and responsibilities, including nurturing and child-rearing. Complicating matters, however, was the rise to power of the samurai during the late medieval and warring states period (1467–1568), which created a privileged male culture centered on warfare. The empowerment of the samurai class and the subsequent emulation of their norms by lesser classes undermined the relative gender equality that Frois mentions or alludes to. Gender inequality was further exacerbated during the second half of the nineteenth century when the Japanese state whole-heartedly pursued

---

1 Keith Thomas, *The Ends of Life Roads to Fulfillment* (Oxford: Oxford University Press, 2010), 20–21, 104–107.

industrialization, relegating women to a cult of domesticity while promoting male education and employment away from home.[2]

As regards this first distich, the Christian church has a long history going back to late antiquity and the "Church fathers" of glorifying female chastity.[3] In Portugal and the rest of Mediterranean Europe, the post-Tridentine Church was obsessed with female chastity.[4] In Japan, by contrast, premarital sex was an accepted part of courting; "night-crawling" (*yobai*) was an ancient practice that continued well into the twentieth century in rural parts of Japan.[5] Some young women also prostituted themselves to support their poor families and gain dowries for their subsequent marriages. They were not criticized for doing so because: 1) coitus had no stigma in a Shinto culture, where, for instance, people sang explicitly bawdy songs while planting rice; 2) the women acted to help others and did not act from selfish desire, something that would be considered bad from a Buddhist point of view; and 3) they were behaving in an exemplary manner from the point of view of Confucian ethics, where assisting one's parents and superiors was the cardinal virtue. Among the upper class, marriages generally were arranged and women were discouraged from intercourse with other men lest their affection be alienated, but virginity *per se* was not at issue.

During the post-World War II occupation of Japan by the United States, many Japanese took on more conservative American values, including a virgin-until-marriage mindset. Indeed, during the 1960s the Japanese press criticized the West for being "sexually promiscuous." However, by the end of the twentieth century Japanese attitudes were similar to Europeans', both of whom, for instance, thought Americans made too big a deal of President Clinton's sexual promiscuity.

2. Women in Europe greatly prize and do everything possible to have blond hair; women in Japan abhor it and do all they can to make their hair black.

Europeans as far back as the Romans apparently believed that "blondes have more fun,"[6] presumably because the hair color is reminiscent of men's other preoccupation: gold. Women in sixteenth-century Iberia were chastised by moralists

2 Issues of gender and our changing understanding of the role of women in Japanese society over time are the subject of two excellent collections of essays: Gail Lee Bernstein, *Recreating Japanese Women, 1600–1945* (Berkeley: University of California Press, 1991); Anne E. Imamaura, ed., *Re-Imagining Japanese Women* (Berkeley: University of California Press, 1996).

3 See, for example, Jerome's letter (22) to Eustochium, *The Letters of Saint Jerome*. Trans. Charles C. Mierow (Westminster, Maryland: The Newman Press, 1963), 134–180.

4 Anne J. Cruz and Mary Elizabeth Perry, "Introduction." In *Culture and Control in Counter-Reformation Spain*, ix–xxiv (Minneapolis: University of Minnesota Press, 1992), xvii–xviii; Isabel M.R. Mendes Drummond Braga, "Poor Relief in Counter-Reformation Portugal: The Case of Misericôrdias." In *Health Care and Poor Relief in Counter-Reformation Europe*, eds. Ole Peter Grell, Andrew Cunningham, and Jon Arrizabalaga, 210–215 (London: Routledge), 207–208.

5 Anne Walthall, "The Life Cycle of Farm Women in Tokugawa Japan." In *Recreating Japanese Women, 1600–1945*, ed. Gail Lee Bernstein, 42–70 (Berkeley: University of California Press, 1991), 51, 63.

6 Richard Corson, *Fashions in Hair: The First Five Thousand Years* (London: Peter Owen, 2001).

such as Fray Luis de Leon for dying their hair blond ("God save us from such ruination"). In Japan, on the other hand, raven black (*nubatama*) hair was *the* classic mark of a beauty.

3. Women in Europe part their hair at the forehead; in Japan they shave their foreheads and conceal the part.

European women not only parted their hair, but some noblewomen also shaved their scalps or used a caustic paste (ceruse) to accentuate their foreheads and lighten their eyebrows.[7] This attention to the forehead was an aesthetic complement to the tall hats with veils (*crespina*) that were fashionable in Portugal and other parts of Europe (e.g., *hennin*).[8]

Japanese women shaved their hairline to create what Westerners might call a widow's peak and what the Japanese call *fujibitai* (literally Mount Fuji-brow). Okada wonders, however, if Frois is referring in this distich to a *naka-zori*, a spot in the scalp shaved for the purpose of inserting a small pillow to construct a hairdo. It is unclear whether this Tokugawa era-style yet existed in 1585.[9]

4. Women in Europe perfume their hair with fragrant aromas; Japanese women always walk about reeking of the oil they use to anoint their hair.

Japanese women in ancient times placed cloves in their hair oil (*mizu-abura*, literally water-oil), which was made from sesame and camellia oil. Okada cites a work of literature where a woman is advised to trade in her sesame oil for less smelly but more expensive walnut oil. How ironic that European women, who bathed infrequently, apparently smelled good thanks to perfume, while Japanese women, who bathed every day, apparently reeked.

5. Women in Europe rarely add hair from other sources to their own; women in Japan buy many wigs brought through trade with China.

It might be more accurate to say that wealthy European women *infrequently* used wigs or hairpieces; some did so for a fuller effect or because their own hair was too thin.[10]

Some Japanese noblewomen did wear several lengths of hair in serial. Okada notes that the Japanese had professionals whose job was to purchase hair lost through brushing, which was recycled as wigs. It is likely that the Chinese "wigs" spoken of by Frois were, properly speaking, *kamoji*, which were large hair buns stuffed with yak hair. Europeans were behind in the wig game, but even as Frois wrote the male wig had begun to take root among English professional men and would soon spread throughout much of Europe.

6. Women in Europe often adorn their heads by covering their hair; Japanese women always leave their hair uncovered, and noblewomen wear their hair loose.

7 Victoria Sherrow, *Encyclopedia of Hair: A Cultural History* (Westport, CT: Greenwood Press, 2006), 115.

8 A.H. De Oleveira Marques, *Daily life in Portugal in the Late Middle Ages* (Madison: University of Wisconsin Press, 1972), 84.

9 Akio Okada, trans. and ed., *Yoroppa-Bunka To Nihon-Bunka* [European Culture and Japanese Culture] (Tokyo: Iwanami Shoten, 1965), 39–40.

10 Richard Corson, *Fashions in Hair: The First Five Thousand Years* (London: Peter Owen, 2001).

As the sixteenth century unfolded European women exposed more and more of their hair; large hats and headdresses gave way to smaller hats, veiled headdresses, and hooded garments that revealed more of the forehead and temples.[11]

When Frois wrote, most women in Japan wore their hair down. Within one hundred years of Frois' observation, Japanese women wore their hair up with enough hairpins to frighten a porcupine, and the hairpin man, with his straw-wrapped pole stuck full of his wares, was an accepted part of Edo culture.

7. Women in Europe tie their hair by braiding ribbons into it all the way to the ends; Japanese women tie their hair using either a small paper ribbon at a single place in the back or they roll it on top of the head using a paper string.

This contrast would seem to contradict Frois' previous observation that Japanese women of nobility wore their hair loose. However, there is no contradiction when it is understood that the tie (something like a half bow-tie, with the loop on the left) was either worn so far down the back that, for all practical purposes, the hair above was loose, or tied at the base so the remainder was a loose ponytail. Frois' contrast is between hair kept tightly tied-up (Europe), and hair which, bound at the end or at the top, was free for the rest of its considerable length (Japan). Presumably, Europeans found the latter "loose" in both senses of the word.

8. Women in Europe wear veil-like coverings on their heads; Japanese women wear wataboshi of silk or a piece of white cloth under a mantle.

Iberian women of means often wore fine *beatilhas* and *volantes* (a large scarf of fine, black lace). Japanese *wataboshi* were made from cloth beaten from substandard silkworm cocoons, and while perhaps not much to look at, they nevertheless were very soft and warm. Similarly, the plain white cloth sometimes worn by Japanese women was absorbent and cool.

9. Women in Europe wash their hair and head in their homes; Japanese women do so in public baths, where there are special lavatories for the hair.

Frois' reference to both hair and head may strike us as strange; today in English we simply say "wash our hair." Yet lice were a common problem in early modern Europe and thus one washed one's head (scalp) as well as hair. With respect to Japan, Frois, for a change, is *not* referring here to Japanese noblewomen, who would not be caught dead in a public bath, not because of a different attitude toward nudity than that of the lower classes, but because high status in Japan implied maintaining distance from ordinary folk.

10. Noblewomen in Europe wear their skirts with long trains; Japanese women in the house of the shogun[12] wear four or five wigs attached one to another that drag about six feet[13] behind them when they walk.

---

11 Ibid.

12 *Kubo*, literally, is a "public-direction = person = way," but it has been used to refer to anything from the Emperor to public officials. In Frois' time, it usually referred to the shogun and could modify his household and those of his close relations, or, at least, that is how Frois used it.

13 Three *couvades*.

The clergy denounced dresses with long trains as bestial: "let them go about with breasts covered, and let them not wear tails like cows ..."[14] Still, the dresses worn by European noblewomen not only had trains but often a hoopskirt, which entailed a cloth bolster or one or more hoops of willow or some other lightweight material that lifted and extended the skirt outward, essentially exaggerating a woman's hips.

The wigs here mentioned by Frois were not actually wigs (*katsura*), serially linked, but instead a single long tress (*kamoji*) that was attached with a decorative cord to a woman's real hair a bit below the shoulders. The tress featured decorative paper, half-bows at intervals. Such long tresses presupposed extremely clean surroundings. They generally rested on the long train of the kimono, which in turn, glided on spotlessly clean *tatami* or floorboards.

11. Women in Europe value eyebrows that are well-formed and shapely; Japanese women pluck theirs out with a tweezers,[15] leaving not a single hair.

Frois is essentially correct in highlighting what was an age-old custom in Japan. Japanese feminists point out that a lack of eyebrows, combined with make-up that minimized the size of the mouth, left women bereft of the signs of an outgoing personality.

12. Women in Europe use makeup to whiten their brows; noble[16] women in Japan paint their foreheads with black paint as decoration.

The same caustic cosmetic (ceruse) that was used to whiten a woman's face also was used by European women to lighten their eyebrows.[17] Japanese women of the nobility painted the edges of their hairline and also painted stubby false eyebrows on the upper part of the forehead, which, significantly, does not move as much as the lower brow. Children of both sexes sometimes also had what we might call displaced eyebrows. As late as 1868 the youthful Emperor Meiji had high artificial eyebrows painted on his forehead when he received European diplomats.

13. The hair of women in Europe turns white in a few short years; Japanese women who are sixty years old have no gray hair because they treat it with oil.

If European men were fortunate to have full beards, Japanese women were blessed with hair with lasting beauty. Walnut oil, in particular, was reputed to keep hair black.

14. European women pierce their ears and wear earrings; Japanese women neither pierce their ears nor do they use earrings.

The Japanese, unlike the Chinese, did not pierce their ears. Perhaps because large ear lobes are synonymous with good fortune the Japanese were hesitant about

---

14 Ronald Rainey, "Dressing Down the Dressed Up: Reproving Feminine Attire in Renaissance Florence." In *Renaissance Society and Culture*, eds. John Monfasani and R.G. Musto, pp. 217–239 (New York: Ithaca Press, 1991).

15 Tweezers, called *ke-nuki* or hair-removers, were a popular item among Japanese street vendors during the Tokugawa era.

16 Note here Frois' reference to *nobres*, apparently court level, which was a higher level than, say, *fidalgas*.

17 Sherrow, *Encyclopedia of Hair*, 115.

puncturing what might be a source of luck. Today, most Japanese women wear earrings, although many still consider ear piercing unnatural and wear only clip earrings.

15. Women in Europe think it unattractive for their face powder and make-up to be noticeable; women in Japan think the more layers of white powder applied, the more genteel.

Cosmetics as well as jewelry were popular in Europe, although the Church frowned on make up, "Because, to give oneself over to the arts of the toilet pertains to a harlot, and not to a woman who is truly good." [18] Certainly Japanese women, on formal occasions, out-did their European counterparts in the foundation department, as the prolific playwright Saikaku has a female character apply two hundred layers of powder. As noted in Chapter 1 (#8), the Japanese from time immemorial have valued white skin, especially for women. Still, it would be wrong to identify Japanese women in masse with heavy make-up. The Spanish merchant Avila Giron, writing a couple decades after Frois, noted that it was primarily married women, "as a mark of honour," who were accustomed to putting on a little powder and a touch of color on their lips, to hide the dye that came off on their lips when they stained their teeth black.

16. Women in Europe make use of methods and concoctions to whiten their teeth; Japanese women use iron and vinegar to make their mouths and teeth as black as [missing].

Black as "pitch" is how fellow Jesuit Rodrigues described the teeth of some Japanese women, particularly nobles. Rodrigues noted that some boys also blackened their teeth, but "the practice has now been given up completely by men and largely by women, who now leave their teeth in their natural condition." As it turned out, the custom of *ohaguro*, which apparently prevented tooth decay, was later revived and continued to the end of the Tokugawa period, with black teeth being the mark of a married woman.

17. Women in Europe wear bracelets of gold and silver on their arms; the noblewomen of Shimo wear thin threads that circle the arm five or six times.

The Japanese lack of interest in gold, silver, and precious stones is unusual, even in Southeast and Far East Asia. Okada speculates that the thin threads described by Frois refer to a charm worn when the arm or fingers were sore. He does not suggest why they might be sore, but young noblewomen wove clothing for their would-be lovers and often played the *koto*, a zither-like instrument that is one of the most muscularly taxing instruments in the world. There is also the possibility that the strings were charms to help attract or retain a lover.

18. Women in Europe wear jewels and golden chains around their necks; non-Christian women in Japan wear nothing, and those who are Christian wear relics or rosary beads.

---

18 Fray Luis De Leon, *The Perfect Wife* (Denton, Texas: The College Press, Texas State College for Women, 1943[1583]), 60.

As suggested above, the Japanese have never been particularly interested in precious stones and minerals (there is a correspondingly small vocabulary to discuss gems in Japanese). In ancient Heian times (800–1200 C.E.) Japanese women wore necklaces that were allegorized in Japanese poetry as their lover and their lover's soul. These necklaces, called *tama-no-o* or "*tama*-string," are based on a homophonic pun: *tama* means soul as well as any round, shiny, or bead-like object.

19. Women in Europe wear sleeves that extend as far as the wrist; women's sleeves in Japan extend halfway down the arm and they do not consider it unchaste to reveal their arms and breasts.

This distich and those that follow reveal a European preoccupation with women's bodies, which needed to be hidden and fully clothed lest they arouse or excite men's passions.

If the Japanese sleeve was long in the sense that it was wide enough to hang almost to the ground (see Chapter 1, #5a), it was short in length as measured from the shoulder to the hand. Thus, if a woman were to extend her arm or arms, one might glimpse the woman's breast through the arm-hole. Note, however, that this was probably more titillating to European men than it was to Japanese men; the latter were more likely to be aroused by the sight of a woman's nape than her breasts.

20. Among us, a woman would be considered mad or shameless if she went barefoot; Japanese women, be they nobles or commoners, walk about barefoot during most of the year.

Europeans turned a woman's feet as well breasts into a fetish, thus explaining Frois' preoccupation here with exposed feet. Note that Frois' Portuguese usage is misleading, as the term *descalças* ("barefoot") implies that Japanese women wore nothing on their feet. What Frois meant to say was that they rarely wore "socks" or *tabi*. They did, however, wear sandals or clogs, which, from a European perspective, exposed too much of the foot. As a literal antipode to Japan, China would seem better than Europe. In China, feet were a woman's surrogate private part! If Japanese women could be considered loose with their feet, Chinese women were tight, and Europeans somewhere in between. This is not only true for the degree of exposure, but for the degree to which the feet were tortured. The Japanese were kind to them, the Europeans, with their pointed and symmetrical toes, hard on them, and the Chinese, with their foot-binding, downright sadistic.

21. Women in Europe wear their belts very tight; Japanese noble women tend to wear them so loosely that they are always falling down.

The belts and girdles worn by elegantly-dressed European women were not only tight, but during some periods the style was to wear them so high that they cinched the bust.[19]

---

19 Marques, *Daily Life in Portugal*, 89.

Okada[20] has pointed out that the reason the *obi* (bands of cloth as stiff and "wide as a horse's girth strap," according to de Avila Giron[21]) was tied loosely, was because of its greater width and the fact that it was wrapped around the body several times. (In television "Easterns," the bad guys strip women by spinning them like tops.) Judging from artwork, the *obi* was usually worn lower in Frois' time than in the twentieth century, when it was so high and so tight that it could literally squash the breasts (an interesting change in fashion that paralleled the loss of freedoms once enjoyed by Japanese women).

22. European women wear gemstone rings and other jewelry; Japanese women wear no adornment or jewelry made of gold or silver.

Marques notes that those Portuguese who could afford it spent enormous sums on jewelry, including rings that decorated all the joints of the fingers.[22] Finger rings seem so natural to Europeans and Americans that it is hard to imagine a people who would have nothing to do with them. The Japanese called rings "finger-metal" (*yubigane*) and acquired them from the Dutch in the seventeenth century to fasten the strings of a pouch (one area where a certain amount of orna-mentation was traditional).[23] How times have changed; today most Japanese wear "finger-rings" (*yubiwa*) as in the West.

23. European women wear purses or keys on their chords or belts; the Japanese tie some strips of thin silk painted with golden leaves [around their obi bands], but they do not attach anything to them.

The image of a housewife or maid with keys dangling from her waist is very European. Japanese houses could only be locked from the inside, and there were no locked rooms or cabinets. Thus, Japanese women had no use for keys. This is not to suggest, however, that theft was not of some concern in Japan. Rather than lock one's home, the Japanese employed a *rusu-ban* or "remain-guard duty" in the house (again locking the doors from the inside) to guard against theft. Purses were not needed, for the partially sewn sleeve ends served in that capacity.

24. The dresses of European women are closed in the front and cover their feet all the way to the ground; those of Japanese women are completely open in the front and extend to the ankle.

During the Tokugawa period (1603–1868) prostitutes on parade walked on high-teethed *geta*, wearing a half dozen or more layers of clothing, all of which were open in the front. However, this was not ordinary women's wear, which usually had inner layers that wrapped around to the side, keeping the legs well covered. In this case "open" does not mean cut away or slit, thus revealing the legs, but that the overlapping panels of the dress separate as a Japanese woman walks, revealing a woman's foot and ankle. Japanese women also walked in short,

20 Okada, *Yoroppa-Bunka To Nihon-Bunka*, 46.
21 In Michael Cooper, *They Came to Japan* (Ann Arbor: University of Michigan Press, 1981), 208.
22 *Daily Life in Portugal*, 89–91.
23 Okada, *Yoroppa-Bunka To Nihon-Bunka*, 47.

mincing steps, with their toes inward as if consciously hiding their insteps, which, together with the nape of the neck, were the focus of men's ogling.

25. Women in Europe wear fine, scented gloves; Japanese women wear silk gauntlets that cover the forearm, leaving all the fingers exposed.

Tight-fitting gloves, particularly of kidskin, were popular with European men as well as women (presumably only the women perfumed theirs).[24] Japanese gloves cover the back rather than the front of the hands; protecting the hands from the sun or cold while not adversely affecting dexterity. (One could eat and write with these gloves on.) In any case, the main intent was to keep the inside of the sleeve clean (see #56a below).

26. Women in Europe wear very long black cloaks; Japanese noblewomen wear short ones made of white silk.

Long and black vs. short and white seem as different as can be, but both European and Japanese cloaks fulfilled much the same function of covering and protecting a woman's hair from the elements. Okada notes that the Japanese scarves or cloaks usually were made of satin or silk crepe.

27. Cloaks in Europe have neither sleeves nor any color; in Japan their color-ful katabiras *also serve as cloaks.*

The image of a light robe serving as a head scarf or cloak might seem strange, but imagine getting caught during the summer in a rain shower without a hat or umbrella and removing your arms from your coat and drawing it up over your head. This is what Frois seems to be commenting on. As noted in the previous chapter (#1a), the *katabira* is summer wear, and most *katabira* were white, "pale-scallion" (light green) "water-pale-scallion" (light blue-green), and other light shades. The Japanese still feel that such colors are cooling and utilize them even today, particularly for window and door screens.

28. European soldiers wear their [troop's] colors when they dress up; Japanese women regularly wear their group's colors on their kimonos, in a four-color design.

It is unclear whether the "four-color design" (*quarteados*) mentioned by Frois refers to the colors of a single item, or four different colored robes that were worn one over another. If it is the latter, a clan crest on the garment may have made it seem even more military. Charles Thunberg visited Japan at the end of the eighteenth century and was struck by how at public baths the Japanese would fold their cloaks and put them in little boxes. Thunberg noted that every cloak had a "coat of arms," perhaps to distinguish one from another.

29. In Europe, men walk in front and women walk behind; in Japan, the men walk behind and the women in front.

As noted at the outset of this chapter, this is the first of numerous distichs that focus more on behavior than appearance. Japanese editions of the *Tratado* by Okada and Matsuda and Jorißsen interpret the "men and women" as "husband and wife (*otto, tsuma*)." This contrast would appear to make more sense, however, if it

---

24 Marques, *Daily Life in Portugal*, 72, 87.

is understood that Frois is referring to the male and female servants who ordinarily accompanied nobles in Japan and Europe. Frois' superior, Valignano, observed that Japanese noblewomen were preceded by their maids (*senoras moças*) and followed by their male servants (*criados*); this is indeed the opposite of European practice.

30. In Europe, property is held in common by husband and wife; in Japan, each owns his or her own, and sometimes the woman lends hers to her husband at exorbitant rates of interest.

European commonality belied the fact that, practically speaking, the property (i.e., land, house, furniture) was controlled by the husband rather than the wife, excepting perhaps clothing or furniture (e.g., chests, tapestries) that a wife may have brought to the marriage as a dowry.[25] At the time Frois wrote, a Japanese woman's *trousseau* remained hers to dispose of as she wished. If and when she divorced (see #32 below), she got her things and money back.[26] "Her" children, unless they were from a previous marriage, remained with her husband's family. However, if a Japanese man married into a woman's family, which was not uncommon, the situation reversed and *her* family kept the children.

If men tended to control the purse strings in Europe, it was indeed the opposite in Japan, where women saved, kept the books, and made the budget. Men in Japan, unless they were merchants, were supposed to be above pecuniary matters. A housewife in all her glory is often called the *daikoku-bashira*, literally the "big-black-post," which is to say the central pillar of the house.

Generations of Japanese men have joked about being cormorants, made to regurgitate their pay for their wives. In modern times, the complaint has gained a new twist. The wedding ring (a Western import) is sometimes jokingly referred to as the neck-choke, worn by the bird to make certain it cannot swallow any fish. In the 1970s and 1980s some Japanese companies reputedly cooperated with their cormorant "salary men" by giving them two paychecks, one of which was kept secret from the wife.

31. In Europe, repudiating a woman is not only a sin but a great dishonor; in Japan, one can repudiate as many women as one pleases without them consequently losing their honor or prospects for marriage.

Today, as in the past, the Catholic Church does not allow divorce. In Frois' day, husbands and wives who did not get along remained together yet essentially lived separate lives. Among the nobility or wealthy business class, this often meant, in the case of the husband, keeping a mistress. A woman in Europe who was

---

25 See for example Malveena McKendrick, *Women and Society in the Spanish Drama of the Golden Age: A Study of the 'Muger varonil'* (Cambridge: Cambridge University Press, 1974), 16–17.

26 Varley would seemingly take issue with Frois, arguing that the many rights and responsibilities that Japanese women enjoyed during the Kamakura period (1185–1333), including equal inheritance of property, had been ceded to men even before the Jesuits arrived. Paul Varley, "Law and Precepts for the Warrior Houses," In *Sources of Japanese Tradition, Second Edition, Volume One: From Earliest Times to 1600*, eds. Wm. Theodore de Bary, D. Keene, G. Tanabe, and P. Varley, 413–433. (New York: Columbia University Press, 2001), 415.

disowned by her husband was "damaged goods" and certainly could not remarry "in the eyes of the Church," which was no small matter in communities where the Church wielded enormous power.

The situation for married women in Japan was somewhat "better," seemingly, in that divorce or repudiation did not have a crippling stigma, except perhaps among the samurai class.[27] A Japanese husband, unless he was a noble and feared scandal and damage to a family alliance, could easily divorce a woman and remarry, while a woman could not remarry without official papers of separation and divorce, which the husband was free to grant or withhold.[28] Presumably, the threat of divorce was used to control women. The seventeenth-century moralist, Kaibara Eiken, in his classic *Onna Daigaku* ("Woman-Great-Study"), gave a handful of reasons for divorce: disobedience to the father or mother-in-law, barrenness (an otherwise good wife might be kept and children adopted), lewdness, jealousy, leprosy or any foul disease, disturbing the household harmony by talking too much and too disrespectfully, or being a kleptomaniac. To promote frugality, the authorities further decreed that "too much sightseeing" or "too much tea-drinking" were just cause for divorce.

After World War II, divorce was strongly discouraged in Japan, both for the sake of the children (the nuclear family now being the norm), and purportedly out of concern that men would use and then throw away their wives for someone younger.[29]

32. In accordance with corrupt nature, it is men in Europe who repudiate women; in Japan it is often the woman who repudiates the man.

The Judeo-Christian origin myth, Genesis, says Eve tempted Adam with the forbidden fruit, which got both of them thrown out of the Garden of Eden. Genesis also says that, as a consequence, "Your [Eve's] yearning will be for your husband, and he will dominate you." Domination and repudiation go hand-in-hand.

While only men in Japan had a general right to divorce, the wife's family could sue when the husband sold off or pawned her possessions without her permission; she could flee to her family and gain a divorce if the husband did not sue for her to return to his family (in this case, the influence of the wife's family was important), or she could become a nun for life.[30] Still, it was not until 1873 that women obtained a formal right to sue their husbands for divorce.

Jesuit and other early visitors to Japan did not note any class difference here, but late nineteenth-century writers made it clear that peasant women often repudiated

27 According to samurai teachings, divorcées were not supposed to remarry; better the wife should commit suicide. Anne Walthall, "The Life Cycle of Farm Women in Tokugawa Japan." In *Recreating Japanese Women, 1600–1945*, ed. Gail Lee Bernstein, 42–70. (Berkeley: University of California Press, 1991), 60.

28 Okada, *Yoroppa-Bunka To Nihon-Bunka*, 49.

29 Since the1960s, the divorce rate has slowly increased and now over 30 percent of marriages end in divorce. See Allison Alexy, "The door my wife closed; houses, families, and divorce in contemporary Japan." In *Home and Family in Japan*, eds. R. Ronald and A. Alexy, 236–254 (London: Routledge, 2011), 238.

30 Ibid., 49.

their husbands, mostly for being hopelessly dissolute drinkers or gamblers, but sometimes for lesser reasons. Writing in the early twentieth century, Douglas Sladen *lauded* the high divorce rate in Japan, noting that it was far more reasonable to allow a working woman to divorce her no-good husband than to chain her to an utterly irresponsible and violent man, as English Law did at the time.[31]

Today, Europeans and Americans have a higher divorce rate than the Japanese. Considering the historically recent reversal, it is ironic that this difference is usually attributed to some inherently Western individualism versus Japanese collectivism. It may well be that both sexes in Japan had more control of their lives in Frois' time, considering that today they face an uphill battle securing a divorce, even in clear-cut cases of abuse or where a married couple has lived separately for a long time.

33. In Europe, the abduction of a female relative results in the entire family placing their lives on the line; in Japan the fathers and mothers and siblings dissimulate and pass over this lightly.

Okada believes Frois was referring to *yukai*, meaning "abduction" or "enticement." Japan was not a place where women worried about being overpowered and carried off, either physically or symbolically, but lovers could and did elope, something that was usually hushed up for a while and later forgiven.

Both abduction (lovers running off together) and rape, meaning the physical violation of a woman, was much more common in Europe as compared with Japan. We in the West forget that the family was very much a "private enterprise" during the sixteenth-century; it wasn't necessarily or solely a loving support group. Women were of great value to fathers, uncles, brothers, and other male relatives; the latter understood that their female kin were valuable assets that could realize great economic and social gains if properly "invested," that is, married into the right family. So, forced or not, a woman's rapture was serious business.[32] A rape in the modern sense of the word would have undermined a woman's chances for marriage in the West, but not in Japan, where virginity *per se* was not an issue. While women of the warrior class were expected to defend their own honor to the death (see #35 below), not all commoners would have been so proud.

34. In Europe, the confinement of daughters and maidens is very intense and rigorous; in Japan, daughters go unaccompanied wherever they please for an entire day, and many do so without informing their parents.

Women in Japan were not in fact as secluded as in most Asiatic countries or in sixteenth century Spain or Portugal, where a quarter or more of the female population lived in convents. Walthall recounts how in eighteenth century Japan it was not uncommon for the daughters of wealthy peasants to make lengthy pilgrimages

---

31 *Queer Things About Japan* (Detroit: Singing Tree Press, 1968[1913]). See also Walthall, "The Life Cycle of Farm Women," 60–62.

32 Merry E. Wiesner-Hanks, *Women and Gender in Early Modern Europe* (Cambridge: Cambridge University Press, 2008), 75–81.

to Shinto shrines for religious purposes as well as for sightseeing and simply experiencing the world beyond one's home town or village.[33]

35. Women in Europe never leave the house without their husband's permission; in Japan the women are free to go where they please without their husbands' knowledge.

Beyond the different gender constructions already noted, the differential freedom of women may also reflect different levels of public safety. While war made Japan unsafe for male combatants, the greater emotional self-control of the Japanese meant that there was less random violence as compared with Europe (see Chapter 14). Japanese women (at least in the warrior classes and among the towns-folk, who strove to emulate the samurai) were not only more likely to read and write than their European counterparts (see #45 below), but also were more likely to have studied martial arts. Japanese literature or drama do not feature Japanese women who "faint away" like their European counterparts. Perhaps more importantly, if overpowered, Japanese women of the samurai class were prepared to kill themselves.[34] On television "Easterns" at least, the instant the "bad guy" touches a woman she stabs herself, or if the dagger is taken away from her, she bites off her tongue and bleeds to death. (This inevitably brings on the avenging hero or her vengeful ghost.) Television exaggerates, but the threat of suicide may have been a significant deterrent of violence against women. Japanese women were, then, "free" to move about as they pleased.

Still, lest these women appear braver than they probably were, it should be noted that if a woman was anything more than a servant, she probably did *not* go out alone. A letter of Gaspar Vilela from 1565 put it this way: "They [noble-women] are not used to being accompanied by men when they go out, but with many other women with whom they have been raised."

36. In Europe the love felt between male and female family members is very strong; in Japan it is weak and they treat each other like strangers.

Frois seems to imply that marriage in sixteenth-century Europe was a lot like marriage today, where couples ideally are best friends as well as lovers. It is not clear that this was indeed the case in 1585, as many Europeans seemed to view marriage as a practical necessity. Men, in particular, often had another man as their "best friend."[35]

Today, as in the past, the Japanese, particularly of the upper classes, do not center their lives around the biological family and blood relatives (as compared with Europeans and Americans). The Japanese have traditionally favored those nearby over blood kin. "Out of sight, out of mind" makes more sense to the Japanese than "absence makes the heart grow fonder." Thus, Japanese families were more liable to adopt children (or husbands) to carry on the family line, despite their pride in lineage. In Japan, the idea of lineage or heredity had less to

33 Walthall, "The Life Cycle of Farm Women," 48.
34 Catharina Blomberg, *The Heart of the Warrior* (Sandgate, UK: Japan Library, 1994), 123.
35 Thomas, *The Ends of Life*, 187–225.

do with blood and more to do with actual relationships, including those where a craftsmen would pass on his skills to a loyal apprentice or adopted son-in-law.[36] Some have argued that this Japanese attitude was conducive to modernization in general and the building of effective corporations in particular.

37. In India, foot servants carry umbrellas for the women [to protect them] against the sun and the rain; in Japan, women hold up umbrellas for each other.

Frois lived for years in India and Malacca before he was assigned to Japan. This is one of a few instances in which he refers to India instead of Europe, presumably because Europeans did not yet make use of umbrellas. Nowadays in Japan, everyone holds up their own "bat-umbrellas," as Western-style umbrellas are called.

38. In Europe, while they do exist, abortions are infrequent; in Japan this is so common that there are women who have had twenty abortions.

Frois seems to understate the frequency of abortions in Europe, particularly as most abortions presumably went unreported. Somewhat surprisingly, Church law was rather lenient, allowing abortions for unwed women as late as the fifth month of pregnancy or before "quickening" and "ensoulment."[37]

With respect to Japan, *risqué* poems (*senryu*) written two centuries after Frois actually joked about abortion. Even today, the abortion rate in Japan is relatively high, owing to a belief that the child of an unwed mother will be stigmatized and have a difficult life.[38] Still, abortion was no laughing matter for the Japanese woman who drank poisonous drugs, put pressure on their stomachs, and so forth. Moreover, the complex emotions felt by Japanese women, today as in the past, is evident from the fact that some Buddhist temples secure high fees praying for a "water-baby's" soul. At these temples, one can see thousands of small stone statues, many with bibs and candy or toys placed before them.[39]

39. In Europe, an infant is rarely or almost never killed after birth; in Japan, the women step on the neck and kill any children to whom they give birth that they believe they cannot feed.

Europeans considered infanticide an offense to God, an unspeakable crime in the same general category as witchcraft, incest, and sodomy. Although the Counter-Reformation is sometimes cast as a defensive reaction to criticism of the Church, it was itself reform-minded and encouraged confraternities and new

36 Jordan Sand, *House and Home in Modern Japan* (Cambridge: Harvard University Press, 2003).

37 Londa Schiebinger, *Plants and Empire, Colonial Bioprospecting in the Atlantic World* (Cambridge: Harvard University Press, 2004), 116–128.

38 Ekaterina Hertog, "I did not know how to tell my parents, so I thought I would have to have an abortion." *In Home and Family in Japan*, eds. R. Ronald and A. Alexy, 91–112 (London: Routledge, 2011).

39 Bardwell Smith, "Buddhism and Abortion in Contemporary Japan: Mizuko Kuyō and the Confrontation with Death." In *Buddhism, Sexuality, and Gender*, ed. José I. Cabezón, pp. 65–90 (Albany: SUNY Press, 1992).

religious orders dedicated to the poor, orphans, and foundlings.[40] That said, Frois understates the extent of infanticide in Europe, where innumerable infants died in foundling homes or at the hands of wet nurses or helpless mothers.[41]

Okada[42] cites a late Ming (1368–1644) Chinese source to the effect that there were more women than men in Japan because the fief administrators cruelly encouraged the strangulation of boys born to poor women at birth because they only desired a supply of women to serve as common-law wives and mistresses. Frois, however, writes in a letter of April 4, 1565, that it was girls who were liable to be killed. Perhaps both are correct and different practices of infanticide obtained in Japan at different times and places.

The Japanese were mostly a farming people and correspondingly referred to infanticide as "thinning" (*mabiki*). You do not thin for reasons of cruelty. When crops failed or did not keep up with taxes, parents had to make hard choices on how to maximize the chances of survival for their offspring. Because bad years could not be predicted, abortion was not always an option. In 1557, Frois' fellow Jesuit, Vilela, wrote with obvious sympathy, "We fear the lean cows of Pharaoh[43] and pray the Lord will not let them come, because it is a heart-breaking thing to see children killed in similar times, ..."[44] Although scholars who have studied infanticide in early modern Japan have concluded that peasants lost far more children to natural causes than to induced death,[45] the Jesuits as early as 1557 opened a foundling home in Funai, their base of operations in Japan and one of the two largest cities in the province of Bungo.[46]

40. Pregnant women in Europe loosen and relax their belts so as not to hurt their unborn babies; the Japanese wear a belt up until the time of birth that is kept so tight that it is impossible to slip a hand between the belt and the skin.

Frois' Jesuit superior noted that the Japanese, "from experience" rather than, say, ignorance, had come to believe that the tight belt brought good luck in birthing. The tight *obi* was put on ceremoniously in the fifth month of conception and was thought to prevent miscarriage and premature birth.

40 John Henderson, "Charity and Welfare in Early Modern Tuscany." In *Health Care and Poor Relief in Counter-Reformation Europe*, eds. Ole Peter Grell, Andrew Cunningham, and Jon Arrizabalaga, 56–87 (London: Routledge).

41 Maria W. Piers, *Infanticide* (New York: W.W. Norton & Company, 1978), 122–123; Linda A. Pollock, "Parent-Child Relations." In *The History of the European Family, Volume I, Family Life in Early Modern Times*, 1500–1789, eds. David Kertzer and Marzio Barbagli, 191–220 (New Haven: Yale University Press, 2001), 217–218.

42 Okada, *Yoroppa-Bunka To Nihon-Bunka*, 1.

43 "The lean cows of Pharaoh" refers to a time of famine and poverty as per the Book of Genesis (41:3).

44 *Cartas que os Padres e Irmãos da Companhia de Iesus Escreuerão dos Reynos de Iapão & China aos da Mesma Companhia da India & Europa, des do Anno de 1549 Até o de 1580*. 2 Vols. Facsimile edition by José Manuel Garcia (Maia: Castoliva Editora, 1997), I, 60.

45 Laurel L. Cornell, "Infanticide in Early Modern Japan? Demography, Culture, Population Growth," *Journal of Asian Studies* 55 (1996): 22–50.

46 Jurgis Elisonas, "Christianity and the Daimyo." In *The Cambridge History of Japan, Volume 4, Early Modern Japan*, ed. J.W. Hall, 30–373 (Cambridge: Cambridge University Press, 1991), 317.

41. After giving birth, women in Europe lie down and rest; Japanese women are required to remain in a seated position day and night for twenty days after birth.

Child-birthing in both Europe and Japan often was done sitting, as it is in most cultures. European women made use of horseshoe-shaped or elongated chairs or stools. In Japan, the wealthy sat on special legless chairs covered with cushions. (If we can call something legless a sofa, then they invented the sofa or soft armchair.) Poor farmers improvised with straw.[47]

42. In Europe we are very careful after childbirth to guard against the air and wind; as soon as they have given birth, the Japanese wash themselves and open doors and windows.

In Europe, immediately following a birth, both mother and child were quickly washed and dressed to protect them from chills as well as outside air.[48] The Japanese opened doors and windows to "vent the pollution of birth." For most of Japanese history, delivery took place in a separate birth hut so the main house would not be "polluted." However, the Japanese also were wary of the wind, for the very word for the common cold in Japanese is "wind." Rodrigues' Japanese-Portuguese Dictionary includes *ubukaze*, or "birth-wind," meaning a cold caught by a newborn. The bath after birth is almost always called *ubuyu*, "birth-warm water." Only rarely was it called *ubumizu*, "birth-coldwater," and that was in Shikajima prefecture, which happens to be where the Jesuits began their mission-ary work. But even then, it was only a little cold water and it was used after a bath in warm water.

43. In Europe, the cloister and confinement of nuns is strict and rigorous; in Japan the monasteries of the bikuni [Buddhist nuns] function almost like a red-light district.[49]

Again, Frois overstates the case for Europe, for not all nuns were bound to convents, nor did they all lead lives of strict religious observance. Recently we have learned that many women who entered convents had male guests and serv-ants and some wrote love stories and poetry.[50] Indeed, the fact that many convents lacked "rigor" explains the reform movements led by Frois' contemporaries, such as Saint Teresa of Avila (1515–1582).

---

47 Okada quotes a document that mentions no less than twelve bundles of straw covered with a futon.

48 Jacques Gélis, *History of Childbirth, Fertility, Pregnancy and Birth in Early Modern Europe* (Cambridge, U.K.: Polity Press, 1991), 173–183. Lacking a germ theory, Europeans nevertheless perceived correctly at times that disease was transmitted through the air. Thus, diseases like malaria, which is actually transmitted by anopheles mosquitoes, were attributed to bad air (*malaria*).

49 *Rua de meretrices.*

50 For the complex lives of cloistered women see Alison Weber, *Teresa of Avila and the Rhetoric of Femininity* (Princeton: Princeton University Press, 1990); Asuncion Lavrin, *Bodies of Christ: Conventual Life in Colonial Mexico* (Stanford: Stanford University Press, 2008); Stephanie Kirk, *Convent Life in Colonial Mexico: A Tale of Two Communities* (Gainesville: University Press of Florida, 2007); Mónica Díaz, *Indigenous Writings from the Convent* (Tucson: University of Arizona Press, 2010).

Some of the most charming female letters in Japan are the work of devout nuns, who, like poet bonzes, tended to be very witty (again, not unlike nuns in Spain and the New World who penned fabulous poetry, plays, commentaries, and auto-biographical pieces). But nun-prostitutes were also a very visible part of Japan for hundreds of years. There were even "boating nuns" (*funa-bikuni*) who plied the canals. It is clear that some religious authorities actually sponsored these "road-side angels" who were sometimes identified with Kannon, the Buddhist Goddess of Mercy. Frois is only wrong for what he seemingly chose *not* to mention: the vast majority of *bikuni* were chaste and devoted to Buddha.

44. Our nuns ordinarily do not venture outside the convent; the bikuni in Japan are always out entertaining, and sometimes go into military camps.

Frois again focuses on *bikuni* prostitution, which Okada[51] suggests flourished at this time of frequent wars between Japanese nobles (the logic presumably is that during times of war men require or benefit from gratuitous sex).

45. Among us it is not very common for a woman to know how to write; among the elite women in Japan it is considered demeaning not to know how to write.

At the time Frois wrote, high schools and universities were springing up throughout much of Europe and more and more people were learning to read; rag paper, the printing press, and vernacular bibles all inspired and made possible greater consumption of ideas. As Frois suggests, European women rarely were afforded an opportunity to participate in this revolution. Girls might be taught to read, but less frequently learned to write, as learning to write required costly supplies and girls/women were deemed an unlikely source of "great" ideas.[52] If a girl did manage to make it into a lower school, she often was not permitted to study more than the basics or beyond the age of nine. Although women of the lower and middle classes often desired or were required by circumstance to do "men's work"[53] this reality was conveniently ignored in favor of a cult of domes-ticity, which, while no less demanding, required little education.

In a letter from 1565, Frois noted that "in the more cultured parts" of Japan or wherever there were nobility, both men and women knew how to read and write. We would add that not only would both be able to read and write, but they were also expected to write beautifully, in terms of both content and calligraphy. In Murasaki Shikibu's *Tale of Genji*, generally acknowledged as the world's first full-length novel, writing was the key to a lover's heart. In Japan, poetic letters were passed back and forth in the night, and love and literacy went hand and hand.

51 Okada, *Yoroppa-Bunka To Nihon-Bunka*, 54.
52 Wiesner-Hanks, *Women and Gender in Early Modern Europe*.
53 Thomas, *The Ends of Life*, 20–21, 104–107.

Women did not use as many Chinese characters as men and mostly wrote with the visually lighter and more flowing phonetic syllabary.[54] Women also developed argot of their own different enough from that of men that some European visitors in Frois' time mistakenly thought they spoke a different language than men. Even today, there are far greater gender differences in the use of the Japanese language than can be found in English.

46. Among us, letters addressed to a woman are signed by the man who writes the letter; letters to women in Japan do not need to have a signature, nor do women sign their letters, nor do they[55] indicate the month and year.

Letters between Japanese friends, regardless of the sex of the writer or the recipient, need not be signed. The beauty and diversity of Japanese handwriting, which enables instant recognition of the author, may have something to do with this. Note that Frois' knowledgeable contemporary, Rodrigues, wrote in his "Treatise on Epistolary Style" that Japanese men did, in fact, conclude their letters with their name and cipher.[56] Perhaps both Frois and Rodrigues are correct: Japanese men *sometimes* "signed" their correspondence with women.

47. Among us, women's names are taken from the saints; the names of Japanese women are: kettle, crane, turtle, sandal, tea, bamboo.

As Michael Cooper[57] has pointed out, Frois seems to have gone out of his way to mention the least flattering Japanese names; he could just as easily have cited names that remain popular to this day, such as Spring (*Yuki*), Snow (*Hana*), Blossom (*Kiku*), or Chrysanthemum (*Gin*), to name but a few.[58] The Japanese have a far greater variety of personal names (over a million) than Europeans and Americans, whose first names until recently were derived largely from a select group of biblical figures and saints. On the other hand, the ethno-diversity of America, in particular, is reflected in the fact that it has far more family names than in Japan.

48. Women in Europe wear slippers of leather or Valencian gilt; Japanese women wear footwear made of lacquered wood, with the big toe separated from the others.

The *chapim* or slippers mentioned by Frois presumably were of goatskin or "Cordovan leather," which could be dyed and decorated with gold and silver.[59] The beautifully lacquered (shiny black) female footwear in Japan usually had a triangular front stilt tapering out to the tip and is called *bokuri* (rather than *geta*).

---

54 Joan E. Ericson, "The Origins of the Concept of "Women's Literature." In *The Woman's Hand, Gender and Theory in Japanese Women's Writing*, eds. Paul G Schalow and Janet A. Walker, pp. 74–116 (Stanford: Stanford University Press, 1996), 77–82.

55 The Portuguese is imprecise here as to whether it is both men and women who do not date their correspondence.

56 Jeroen Pieter Lamers, ed. and trans., *Treatise on Epistolary Style, João Rodriguez on the Noble Art of Writing Japanese Letters* (Ann Arbor: Center for Japanese Studies, 2002), 72–73.

57 *They Came to Japan*, 246.

58 Lafcadio Hearn, *Shadowings* (Boston: Little, Brown, and Company, 1900) left us forty-eight charming pages with hundreds of fine examples of Japanese women's names.

59 Marques, *Daily Life in Portugal*, 66–67.

All varieties of Japanese footwear came to have the toe separation mentioned by Frois. The thong, which is *not* mentioned by Frois, generally is the most decorated part of the *geta* or *bokuri*, as that is what is seen above the *tabi*-encased foot.

49. Women in Europe ride sidesaddle or on a seat; Japanese women ride in the same manner as men.

In Japan, where horses were relatively few in number, it was primarily the nobility who rode them (see Chapter 8). As Frois notes, noblewomen or the female kin of high-ranking samurai rode in the same manner as their male relatives. The Japanese did not consider the separation of a woman's legs to be obscene. Note that it was illegal for "lesser" Japanese (i.e., middle-class townsmen, wealthy farmers, brides, and so forth) to ride in the manner of the nobility. Common women did not really ride at all.

50. In the case of [our] women, cushions are placed on the seat on the back of the mule; in Japan, a white cloth is placed over the saddle of the horse of a noblewoman.

A 1560 Japanese text cited by Okada[60] refers to the sheet as an "oil-cloth" and "dust-remover" (*aka-tori*) and cites another source to the effect that these hung way down like skirts. Frois' contrast would seem to refer to something soft and practical pampering European behinds versus a show of purity and cleanliness on the part of the Japanese.

51. In Europe, women ordinarily prepare meals; in Japan, men do the cooking, and noblemen consider it something excellent to go into the kitchen to prepare food.

Although European nobility made a great deal of feasting and appreciated a good chef, cooking was not perceived as a "liberal art." European elites may have learned to paint, recite poetry, or play the viola, but cooking remained for the most part "beneath them."[61]

Fellow Jesuit Rodrigues provided a detailed description of the "public kitchens" in the palaces of Japanese lords and nobility. The kitchen was one of the best parts of the house, and the preparation area was beautiful and clean. That cooking was deemed dignified and honorable is consistent with the fact that carving was a major activity in the kitchens of nobility, owing to plentiful game and fish. In Japan, where nearly everything is carried to the table bite-sized (see Chapter 6), carving was one of the ten principal "liberal arts." In fact, there were even competing schools of professional carvers, with the prestigious "*shi*" suffix for their title. These finely attired pros could even be found putting on a practical show in the dining room.

Nevertheless, Frois' contrast is overdone, for women did much of the cooking in Japan as well as served and removed the food. Not much has changed in this regard, as suggested by a late twentieth-century Japanese commercial in which a woman says, "I'm the one who makes it" (literally "I'm a making-person")

60 Okada, *Yoroppa-Bunka To Nihon-Bunka*, 55–56.
61 Brian Cowan, "New Worlds, New Tastes, Food Fashions after the Renaissance." In *Food: The History of Taste*, ed. Paul Freedman, pp. 197–232 (Berkeley: University of California Press, 2007), 212.

and the man says "I'm the one who eats it" (literally "I'm an eating person"). The mass media generally slight feminist complaints in Japan, but complaints about this ad developed into a national controversy, or rather, reflection, because it called attention to a sad but true fact: few Japanese men do any cooking at home.

52. In Europe tailors are men; in Japan they are women.

Throughout the Middle Ages and well into the modern period European women spun cotton and wool and sewed, first in their homes and then in workshops and factories, coincident with mercantilism and the rise of capitalism in the sixteenth century. Men did the weaving and dying and monopolized the higher-skilled profession of tailoring, meaning the actual design and assembly of clothing and fabric, which was big business in sixteenth-century Europe.

With respect to Japan, the production of clothing provides one example of how differing gender roles may have helped Japan preserve separately, rather than fuse and lose, items of Eastern and Western culture. For most of modern times, Japanese-style clothing (*wafuku*) was generally made by women,[62] while many, if not most, tailors of Western-style clothing (*yofuku*) were men. Men adopted Western clothing in the nineteenth century and became tailors because a tailor might have to deal with foreigners. Japanese women retained their native garb much longer than men, so Western dress became essentially synonymous with menswear.

In one sense, however, Japanese men *always* had a hand in the sewing business, as the Japanese did not buy their kimonos; they bought rolls of cloth produced by manufacturer-dyers that were generally run by males. This cloth was very good and equally expensive. Labor, however, was cheap, so in-house "tailors" finished the product for free. In this sense, Japanese women were not really tailors (an independent calling) but seamstresses.

53. In Europe men eat at high tables and women at low ones; in Japan women eat at high tables and men at low ones.

Among the upper class in both Europe and Japan, men and women of the same household often ate separately. Men in both societies not only ate more and better food, but in the case of Europeans, they often were afforded a privileged seat and place at the table ("the head"), if not a table of their own. European women often ate at a work table in the kitchen.

Okada's edition includes a picture of a Japanese nobleman, legs folded, eating with his table (more like a portable writing desk) directly in front of him, while the woman diagonally across the small room has a table by her side that is about eight inches high. Because both sit on the floor (as per Chapter 6), no one is really looking down on anyone.

---

62 During the Tokugawa period Japanese girls from age fourteen to marriage attended compulsory "needle shops" and "girl's rooms" where they learned sewing from other women. Walthall, "The Life Cycle of Farm Women," 46.

54. In Europe it is considered offensive for women to drink wine; in Japan it is very common, and on festive occasions the women sometimes get drunk.

Not all European women were as proper as Frois suggests. One need only glance at one of Dürer's paintings of European peasant life to know that clerical preferences and societal prescriptions were not empirical reality. In Frois' Portugal, the Crown regularly tried to do away with taverns that were frequented by "women of low repute" as well as ladies and maidens who enjoyed gambling more than embroidering and sewing.[63]

With respect to Japan, older women in particular were almost as free to imbibe as the men for whom they heated sake.[64] Still, in Japan as in the West, a woman was supposed to "stand by her man," not lie plastered next to him. The Spanish merchant Avila Giron summed it up quite well: "The women drink very little, although their men folk are like Frenchmen."[65]

55. Women in Europe generally eat both meat and fish; Japanese noblewomen usually do not eat meat and many do not eat fish either.

This is an exceptionally nuanced contrast on the part of Frois, as it includes three qualifications (generally, usually, many). As Okada points out, noblewomen were more likely to refuse fish and meat because of their Buddhist upbringing. Japanese men conveniently construed four-legged animal meat as "medicine," and thus put health above karma. (Interestingly, sixteenth-century Europeans often cast chocolate, which was otherwise "sinful," as medicine). Japanese peasant women ate fish if they could, although they seemingly got little of anything tasty because they put others (i.e., their mother- and father-in-law, husband and children) first.

56. If women in Europe are wearing a head covering, they cover their faces even more when they are speaking with someone; Japanese women must remove their scarf, for it is discourteous to speak with it on.

As noted, European women were discouraged from revealing their bodies in public, including their faces. Ironically, the Council of Castile complained to Philip II that the veil had become something of a double-edged sword, inasmuch as men were "mistakenly" accosting innocent girls and other men's wives, while prostitutes were passing for good women. Although Okada[66] points out that Japanese dramas of the time show women carrying on a discussion with their mantle in place, these dramas were *kyogen*, meaning "crazy-talk."

57. European noblewomen do not conceal themselves when speaking with someone who has come to pay them a call; in Japan, if the caller is unknown, the lady of the house speaks from behind a screen[67] or a bamboo blind.

As readers of the *Tale of Genji* know, the custom of a Japanese noblewomen conversing from behind a screen went back at least five hundred years before Frois

63 Marques, *Daily Life in Portugal*, 253–254.
64 Joy Hendry, "Drinking and Gender in Japan." In *Gender, Drink and Drugs*, ed. Maryon McDonald, 175–191 (Oxford: Berg, 1994).
65 Cooper, *They Came to Japan*, 40.
66 Okada, *Yoroppa-Bunka To Nihon-Bunka*, 58.
67 *Biobus. Byōbu,* which are standing screens of paper.

wrote. There also was a tendency for all Japanese women to hide their faces; one sees this still today, particularly when Japanese women laugh. Still, women (at least townswomen during the Tokugawa era) began showing their faces more and more (nobles held out until the late 19th century). While American and English feminist scholars often have equated attention to personal beauty with female oppression, some Japanese feminist writers see the cult of public beauties (represented by the *bijin-e*, which are prints of beautiful women, mostly, but not all, courtesans) as a mark of a new freedom for women to exist as individuals rather than as faceless belongings of men. When a courtesan or female street vendor caught Edo's imagination and even initiated new styles, she had something modern: her own identity.

58. In Europe, women are free to enter any church they want; in Japan, noblewomen cannot enter certain temples that are prohibited to them.

Although Japan on the whole offered more freedom of worship than Europe (see Chapter 4), for "reasons of purity" *all* women were taboo at shrines during periods when they were menstruating (officially this was seven days per month). Moreover, one can still find temples (usually on mountains) where women are taboo except for one day a year. In Japan, the mountains and the seashore have official "openings," i.e., times of the year when certain activities such as visits by women are acceptable. The famous haiku poet Issa fondly observed that the first thing old women did when they visited Mitsui temple was look at the sea. If they were farm wives, chances are it was their only look at the sea for the entire year.

59. Among us it is very unusual for a woman to carry anything using poles[68]; in Japan it is normal for female servants to carry pails full of water.

This is one of Frois' stranger contrasts, although it is perhaps less so when one recalls that Frois is mostly thinking about European women of nobility who had servants or slaves who fetched water and handled other domestic chores. Marques notes that Lisbon in circa 1550 had some 3,500 women who made a living washing clothes (not included in this figure are household slaves).[69] European women of modest means who washed their own clothes presumably relied on children to fetch and carry water.

The editors of the French-language edition of the *Tratado* have suggested that *pinga[h]* is a Malay word used in Macao (a Portuguese colony in 1585) for poles of bamboo or wood that were shouldered to carry things suspended from the ends.[70] The Japanese term for the same is *tenbinbo* (literally "scale-pole"). Japanese prints or illustrations feature few freshwater-carrying maids (as implied by Frois) and many more "brine maidens" (*shikumi*), who used poles to carry buckets of brine to the vats at salt works. It should be noted that Japanese men also used poles to shoulder heavy loads.

60. In Europe, women stand up to greet their guests; in Japan, they receive them while allowing themselves to remain seated.

---

68 *Levarem as molheres couza à pinga.*

69 Marques, *Daily Life in Portugal*, 137–138.

70 Xavier de Castro and Robert Scrhimpf, trans., *Traite de Luis Frois, S.J.(1585) sur les contradictions de moeurs entre Europeens & Japonais* (Paris: Chandeigne, 1993).

Europeans think of snapping to attention as the ultimate in formal posture, as opposed to actual gestures of greeting such as bowing, tipping one's hat, or curtsying. The Japanese posture of proper seating puts the entire body into a tight rectangle and has a formal name, *seiza* (literally correct-sit), which is difficult to maintain because the weight of the body rests entirely on folded legs (see #63 below). Frois' contrast is correct as it is written, but faulty in failing to note that both Europeans and the Japanese make an equally active effort at being polite. While the physical gestures are clearly opposite, both are stiff postures, showing attentiveness toward the guest.

61. In order to go out in public unrecognized, women in Europe wear a hooded cowl; in Japan when they go out in public, women tie a towel on their head so that the two corners hang down in front of their face.

In a society that enclosed and otherwise restricted women's freedom, being able to lose oneself in a crowd provided a convenient way for European women to engage a world that was otherwise off-limits. Japanese women generally draped their light robes (*katabira*) over their heads, but some also wore *zukin* (literally head-clothes). Today, these light, usually colorful, two-foot long pieces of cloth are used for headbands at work or as neckerchiefs and for removing sweat at *bon* dances. Perhaps the "towels" spoken of by Frois had similar practical uses rather than functioning as concealment.

62. European women conserve their hair until they die; in Japan the old women and widows shave their hair in place of grief and mourning.

Frois' use of "in place of" (*em lugar de*) in the second half of the distich wrongly implies that Japanese women cut their hair, rather than actually mourn the loss of a loved one. We are reminded of the *nihonjinronka* (modern writers who define Japanese identity and culture in terms of contrasts with the West) who wrote that by saying "thank you" a Western person had no lingering feelings, whereas the Japanese still feel much obliged. Perhaps what Frois meant to say was that Japanese women often in old age cut their hair and retired to a convent, there to pray for the souls of their family and to die gracefully (see Chapter 4). Similar practices were not uncommon in Europe and the New World, where widows often "withdrew from the world" and joined convents.[71]

63. Women in Europe sit on divans, chairs, and stools; women in Japan always kneel on the floor with their feet turned up together behind them, with one hand on the tatami, supporting them.

In a formal setting both Japanese men and women fold their legs straight back under them, with their shins resting on the tatami and with their hands resting symmetrically on their respective thighs (or in front if the person bows). What Frois describes here is actually an informal posture adopted by women (and which men never use as they sit informally with crossed legs). In this informal position,

---

71 Natalie Zemon Davis, *Women on the Margins, Three Seventeenth-Century Lives* (Cambridge: Harvard University Press, 1995), 63–139; Kathleeen Myers and Amanda Powell, eds., *A Wild Country Out in the Garden* (Bloomington: Indiana University Press, 1999).

the arm is needed to support the body because the legs are allowed to stray to one side. Even more informally, some women let their legs, still bent back, slip out one to each side so that their seat comes in direct contact with the tatami. This form of sitting (used by Chinese Taoists while meditating) is even harder for most Westerners than sitting on their heels. How do they do it? Here is Alice Bacon, writing at the end of the nineteenth century:

> The flexibility of the knees, which is required for comfort in the Japanese method of sitting, is gained in very early youth by the habit of setting a baby down with its knees bent under it, instead of with its legs out straight before it, as seems to us the natural way. To the Japanese, the normal way for a baby to sit is with its knees bent under it, and so, at a very early age, the muscles and tendons of the knees are accustomed to what seems to us a most unnatural and uncomfortable posture.[72]

64. Among us, women pick up a cup of water with the right hand and drink with the same; Japanese women pick up the sake cup[73] with their left hand and drink with the right hand.

Japanese men hold the small *sake* cup with both hands when someone is filling it for them and formally drink that way as well (see Chapter 6, #28). Japanese women use only one hand. Frois' contrast is not between one hand or two hands but between drinking with the same hand the drink is received in and drinking with the opposite hand. It may well be due to the fact that women conventionally waited to the right of men and, facing the tables, received *sake* with the left hand and drank with the right.

65. Women in Europe braid their hair with silk ribbons; the Japanese tie theirs in the back in a single place, sometimes with a very dirty cloth.

This contrast is nearly identical to #7 above, but one wishes that Frois was more specific about the class of women he is contrasting. After all, in #28 we are told of Japanese women who appear like European soldiers in dress attire. Working women in Japan often tied their hair back with a *tenugui*, a simple piece of cloth that often boasted interesting designs. Frois may have considered favorite well-worn *tenugui* "very dirty" or he may have observed "lucky" hair-ties worn by samurai women whose husbands were off on campaigns. These ties were not washed until a loved one returned to untie it.

66. In Europe one case of face powder would be sufficient for an entire kingdom; in Japan, despite importing many boatloads from China, there is still a shortage.

72 Alice M. Bacon, *Japanese Girls and Women* (London: Kegan Paul, 2001[1892]), 8. For all her cultural relativism, Bacon noted in a footnote that the Japanese way of sitting was "unnatural and unhygienic." This notion is still current today, even in Japan, and yet it is Americans, not the Japanese, who seem to suffer from bad knees.
73 *Sakazuki.*

This is a more poetic restatement of the contrast offered in #15 above. Japan at this time (and later, when it began to industrialize) still had sufficient reserves of most minerals. The idea of Japan as a nation which is exceptionally poor in natural resources that "has to be diligent" is a modern invention and, in Japan today, a useful tool of government. Still, Japan did import mercury and lead from China. Okada[74] notes that the two were ground and combined to make a popular powder that was called "Chinese dirt."

67. European women do their sewing with copper thimbles on their fingertips; Japanese women do theirs with a strip of leather in the palm of their hand or with a little bit of paper wrapped around the middle of the finger.

Europeans and Americans sew by pushing the needle and thread through the fabric. In Japan, a long needle is held steady with its butt against a piece of leather or paper, and one uses one's finger tips to push the cloth onto the needle. (This is called "grab-needling" or *tsukami-bari*).[75] Today, like most everyone else, the Japanese rely on sewing machines. However, when replacing buttons or mending torn cloth, they still use broad-banded rings called *yubi-nuki* or "finger-pass [through]" rather than the closed, cap-like Western thimble.

68. Among us, when we want to take apart a garment, we do so by cutting the seams with a knife; Japanese women pull out the whole line of stitching.

If you have ever taken apart an old kimono, you know that it is simply far easier and faster to pull out the thread than to cut it and risk damaging the material.

74 Okada, *Yoroppa-Bunka To Nihon-Bunka*, 60.
75 During the Edo era a small round metal dish was used instead of a piece of leather or paper.

3 Concerning children and their customs

1. Boys in Europe wear their hair short; in Japan, they all let it grow freely up to the age of fifteen.

This chapter reflects the fact that the education of children was absolutely central to the Jesuit program for directed culture change, be it in Asia, the Americas, or Europe itself.[1] If the Jesuits were to transform Japanese society it was imperative that European Jesuits understand how Japanese children were reared.

In paintings such as "Saint Francis Xavier Preaching," Portuguese artist André Reinoso clearly depicted boys with hair that was off the ears.[2] Recall that Europeans equated long hair with virility and thus it was more appropriate for adult men.

In Japan a baby boy's head was shaven four to five times a month until age three, when there was a ceremony called "hair placing" (*kami-oki*). Henceforth the boy's hair was allowed to grow until age five, when it was trimmed neatly around the edges in the manner of a bowl-cut. The child's hair was not cut again until the boy's coming of age, roughly between the age of eleven and sixteen. The hair was not, however, allowed to hang freely, for a shock of loose hair was considered to be the mark of an outlaw or a vengeful ghost. It was generally bound in a ponytail until adulthood, at which point the front of the pate was shaven and the remaining hair bound and set as described previously in Chapter 1, #6.

2. European babies spend a long time in swaddling clothes with their hands tucked inside; in Japan they wear kimonos from the time they are born and their hands are always free.

It was common in Europe to swaddle infants, that is, to keep them tightly wrapped in cloth or linen for upwards of nine months (if not too restrictive, the swaddling seems to comfort babies).[3] With respect to Japan, Frois is correct that the robe worn by infants was similar to adult robes. However, the Japanese would say the infant is put into *ubugi* or *ubuginu,* which literally translates as "birth-robe." These robes often were decorated with auspicious motifs appropriate to the infant's sex and are fastened from behind by two ribbons. At age three, the child changes to a *kimono* with a girdle-like *obi.*

1 Daniel T. Reff, *Disease, Depopulation, and Culture Change in Northwestern New Spain, 1518–1764* (Salt Lake City: University of Utah Press, 1991), 252–253.
2 Jay Levenson, ed., *Encompassing the Globe, Portugal and the World in the 16th & 17th Centuries* (Washington, D.C.: Sackler Gallery, Smithsonian Institution, 2007), 245.
3 Daniel Beekman, *The Mechanical Baby* (Westport CT: Lawrence Hill and Company, 1977), 7–8; Linda Pollock, "Parent-Child Relations." In *The History of the European Family, Volume I, Family Life in Early Modern Times, 1500–1789*, eds. David Kertzer and Marzio Barbagli, pp. 191–220 (New Haven: Yale University Press, 2001), 193–196.

3. In Europe, children sleep in cradles and they use little carts to teach them to walk; in Japan, they have none of these things and use only the aids that nature provides.

Manuscripts from the Middle Ages describe a three-wheeled walker that was used in Europe to teach infants to walk. One of these "baby walkers" is depicted on a tapestry dating to 1390.[4] The Japanese did not have "walkers" and used cocoon-like wicker baskets instead of cradles. Today, Euro-American style cribs are common in Japan and are called by the descriptive term *beibi-sahkuru*, or "baby circles." Note, however, that at night Japanese infants ordinarily sleep with their parents, not in a crib.[5] Japanese parents do not feel obliged to teach their children to sleep alone, nor do they worry about infants being suffocated or otherwise hurt in a family bed. (The American belief that infants and young children should sleep by themselves is unusual, as cultures go).

4. Among us, it is ordinarily grown women who carry the babies, on their bosom; in Japan, it is nearly always very young girls who carry the babies, on their backs.

Here Frois contrasts commoners; the nobility in both Japan and Europe generally had grown nursemaids who looked after infants. According to Bacon, there was even a particular village in Japan of large, extremely fit, red-cheeked women who performed this service as a hereditary calling for the Emperors' children. Be that as it may, Frois makes two generally valid contrasts in one: 1) the different manner of carrying the baby, and 2) the different age of the carrier. Although today in Japan one rarely sees siblings carrying tiny tots on their backs, one does occasionally see infants being carried on their mother's or, more commonly, grandmother's back.

5. Among us, infants wear only a single cloth belt, cinched and tied in front; infants in Japan wear kimonos with a ton of ribbons, all tied in back.

One might think the knot uncomfortable, but the Japanese did not have chairs to lean back against, and back-ties made sense for those who carried infants (the knots did not come between the child and its mother or older sister). Although Frois' usage—"a ton"—prosaically conveys the number and size of the knots, they came undone in an instant because they were tied in a bow.

6. Among us, a four-year old child still does not know how to eat with his own hands; in Japan a three-year old already eats by himself using chopsticks.[6]

Frois' contemporary, the Spanish merchant Bernardino de Avila Giron, noted with amazement that a Japanese child of four could remove the bones of a sardine with chopsticks. In the economic "bubble" days, when Ezra Vogel's (1980) *Japan as Number One: Lessons for America* was still selling like hotcakes, Morita Akio,

---

4 Irina Metzler, *Disability in Medieval Europe* (London: Routledge, 2006), 174. See also Beekman, *The Mechanical Baby*, 4–5, 24.

5 Joy Hendry, *Becoming Japanese, The World of the Pre-School Child* (Manchester: Manchester University Press, 1986), 19–22.

6 *Faxis*, from the Japanese *hashi*.

the head of Sony, suggested that because chopsticks were more difficult to use than Western silverware, Asian minds were better developed, hence the success of the Far East.

7. With us, it is normal to whip and punish a child; in Japan this is very rare and they only reprimand them.

Daily life in sixteenth-century Europe was filled with danger. Many parents viewed corporal punishment as a Biblically-sanctioned means of insuring that children did not repeat behavior that might get them killed by a horse, burned by a fire, or run over by a cart. The Jesuits were amazed that Japanese parents disciplined their children solely with words, spoken to a child of six as if he or she was a seventy year-old. Even today visitors and researchers alike remark on how Japanese mothers squat down and explain things at length to children,[7] rather than simply demand obedience.

8. Among us, one learns to read and write from secular teachers; in Japan, they all learn at the temple-schools[8] of the Buddhist monks.

Cities and towns in Europe, particularly in northern or Protestant Europe,[9] often established neighborhood schools (*gymnasia, ludi litterarii*) where the children (particularly boys[10]) of commoners and the petty bourgeoisie received a basic education. Frois may overstate the extent to which schools were staffed by secular teachers, as elementary education in sixteenth-century Europe often fell to priests or religious. Indeed, during the sixteenth century (albeit after Frois left Portugal in 1548[11]) the Jesuits became largely a teaching order, establishing schools throughout Catholic Europe as well as Asia and Latin America

With respect to Japan, Frois' fellow Jesuit, Rodrigues, observed that the sons of nobles were tutored at home while the rest of the gentry studied in temple schools. According to Rodrigues:

> Some stay at the monasteries for their studies, but others return home daily if the monastery is near their homes. These monasteries of the bonzes also serve

---

7 Hendry, *Becoming Japanese*, 51–57; Shing-Jen Chen, "Positive Childishness: Images of Childhood in Japan." *In Images of Childhood*, eds. C.P. Hwange, M.E. Lamb, and I.E. Siegel, pp.113–128 (Mahwah, N.J.: Lawrence Erlbaum Associates, 1996); Anne Allison, "Producing Mothers," In *Re-Imagining Japanese Women*, ed. Ann E. Inamura, pp. 135–155 (Berkeley: University of California Press, 1996).

8 *Varelas,* a Portuguese term for Buddhist temples, derived from Malaysian or Javanese. The Japanese called the schools *terakoya*, "temple-small-room" or "temple-child-room."

9 Luther and other reformers argued that Christians should read the bible rather than have it read to them. This imperative, rather than a desire to promote social mobility, seems to have prompted the establishment of schools for commoners. Keith Thomas, *The Ends of Life* (Oxford: Oxford University Press, 2009), 18–19.

10 As previously noted, girls generally were taught to read but not write. Merry E. Wiesner-Hanks, *Women and Gender in Early Modern Europe* (Cambridge: Cambridge University Press, 2008), 147. See also Paul F. Grendler, *Schooling in Renaissance Italy* (Baltimore: Johns Hopkins University Press, 1989), 87–109.

11 That very year the Jesuits opened their first school in Messina, Italy.

as universities for those who study philosophy and the sciences and want to follow an ecclesiastical career. In the district of Bando, in the kingdom of Shiomonotsuke, there is a university called Ashikaga, whither students flock from all over Japan in order to study all the sciences which are taught there *gratis*.[12]

9. Our children learn first to read and then to write; in Japan they commence with writing and then learn to read.

Japanese children did indeed write Chinese characters before they could read them. Because most Chinese characters have multiple pronunciations in Japanese, mastering the various possibilities, that is, reading, does indeed take much more time than writing (excepting a significant number of very complex characters, which most Japanese learn to read but never learn to write). Today the Japanese still are big on memorizing by writing. The thick, brushed line seemingly impresses the visual memory, and it is important to learn the order of the strokes. Moreover, such writing can be art. The calligraphy of elementary school children (usually just one or two large brushed characters) frequently is on exhibit in Japanese rail and subway stations.

10. Our instructors teach our children the catechism, [the lives of] the saints, and virtuous habits; the bonzes teach the children to play music, sing, play games,[13] fence and carry out their abominations with them.

The catechism and lives of the saints were a major component of primary education in Europe, which, as noted, often was in the hands of clergy and religious orders such as the Jesuits. Frois' allusion to pederasty ("their abominations") hints at his less-than-objective attitude toward Buddhist temple-schools. The mastery of hundreds of Chinese characters clearly occupied most student's time. And yet Frois is correct in suggesting that pederasty was a part of temple-school life (see Chapter 4). Indeed, judging from the literature, which goes back a thousand years, there was rather intense competition among temple-schools to recruit attractive boys. Although pederasty was not uncommon in Europe, particularly in school settings, Europeans ignored it or made a great show of horror when it was discovered.[14]

11. Young men in Europe do not know how to deliver a message; a Japanese child of ten can do so with the wisdom and prudence of a fifty year-old.

This contrast, like others in this chapter (e.g. #6, #13, #14) show that Frois is not just following an agenda to idealize Europe. Nowadays, the "messenger boy" is

---

12 Michael Cooper, *They Came to Japan, An Anthology of European Reports on Japan, 1543–1640* (Ann Arbor: University of Michigan Press, 1965), 242.

13 *Jugar*. Frois is probably referring here to board games such as *shogi* and *go*, which are similar to chess.

14 Isabel M.R. Drummond Braga, "Foreigners, Sodomy, and the Portuguese Inquisition." In *Pelo Vaso Traseiro*, eds. Harold Johnson and Francis Dutra, pp. 145–165 (Tucson: Fenestra Books, 2008), 156–158; Thomas, *The Ends of Life*, 205–206.

an anachronism; so, too, is his skill at recalling details of a message or supplying contextual information that would clarify or amplify a hastily penned dispatch. Not long ago in both Japan and the West messenger boys were crucial to the functioning of any town or city. The English verb "to page" testifies to this fact, as does the Japanese term for message, *kojo*, which literally means "mouth-above."

12. Among us, a man can reach the age of twenty and still not carry a sword; in Japan, twelve- and thirteen-year old boys carry a sword and dagger.[15]

As noted in Chapter 1, Europeans during the sixteenth century increasingly equated privilege with education, rather than martial prowess. Soldiering, in fact, became a profession and many a European army was made up of mercenaries. Correspondingly, young boys of the middle and upper class were raised to appreciate rather than pursue military service.[16]

Frois was certainly not exaggerating the situation in Japan.[17] Others (e.g., Alvarez and Gago) claimed that boys of eight or ten carried arms. In a letter from 1565, Frois noted that Japanese boys slept with their swords and daggers next to their pillow. What neither Frois nor his European contemporaries pointed out was that it was primarily Japanese boys of the *buke* or samurai class who donned swords and daggers at an early age, although even little commoners as well as their parents could wear a single sword if they so wished. Until the modernization of Japan in the late nineteenth century, tykes far younger than twelve or thirteen wore the standard "big and little" sword set.

This contrast reflects both the utterly martial orientation of the Japanese gentry and the same precocious self-control suggested by other contrasts. The young Japanese who could be entrusted with a message could also be entrusted with a lethal weapon. Why? For one thing, Japanese children quarreled infrequently, and this is largely true even up to the present day. There was a downside, however, to armed precocity. Frois' Jesuit superior, Valignano, noted that it sometimes happened that small children would have a temper tantrum and commit *hara-kiri* by slitting open their stomachs.

13. Our children have little command and excellence in their manners; children in Japan are exceedingly thorough in their manners, so much so that they are amazing.[18]

Western visitors from Frois' day to the present have been amazed by the polite manners of Japanese children.[19] By contrast, authors such as Keith Thomas have

---

15 *Catana. ... vakizaxi.*
16 Thomas, *The Ends of Life*, 62–77.
17 In their Japanese-language edition of the *Tratado*, Matsuda and Jorissen write that Frois exaggerated, inasmuch as the teenage Japanese ambassadors who left Japan in 1584 to travel to Europe recounted meeting three teenage sons of a Portuguese count who all wore swords. *Touché*? Not quite. A formal occasion is not the same as wearing a sword or swords all the time, as was the case for little samurai.
18 ....*os de Japáo sáo nisto estranhamente inteiros, em tanto que poem admirasáo.*
19 See Hendry, *Becoming Japanese*, 85–96.

written about children in early modern England who ran wild, peeing in the aisles of churches to make ice to skate on.

14. For the most part, our children are embarrassed to participate in public dramas and performances; in Japan they are uninhibited, relaxed, charming, and very graceful in their performances.

The Jesuits were unusual as a religious order in their warm embrace of the theatre, which they viewed as a great tool for teaching their students and the laity about Catholicism.

Okada[20] believes that the Japanese side of the contrast refers specifically to children of the samurai class and child actors in *No* drama (see Chapter 13). Frois may nevertheless describe a more general trait, for the ease with which the Japanese of all ages perform in front of audiences is still apparent today and is by no means restricted to drama. In formal or public situations, it is the Western man or woman who is far more likely to blush when asked to give a speech at a wedding or to sing a song in front of colleagues. Many, if not most, Japanese do so with the aplomb of an old pro. They seem to find what is essentially role-playing (acting out a public *persona*) less stressful than informal conversations, which most Westerners find relaxing rather than stressful. In informal situations, or when asked for their opinions, Japanese individuals above the age of eight tend to be more uptight than Americans and, possibly, most Western peoples. Indeed, the Japanese see themselves as extremely bashful and even lacking in self-expression compared to "outgoing and brave" foreigners. Lacking the unstated agreement to disagree found in much of the West, lively discussion in much of Japan seems all but impossible in many contexts.

15. Children in Europe are reared with many kindnesses, tenderness, and good food and clothing; in Japan they grow up half-naked and essentially lack all kindnesses and pleasures.

Here "Children in Europe" refers to the offspring of the nobility and the emerging bourgeoisie. The vast majority of European children (i.e. the children of peasants and townspeople) were too busy working for their parents or outside the home to be pampered. Okada[21] quotes a Japanese period book of instruction for child rearing that states that it was best for small children to be "starved by a third and frozen by a tenth." This was thought to be good for long-term health and character. Such advice was doubtlessly for the upper classes and wealthy townsmen. As was the case in Europe, the majority of Japanese children (i.e. the sons and daughters of farmers and townspeople) received these "benefits" automatically. In both early modern Japan and Europe the vast majority of children were not simply

20 Akio Okada, trans. and ed., *Yoroppa-Bunka To Nihon-Bunka* [European Culture and Japanese Culture] (Tokyo: Iwanami Shoten, 1965), 66.
21 Ibid., 67.

dependents but were important contributors to the preservation and prosperity of households.[22]

As for gifts and treats, the Japanese had no tradition of lavishing affection on a child's birthday. Children received gifts of money and new clothing only on New Year's Day. Still, young children enjoyed festivals on what today are referred to as "Girl's Day" and "Boy's Day,"[23] as well as visits to local shrines or temples where there were booths selling fun things or offering challenges for children. One of the most common booths today is the *kingyo-ya*, where children use paper spatulas to catch (and take home) goldfish. It is pretty tricky catching a fish before the wet paper breaks, but the seller always gives the smaller children a hand when necessary, so that nearly everyone gets something.[24]

16. European parents handle affairs directly with their children; in Japan everything is carried out using messages and a third party.

The Jesuits as a whole were struck by Japanese reluctance to discuss important matters face to face and their reliance on third parties. Although Okada[25] has suggested that maintaining distance between parents and children was specific to the samurai class, reliance on surrogates seems to have been a more general phenomenon that has persisted into modern times. Anthropologist Takie Sugiyama Lebra has noted that the Japanese make use of surrogates (*migawari*) in various social contexts, and she suggests that letting another act in one's place is consistent with the Japanese understanding of self, which is "*dividual*" (rather than individual) and integrally related to a particular kin group.[26] Today, as in the past, the Japanese hate confrontation; even when they talk face to face, it was, and still is, generally not eye to eye, but with the eyes facing down, off to the side, or past one another.

17. Among us, one acquires godparents at baptism or confirmation[27]; in Japan, this occurs when a youth once again girds his sword and takes on a new name.

The Christian sacraments of baptism and confirmation entail the acquisition of fictive kin or "godparents" who assist with the rearing of a child. In Portugal,

---

22 There is some evidence from the seventeenth century that suggests that the lives of most Japanese children under five were made as pleasant as possible and afterwards the children were treated more strictly and given age and gender specific tasks. Anne Walthall, "The Cycle of Farm Women in Tokugawa Japan," in *Recreating Japanese Women, 1600–1945*, ed. Gail L. Bernstein, pp. 42–70 (Berkeley: University of California Press, 1991), 45. See also Kathleen S. Uno, "Women and Changes in the Household Division of Labor." In *Recreating Japanese Women, 1600–1945*, ed. Gail L. Bernstein, pp. 17–42. Berkeley: University of California Press, 1991), 22.

23 In Frois' time these festivals were called Doll-festival (*Hinamatsuri*) and Carp-banner (*Koinobori*) and were celebrated on March 3 and May 5, respectively.

24 Edo (Tokyo) during the seventeenth century is said to have had innumerable vendors of services and toys catering to children, with everything from soap bubbles (*shabon*) to tiny kinetic toys like those for which Japan became famous during the immediately post-World War II era.

25 *Yoroppa-Bunka To Nihon-Bunka*, 67.

26 Takie Sugiyama Lebra, "Migawari: The Cultural Idiom of Self-Other Exchange." In *Self as Person in Asian Theory and Practice*," eds. Roger T. Ames, Wimal Dissanayake, and Thomas P. Kasulis, pp. 107–125 (Albany: SUNY Press, 1994).

27 *Crisma.*

boys at baptism generally acquired two men and one woman as godparents; girls received two women and one man.[28]

At the Japanese coming-of-age ceremony called *genbuku*, the youth wears a "crow-hat" (a tall, black, phallic-looking thing) and acquires a "crow-hat-parent." The youth at the same time drops his birth name and takes a new name, usually a character from the name of the crow-hat-parent.[29] This coming-of-age ceremony was adopted from China in the Heian era (794–1185) and is delightfully translated in Kenkyusha's Japanese-English dictionary as "assuming the *toga virilis*." This was also the time when a youth assumed an adult hairstyle and clothing and acquired a valuable sword. The ceremony was held when a boy was between twelve and sixteen. Girls of the same age had a simpler *genbuku*, during which their hair was put up in an adult hairdo for the first time. As a Chinese-derived ceremony, *genbuku* might be called Confucian, but as was the case for most celebratory rituals in Japan, it probably was informed by Shinto.

18. Among us, sons accompany their mothers when they go out; in Japan they rarely or never accompany them (because they are grownups).

As was noted in Chapter 2 (#34, #35), European women, particularly of the middle and upper classes, were thought to require male guidance or protection; sons who accompanied their mothers out in public presumably discouraged unwanted advances from adult males. The fact that Japanese boys did not accompany their mothers may reflect the fact that Japanese women usually accompanied each other in public. Also, as discussed in Chapter 2, Japanese women could venture out in public without fear of harassment.

19. Among us, names don't change after confirmation; in Japan, as one ages, the name changes five or six times.

Frois is again referring to Japanese men at relatively high levels of Japanese society. Three or four name changes probably were more the norm in Japan: a childhood name, the name received at adulthood, occasionally a name to reflect a new station in life, and one for retirement. Commoners generally did not share in this plethora of name changes, but men active in administration who changed posts could enjoy upwards of a half-dozen names. Names were a sort of title granted by superiors to inferiors to show they had achieved a higher rank. João Rodrigues counted ten categories of names. François Caron noted a contrast that was so obvious that Frois must have imagined that he had already made it, when, in fact, he had not:

> The surnames are first pronounced, for being their parents were before them, they think it but reasonable that their names should likewise preceed.[30]

---

28 Marques, *Daily Life in Portugal*, 206.
29 Okada, *Yoroppa-Bunka To Nihon-Bunka*, 67.
30 Cooper, *They Came to Japan*, 237. The Sino-Japanese system of address (country-state-city-street-number-name) and dating (era-year-month-day) follows the same logic.

20. Among us, children often visit their relatives, with whom they are close; in Japan, they rarely visit relatives and they are treated as strangers.

As noted in Chapter 2 (#36), the Japanese do not feel compelled to maintain strong family ties to blood relatives. It is perhaps not surprising that an Iberian Jesuit like Frois would be struck by this, particularly as grandparents, aunts and uncles, and cousins were, and are, an important part of an individual's life in Mediterranean Europe.[31]

21. In Europe, children[32] inherit upon the death of their parents; in Japan, parents relinquish their estate early in life in order to hand over the inheritance to their children.

This contrast can be interpreted in different ways. One is that wealthy Japanese parents do not selfishly (and often with disastrous consequences, especially when they begin to lose their judgment) hold on to the family fortune, but share it early enough to improve the lives of their loved ones, and probably improve the family business. However, it is also possible to say that by handing over the business and retiring, the Japanese parents are selfishly getting out of work and onto the dole while they still are well enough to really enjoy themselves. Both interpretations are perhaps equally true.

So why has the West behaved differently? Bacon[33] thought that, at least in the case of America, it was because of a dread of dependence on others. But how times and people change. Today, the Japanese are notoriously bad at retiring. Like many Western men and women, work is everything to them. This was not true a hundred or four hundred years ago.[34] Then retirement was a quasi-religious experience: a retreat into a world of leisure, a world of writing provided by the bottomless well of Chinese characters, pilgrimages along narrow roads to mountain shrines, and the game of *go*.

22. For our children's health, we scarify and bleed them; in Japan this is not done; rather, they are treated with buds of flame.

As discussed in Chapter 9 (#2, #3), educated doctors in Europe often used "bleeding" to prevent and treat sickness, which was thought to result from an imbalance of various bodily humors (e.g., phlegm and blood). Scarification is a less invasive form of bleeding that involved making small puncture wounds rather than actually opening a vein and draining off copious amounts of blood (venesection).

The expression "buds of flame" refers to moxibustion, which involves placing a pinch of burning *moxa* (mugwort leaf) on a particular part of the body or skin (again, see Chapter 9). Medical practitioners in China and Japan theorized about where on the body the moxa should be placed to achieve the best effect. According

---

31 And perhaps most parts of Europe. See Thomas, *The Ends of Life*, 190.

32 *Os filhos.*

33 *Japanese Girls and Women* (London: Kegan Paul, 2001[1892]).

34 Neither Europeans nor Japanese living in the sixteenth century were "workaholics;" most people worked because they had to and preferred to be idle. Thomas, *The Ends of Life*, 81–82.

to Okada,[35] a pellet of *moxa* was ritually burnt on the three-day old infant's head and on the end of the navel cord to prevent future illness. There was also an annual treatment ritual that functioned in the manner of a "booster shot," supplementing the initial moxibustion. Children in Japan did not like this any more than children in the West like getting shots. In one of his haiku, Issa relates how a naked child fled from his "medicine," despite it being the coldest part of the year. In partial contradiction of #7 above, while Japanese children were not whipped, they were *sometimes* threatened with corporal punishment in the form of moxibustion.

23. Among us, only women use rouge and face powder[36]; in Japan, some of the sons of nobles, up to the age of ten, also wear makeup when they go out.

Although European men would one day powder their wigs, Frois is correct that men of his time used no powder or make-up. In Japan, make-up was essentially restricted to boys from the samurai class or nobility. As noted in Chapter 1, #46, noblemen spent a lot of time on their toilette. Thus, boys were only aping their fathers. Okada[37] cites a Chinese report of "barbarian (i.e., Japanese) boys made up with thick powder like women," which suggests that this idea arose in Japan.

In the 1990s, Japanese youth began to wear makeup at a faster rate than their Western counterparts. Male *tarento* (minor television personalities who only last until the proverbial bloom is off their adolescent cheeks) pluck and darken their eyebrows and use eyeliner, which was even advertised on TV in at least the Tokyo area. This use of make-up is not necessarily or normally equated with femininity, but with looking attractive.

24. Among us, children's clothing has sleeves that are narrow, with the seams sewn closed [all the way] around the shoulders; in Japan, the sleeves are very loose and under the arms they are open from front to back.

The young Japanese samurai who toured Europe at the time Frois wrote his *Tratado* were delighted when they encountered youth in Evora, Portugal who wore clothing with broad sleeves like the ambassadors' kimonos. This delight suggests that such sleeves were unusual in Europe and that Frois' observation was, on the whole, valid. Open underarm seams still are found in some traditional Japanese garments, perhaps because they are very cooling in sultry weather.

---

35 *Yoroppa-Bunka To Nihon-Bunka*, 68–69.
36 *Arrebige e alvayade.* Although arrebique generally meant "makeup," in this case it may refer to rouge, inasmuch as the term appears along alvaiade, a powder made from white lead.
37 *Yoroppa-Bunka To Nihon-Bunka*, 69.

4 Concerning the *bonzes*[1] and their customs

1. Among us, men enter religious life in order to do penance and to save their souls; the bonzes enter religious life to live in pleasure and ease and to escape hardships.

Frois' own life choices and identity as a Jesuit, not to mention the fact that superiors saw everything he wrote,[2] made it seemingly impossible for him to acknowledge the worth of another religion, never mind the shortcomings that accrued to his own Catholicism.[3] Of course, by 1585 Protestant reformers had compiled a long list of Church shortcomings. Frois was not about to repeat such complaints.

Frois was well aware that some men in Europe became clerics or joined religious orders to enjoy a life of relative leisure and to, in effect, escape hardship.[4] What was true of Christianity was true of Buddhism. For instance, various Zen sects (not unlike the Jesuit order) attracted large numbers of novices from wealthy and powerful families. Like Jesuit novices, many or most of these would-be monks were animated by a desire for enlightenment or "salvation." Still, others became bonzes to escape (at least in part) difficult family situations or to enjoy a life free from manual labor.

2. Among us, one subsequently professes vows to be pure of soul and chaste of body; the bonzes profess vows to all manner of inner filth and all the nefarious sins of the flesh.

In his eleventh century treatise on sodomy, *The Book of Gomorrah*, St. Peter Damian acknowledged that sodomy was commonly seen as "the vice of

---

1 With *bonze/s* we follow the customary Anglicization of the Iberian *bonzo/s*. Like all Japanese words, *bonso* or *bonzo* has no number. *Bonzo* is properly a low-ranking Buddhist monk, while Frois uses it to refer to *all* Buddhist monks. Japanese editions of the *Tratado* change Frois' references to *bonzos* to the common general term *bozu*, which includes higher ranking monks, or the Chinese characters for a rare word for the same, *butsuso*, with the pronunciation indicated as *bonzo*. Frois' denigrative tone is captured by affixing a rude plural suffix ~*ra* to these terms.
2 It is hard to overstate the extent to which Jesuit authors were "governed" by superiors; the latter saw most everything and edited or otherwise approved any and all texts that circulated within the order or that were published. See Lionel M. Jensen, *Manufacturing Confucianism* (Durham: Duke University Press, 1997), 67–68.
3 As regards Portugal in particular, see A.H. de Oliveira Marques, *Daily Life in Portugal in the Late Middle Ages* (Madsion: University of Wisconsin Press, 1971), 224–225.
4 This seems to have been particularly true of parish priests and more senior members of the ecclesiastical Church. Marcelin Defourneaux, *Daily Life in Spain In the Golden Age* (Stanford: Stanford University Press, 1979), 109; A.R. Disney, *A History of Portugal and the Portuguese Empire* (Cambridge: Cambridge University Press, 2009), 158–160.

the clergy."[5] At the time Frois wrote, *pecado nefando* (unspeakable sin) remained widespread among Catholic clerics, monks and religious, even if the Church and inquisition railed against it.[6] Sodomy certainly seems to have been less controversial among Buddhist monks and the Japanese as a whole,[7] but it is hardly true that Buddhist monks took vows to "all inner filth."

3. Among us, a vow of poverty is made to God and worldly riches are shunned; the bonzes fleece their followers and seek countless ways to increase their wealth.

Frois' contemporary, the Florentine voyager and merchant, Francesco Carletti (1573–1636), offered a perfect foil to this unfair contrast of the best Christians and the worst Buddhists. In an aside he commented on an austere sect of Buddhism that rivaled the asceticism of an Antony and other Christian ascetics:

> They all lead a sterile life, in imitation of the founder, who introduced it [to Japan]. They say of him that he never ate anything but cooked rice, and sometimes raw rice, and that to do greater penitence he always wore an iron chain tight against his flesh, where it had made such a sore that it became putrid, generating and nourishing a quantity of worms. And if one of these worms happened to fall to the ground, he would pick it up lovingly and with charity and put it back in the sore, saying: 'Why are you fleeing? Are you perhaps lacking something to eat?'[8]

4. Among us, one professes and vows obedience to his superior; the bonzes each do as they please and obey their prelate only by happenstance, as they see fit.

Most Buddhism in Japan was hardly that anarchistic. Some Zen sects, however, made a point of free thinking and independence, even going so far as to abuse the Buddha and the Patriarchs. The way they flaunted disobedience must have horrified the Jesuits. Frois' generalized contrast between Western religion, with its strict order, and a more individualistic Eastern religion, is a welcome counterpoint to the orientalist depiction of the obedient oriental, even if Frois did not intend it as a compliment.

5. Among us, the temporal possessions of religious are held in common; the bonzes all have their own property and earn [money] in order to acquire [property].

It is perhaps true as a generalization that Japanese religious enjoyed more personal effects than their Western counterparts. For instance, most Japanese had their own bowls, chopsticks, tea cups, writing equipment, bedding, clothing, and, within limits, spending money.

5 Luiz Mott, "My Pretty Boy: Love Letters from a Sodomite Friar, Lisbon (1690)." In *Pelo Vaso Traseiro*, eds. Harold Johnson and Francis Dutra, pp. 231–262 (Tucson: Fenestra Press, 2008); John Boswell, *Christianity, Social Tolerance and Homosexuality* (Chicago: University of Chicago Press, 1980), 187.

6 Federico Garza Carvajal, *Butterflies Will Burn* (Austin: University of Texas Press, 2003).

7 Tsuneo Watanabe, *The Love of the Samurai: a Thousand Years of Japanese Homosexuality*, trans. D.R. Roberts (London: Gay Men's Press, 1989).

8 Francesco Carletti, *My Voyage Around the World*, trans. Herbert Weinstock (New York: Pantheon Books, 1964[1610]), 173.

By now the reader should suspect that Frois is not about to say anything nice about Buddhist priests or monks. The Jesuits believed they were on a mission from God, and as noted in the critical introduction, they were delighted when Japanese converts, particularly *daimyo*, seized or destroyed Buddhist temples, causing the *bonzes* to flee or apostatize.

6. *Among us, the faithful belong to a parish and not to a particular clergyman; the bonzes divide the people amongst themselves so that each is fed by those under his charge.*

You would never know from Frois that being a parish priest or cathedral canon in Europe was a desirable position, often because parishioners gave generously or paid handsomely for a funeral mass or a special petition to the Virgin Mary.[9] The territoriality of the *bonzes* (at least young *bonzes* and begging bonzes, who went door to door) was recorded as late as the Meiji period (1868–1912). A haiku by Shiki, known as the father of modern haiku, jokes of an alms-gathering monk walking into a dead end: another alms-gathering monk.

7. *Among us, religious condemn their congregations' sins without regard for social niceties; the bonzes court their followers and praise their sins so that they will not strip them of their income.*

Frois again speaks of the ideal situation with respect to Europe and the sordid reality of Japan. During his lifetime many of his fellow Jesuits became advisors and confessors to Europe's rich and powerful. Jesuits as a whole were advised to seek out the powerful, since one devout Catholic noble could provide enormous help funding Jesuit schools, residences, or missionary activities. It is hard to believe that Jesuit confessors did not, on occasion, refrain from condemning the sins of the kings, dukes, and other elites whom they served as spiritual advisors.

8. *Among us, religious do not wear silk clothing out of contempt for the world; all the bonzes who can, wear silk to better display their pride and vanity before the world.*

This contrast beautifully reverses the Orientalist idea of Far Eastern religion as other-worldly nihilism. Japanese Buddhists were one of the most proselytizing groups in Asia. Buddhist or Christian, attractive clothing (and for that matter, good looks) never hurt a preacher man. Writing toward the end of the tenth century, Sei Shonagon commented:

> A preacher ought to be good-looking. For, if we are properly to understand his worthy sentiments, we must keep our eyes on him while he speaks; should we look away, we may forget to listen. Accordingly an ugly preacher may well be the source of sin ...[10]

9. *Among us, good religious abhor and have great fear of honors and being promoted to positions as dignitaries; the bonzes in Japan spend great sums of money on these things and all of them avidly pursue these promotions.*

9 See, for example, Natalie Zeamon Davis, *The Gift in Sixteenth-Century France* (Madison: University of Wisconsin Press, 2000), 25.
10 Sei Shônagon, *The Pillow Book of Sei Shônagon*, trans. Ivan Morris (New York: Columbia University Press, 1991[1000]), 53.

Frois, to his credit, finally qualifies the European side of this distich, implicitly acknowledging that some Catholic religious were not observant of their vows. As usual, however, he makes no such distinction for the bonzes, saying they were *all* bankrupt. Qualifications aside, the Jesuits in particular made it a rule not to accept titles and honors. However, not all Christian religious were so humble; many Franciscans and Dominicans, and even the Jesuits, on rare occasions, accepted privileges that went with titles and ranks.[11] The question then becomes whether the *bonzes* differed greatly from Christian religious; arguably the difference was one of degree not kind.

10. Our religious always desire peace and war causes them great sorrow; the Nengoros[12] profess warfare and are hired by lords to go and fight in battles.

While Jesuits did not fight or carry weapons, clerics who brandished knives or swords apparently were a significant problem in Portugal at the end of the fifteenth century.[13] Moreover, in places like Mexico or Brazil, the Jesuits and other religious (i.e. Franciscans, Dominicans) often accompanied and lent moral support to Spanish and Portuguese forces. In the 1580s, Frois' superior, Valignano, actually contributed gunpowder and other logistical help to Japanese *daimyo* who favored the Jesuits. After Hideyoshi's crackdown on Christians in Nagasaki (1587), Valignano realized that providing material support to particular *daimyo* was a losing game. In his *obediencias* of 1592, Valignano "laid down that on no account were the Jesuits to encourage or foment any fighting among the Japanese even if it was in support of a Christian *daimyo* against a heathen, or Christian vassals oppressed by a heathen overlord...."[14]

Martial arts were introduced to Japan from China along with Buddhism beginning in the sixth century. It was not uncommon for Buddhist monks to know and use martial arts. When Nobunaga razed the Enryakuji temple in 1571, he wiped out a tradition that had lasted for almost eight centuries. Founded on Mt. Hiei in 807, Enryaku-ji was one of a number of temples of the Tendai sect whose fighting *bonzes* (*sohei*) opposed the excesses of the powerful warrior clans.[15]

The *bonzes* of the True Word (Shingon) sect on Mount Negoro, who were actually called *Negoro-houshi* or *Negoroshu*, had a tradition of fighting that predated the Sengoku or "warring states era" (ca. 1350–1650). At their peak, the *Negoro-houshi* had a coalition of two thousand temples. Quick to adopt and make firearms, they played an important role in the major battles of the warring era.

11 Ignatius Loyola understood this problem and thus the Jesuit "formula" (founding rules of the order) mandated that Jesuits *not* accept ecclesiastical appointments. The rule, however, at times was broken, inasmuch as the Jesuits found it difficult to deny requests from kings and other powerful leaders who asked them to accept ecclesiastical positions that came with titles and honors.

12 The word *Negoro* (not *Nengoro*) might have sometimes been used by the Japanese to refer to the monks of said place, but it is not, strictly speaking, correct.

13 Marques, *Daily Life in Portugal*, 223.

14 C.R. Boxer, *The Christian Century in Japan, 1549–1650* (Berkeley: University of California Press, 1951); see also Josef Franz Schütte, *Valignano's Mission Principles for Japan 1573–1582*. Vol. I, Part II, trans. J. Coyne (St. Louis: Institute for Jesuit Sources, 1985), 168, 304.

15 Boxer, *The Christian Century in Japan*, 70–71.

11. Among us, an effort is made to fully keep whatever promises are made to God; the bonzes publicly profess not to eat meat or fish, but almost all of them do so in secret, unless they fear being seen or are unable to.

About thirty years earlier, in 1552, Xavier wrote that "formerly the bonzes or bonzesses who had broken one of their five precepts [sex, theft or lying, homicide, killing any creature or eating the same, or drinking wine] were punished with death by the princes and nobles of the place where they lived.... But at present, this discipline is entirely relaxed and corrupted; the greater number drink wine, eat meat secretly. ..."[16] So even when bonzes observed their vows the Jesuits attributed it to fear of physical punishment rather than piety.

12. Our religious never serve as diplomats for princes or lords; feudal lords[17] *in Japan use the bonzes as diplomats as well as military strategists.*[18]

Valignano's order to his fellow Jesuits forbidding them to act as intelligence agents, even if it was in the interests of a Christian daimyo,[19] clearly suggests that the Jesuits were not entirely outside the intelligence business. In fact, the Jesuits undertook numerous diplomatic missions on behalf of the Crown of Portugal.[20] Perhaps what Frois meant to say was that some bonzes essentially were employed as envoys, whereas the Jesuits mostly dabbled in the information business (for instance, conveying information or correspondence from a secular ruler while travelling on religious "business"). Okada[21] points out that each Shogun had a respected bonze-envoy or diplomat (*shizo*, meaning messenger bonze).

13. Among us, a religious who gets married becomes an apostate; when the bonzes get tired of religion, they either marry or become soldiers.

For the Jesuits and other Catholic religious and clerics the decision to embrace a religious life essentially was irrevocable. To quit the order or Church was to go back on your word; as Frois phrased it, to apostatize. While celibacy was a serious vow, it was not uncommon for secular priests, bishops, cardinals, or even the Pope to have a mistress and children.[22] Indeed, Martin Luther, who quit the priesthood and married a former nun in 1525, argued that enforced celibacy was one reason why so many Catholic clerics had hidden concubines and tolerated prostitution.

A few Buddhist sects did permit marriage, but the majority did not. During the disordered or dynamic period when Frois wrote, one suspects that even *bonzes* who were not supposed to marry, sometimes did. In fact, Frois and his Jesuit mentor, Organtino, devoted almost a year to studying The Lotus Sutra of the Tendai and Nichiren sects under the tutelage of an erudite and highly cultured former *bonze* who was married. Whatever "slack" existed in Frois' day would tighten up in the

---

16 Henry James Coleridge, *The Life and Letters of St. Francis Xavier*. 2 vols. (London: Burns and Oates, 1881), II, 340.

17 *Tonos.*

18 *Buriaqos,* or strategists, derived from *buryaku,* or strategy.

19 Boxer, *The Christian Century in Japan.*

20 Dauril Alden, *The Making of an Enterprise, The Society of Jesus in Portugal, Its Empire, and Beyond 1540–1750* (Stanford University Press, 1996).

21 Akio Okada, trans. and ed., *Yoroppa-Bunka to Nihon-Bunka* [European Culture and Japanese Culture] (Tokyo: Iwanami Shoten, 1965).

22 Marques, *Daily Life in Portugal,* 176–177.

Tokugawa era, when new national sartorial regulations forced Buddhist religious to comply with their own rules.

14. Among our religious, there is no succession by means of inheritance, only by vote and virtue; among the bonzes, succession is inherited by the disciple whom the superior chooses as a child and rears.

When an individual enters the Jesuit order he undergoes a two-year novitiate, during which time superiors make a decision about the novice's potential as a religious, particularly whether the individual should receive advanced training in theology, which would enable that Jesuit later to be admitted to the rank of the "professed." Only professed Jesuits can fill the highest positions within the Society of Jesus and participate in convocations to amend the constitution and set policy. Lesser Jesuits, spiritual coadjutors (educated priests) and temporal coadjutors (non-ordained "brothers" who serve as cooks, artisans, nurses, etc.) follow, rather than make the rules. During the century following the founding of the Jesuit order (1540–1640), the ranks of the professed were dominated by Spaniards and Italians from aristocratic families who discriminated against Jesuits born elsewhere. Frois is disingenuous when he implies that succession within the Jesuit order was strictly a matter of virtue and common assent. Frois' own superior, Valignano, came from a respected Italian family with close ties not only to the Jesuit Father General but also the Pope, and despite having once done jail time for purportedly slashing a woman's face,[23] Valignano shot up like a rocket within the Jesuit order, becoming at age thirty-seven *Visitador* in charge of all the East Indies (churches from India eastward). Granted, Valignano was brilliant, but his brilliance became more apparent after, rather than before his appointment as a Jesuit superior. Frois, by contrast, despite many years of experience and unparalleled knowledge of Japan, never was promoted to the rank of Professed.

In Japan, as Okada notes, a disciple might be chosen from a large number of young bonzes (or bonzes-to-be) on the basis of intelligence and ability. He was indeed groomed for succession, but it was hardly so arbitrary a process as this contrast implies. This is not to deny that some Zen monasteries accepted the younger brothers of samurai families who gave up their inheritance and expected, in exchange, promising opportunities. In this case, Frois may be correct.

15. Among us, one becomes a religious out of devotion and an inner calling to virtue; the bonzes do so to inherit one another's wealth and gain worldly glory.

This contrast essentially is a repeat of #1 above. To reiterate our own caution—individuals in both Europe and Japan became religious for various reasons, including an "inner calling to virtue."

16. Our religious focus their principal efforts on interior purity and cleanliness; the bonzes keep their dwellings, gardens and temples extremely clean, but keep their souls abominable.

Christianity has a long tradition of ascetics who sacrificed their bodies and cleanliness to get close to God. Indeed, lice were said to be the inseparable companions of monks and soldiers. In Japan, the Jesuit superior, Valignano,

23 Andrew C. Ross, *A Vision Betrayed* (New York: Orbis Books, 1994), 33.

restricted all novices and ordained Jesuits (except the sick or aged) to no more than one bath every eight days.

In drafting this contrast on cleanliness, Frois again alludes to sodomy ("keep their souls abominable"), suggesting that it was central to the lives of Buddhist monks. As noted, sodomy was indeed common and widely accepted, but it is unfair to suggest that it was central to the religious lives of many bonzes (just as it would be unfair to dismiss the religious lives of Catholic monks because of the prevalence of sodomy in European monasteries).

In Japan, cleanliness and godliness were inseparable. Frois could not accept that cleansing and (self) reflection were one and the same and that Japanese Buddhism and Shinto aimed for "inward purity of heart." The mirror is one of Shinto's main symbols, and keeping it clean was identified with keeping a pure soul. When Buddhism was introduced to Japan it had no choice but to emphasize cleanliness, both material and metaphorical, to take root in the land of Shinto. The Buddhists cherished the moon, which was identified with the "wheel of the Law" (the teachings of the Buddha), likening it unto a mirror that had to be kept free of dust. In Japanese, *kirei* means "clean," "pretty," and "right," as in "doing it right" (*kirei-ni-shite*).

17. Among us, we are keen to avoid deceit, hypocrisy and adulation; the bonzes of Japan live off these and consider them an extremely powerful means of making a livelihood.

The Jesuits clearly saw Buddhism as a sham, inspired by the devil, but profitable to the *bonzes*. In his letter of January, 1552, Francis Xavier was quite explicit:

> ... our greatest enemies are the bonzes, because we expose their falsehoods.... they used to make the people believe that it is impossible for persons in general to keep those five commandments ... and that, therefore, they would observe them for the people, on the condition of the people giving them maintenance and honour. They give their word that if anyone goes down into hell he will be delivered by their intervention and labour. We, on the contrary, proved to the people that in hell there is no redemption, and that no one can be rescued from it by the bonzes and bonzesses.[24]

Xavier's argument against the bonzes is like the kettle calling the pot black. Throughout the history of Christianity, religious have functioned much like the bonzes described by Xavier, observing vows and commandments that ordinary people struggle with in order to draw close to God, in part to present petitions from ordinary folk concerned with their own souls and the souls of the departed. Like the bonzes, priests and nuns are quick to point out that they have no power to rescue a soul from purgatory or hell, yet they rely on money from masses, rosaries, and prayers offered to God in the hopes of winning his mercy.

In one sense, Frois and Xavier were correct. Most Japanese, including the bonzes, were not supremely confident and absolutely sure of their faith and the existence of God and Heaven. This seems to be a Christian luxury. Arguably, many

24 Coleridge, *The Life and Letters of St. Francis Xavier,* II, 339–340.

bonzes were emotionally and intellectually mature and humble enough to know they did not know everything. And yet clearly they knew quite a bit, as on numerous occasions the Jesuits themselves admitted to being bowled over by the bonzes' philosophical disputations.

18. Our religious wear no beard and have tonsured heads; the bonzes shave their heads and beard every four days.[25]

The Jesuits did not tonsure, presumably to emphasize that they were neither monks nor secular priests, attached to a monastery or parish, respectively. While tonsure is uncommon today, in Frois' time members of monastic orders and many secular clergy shaved all or part of the head to signal their religious calling. Apparently not all clergy were as attentive to their hair as Frois suggests, for Marques notes that the Archbishop of Lisbon found it necessary in the early fifteenth century to mandate regular hair cuts for priests and monks.[26]

The *bonze* turned his whole head into a round object, which, in Japan was a similitude for the soul itself (as noted, *tama* means "soul," "gem" or any round smooth object; *atama* means "head").

19. Among us, religious wear cowls or caps; most of the time the bonzes do not wear anything. When it is cold they wear sack-like caps, orvataboxis, and some of them wear a cowl-like article that looks like the neck and head of a horse with ears.

When outdoors or traveling, *bonzes* usually wore large umbrella-like hats, which provided relief from the sun. These hats were never worn indoors. Here Frois appears to be referring to *wataboshi*, a cotton hat of sorts, which sometimes had a neck-piece that protected the neck and presumably suggested to Frois the horse simile. One can imagine "ears" appearing if the weight of the neck piece caused the top of the cap to become slightly concave, leaving the corners sticking up a bit. Frankly, Frois seems to be trying too hard for a contrast that hardly exists.

20. Our religious place great value on decency and setting a good example; the bonzes always walk around with their legs exposed, and during the summer they wear robes that are so thin that they show everything, which they do not find the least bit embarrassing or shameful.

In Japan and China, where bodies were less likely to be mortified, or alternatively, celebrated as in Renaissance art, no one was bothered by thin clothing in hot muggy weather. And when the penis itself was involved, the Japanese were not the least bit offended by God's handiwork. Even today, Shinto parades feature large straw or wooden phalluses.

21. Our religious show great sobriety and temperance in what they drink, especially wine; despite its being prohibited, the bonzes often are encountered on the road drunk.

Water drawn from wells or cisterns in sixteenth-century Europe often was contaminated (the "sewer system" is many towns and cities often amounted to throwing human waste and garbage into the street at night). Beer, ale, and wine were for sixteenth-century Europeans what bottled water is for people today.

---

25 The frequency of shaving actually depended on the particular sect of Buddhism.
26 Marques, *Daily Life in Portugal*, 223.

Although as Frois suggests, priests and religious ideally were supposed to avoid over-consumption of alcohol, many apparently were not successful in doing so. In his fourteenth-century *Libro de buen amor*, the archbishop of Hita, Juan Ruiz, implied that quite a few clerics were intemperate.[27] Marques cites records from one monastery in Portugal where the daily ration of wine was at least a quart and a half per person.[28]

In Japan, Frois may well have encountered a good number of "fake" bonzes, in part because superficially speaking, being a *bonze* (essentially wearing a robe, carrying a string of beads, and shaving one's head) was a good way for professional poets (e.g. Matsuo Basho[29]) to move about the countryside and more easily get through fief checkpoints. We cannot know how many of the drunk *bonzes* seen by Frois were the "real" thing (and not that it matters). The prohibition in Japanese Buddhism on drinking had more to do with sartorial restrictions than morality. Taking rice out of circulation to make *sake* was, on the whole, at odds with feeding a large population. Like meat, alcoholic beverages are a relatively inefficient food source. The Japanese saw, and still see nothing wrong with being drunk *per se*, particularly as there never have been as many mean and violent drunks in Japan as in the West.

22. Our religious do not usually sing, nor do they perform in profane plays or farces; the bonzes consider these a delight and take regular recreation in them.

Most bonzes were no more performers than they were warriors (as per #10 above), but part of the Pure Land (*Jodo*) school, called the *Ji-shu*, was particularly noted for its rousing performances of the *Nembutsu* or Buddhist prayer acknowledging Amida Buddha and his saving grace. The founder of *Ji-Shu*, Ippen (1239–1289), pioneered the use of dancing while preaching. Not only were the Jesuits in Japan opposed to performing themselves, but worse, they could be "wet blankets" for those who embraced dramatic dance. In a letter written in 1565, the Spanish doctor turned Jesuit, Luis de Almeida, recounted how a group of Japanese Christians who had been visited by some dancing gentiles returned the favor, creatively making up a dance lauding the Virgin Mary. On their way home, the Christians dropped by the church to show off the dance to Father Cosme de Torres. Torres was dismayed and laid into his neophytes for disgraceful behavior. A Japanese nobleman took full responsibility for the dance, disciplining himself so strongly "that he was left bathed in blood." This sense of personal responsibility greatly impressed Almeida, although he said nothing about whether Cosme de Torres may have overreacted.[30]

---

27 Olivia Remie Constable, *Medieval Iberia* (Philadelphia: University of Pennsylvania Press, 1997), 288–292; see also distich 36.

28 Marques, *Daily Life in Portugal*, 28.

29 *Matsuo Basho: The Narrow Road to the Deep North, and Other Travel Sketches*, trans. Nobuyuki Yuasa (New York: Penguin Books, 1966[1684–94]), 54.

30 *Cartas que os Padres e Irmãos da Companhia de Iesus Escreuerão dos Reynos de Iapão & China aos da Mesma Companhia da India & Europa, des do Anno de 1549 Até o de 1580*. 2 Vols. Facsimile edition by José Manuel Garcia (Maia: Castoliva Editora, 1997), I, 171v.

23. We take on faith [the existence of a] future heaven and hell and the immortality of the soul; the Jenxu³¹ bonzes deny all this and believe there is nothing more than being born and dying.

Frois in his *Historia*³² described a debate between a Father Lourenço and a Zen *bonze* named Shozaemon that began with Lourenço describing the "great differences" between the Japanese kami (gods) and *hotoke* (Buddhas) and the Christian *Deus* (God). Shozaemon smiled and then commented that "... all that is a laughable illusion, which wise and knowledgeable men value not a whit." That was a fair representation of the Zen position. The idea that "getting born means you die, and that is it" was standard Zen teaching.

Zen or Ch'an Buddhism bears a resemblance to Christian asceticism in its rigorous discipline of meditation and silence, its aim of unity with the *all* and *nothing*, and in the free behavior of the enlightened. Frois, of course, acknowledged none of this, but not so his fellow Jesuit João Rodrigues:

> Their vocation is not to philosophize with the help of books and sermons written by illustrious masters and philosophers.... Instead, they give themselves up to contemplating the things of nature ... Thus, from what they see in things themselves, they attain by their own efforts to a knowledge of the first cause, and putting aside what is evil and imperfect in the mind and reasoning, they reach the natural perfection and being of the first cause.... the monks of this sect are of a resolute and determined character, without any indolence, laxity or effeminacy.... they do without a great number of things which they consider superfluous and unnecessary. They maintain that a hermitage should first of all be frugal and moderate, with much quietness, peace of soul and exterior modesty.³³

24. We profess only one God, one faith, one baptism and one Catholic Church; in Japan there are thirteen sects and almost all of them disagree on worship and veneration.

During Frois' lifetime (1532–1597) the Catholic Church was torn apart by disagreements over what Frois casts as "one faith." Catholics and former Catholics, now known as Protestants, were killing each other in the streets over grace,

---

31 *Zen-shu,* or the Zen school was one of the three main schools of Buddhism in Japan. Perhaps the most salient difference among the three schools centers around how to realize enlightenment. Whereas Zen held fast to the traditional Buddhist emphasis on meditation, the Pure Land and Nicheren schools argued that this path (and others more esoteric) were unrealistic. The only real hope for salvation rested with Amida Buddha and his promise of saving any and all who placed their trust in Him. Yoshiro Tamura, *Japanese Buddhism: A Cultural History* (Tokyo: Kosei Publishing, 2001); Kazuo Kasahara, *A History of Japanese Religion* (Tokyo: Kosei Publishing, 2002).

32 Luís Fróis, *Historia de Japam,* ed. José Wicki, S.J. 5 vols. (Lisbon: Biblioteca Nacional de Lisboa, 1976–1984[1597].

33 Cooper, *They Came to Japan,* 23. Rodrigues went on to say that Zen was so much "hypocrisy," but one wonders, given his frequently expressed cultural relativism, whether he wrote this to please superiors.

predestination, baptism, the Eucharist, and a host of other Christian beliefs and practices.[34]

Buddhists certainly disagreed, sometimes violently. Thus, there were numerous Buddhist sects offering different approaches to the divine.[35] Members of the same family might belong to different sects, and in one sense, they all embraced more than one religion (if Shinto is included).

25. Above all things we abhor and abominate the devil; the bonzes venerate and worship him, building temples and making great sacrifices to him.

As noted, Frois and other Jesuits believed that the devil was the architect of Shinto and Buddhism. In Buddhist temples from India to Japan one does often find the closest thing the Buddhists have to the devil, known as Jemma O, Yama, or Emma. This devil, however, is quite unlike the Christian version, who actively pursues souls and makes trouble. Kaempfer,[36] writing in 1690, aptly described Jemma O as a severe judge and sovereign commander of a place of horror and heinousness who observed all through a large looking-glass, placed before him and called *Sofarino Kagami*, or the looking-glass of knowledge. Kaempfer went on to explain that unhappy souls in hell may receive great relief (lighter punishment, early release, etc.) by the virtuous life and good deeds of family, friends, and relatives, and through prayers and offerings to the great and good Amida. (Amitabha Buddha was as central to the Pure Land faith as the Virgin Mary was/is to Catholicism.) It was also possible to appeal for mercy directly to the Judge, and doing so had none of the nefarious connotations of making a deal with the devil. In a long letter from 1565, Frois himself described a temple dedicated to the god and judge of hell where people sought mercy:

> On the walls are painted the many kinds of torments in hell, with many figures of men and women suffering these pains, and of the demons inflicting them. Many people visit this temple to pray and give alms, and they usually repair there to beg the king of hell to deliver them from these torments.[37]

Note that the reason the Japanese could pray to Emma is simple: Emma was not evil. He did not pursue people and try to lure them into sin. He did not delight in bad behavior nor seek to increase it. He only judged people for their sins.[38] Thus, if the Japanese Buddhist hell was equally full of demons, fire, poking and cutting,

34 For instance, thousands of Protestants and Catholics died during the "Saint Bartholomew's Day massacre" in August of 1572. Luc Racaut, *Hatred in Print* (Burlington: Ashgate, 2002).

35 A contemporary dictionary indicates that there were traditionally thirteen sects in China and eight in Japan. However, the number eight suggests "many" in Japanese.

36 Englebert Kaempfer, *The History of Japan, Together With a Description of the Kingdom of Siam, 1690–92*. 3 Vols. (Glasgow: James MacLehose and Sons, 1906[1690–92]), II, 60–62.

37 Cooper, *They Came to Japan*, 340.

38 In addition to Emma, there also were horrifying demons that served to ward off evil spirits or guard this or that Buddhist treasure. Perhaps the closest Christian equivalent is the cynocephali St. Christopher, whose beastly powers were enlisted on behalf of his new religion. Most sects did not make a big deal of these demons; only the *Konpira* sect centered on images of the powerful *tengu* goblin. Like St. Christopher, he was the patron "saint" of travelers and, most of all, seafarers.

and so forth, how you got there and how long you stayed was another matter. With Christianity, anyone who is not saved ends up in hell forever. (As Xavier noted in his letter of 1552, this did not go over well with the Japanese, who were told by the Jesuits that their pagan relatives and ancestors would burn forever.)

26. Among us, the temples and the facilities of a monastery belong to the universal Religion; in Japan, if a bonze becomes tired [of a religious life], he sells off the temple and its facilities and [everything else?].

When Buddhist temples lost their backing, or the prelate retired, it was declared a *haidera*, or derelict temple, and might even be bought for use by a different sect. This is apparently what Frois is alluding to.[39]

27. Our priests wear a stole to administer the sacraments; the bonzes wear one as a refinement when they go out to make their visits.

Catholic priests wear a stole or scarf-like garment whenever they are fulfilling their priestly duties; the stole is a symbol of the priest's authority. *Bonzes* generally wore a surplice over their robe when they went out on official religious duties such as conferencing with other *bonzes*. Frois, rather unfairly, seems to be saying, "We adorn ourselves to do God's work; they do so to impress people."

28. Our priests wear the stole draped across the nape of the neck; the bonzes wear theirs crosswise, over one shoulder and under the other, and it is broader and sewn in a different manner.

The fact that priests and bonzes wore something similar enough to warrant Frois using the same term is perhaps more remarkable than any difference or similarity in the stoles themselves. The Buddhist equivalent of a stole is called a *kesa*.

29. Our religious, if they know how, administer medical treatment for free, out of a love for God; most physicians in Japan are bonzes who live off their fees.

The Jesuits did indeed distinguish themselves as tireless caretakers of the sick; Jesuit novices often were required to spend time each week working in hospitals.[40] Okada[41] writes that while there were bonzes who attended to medical matters in the large temples in Kyoto and Nara, most doctors in Japan shaved their heads and otherwise looked like bonzes. Frois perhaps assumed (wrongly) that many doctors were also priests.

30. If our religious were to go about carrying a gilded fan in their hand, they would be considered mad; the bonzes, as a refinement, must carry a golden fan in their hand whenever they preach or go out.

These fans belong to a class of fans called *suebiro* or "end-wide/open" and were called *chukei* ("mid-open"), with the Chinese character for "open" not the usual one, but one that means "enlightened." But even without this apparent symbolism, the elegant appearance of these fans in the closed position (unique in the way that the ends remain partially spread open) more than justifies their being carried as a symbol of authority. These gilded fans were only carried by elders and

39 Okada, *Yoroppa-Bunka to Nihon-Bunka*, 76.
40 One of the first Jesuits to be canonized as a saint was Luis Gonzaga, who gave his life in 1594 caring for the sick during an epidemic in Spain.
41 Okada, *Yoroppa-Bunka to Nihon-Bunka,* 77.

by Buddhist clergy with that authority, not by those whom the Japanese would call *bonzo*. The fans often were used to emphasize points in conversation.

31. We preach standing up, and we gesture by moving our hands; the bonzes preach sitting down gesturing with their heads, without moving their hands.

The Japanese move their heads a lot more than their hands, in comparison to Southern Europeans, who might be said to talk with their hands. Professional storytellers in Japan whack their closed fans smartly upon their thighs to emphasize points, but this was apparently beneath the dignity of *bonzes*.

It is interesting that the Japanese should be more liable to sit, given that Westerners use chairs. Frois never does contrast our respective positions for meditation (kneeling versus cross-legged).

32. In Europe we preach wearing a white surplice and no stole; the bonzes preach wearing a black koromo[42] *and a stole, with a gilded fan in their hand.*

A surplice is a loose-fitting, full-sleeved white vestment worn by Christian clergy over their cassocks (the latter is a black vestment that has the appearance of a combination of a shirt and skirt, extending as it does to the top of the shoes). The bonze's stole is a short surplice; the Chinese characters for stole ("shoulder" and "added + clothing") make the meaning transparent to those unfamiliar with the item. The *koromo* is a black robe of fine hemp with wide sleeves that almost reaches to the ground. It was worn over a very clean white robe. Until recently, *koromo* was the traditional generic term in Japanese for clothing; today *yofuku* or "Western-dress" is the generic term.

The religious use of white in Japan was pretty much reserved by Shinto. Not only priests and shrine maidens, but also people on pilgrimages stick to white. It is part of their orientation toward purity and provides a powerful visual contrast, not so much with Buddhists, but with all the corporate soldiers in dark suits.

33. We preach from pulpits; the bonzes do so from chairs, like our lecturers.

It is somewhat surprising, given that the Japanese are generally a chair-less culture, to learn that Frois is correct in noting the *bonzes'* use of a chair for preaching. The chair, called a *kyokuroku*, apparently was a Chinese design. It was tall, with a finish of vermillion or black lacquer and X-shaped legs, suggesting that the chair could be folded. The chair also had parallel runners extending between the front and rear legs, as well as a foot rest.

34. Free of charge, we give others rosaries that have been blessed as well as relics from saints; the bonzes sell for a very good sum of money a great number and variety of amulets in the form of a written piece of paper.

It is true that the Jesuits never charged their neophytes for relics, medals, and rosaries. Still, relics and indulgences were big business in Europe and a major point of contention between Catholics and Protestants (Luther and other Church critics railed against the "magical thinking" and profiteering behind the sale of relics and indulgences). When Phillip II lay mortally ill, he asked for and received the entire knee of Saint Sebastian (skin as well as bone) in addition to the rib

42 *Koromo* = robe, in this case, a religious habit or priestly garment.

of Saint Alban and the arm of Saint Vincent Ferrer.[43] Today visitors to Lourdes, Fatima, Tours, and many other shrines purchase rosaries, ashes, holy water, and similar items that are thought to facilitate recovery from illness and other of life's setbacks.

The bonzes did sell charms to deal with illness, heartbreak, etc., and some apparently went overboard, offering what amounted to "tickets to paradise," which are perhaps analogous to the plenary indulgences that Christians can obtain during Jubilees and other special occasions.

35. The Franciscan friars bestow their order's habit on some deceased [non-members] at no charge; the bonzes compel men and women, while they are living, to acquire some paper catabiras with foqeqio[44] written on them, so that they can be worn when they die, in order for the bonzes to thereby profit.

The Franciscan order of friars, founded by St. Francis at the outset of the thirteenth century, actually was part of a much broader religious movement that encompassed lay people who came to form a "third order" of the Franciscans. Within a decade of St. Francis' death in 1226, wealthy knights and ladies, and in Frois' time, explorers such as Columbus, embraced the "rule" of the third order and were honored with burial in the simple sackcloth habit of St. Francis. Theologically speaking, the robes were nothing more than a statement that the individual had endeavored to live a good life, following the example of Christ and Saint Francis. Implicitly it was understood (based on medieval traditions) that the robes provided a protection of sorts from damnation or the fires of hell (perhaps experienced en route to the pearly gates).

In his *Historia*, Frois recounts Nobunaga's brutal execution of everyone related to a political rival, Araki, including 120 women who went to their death wearing sutra-embossed paper undergarments. These paper *catabira* or robes, which were sold by the *bonzes*, were painted with Chinese characters denoting "The Sutra on the Lotus of the Wonderful Law" (*Myohorenge-kyo* or *Saddharma Pundarika Sutra*).[45] Because written language in the Sino-cultural world need not be evoked to be invoked, it was enough to skip the sutra itself and just say or write its name. The writing could be burnt or exploded to float up into heaven; vibrated into heaven by being written around the bonze's hand-drum or upon a temple bell that is struck; "read" to the universe by rotation using human, hydraulic or wind power; cast upon the wind, each flutter of a sutra-lettered flag comprising a reading; dissolved and drunk; or simply worn, like the robes mentioned here by Frois.

36. Our priests conduct funeral rites for the deceased in churches; the bonzes quite often hold them in the home of the deceased, in order to eat and drink there.

While it is true that the most solemn part of a Catholic funeral, the funeral mass, takes place in church, it is not uncommon for the participants, including the

---

43 Carlos M.N. Eire, *From Madrid to Purgatory, The Art and Craft of Dying in Sixteenth-Century Spain* (New York: Cambridge University Press, 1995).

44 *Hokekyo* is the short title of the Lotus Sutra.

45 As noted, Frois devoted almost a year to studying The Lotus Sutra of the Pure Land and Nichiren sects.

priest, to adjourn to a banquet. The picaresque classic, [The life of] *Lazarillo de Tormes* (1554),[46] pokes fun at what was obviously a tendency in sixteenth-century Iberia for priests to overindulge at funerals. Hired by a priest as an assistant, the perpetually hungry Lazarillo found that "... at the meetings of religious societies and funerals where we prayed, if someone else was paying, he [the priest] used to eat like a wolf and drink more than a faith healer."

With respect to Japan, while important people often had memorials said at Buddhist temples, Frois is essentially correct in emphasizing the central role of the home in Japanese funerals. Prior to burial or cremation, the Japanese hold long wakes or vigils at their homes.[47] Relatives gather and help with the cooking, cleaning, reception of people, recording of gifts received, and so forth. People sit around and reminisce about, and occasionally view, the deceased. The *bonzes* may have played a greater role in these affairs in Frois' time than today and, naturally, enjoyed the repast. Still, to claim the whole affair was for the sake of the *bonze's* bellies is ridiculous. There is a fine story in Eliza Scidmore's *Jinrikisha Days in Japan* that suggests something other than selfish Buddhists:

> When the American man-o-war *Oneida* was run down and sank with her officers and crew by the P. and O. steamer *Bombay*, near the mouth of Yeddo Bay, January 23, 1870, our Government made no effort to raise the wreck or search for it, and finally sold it to a Japanese wrecking company for fifteen hundred dollars. The wreckers found many bones of the lost men among the ship's timbers, and when the work was entirely completed, with their voluntary contributions they erected a tablet in the Ikegami [temple] grounds to the memory of the dead, and celebrated there the impressive Buddhist *segaki* (feast of hungry souls), in May, 1889. The great temple was in ceremonial array; seventy-five priests in their richest robes assisted at the mass ... The scriptures were read, a service was chanted, the Sutra repeated, incense burned, the symbolic lotus-leaves cast before the altar.... No other country, no other religion, offers a parallel to this experience ...[48]

Here, *pace* Shakespeare, we see it is not birth but *death* that makes all men kin. "No other country" is overdoing it, but Scidmore's point is that the Buddhists very often were kind. They lived, and still live, for the repose of souls.

37. Among our religious yellow is a garish and indecent color; the bonzes consider it a virtuous color and enjoy wearing yellow or green.

Christians divide the year into liturgical seasons such as Advent and Easter, which have different theological emphases that are conveyed, in part, through the different colored vestments worn by priests (e.g. purple during Lent). Although ecclesiastical vestments of yellow (and blue) were known during the Middle Ages in Portugal, by Frois' time green and yellow were deemed inappropriate colors

---

46 Anonymous, *Lazarillo de Tormes*, trans. Stanley Applebaum (Mineola, N.Y.: Dover, 2001 [1554]), 33.
47 See Hikaru Suzuki, ed., *Death and Dying in Contemporary Japan* (London: Routledge, 2013).
48 New York: Harper & Brothers, 1897, 139.

for clergy.[49] Buddhist sects wore different colors depending on the season, and the yellow and green robes mentioned by Frois probably were closer to moss and manilla. Today, at least, only esoteric Buddhist high-priests, *hari-krishna* evangelists, and members of marginal cults go in for truly bright colors.

38. Among us, there is no hatred between one religious order and another; the bonzes of one sect abhor those of other sects, for the good of their own authority[50] and advantage.

Maybe not hatred, but Jesuits, Franciscans, and Dominicans—not to mention secular clergy—frequently fought with each other over matters of faith, power, and influence. Indeed, the Mendicants and Jesuits fought with each other for Papal and Crown support of missions to China and Japan as well as in the Americas. Franciscans and Dominicans who returned to Europe from China in the 1630s accused the Jesuits of allowing the Chinese to retain many of their "superstitions."[51]

Okada points out that the precepts of the egalitarian Pure Land sect (written about 100 years before the *Tratado*) include an admonition from its founder, Rennyo (1415–1499), against badmouthing other sects. Yet it is clear that Rennyo's advice largely was ignored during the sixteenth century by both his own sect (known by its detractors as *Ikko-shu*, or One-way-cult!) and others. Apparently the recent political upheavals and the effect of centuries of civil war (driving out those in the middle and encouraging fanatics) was reflected in the behavior of some Buddhists, who took their differences of interest and in catechism into the streets. In 1536, for instance, an army of militant monks of the Tendai school from Mt. Hiei attacked and destroyed Nicheren temples in Kyoto.

39. Among us, sorcerers are punished and castigated; the bonzes of the Ikkoshu and Yamabushi sects enjoy their company because they [themselves] are sorcerers.

During Frois' lifetime, Europe witnessed the great witch craze that cost the lives of tens of thousands of women, in particular. While Mediterranean countries such as Spain, Portugal, and Italy accounted for a small percentage of witch trials and executions[52] (eastern France, Germany, and Switzerland had the majority), the Church in Iberia, and more precisely, the Inquisition, was quick to investigate accusations of sorcery or witchcraft. While the accused got off with a warning and mild penance most of the time, there were occasions when the punishment was severe: In 1507, thirty women accused of sorcery were burned to death in Calabarra, Spain.

Sorcery was not an issue in sixteenth-century Japan. The *Yamabushi*, literally meaning "mountain warriors," actually look wizard-like in their unique clothing. They combine elements of esoteric Buddhism and shamanism and can hardly be considered a sect. After undergoing terrifying ordeals and inhuman austerities in their mountain headquarters, they wander around the country, to put it crudely,

49 Marques, *Daily Life in Portugal*, 222–223.

50 *Isei* = authority.

51 J.S. Cummins, *Jesuit and Friar in the Spanish Expansion to the East* (London: Variorum, 1986).

52 Italian and Iberian theologians and inquisitors attributed most acts of sorcery or witchcraft to ignorance or superstition, rather than a rational, conscious decision to enter into a pact with Satan.

exchanging magic for money. In 1583 Frois devoted almost an entire letter to a discussion of the *Yamabushi*, explaining how the "monks" with curled and straying hair made a profession out of selling curses as well as blessings and finding things that were either lost or stolen.[53]

The large *Ikko* "sect" practiced a form of "sorcery" that is more like Pentecostal Christianity, where, in a spiritually charged atmosphere, a charismatic leader heals the sick and works other "miracles." The head was venerated as a reincarnation of *Amida (Amithaba Buddha)* himself. Frois' fellow Jesuit, Vilela, offered this telling description of the *Ikko*:

> They give this *bonze* so much money in alms that he controls a large part of the country's wealth. Every year a great festival is held in his [i.e., Amidabutsu's] honour, and so many people wait at the gate of the temple to enter that many die in the stampede which results when they open the gates. Such people, however, are considered very lucky to have died in that way and some at their own request are dropped into the crowd around the gates and are thus killed. At night he preaches them a sermon during which they shed many tears.[54]

40. The tabi [socks] worn by laymen are black or mastic[55]colored; the bonzes and noblewomen wear white tabi made of cotton.

It is not clear what Frois intended with this contrast, except perhaps to suggest that the *bonzes* in Japan enjoyed wearing *tabi* of cotton, whereas religious in Europe wore poor-quality socks. Today in Japan white cotton is cheap, as it is in the West, but in Frois' day most *tabi* were leather and those of white cotton were a luxury.

41. In Europe when a master dies, his servants weep as they accompany his corpse to the gravesite; in Japan, some cut their stomachs and many others cut off the tips of their fingers and place them on the fire to burn.

Committing suicide by *hara-kiri* or "belly cutting" seems to have been uniquely Japanese. Finger joint cutting (today seen only in films and practiced mostly by apologetic *yakuza*) is found among many Pacific Island peoples. While the practice of self-injury and "retainer sacrifice" is found in many cultures,[56] in Japan's case it continued much longer than elsewhere. There were, nevertheless, many types of funerals in sixteenth-century Japan, and Frois here focuses on the more outlandish. Indeed, elsewhere Frois describes a sumptuous funeral with no split bellies or chopped fingers.[57]

53 *Cartas de Japáo & China*, II, 85v–88v; See also Cooper, *They Came to Japan*, 324
54 Ibid., 319.
55 Mastic here refers to a transparent resin that is pale yellow to green in color.
56 Bruce Trigger, *Understanding Early Civilizations* (Cambridge: Cambridge University Press, 2003), 88–89.
57 See Cooper, *They Came to Japan*, 363–366.

42. In Europe, we Christians beat our chests while asking God for forgiveness; in Japan the non-Christians vigorously rub their beads in the palms of their hands.

One of the prayers (*confiteor*) of the Latin mass has participants utter "*mea culpa, mea culpa, mea maxima culpa* (I am at fault; I am at fault; I am entirely at fault)," while striking the chest. Perhaps because of the absence of an icon such as the crucifix (to which Christians direct their guilty pleas), Japanese Buddhists rub their prayer beads as they contemplate their shortcomings and request mercy. Note that Frois wrote gentiles rather than *bonzes* because Japanese Buddhist laymen also had beads. Frois does not exaggerate when he says "vigorously." A group of Buddhists who pray in this way can sound like a tree filled with cicada. Rubbing and prayer or supplication went hand in hand. One of Issa's most famous haiku (*yare utsu-na*) features a fly rubbing his hands and feet for mercy. Another of his haiku, less famous, has them copying the people in the temple, rubbing their prayer beads (*dô no hae juzu suru hito no te o mane suru*).[58]

---

58 Robin D. Gill, *Fly-ku!* (Key Biscayne, FL: Paraverse Press, 2004), 41.

5   Concerning [Buddhist] temples, images and things pertaining to the practice of their religion

1. Our churches are long and narrow; temples in Japan are broad and shallow.[1]

Frois' perspective is from the front of the building. When you enter a church you essentially enter a long hall with an altar at the end. Here the most important Catholic belief—that God became man—is celebrated during mass. Catholicism is very much a religion centered on sacraments (i.e. baptism, confession, communion, marriage) that take place in a church. The altar in a Catholic church is not just a stage of sorts; it is understood as a sacred space by virtue of a holy relic within the altar and the consecrated host, which is kept secure in a tabernacle.[2]

Isabella Bird, who visited Japan during the mid-nineteenth century, offered one of the best summary descriptions of Buddhist temples:

> Writing generally, it may be said that in design, roof, and general aspect, Japanese Buddhist temples are all alike ... There is a single or double-roofed gateway, with highly coloured figures in niches on either side; the paved temple-court, with more or fewer stone or bronze lanterns; *amainu*, or heavenly dogs, in stone on stone pedestals; stone sarcophagi, roofed over or not, for holy water; a flight of steps, a portico, continued as a verandah all around the temple; a roof of tremendously disproportionate size and weight, with a peculiar curve; a square or oblong hall divided by a railing from a "chancel" with a high and low altar, and a shrine containing Buddha, or the divinity to whom the chapel is dedicated; an incense burner, and a few ecclesiastical ornaments ... Some temples are packed full of gods, shrines, banners,

---

1 In Romance languages and English the word "church" refers to a Christian place of worship, while temple is a more generic term. The Japanese use completely different terms for native and foreign "houses of worship." A Shinto shrine (often a simple wooden building with roof-beams crossing in the fashion of a two-dimensional tepee) is a *yashiro* or *jinja*; a Buddhist temple is a *tera* or *otera*; a church is a *kyokai*.

2 Despite being a sacred space, particularly during mass or when the Blessed Sacrament is exposed, churches also were multi-purpose centers for a variety of secular activities. See A.H. De Oliveira Marques, *Daily Life in Portugal in the Late Middle Ages* (Madison: University of Wisconsin Press, 1971), 224.

bronzes, brasses, tablets, and ornaments, and others, like those of the Monto sect,[3] are so severely simple, that with scarcely an alteration they might be used for Christian worship to-morrow. [4]

Japanese Buddhists do not go to temple for regular services or sacraments the way Catholics attend church. In Frois' time, they went mostly for the anniversaries of Buddha's death, the sect founder's death, or the recent death of a relative (hence the often-repeated truism about Japanese religion: Buddhism is for dying, Shinto is about living).[5] During funeral services, the head priest does not face the congregation, but sits closest to and faces the honzon—statue of the Buddha.[6] Behind him sit fellow priests, with the mourning family in a row behind them, and relatives in a row behind them, and so forth.

Despite widespread agnosticism in Japan today, seemingly every Japanese family has an altar in their home that serves "religious" purposes.[7] These altars often consist of a small cabinet with images of deceased relatives, the Buddha, or any item or icon (e.g. a dried flower) that facilitates contemplation. The altars provide a focal point for Shinto reflection, Confucian ancestor reverence, and/ or Buddhist prayer. The popularity of these altars and a lack of temple-centered sacraments such as confession or communion explain in part why the Japanese do not go to temples regularly the way Christians go to church. Following the expulsion of Christians from Japan during the early seventeenth century, the Tokugawa rulers made owning an altar mandatory. This also contributed to the embrace of altars.

Note that while the Jesuits under Valignano embraced Japanese architectural styles for Jesuit residences and schools, Valignano warned against constructing Catholic churches that might resemble a "devil's temple."

2. Our churches have choir lofts with pews or chairs to sit on; the bonzes pray before their altars seated on tatami.

As we have seen, the Japanese attach great significance to the relative heights of people and things. Thus, even if Japanese Buddhists had a choir, its members would not be seated above the altar and the abbot.[8]

---

3 In 1585, the Monto, an informal congregation of the Pure Land school, was perhaps the most influential Buddhist sect in all of Japan, owing in part to its main doctrine articulated by Shinran (1173–1263): salvation did not require abandoning "delusional" attachments and mastering difficult meditative practices; it was as "simple" as whole-heartedly embracing Amida. Dennis Hirota, *Asura's Harp, Engagement with Language as Buddhist Path* (Heidelberg: Universitätsverlag, 2006), 5–13.
4 Isabella L. Bird, *Unbeaten Tracks in Japan* (Boston: Beacon Press, 1987[1880]), 25.
5 Jacqueline I. Stone and Mariko Namba Walker, eds., *Death and the Afterlife in Japanese Buddhism* (Honolulu: University of Hawai'i Press, 2008).
6 The *honzon* of a particular temple could also be an image of a bodhisattva, or especially in the Shingon or Tendai schools, an esoteric deity (usually of Indic origins).
7 Hirochika Nakamachi, *Japanese Religions At Home and Abroad* (London Routledge, 2003), 14–16.
8 Japanese Buddhism did not have choirs during Frois' time, but Soka Gakkai (an offshoot of Nichiren Buddhism) does today.

3. We put our books on a bookstand so that everyone can sing together; each bonze has a little stool in front of him with his own book.

Perhaps this reflects the difference between the private devotion that seems to be at the heart of Buddhism and Christian rites and rituals that emphasize community, such as communion, where Christians share the body of Christ. In fact, despite an occasional small bell being struck, Japanese chanters are usually out of synch with each other, as chanters freely pause to catch their breath. Be that as it may, it is more likely that the difference stems from the fact that there was more and cheaper printed matter in Japan than in Europe. It may also derive from the Japanese practice of sitting: It is easy to share a book while standing (as Europeans usually do when singing), but it is clumsy when sitting cross-legged.

4. Our books are made by folding the pages and they are closed with a clasp; the bonzes' books are rolled up and tied with a ribbon.

"Our books" presumably refer to Holy Scripture and the works of the Latin Church Fathers, which often were bound in leather volumes that had hinged metal clasps to guard the contents from unauthorized readers as well as silverfish, the wingless insect that eats paper and the glue in book bindings. Much to the consternation of Martin Luther and other reformers, the Church insisted that only clergy were properly trained to read and interpret the Bible or the Latin texts of Augustine, Thomas Aquinas, and other Christian theologians.

The scroll, which was popular in the West during antiquity and the Middle Ages, continued in use longer in Japan, probably because the vertical ordering of Japanese characters (rather than the left-to-right ordering of written Latin) permitted the scroll to be rolled open horizontally, which is no more tiring or less efficient than turning a page. But the Japanese also had folded books at this time, and before long most sutra would be printed on long pages folded accordion style into books. Since the paper was thin, the pages were printed on only one side.[9]

5. Our images for the most part are painted retablos; all of the images[10] in the bonzes' temples are sculpted.

Frois is probably correct that most Catholic devotional images were *retablos*—panels of wood with low-relief paintings of scenes from the Bible and the lives of the saints. Note that canvas was only beginning to replace walls and wood panels as the preferred substrate for painting. Today in Lisbon's Ancient Art Museum one can view Nuno Gonçalves' multi-panel *retablo* of the Adoration of Saint Anthony of Padua, who hailed from Portugal. Gonçalves' work is an outstanding example of fifteenth-century Portuguese painting. During Frois' lifetime Portugal also imported thousands of *retablos* by Flemish painters. Indeed, the demand was so great that Flemish artists moved to Lisbon and Evora, where they adopted Portuguese names (e.g. Francisco Henriques)

9 For a discussion of scrolls and books, see Andrew Pettegree, *The Book in the Renaissance* (New Haven: Yale University Press, 2010), 4–9.
10 *Varelas.* As noted in Chapter 3, the term *varela* is probably derived from the Malay *berhala* or the Javanese *brahala*, meaning "idol"; *berhala* alone may have been used elliptically by the Malay or misunderstood by the Portuguese.

and opened workshops that made Portugal a center of painting on wood.[11] Still, Catholic churches in sixteenth-century Portugal and elsewhere were well known for their three-dimensional images created in stone or on polychrome wood, depicting various saints and, of course, the crucified Christ.[12] Indeed, Protestant reformers pointed to an abundance of these lifelike images as proof that the Church had promulgated idolatry.

Buddhist images (and to Frois' credit he did not use the pejorative term idol) were generally cast or carved in wood. Note that this contrast makes sense so long as one is focusing on the altar; paintings and images appear elsewhere in Buddhist temples. These paintings range from the black and white Zen *daruma* (i.e. a depiction of Bodhidharma, the Indian monk who purportedly brought Ch'an/Zen to China) and portraits, which are usually in a side room or office rather than the main temple, to luridly colored paintings of hell, which Frois himself comments on elsewhere (Chapter 4, #25). Curiously, neither Frois nor any other Jesuit (as far as we know) mentioned the most important painted image of esoteric Buddhism, the *mandala*. Whereas Christians come close to God through scripture[13], Buddhist monks meditate upon true nature or cosmic principles using this complex abstract painting, which can be mesmerizing.

6. We paint our images with a variety of colors; theirs are gilded from top to bottom.

Oil-based paint became popular among Flemish painters in the early fifteenth century and subsequently was embraced by artists elsewhere in Europe, in part because oil paints were much easier to mix than tempera and yielded the rich variety of colors emphasized by Frois. Portuguese painters such as Grão Vasco, who developed the Manueline art style, were noted for their use of gem-like colors.

Generally, the manifestation of the Buddha best reflecting the philosophy of a particular sect (and/or the founder, who was himself such a manifestation) was covered in gold. Images of the founder often took up as much space in a Buddhist temple as images of Christ or the Virgin Mary in Catholic churches of the sixteenth century. These figures were indeed gilded, as were decorative lotus leaves and flowers. But, as Frois knew, not all Buddhist statues were covered with gold. For instance, Buddhist temples generally feature guardian demons that are usually

---

11 Pedro Dias,"O Manuelino." In *História da Arte em Portugal*, Vol. 5. (Lisbon: Alfa, 1986); "Manueline Art." In *Museum With No Frontiers Exhibition The Manueline: Portuguese Art During the Great Discoveries*, pp. 22–38 (Lisbon: Programa de Incremento do Turismo Cultural, 2002), 30–31. See also Gauvin Alexander Bailey, "Italian Renaissance and Baroque Painting Under the Jesuits and Its Legacy Throughout Catholic Europe, 1565–1773." In *The Jesuits and the Arts*, eds. John W. O'Malley, S.J., Gauvin A. Bailey, and Giovanni Sale, S.J.(Philadelphia: Saint Joseph's University Press, 2005), 125–201.

12 The Council of Trent (1545–1563) encouraged church art that moved the masses by appealing to the senses.

13 The great Christian theologian and Jesuit favorite, Thomas Aquinas, argued that natural reason and contemplation of nature (which is the emphasis in Zen Buddhism) revealed the existence of God but not his nature; the latter was knowable only from the study of scripture and, ultimately, an infusion of God's grace.

painted red. Many temples also have images carved of plain stone depicting "the 500 followers of Buddha" who realized enlightenment, as well as the bodhisattva Jizo[14] (a "patron saint" of children, women, and travelers who was/is particularly popular in Japan as well as Korea). Sometimes the lifelike sculptures of Buddhist saints had simulated pores and implanted hair.

Frois clearly exaggerates to suggest that Buddhists really worship either gold or deities whose spiritual worth has been conflated with material preoccupations. This is like the pot calling the kettle black, given the enormous amounts of gold and silver looted from places such as Mexico that was applied to images and the interiors of Catholic churches during the sixteenth and seventeenth centuries. But maybe Frois knew little of this extravagance, as he left Portugal in 1548, just about the time the Baroque period was getting under way.

7. Our images are all created in proportion to the physical stature of men; some of theirs are so large that they appear to be giants.

Many Europeans were impressed, some of them favorably (e.g. Kipling) and others less so (e.g. Vivero y Velasco) by the immense statues of Buddha (*daibutsu*, literally 'large Buddha') that were cast or carved in various parts of Japan beginning as early as the seventh century (i.e. the Asuka *daibutsu* in Nara). The great size of the statues conveyed in part the salvific power of the Buddha, and perhaps more so, the power and authority of the Japanese rulers who commissioned them.[15] Perhaps because Christianity is about God becoming man and saints who remain human despite infusions of grace, it has favored religious images that approximate human proportions. (Michelangelo's Pieta follows human proportions, whereas his David, unveiled in Florence in 1504, is some seventeen feet tall). Interestingly, in Frois' own Lisbon, the people seemingly broke with this tradition in 1950 when they erected an enormous statue of Christ the King (itself inspired by the enormous statue of Christ the Redeemer in Rio de Janeiro completed in 1931).[16]

Considering the fact that there were also countless small *rakan* and *Jizo* sculptures, which Frois never mentions, one might ask Frois: Why give only one side of the story? Clearly it was to suggest that Buddhism was about worshipping fantastic figures in gold more akin to the devil than the one true God.

8. Ours are beautiful and inspire devotion; theirs are horrendous and frightening, with images of demons engulfed in flames.

Tengu, or minor guardian demons, are regularly found standing guard in Buddhist temples (they drive away evil spirits or guard this or that Buddhist treasure).

14 A *bodhisattva* is a follower of the Buddha who devotes his or her life to freeing others from suffering. Bodhisattvas are a lot like Catholic saints in that they are not supposed to be worshipped, but rather embraced as models to emulate, thereby quickening the enlightened qualities inherent in everyone.

15 Patricia J. Graham, *Faith and Power in Japanese Buddhist Art 1600–2005* (Honolulu: University of Hawai'i Press, 2007), 19.

16 Although European artists during the Middle Ages often exaggerated the size of the most important characters appearing in a painting, a stained-glass window, etc., the exaggeration is usually a matter of degree rather than kind (i.e. *diabutsu* are not just big, they are colossal).

However, not all these fearsome red statues were of such minor figures. Many if not most of Buddhism's "horrid and frightening demons" are converted or appropriated local deities, not unlike "our" cynocephalic Saint Christopher, who, according to legend, was from a race of dog-headed people.

Demons are a peripheral aspect of most Buddhist sects and temples, although in some places their significance can loom large. Many fishing villages in Japan, for instance, recognized and prayed to a powerful *tengu*, depicted as a long-nosed goblin with mountain, and hence, wind-influencing ability. Then there is the patron god of the blacksmith, the "Metal Mountain God." His better-known manifestation, *Fudomyo-o*, literally "the unmoving-light=bright-king" (perhaps better known as a manifestation of Mahavairocana, the central Buddha in the Shingon esoteric worldview), was thought to sit fast upon a metal-filled mountain, his countenance glaring like molten ore, with an upraised sword in hand to sever the deep-seated appetites of the flesh.[17]

Frois knew from first-hand experience that Buddhist images were not only diverse and complex but that some were actually beautiful. In one of his early letters he described a thousand gilded sculptures of "Kannon, the son of Amida": "There is a shining halo behind each statue ... The beautiful faces are so well carved that, but for the fact that it is a temple of Amida, this scene would make a good composition of place for a meditation on the ranks and hierarchies of the angels."[18] Note that Kannon, rather than being the son of Amida, was understood by the Japanese to be a manifestation of Amida's compassion; often Kannon is depicted as an attendant to Amida together with the bodhisattva Seishi. In the Japanese Buddhist imaginary, local (and imported) deities were seen as manifes-tations of a particular Buddha who took on "local" forms to better affect human lives. Buddhism, rather than compete with Shinto kami and shrines, incorpo-rated them into the Buddhist worldview. Thus, most Shinto shrines and deities were given a place within the Buddhist system, which was dominant up until the Meiji Revolution.

9. We keep our bells in very high towers; they keep them down low, very close to the ground, within arm's reach.

The reason why Japanese bells are close to the ground is made apparent in the following contrast.

10. Our bells toll and have a clapper on the inside; the bells in Japan do not move and are struck on the outside with a pole that is drawn outward away from the bell and brought forward again to strike it.

Frois does not exaggerate. The largest bells (and they are genuine concave bells) are struck by logs measuring one foot thick by ten feet long that are swung by a group of men. Kipling, at the end of the nineteenth century, wrote of being awoken by what he thought was an earthquake in Kyoto and discovering it was a twenty-foot bronze bell hanging five feet from the ground on a nearby hillside.

---

17 Kohei Sugiura, *"Futo—" no geijutsu kōgaku* (Tokyo: Kōsakusha, 1999), 162–163.
18 Michael Cooper, *They Came to Japan* (Ann Arbor: University of Michigan Press, 1965), 340.

The bell at the Buddhist temple of Chion-in weighs more than seventy tons and is two meters in diameter and six meters tall.[19]

Shinto shrines and Buddhist temples with Shinto connections have yet another, quieter type of bell that visitors gong by swinging a rope with a knot, which functions like a clapper. These bells, which are usually hung about ten feet off the ground, are rung after making an offering or a wish, or just for the fun of it.

11. We celebrate with a continuous tolling of bells; Japanese bells never toll, because they do not have clappers.

Church bells were first used in Europe to summon worshippers and sound an alarm. Christians under Muslim rule in what was to become Portugal (in Gharb al-andalus) were not allowed to ring church bells.[20] As Frois suggests, following the reconquest (circa. 1249), Christians rang their church bells with gusto.

Even if Japanese bells could toll, they probably would not have been used for celebration, since continual loud noise meant a state of emergency. (The Japanese were shocked at a related European practice, the use of cannon or gunfire to salute a visiting dignitary.) In Japan, watchmen in towers hit smaller bells rapidly with a stick in the event of robbery or fire.

12. In our monasteries we have clocks made of iron; the Japanese have only water clocks.

In both cultures monks marked the passage of time, although Christian religious may have done so making finer temporal distinctions, using mechanical clocks.[21] During the fourteenth century gear-driven clocks with their own escarpment or power source (previously clocks were powered by the gravitational pull of water or sand) became widespread in Europe. Clocks and clock towers were coincident with the rise of towns and the beginnings of mercantilism, when men and women increasingly began working away from home in small factories and were paid an hourly rather than a day's wage. Clocks that marked each hour of the day also became common in monasteries, where religious life already centered on chanting prayers and psalms at appointed times of the day (i.e. the Divine Office).

In 1551 Francis Xavier introduced the mechanical clock to Japan, giving it as a gift to feudal lord Yoshitaka Ohuchi of Suo (the old name for the eastern part of what is now Yamaguchi Prefecture). It seems that in this contrast and the two that follow, Frois sought not only to emphasize the distinctive way the Japanese marked time, but to suggest ("the Japanese have only ...") that the Japanese system was somehow deficient or an impediment to the time-conscious life led by religious in Europe. And yet neither Frois nor other Europeans complained about the Japanese being late (excepting perhaps nobles who stayed up all night talking and partying). The water clock mentioned by Frois (*rôkoku* in Japanese) had been in use in

19 William E. Deal, *Handbook to Life in Medieval and Early Modern Japan* (Oxford: Oxford University Press, 2006), 213.

20 A. R. Disney, *A History of Portugal and the Portuguese Empire, From Beginnings to 1807 Volume I: Portugal* (Cambridge: Cambridge University Press, 2009), 63.

21 Giorgio Agamben, *The Highest Poverty, Monastic Rules and Forms-of-Life* (Stanford: Stanford University Press, 2013), 18–27.

China and Japan for over a thousand years before Frois arrived, and according to the *Nihon-shoki* (the "Chronicles of Japan"), Emperor Tenchi produced a water clock in 671. Sand clocks, similar to the European hourglass, also were becoming popular during Frois' time, and Rodrigues mentions *bonzes* using "very ingenious fire clocks" that burnt a dry scented powder that was laid out in furrows.[22] Rodrigues went on to suggest that these fire clocks were used effectively to "know the hour of prayer and when to ring or sound the bells in their temples."

13. Our day and night come to a total of twenty-four hours; the Japanese have but six hours of day and six of night.

During the Nara and Heian eras (710–1185) the Japanese actually followed a twenty-four hour system called *teijiho*, which was similar to what Europe was using when Frois wrote. Several centuries before the arrival of Europeans, Japan's ruling elite switched to a varying-length system (*futeijiho*), which better accommodated the common folk, who marked time using the sun or a sundial.

The Japanese system referenced here by Frois could arguably be said to denote the same twenty-four hours recognized by Europeans, since each set of six hours was actually subdivided into a total of twelve units. Each hour marked the midpoint of a time unit denoted by an animal in the Chinese zodiac. This meant that when the hour struck, one-half of the zodiac animal's time was over and one-half still remained. If we think of the 'before' and 'after' portions as distinct halves of the same hour (e.g. the pre-rat and the post-rat portions of the hour), the total number of hours comes out to a dozen for the day, and a dozen for the night.

In the older uniform hour system first promulgated by the Japanese Court, each of the twenty-four hours in a day (called *shinkoku*) was subdivided into four quarters, so one could speak of Rat one or Cow three and thus be specific to within thirty minutes. Thus, if the Japanese of Frois' time can be said to have had half as many hours as we do, at one point in time the Japanese had twice as many.

14. We count the hours from one, two, three, up to twelve; the Japanese count them in this manner: six, five, four, nine, eight, seven, six, etc.

This distich and the previous one clearly leave a lot unsaid with respect to how the Japanese kept time. They provide further evidence that the *Tratado* was intended as a teaching tool, a collection of statements that served as a point of departure (rather than a definitive statement) for understanding Japanese society and customs.

Frois might have explained that the Japanese made no use of the notions of one, two, or three o'clock because the first three strokes of the bell were for getting one's attention.

When using their fingers to count, the Japanese consistently fold their open fingers down. Counting down was a practice common to many cultures, including the Romans, who did it in a more confusing, partial manner. But why does Frois begin his count at six? The answer may be that dawn (the sixth hour) was considered the start of a new day.

---

22 Cooper, *They Came to Japan*, 230–231.

15. We adorn our churches with branches and strew them with rushes or flowers; the Japanese scoff at this, saying that we turn our churches into thickets or gardens.

There is a wonderful irony here, considering that Buddhist temples and Shinto shrines long occupied and thus protected old-growth forests, while Christians often toppled trees worshipped by pagans and viewed forests as the haunt of thieves (e.g. Robin Hood), ghosts, and evil spirits. While the Christian tradition of adorning churches with boughs, rushes, and flowers stemmed in part from Celtic and Germanic traditions that sacralized nature, perhaps more important was the Gospel of John (12:13), which relates how Jesus was met by a large crowd waving palm fronds while en route to Jerusalem for the Passover before his crucifixion.

With "windows" as tall as doors and as wide as walls the Japanese temple or house is open wide to nature.[23] Compare this with a Christian church, where the windows function not to reveal nature but to harness sunlight for the purpose of relating a narrative in stained glass.

16. Our candles are thick at the base and thin at the top; in Japan they are thick at the top and thin at the base.

Candles in Europe were made from tallow and less smelly and more expensive beeswax, using the dip-and-drip method, hence the thick base and taper. The Japanese relied on sebiferous trees (mostly the "wax tree" or sumac) for vegetable tallow, which was best shaped by hand. Japanese wax tends to drip less and runs just enough to look good hanging down from the upper edge, while not covering the surface of the candle, which often was decorated with an auspicious and artistic motif.

17. Ours have a wick made of string; theirs are made of the wood and heart of a reed.

Edward Morse, who visited Japan in the late nineteenth century, suggested that the wick used by the Japanese was made from the dried pith of a woody shrub or rush belonging to the *Junaceae* family (the rush plant is also used by the Japanese to make their *tatami*).[24] The reed not only burned slowly and consistently, but as the candle got low one could place the remaining inch or so on top of a new candle, meaning there was very little waste.

18. As we pray, we advance our rosary beads outward away from us; they always pray pulling successive beads toward themselves.

The Japanese pull their beads (*juzu*, literally "bead count"), which are arranged in a circle, down into the hand with the right thumb, one bead at a time, one for every syllable of the sutra. While the Japanese who use beads today still pull them down in this way, Catholics no longer consistently push theirs forward. Many unwittingly work their rosaries in the "Japanese" way. Perhaps the biggest

---

23 The Japanese are not completely averse to using greenery for adornment. They stand two cut pine boughs in artistically cut green bamboo vases in front of their houses on New Year's Eve (one red pine, one black pine, *yin* and *yang* respectively).

24 Edward S. Morse, *Japan Day By Day, 1877, 1878–1879, 1882–1883*. 2 Vols. (Boston: Houghton Mifflin, 1917).

difference is that whereas the Japanese move along at high speed (the beads of fast chanters make a gear-like noise as they rapidly hit together), Catholics move their beads rather slowly, one prayer at a time.

19. Our deceased depart with their hair as it is when they die; in Japan the deceased (both men and women) must go with their heads entirely shaved.

Buddhists identified hair with worldly desire. Shaving the head also was thought to help ensure a favorable rebirth, hence the custom of referring to a person's death as *jobutsu*, or "attaining Buddhahood." This was part of the appeal of Buddhism as a religious system that managed death and the afterlife.

During the Edo period (1603–1868) this custom of shaving the dying was relaxed somewhat, allowing the shaving to occur after, rather than before, death. Eventually, the practice of shaving the head of the deceased was minimized to only a portion of the head, or even simply going through the motions of shaving.

20. Our caskets are elongated; theirs are round, that is, in the form of a half-barrel.

The elongated casket remains the preferred packaging for Europe's dearly departed, although the quality of the casket still tends to vary by class. "Theirs" refers to the coffins of the commoners in some, and possibly most parts of Japan. Cornwallis, writing in 1857, described the Japanese casket as "a sort of tub" about three feet high, two and half feet in diameter at the top, and two feet at the bottom.[25] These caskets, which were once made of pottery, in the nineteenth century were made of wood. They were known as "quick-tubs" (*haya-oke*) because they could be constructed on the spot by a specialist in barrel making (there were no undertakers *per se*).

21. Our deceased are buried face up in a reclining position; theirs are seated and bound with their face between their knees.

Christians anticipate the resurrection of the dead, which some scripture (e.g. 1 Thessalonians 4:13–18) suggests will begin with a trumpet call and other great signs in heaven, hence the logic of being buried face up, preferably with the body oriented east-west with the deceased's head positioned so as to view the dawn of the "day of judgment." With respect to the Japanese, Frois wrote in 1565 that the hands of the deceased were pressed together like someone praying, with the head bent toward the ground. The hands were not always in this position, but the fetal position was standard in Japan. With the hair shaved off, we get an image of a baby in the womb of the earth. Practically speaking, the fetal position reduces the size of the casket and the labor involved in excavating and then backfilling a grave. This also made it easier to transport the deceased; Japanese art shows the casket dangling from a pole that is carried easily by two men.

22. We bury our dead; the Japanese generally cremate theirs.

Christians long have favored burial over cremation, partly because of a belief in the inseparable nature of body and soul (affirmed theologically in the

25 Kinahan Cornwallis, *Two Journeys to Japan., 1856–57* (Bristol, U.K.: Genesha Publishing Ltd., 2002[1856–57]).

fourth century CE), and partly because of the early and enduring importance of the cult of the saints and their relics, which emphasized preservation of the body (or body parts).[26]

The Japanese have an equally long tradition of burying their dead (the corpses of nobility often were left in mountain caves, a custom also practiced by Old Testament Jews). The Buddhist priest Dosho (628–700 CE) is said to have been the first person cremated in Japan. The practice subsequently spread with the embrace of Buddhism, particularly *Jodo-shinshu*, which held that prompt dissolution of the body facilitated transmigration and rebirth. Although the embrace of Confucianism by Japanese elites during the Edo Period (1603–1867) led to a prohibition on cremation among commoners, the practice quickly became the norm once the prohibition was lifted in the late nineteenth century.[27]

Today close to 95 percent of Japanese dead are cremated.[28] Most families, nevertheless, have "grave" sites, where a portion of the cremated remains may be interred. As noted earlier (see 1 above), what Frois never mentions is that there is a device common to most of the Far East but not found in the West by which the dead and the living may be consoled without going all the way to the cemetery: a fine wooden shrine, usually about the size of a bathroom medicine cabinet, with doors that swing open in front. Inside there is a place for a picture or, nowadays, photograph of the deceased, as well as shelves in front where one can burn incense and place offerings and flowers. It often holds a small urn with some of the aforementioned remains, generally including the *nodobotoke*, a bone called literally the "throat-Buddha," which we know as the Adam's apple. Often this warm custom ignorantly has been portrayed as "ancestor worship."

23. We keep our images and printed sayings within our chambers; the Japanese nail them up outside their doors, facing the street.

Homes in Europe and the United States still display religious images such as the Last Supper or placards bearing "God Bless this Home." Europeans also once placed gargoyles, crosses, and other Christian and pagan symbols on the outside of homes, churches, and castles to ward off evil spirits.

The Japanese, perhaps like most people, concentrated their efforts on keeping out the bad and bringing in the good. Thus, gates, doors, and doorframes were and are the most common places to post images and sayings. In 1690 Kaempfer observed many of these protective devices, which were printed on a half-sheet of paper:

> The most common is the black-horn'd [sic]Giwon ... the Ox-headed Prince of Heaven, whom they believe to have the power of keeping the family from distempers, and other unlucky accidents, particularly from the Sekbio, or Smallpox, which proves fatal to great numbers of their children. (Fig.99.). Others fancy they thrive extremly [sic] well, and live happy, under the protection of

26 Peter Brown, *The Cult of the Saints* (Chicago: University of Chicago Press, 1981).
27 Deal, *Handbook*, 359.
28 See Hikaru Suzuki, *Death and Dying in Contemporary Japan* (London: Routledge, 2013).

a countryman of Jeso, whose monstrous frightful picture they paste upon their doors, being hairy all over his body, and carrying a large sword with both hands, which they believe he makes use of to keep off, and as it were to parry all sorts of distempers and misfortunes, endeavoring to get into the house. On the fronts of the new and pretty houses, I have sometimes seen Dragons, or Devil's heads painted with a wide open mouth, large teeth and fiery eyes.[29]

24. Among us, following a funeral the relatives of the deceased withdraw into the privacy of their home; in Japan, they give a banquet for the bonzes and everyone else who attended the burial.

In Chapter 4 (#36) Frois makes it seem like the food at these funerals was all for the bonzes. That is not the case, as there were/are many guests other than the *bonze* (or *bonzes*). Today in Europe and America it is not at all uncommon to follow a funeral, particularly for someone who has lived a full life, with a "party" where relatives and friends of the deceased eat, drink, and are respectfully merry. Such funeral banquets have a long history dating back to the Middle Ages; they provide a symbolic way of reconstituting a community that had been fragmented by death.[30]

While the Japanese do not practice complete seclusion and find the laying in period and funeral a good time to see old friends and receive their condolences, there was and still is a type of limited seclusion called *mo*, or mourning. It is virtually universal for the bereaved to refrain from marrying and from exchanging the customary greeting cards or visits on the following New Year; they send out a special card ahead of time asking others not to send them greetings.

25. Among us, someone who turns away from the faith is considered a heretic[31] and an apostate; in Japan they change from one sect to another whenever they want, without any infamy.

Today one might suggest that the Japanese side of this distich bespeaks the greater religious tolerance of the Japanese as compared with European Christians. Here, as elsewhere (see Chapter 4, #13, #24), Frois chose to cast the Buddhist "search for truth" as unprincipled eclecticism.

26. Our baptism is rich in ceremonies and solemnities; in Japan it suffices to place a book on the head of the person in order for him to become a member of that sect.

Frois is seemingly referring to the public part of the first step to becoming a *bonze* (there is more going on in private that Frois ignores, including long hours of meditation and mastery of sutras). Rather than the novice simply putting a

29 Engelbert Kaempfer, *The History of Japan, Together With a Description of the Kingdom of Siam, 1690–92.* 3 Vols. (Glasgow: James MacLehose and Sons, 1906[1690–92]), II: 313.

30 Antoni Riera-Melis, "Society, Food, and Feudalism." In *Food, A Culinary History from Antiquity to the Present,* eds. Jean-Louis Flandrin and Massimo Montanari, pp. 251–268 (New York: Columbia University Press, 1999), 265.

31 *Elche.* Traditionally this Portuguese term referred to an individual who had converted from Christianity to Islam. Antônio Houaiss, Mauro de Salles Villar, and Francisco Manoel de Mello Franco *Dicionário Houaiss da língua portuguesa* (Rio de Janeiro: Objetiva, 2001), 107.

book on his head, the novice lifts a book containing the cherished sutras of the sect over and slightly in front of the head, as if offering something to a superior or receiving something from the same, thus showing reverence for the teachings of the sect.

27. We beseech one single God Almighty for the blessings of this life and the next; the Japanese beseech the kamis[32] for earthly blessings and the fotoques[33] for salvation only.

Frois ignores the fact that Catholics beseeched innumerable saints, particularly Mary, for favors in this life and the next. Technically, that is according to Catholic theology, the saints had no power other than access to God Almighty. Arguably, many Catholics lost sight of this fact when they established a special relationship with Mary, Saint Ann, Saint Sebastian, Saint Roque, etc.

In Japan, the native religion (Shinto) and the imported religion (Buddhism) managed to retain separate niches: gods for this life and gods for the next, respectively. When Buddhism first came to Japan, there was considerable friction, as rulers who favored different belief systems argued over the merits of each and their respective efficacy or responsibility for epidemics and other natural disasters. In the end, "live and let live" won out and there was some amalgamation and a division of interests (call it specialization). The introduction and spread of Christianity in Europe during the early Middle Ages also entailed accommodation with paganism (hence the Christmas tree),[34] although the Church as an institution never has been comfortable with this reality and on occasion (e.g. the witch hunts of the sixteenth and seventeenth centuries) has violently sought to "purge" itself of paganism.

Today in Japan, it is more common to hear people speak of "Shinto for birth and Buddhism for death" (or Shinto for happy occasions and Buddhism for sad ones). However, this division is dynamic rather than absolute. Thus, every year there is a political debate in Japan about the propriety of politicians visiting one of Japan's main Shinto shrines (the *Yasukuni-jinja*) to honor those who fought and died for their country.

This is the only distich in these two faith-related chapters that even mentions Shinto. It is not clear why the Jesuits paid so little attention to this somewhat regionally-specific folk religion (although there are prominent national Shinto shrines such as Ise). Perhaps it was because Shinto at the time had an informal priesthood (i.e. prominent families led rituals) and lacked a doctrinal system. Shinto's profound yet simple belief in powerful yet mysterious forces that manifest themselves in life (*kami*) gave rise to innumerable local shrines where people engaged the divine, purifying their souls and seeking renewal.[35]

---

32 *Kami* = Shinto god/s.
33 *Fotoque* or *hotoke* = Buddha/s.
34 See Valerie Flint, *The Rise of Magic in the Early Middle Ages*, (Princeton: Princeton University Press, 1991); Daniel T. Reff, *Plagues, Priests, and Demons* (Cambridge: Cambridge University Press, 2005).
35 Ichiro Hori, *Folk Religion in Japan, Continuity and Change* (Chicago: University of Chicago Press, 1968); For contemporary Shinto see Nakamachi, *Japanese Religions At Home and Abroad*, 55–75.

28. Our images are painted on wood; theirs are painted on paper scrolls.

As noted earlier, in 1585 most European religious art or painting still was being done on wood panels (*retablos*) rather than on canvas. Wonderful examples of this religious art from Frois' lifetime are on display in Lisbon's National Museum of Antique Art (Museu Nacional de Arte Antiga), including Nuno Gonçalves' "Adoration of Saint Vincent," six-panels of oak done in oil or tempera celebrating Saint Vincent of Saragossa, who is Lisbon's patron saint.

Although painting on paper might not seem very permanent, Japanese pictures were commonly rolled up and stored when not hung up for viewing, which minimized their exposure to the elements. The scrolls usually have a cloth backing and margins, and wooden ends, which not only help hold the scroll open but improved the image in the same way that a frame improves an oil painting.

29. Among us, a good retablo done in oils is at times worth quite a lot; in Japan, oil paints are not used, but a figure done in black ink can be worth many thousands of cruzados.

One can find wonderful black and white sketches in European art (e.g. Michelangelo's notebooks or Rembrandt's Portrait of Saskia), although these generally were not considered finished works of art, but rather studies in preparation for a painting in oils, hence Frois' unstated wonder at the fact that Japanese ink drawings were worth so much. Had the Japanese drawings conveyed a Christian theme, Frois presumably would have acknowledged their aesthetic beauty. Some seven years after the *Tratado* was written, Frois noted in a later volume of his *Historia* that Japanese students being trained by the Jesuits were reproducing paintings from Rome so perfectly that it was impossible to tell the original from the copy. "So, with God's help," Frois concludes, "Japan won't lack men who can keep all her churches full of fine images and satisfy the [aesthetic needs of the] gentry."

30. Our prelates travel on mules; Japanese prelates travel in sedan chairs.

Frois' word choice here (*amdão em mulas*) evokes an image of a parish priest astride a mule. While perhaps accurate, some Catholic prelates such as bishops often travelled in litters—picture a comfortable closet of sorts suspended from poles that was carried by humans or mules.[36]

In Japan, Xavier made a point of walking so as not to be perceived as being yet another Buddhist high priest, who, like other well-off Japanese, were carried in sedan chairs. These chairs hung from two poles and were generally carried by two men.

---

36 Marcelin Defourneaux, *Daily Life in Spain in the Golden Age* (Stanford: Stanford University Press, 1979), 15.

6   The Japanese way of eating and drinking

1. We eat everything with our hands; the Japanese—both men and women, from the time they are children—eat with two sticks.[1]

Europeans at the time ate mostly with their hands; a knife might be used to cut meat and spoons were used to eat gruel, soups, stews, and pudding. It was customary to wash your hands before and after eating, and books of manners advised against petting the dog or cat during dinner. During the sixteenth century napkins started showing up on European tables and the table cloth became more decorative than functional, meaning you no longer used it to wipe your hands. It was the wealthy and aristocrats who were likely to own silver forks and spoons, although they too mostly used their hands.

The Jesuits and most other Europeans were dumbfounded by the skill with which the Japanese ate with chopsticks. To quote Valignano: "... there are no tablecloths, napkins, knives, forks or spoons. All they have are two small sticks, called *hashi*, which they manipulate with such cleanliness and skill that they do not touch any of the food with their hands nor let even a crumb fall from their plate on to the table."[2]

2. The staple of our diet is bread made from wheat; the Japanese ordinarily eat rice cooked with no salt.

Bread was indeed a staple for many Europeans,[3] although it was not always an inexpensive food item. The price of wheat-flour often skyrocketed in early modern Europe, in part as a function of poor harvests and steady growth in Europe's population.[4] When Frois was a child in Portugal, the grain harvest fell below expectations one year in three[5]; after 1530 the demand for wheat increasingly outstripped supply.[6]

Perhaps the most fundamental principle underlying Chinese and Japanese cuisine is the *fan-cai* principle, which dictates that a good meal should include a proper balance of carbohydrates (i.e. rice, bread, or noodles) and protein and

---

1 *Paus*, a *very* broad term including sticks, twigs, poles, pieces of wood, and even lumber.

2 Michael Cooper, *They Came to Japan* (Ann Arbor: University of Michigan, 1995[1965]), 193.

3 In some parts of Europe bread made up between 70–80 percent of the diet of peasants and townspeople. Laurence Brockliss and Crolin Jones, *The Medical World of Early Modern France* (Oxford: Clarendon Press, 1997), 58.

4 After the Black Death, many parts of Europe experienced steady population growth that continued for several centuries.

5 Eric Jones, *The European Miracle*. Third Edition (Cambridge: Cambridge University Press, 2003), 78.

6 A.R. Disney, *A History of Portugal and the Portuguese Empire, From Beginnings to 1807 Volume I: Portugal* (Cambridge: Cambridge University Press, 2009), 146.

fiber (meat/fish and vegetables).[7] As Frois suggests, rice satisfied the *fan* half of the principle. In Japan during the 1970s one frequently encountered a different distich: "We Japanese eat rice, you Westerners eat meat."[8] This was also true in the sixteenth century, as Europeans, apparently of all classes, ate a good deal of meat,[9] and the Portuguese perhaps more so, owing to their extensive game preserves and uncultivated lands.[10] Eggs, butter and cheese also were an important source of protein for Europeans, and thus the olfactory adjective that the Japanese used with reference to Europeans was "butter-stinking" (*bata-kusai*).[11]

3. Our tables are already set before the meal is brought out; their tables are brought out from the kitchen along with the meal.

In the fifth century the Merovingian king, Meroavaeus, ushered in a new custom for Europe's elite; where previously Romans reclined, Europeans now sat upright in a chair or on a bench at a table, or what was actually a board laid across two trestles.[12] In Frois' Portugal and most of Europe it was common for guests to pair-up around the table and eat with their hands from the same bowl or dish, thus the Portuguese idiom signifying that two people are good friends: "*comer com alguém no prato*" ([they] eat from the same plate).[13] It is still common practice in parts of Portugal and Spain for friends and family to literally share one large salad, with everyone diving in from wherever they are sitting, albeit with forks rather than their hands.

The lacquered tables used by the Japanese were small—"Tea-trays, with legs like dachshunds"[14]—and were brought from the kitchen by the woman of the

7 Joanna Waley-Cohen, "The Quest for Perfect Balance, Taste and Gastronomy in Imperial China." In *Food: The History of Taste*, ed. Paul Freedman, pp. 99–132. (Berkeley: University of California Press, 2007), 108–109.

8 The title of Chikuba Joji's book was all too typical of the times: "Rice-eating Civilization, Meat-eating Civilization" (*Beisshoku, Nikushoku-No Bunmei*). An earlier best-seller, and far more original book by Sabata Toyoyuki, titled "Carnivore Thoughts" (*Niku-Shoku-No Shiso*), also set pastoral meat culture against rice paddy culture, and bread against rice. See also Emiko Ohnuki-Tierney, "McDonald's in Japan," In *Golden Arches East, McDonald's in East Asia*, ed. James L. Watson, pp. 161–183 (Stanford: Stanford University Press, 1997), 167.

9 Fernand Braudel, *Capitalism and Material Life 1400–1800* (New York: Harper Colophon, 1973[1967]), 128. See also Ken Albala, *Food in Early Modern Europe*; Barbara Ketcham Wheaton, *Savoring the Past* The French Kitchen and Table from 1300 to 1789 (Philadelphia: University of Pennsylvania Press, 1983); and Joan Thirsk, *Food in Early Modern England* (New York: Hambledon Continuum, 2007).

10 António Henrique de Oliveira Marques, *Daily Life in Portugal in the Late Middle Ages* (Madison: University of Wisconsin Press, 1971), 17.

11 Ironically, during the 1970s it was not uncommon to see Japanese men eating butter in bars. Thick slices of butter, with two or three raisins embedded in each, were eaten with tooth-picks as an appetizer, or *pupu* (the Hawaiian term for such).

12 Suzanne Von Drachenfels, *The Art of the Table* (New York: Simon & Schuster, 2000), 331. According to Sarti, as late as the eighteenth century it was not uncommon for poor households in Europe to lack chairs and even a table. Raffaella Sarti, "The Material Conditions of Family Life," In *The History of the European Family, Volume I, Family Life in Early Modern Times, 1500–1789*, eds. David I. Kertzer and Marzio Barbagli, pp. 11–23 (New Haven: Yale University Press, 2001), 6, 10; Marques, *Daily Life in Portugal*, 130.

13 Marques, *Daily Life in Portugal*, 30.

14 Douglas Sladen and and Norma Lorimer, *More Queer Things About Japan* (London: Anthony Treherne & Company, 1905), 375.

house as easily as a waitresses carries trays of food. Writing around 1880, Isabella Bird observed that each person was served from four to twelve dishes or bowls of edibles.[15] In Japan, today, this manner of eating is only true for some traditional-style restaurants. At home, most people eat around a Western-style table. In Korea, however, food is still often served in the manner described by Bird.

4. Our tables are high and have tablecloths and napkins; Japanese tables are lacquered panels of wood, rectangular in shape, low, with no tablecloths or napkins.

Wealthy Europeans actually sat at tables with what amounted to several table-cloths. The bottom-most cloth hung down like a swag and was used as a commu-nal napkin. On top of this cloth were one or more "over cloths," which were sequentially removed before each new dinner course. As noted, during Frois' life-time napkins became somewhat popular, again particularly among the wealthy. Arguably, most Europeans lacked the resources to buy tablecloths and napkins and continued a medieval tradition of wiping their mouths with their clothing, the back of the hand, or a piece of bread.[16]

Japanese tables were generally four to eight inches from the floor or *tatami*. Japanese reliance on chopsticks and consumption of bite-sized edibles made napkins unnecessary. Actually, the Japanese found napkins disgusting, apparently because the Jesuits re-used them or washed them irregularly.

5. When we eat, we sit on chairs so that we can extend our legs; they sit on the tatami or on the floor, with their legs crossed.

In sixteenth-century Japan men began meals in the *sei-za* or "proper-seat" posi-tion (knees on the floor and sitting back on the heels), but rarely ate entire meals that way. They switched to the informal cross-legged style described by Frois. Both then and now, women almost never sit cross-legged; they sit more or less formally all the time.

6. Their dishes are served either all together or on three tables; our dishes are served with one course following another.

Note that this is a rare instance in the *Tratado* where Frois reversed the order of the distich, presenting the Japanese custom first (perhaps Frois had grown fond of this particular Japanese custom). Elites in Portugal were accustomed to eating twice a day: "dinner" around mid-day and a light "supper" in the evening. Dinner was the main meal of the day and usually came in three sepa-rate courses, which might include items such as sausage, boiled and fricasseed chicken, and roasted meat or poultry (lesser nobility or peasants might have two or one main course, respectively).[17] A clerical sumptuary edict from England in 1541 indicated that archbishops might have up to six kinds of meat at a meal, bishops no more than five, deans and archdeacons four, and all other clergy no more than three.[18]

15 Isabella L. Bird, *Unbeaten Tracks in Japan* (Boston: Beacon Press, 1987[1880]).
16 Von Drachenfels, *Art of the Table*, 331–355.
17 Marques, *Daily Life in Portugal*, 16–17.
18 Keith Thomas, *The Ends of Life* (Oxford: Oxford University Press, 2009), 115.

Frois' fellow Jesuit, Rodrigues, noted that the Japanese had five different types of formal banquets, including a "banquet of three tables," where each guest was provided with many different items rather than merely one item constituting a course. In Frois' time, people eating formally in Japan always began with a few morsels of rice followed by a sip of soup (*shiru*), repeated thrice over. Details of formal three-, five-, and seven-table banquets were provided by Rodrigues. For example:

> in the banquettes of three tables ... there are twenty dishes and they include four *shiru* ... with five tables they serve twenty-six dishes, among which are included six *shiru* ... with six tables or trays, there are thirty-two dishes, among which are included eight *shiru*, that is five of fish, one of shell fish and two of meat; one of these is crane . . .[19]

During the 1980s in Japan, tables full of dishes became a popular type of television quiz show—not one show mind you, but a *genre* found on channel after channel, day and night. A personality would be shown eating, and game-show participants would be asked either to guess the next dish he or she (usually a very pretty she) would reach for, or, harder yet, give the order of the first five or so items.

European banquets of the sixteenth century were equally elaborate, structured events, although as Frois suggests, the presentation of food came more in courses than all at once. A banquet held in 1529 for the Duke of Ferrara featured at least seven courses; the 104 guests dined on everything from antipasto to suckling pig, served on 2,835 plates.[20] The first course at the wedding feast for Portugal's Prince Afonso and Princess Isabel of Spain, in 1490, began when:

> . . . there came to the head of the table a large golden cart which seemed to be pulled by two huge roasted whole steers, with gilded horns and hooves; the cart was completely filled with a large number of roasted whole sheep with gilded horns; the whole thing was on such a low contraption, with little wheels underneath where they could not be seen, that the steers appeared to be alive and walking."[21]

7. We can eat just fine without soup; the Japanese can not eat without soup.[22]

European peasants certainly ate their fair share of pottages and soups, but as Frois suggests, soup was not central to Mediterranean cuisine. The Japanese

---

19 João Rodrigues, *This Island of Japon*, trans. and ed. Michael Cooper (Tokyo: Kodansha International Limited, 1973[ca. 1620]), 236–241.

20 Ken Albala, *Food in Early Modern Europe* (Westport, CT: Greenwood Press, 2003), 124–125; see also Maestro Martino of Como, *The Art of Cooking*, ed. Luigi Ballerina, trans. Jeremy Parzen (Berkeley: University of California Press, 2005).

21 Marques, *Daily Life in Portugal*, 33.

22 *Shiru* is a term which *can* mean "soup" but also means "juice," "stock" (as in "chicken stock"), or "sap." Here it is soup, not as we understand it in the West, but rather more like broth.

believe that slurping soup at intervals during a meal rather than as a separate course helps other food go down, so to speak. While fancy restaurants still serve fish and fowl in *shiru*, as described by Rodrigues above, today this soup is almost always either a cloudy fermented bean-curd soup or one of a number of clear *suimono*—literally "sucking-thing" soups. The ingredients of both are almost entirely vegetable, but tiny shellfish (*asari* or *shijimi*) in the shell are often added to improve the flavor of the former, which is called *miso-shiru* (well known to health-food devotees in the West). In Japan it receives as much good press as wine in France. Hardly a week goes by without the publication of a new study showing some new medical benefits (never the opposite; see #57, below) of *miso*.[23]

8. *Our table service is made of silver or pewter*[24]; *in Japan the table service is made of wood lacquered red or black.*

Europeans used pottery and wooden cups and bowls to consume liquids like soup or ale. Large slices of bread, called trenchers or *manchets*, commonly were used as "plates." The bread absorbed juice from meat or fish and was consumed at the end of the meal or given to the dog or to the poor, as alms. By Frois' time, Europeans also were using round wooden or pewter plates under or instead of *manchets*. The sixteenth century also witnessed mass production of earthenware and more expensive porcelain, which was durable and non-porous. Wealthier Europeans or religious such as the Jesuits were likely to have table service of pewter; the truly privileged had silver or even gold.

Lacquered wood has a hard and durable finish that results from the application of a varnish of tree resin to which iron oxide and other pigments have been added (thus the often-seen red and/or black). Unlike many ceramics, lacquered wood is light as well as non-porous. It also has advantages over pewter or silver in that it conducts little heat. Today in Japan most ostensibly wood-lacquered bowls and spoons (rarely plates) are made of plastic.

9. *We use earthenware pots and porringers*[25] *to prepare and cook food; the Japanese use pots and pans made of cast iron.*

Clay pots and porringers were no doubt used by Frois' mother and grandmother to prepare *caldeirada* (fish stew like *bouillabaisse*) or various bean-and-pork dishes (cozidos) that are the ancestors of Brazilian *feijoada* ("re-introduced" to Portugal and found today on restaurant menus throughout Portugal).

This contrast and the one that follows suggest that the gentry in Japan relied heavily on cast iron cookware. Japan nevertheless has a long history of fine cooking utensils made of clay as well as iron. Long before Frois wrote, the cracked

---

23 Today, most Japanese *do not* ferment their bean curd from scratch, but they still select and mix it with other ingredients to make their *miso-shiru*. Because each mother's *miso-shiru* is different and the only other thing besides rice to appear at every meal, the flavor of that *miso* becomes an important part of the taste identity of every Japanese.

24 *Prata ou estanho*. The Japanese have translated *estanho* as "tin," which is denotatively correct, but in English the connotation would be one of "cheapness." Frois does not appear to have had this meaning in mind. Pewter is an alloy of over 90 percent tin with a little copper or antimony.

25 A porringer is a pot/bowl with a handle.

stew pot was a popular trope for a widow or woman whose virginity was a distant memory. Today it is common in Japan to see stews slowly cooking in earthenware rather than metal pots.

10. The tripod that we use [for cooking] is positioned with the legs pointing down; the Japanese place theirs with the legs pointing up.

During the sixteenth century many Japanese homes had an *irori*, a square, sunken hearth that functioned much like braziers in Iberia and the fireplace set in the wall, which was becoming common elsewhere in Europe.[26] The *irori* provided warmth and heat for cooking using cast-iron pots that were suspended over the coals using a tripod that looks something like a wrought iron stool, minus the seat, turned upside down.

11. Men in Europe ordinarily eat with their women; in Japan this is very rare because their tables are also separated.

One of the things that made Jesus so radical was his commensality, particularly his acceptance of women at the dinner table.[27] Although the Romans encouraged women to eat with men, it was hardly as equals (women serving or entertaining enhanced the meal). By the sixteenth century probably *most* European men and their wives ate together, although in parts of Iberia, Germany, and France it was common for the men to eat separately (served by women or servants), while the women ate in the kitchen or standing up.[28]

In Japan, as in Europe, the two genders were not considered equal and women joined men at the table mostly in a serving capacity. This was particularly true for the gentry (as per Chapter 2, #53). Among the common folk or peasantry, husbands and wives often ate together.

As the twentieth century began, this matter of men and women eating together became part of Japan's national agenda to Westernize and thus gain the respect of the world powers. Yet even today, husband and wife still eat and socialize together far less than they do in the West. The reason, however, has perhaps less to do with traditional segregation of male and female. Japanese working and commuting hours are usually so long that people eat and socialize with their colleagues. The married man who perseveres until he gets home to eat with his wife, might well eat dinner at midnight! (This is especially the case with small companies, where male employees work more hours than is reflected in official statistics.)

12. People in Europe enjoy eating fish that has been baked or boiled; the Japanese enjoy it much more when it is raw.

Going without meat was a big part of life in Christian Europe. In Frois' Portugal there were around sixty-eight days a year when Christians were forbidden to eat meat.[29] In Provence, the number was closer to 150.[30] Marques notes that seafood

26 Sarti, "The Material Conditions of Family Life," 11.
27 John Dominick Crossan, *Jesus: A Revolutionary Biography* (San Francisco: Harper Collins, 1994), 179–181.
28 Sarti, "The Material Conditions of Family Life," 14.
29 Marques, *Daily Life in Portugal*, 21.
30 Louis Stouff, *La Table Provençale: Boire et manger en Provence à la fin du Moyen Âge* (Avignon: A. Barthelemy, 1996), 205.

such as whiting, eels, mullet, sardines, flounder, mussels, and crabs were a regular part of the Portuguese diet.[31]

The "raw" fish preferred by the Japanese was not as raw as one might imagine. In Frois' time the Japanese dipped the fish in boiling vinegar or fermented it in a mustard sauce (*karashi*). Interestingly, few Japanese today seem to realize that pickled or fermented, i.e. semi-raw fish, was once the norm. The diverse and extremely appealing *sushi* that the West recently has come to know and love was one of many gastronomical developments of the Edo era (1615–1868). The advent of refrigeration expanded the possibilities for *sushi* yet further and have made it a world-class food. Vinegary *o-sumono* still survives in the sushi shop repertoire and is not all that different from the pickled herring that the Dutch made a huge industry during the fourteenth century. Still, for many Jesuits in Japan—many of whom were from Iberia—having to eat "raw" fish was a "continual torment."

13. Among us, all fruits are eaten when they are ripe, except for cucumbers, which are eaten green; the Japanese eat all their fruit when it is green, except for cucumbers, which are eaten very yellow and ripe.

Fresh as well as dried and preserved fruit (e.g. biter orange, cherries, peaches, figs) were very popular in Mediterranean Europe, including Portugal. According to Marques, the Portuguese seem to have particularly enjoyed pairing fruit and wine, often in the evening as a light meal.[32]

The Japanese pickled most fruit, with the apparent exception of the cucumber. The Portuguese must not have exercised one iota of influence on Japanese taste in fruit, for the first British ambassador after the "opening" of Japan (1854), Sir Rutherford Alcock wrote:

> Every tea-garden in the vicinity of Yeddo [Edo] tries to rival its neighbour in the beauty and size of the peach blossoms,—but it is very difficult to get good peaches to eat. They are all habitually plucked unripe. It does not seem to me that the Japanese have any idea what ripe fruit means. They certainly never treat themselves to it, and after two years' practice, my market coolie could never be made to understand what constituted ripeness.[33]

Today in Japan one finds ripe nectarines as well as peaches, but no green fruit, with the exception of the large green "plums" that go into *ume-shu*, or "plum liquor." There are also smaller but apparently similar "plums" that are pickled in vinegar and dyed bright red, sold under the name *su-momo*, or "vinegar peach."

31 Marques, *Daily Life in Portugal*, 21.
32 *Daily Life in Portugal*, 25.
33 Sir Rutherford Alcock, *The Capital of the Tycoon, A Narrative of a Three Years' Residence in Japan.* 2 Vols. (London: Longman, Green, and Roberts, 1969[1863]), I, 322. Note that of all Japanese fruits, Alcock found only watermelons, persimmons, and grapes passable. Both he and Frois failed to note that persimmons often are left on the tree until they shriveled up like enormous raisins, turning white with exuded sugar. One cannot get riper than that. (These ripe persimmons are strung on straw cords.)

14. We cut melons lengthwise; the Japanese cut them crosswise.

It makes sense to cut a melon crosswise, particularly if it has not been turned and thus tastes differently on the top and bottom. A lengthwise cut would be best for long melons with a flavor that varies from stem to butt, so to speak.

During the last half of the twentieth century most Japanese gave little thought to which way to slice a melon, as melons of all types were generally very expensive. Despite the high price, they were almost never sold piecemeal at the grocer's. Fruit was mainly sold to be presented as a gift: one melon or a few apples when visiting a house; a watermelon beautifully bound for carrying up a mountain to a Buddhist temple; a platter including pineapple and citrus as well as melon for a funeral display or a wake. Only well-to-do families regularly ate fruit, the exception being tangerines when they were in season.

15. We sniff melons at the stem; they sniff them at the bottom.

The Japanese leave a portion of the stem on their melons (much as Americans do with their pumpkins), which hides the navel and thus makes it unrewarding to sniff the top of the melon. The stem is typically in the form of a "T" and it is profoundly satisfying to the Japanese because that "T" is found upside down in the Chinese character for "melon."

16. We eat the melon first and then throw away the rind; they pare off the rind and throw it away before eating the melon.

Europeans viewed the plant and animal kingdoms in terms of a "great chain of being," which implied that various foods had qualities (e.g. hot versus cold, coarse versus refined) and particular social value.[34] Melon was considered a "cold" fruit that should be eaten at the beginning of a meal.[35] As Frois notes, the savory flesh was eaten while still on the rind.

Although the Japanese tend to completely prepare their food before eating, watermelon is an exception: slices are eaten with rind in hand, as Americans usually eat it. Smaller melons, persimmons and pears are first peeled and then cut into bite-size pieces, which are picked up with either chopsticks or a large bamboo toothpick.

17. We harvest unripe grapes for flavoring our food; the Japanese harvest them to be pickled with salt.

Europeans once used the juice from unripe apples and grapes for a condiment called verjuice, evidently very sour, for a sour-puss was called verjuiced. Where today we use wine or vinegar for salad dressing, deglazing, and sauces, Europeans of the Middle Ages and early modern period often used verjuice.

Pickled grapes are not common today in Japan, although we have no doubt that Frois tells the truth, for there is little that the Japanese have not pickled at one time

---

34 Allen J. Grieco, "Food and Social Classes in Late Medieval and Renaissance Italy." In *Food, A Culinary History from Antiquity to the Present*, eds. Jean-Louis Flandrin and Massimo Montanari, pp. 302–313 (New York: Columbia University Press, 1999).

35 Jean-Louis Flandrin, "Dietary Choices and Culinary Technique, 1500–1800." In *Food, A Culinary History from Antiquity to the Present*, Flandrin, Jean-Louis, and Massimo Montanari, eds., pp. 403–418. New York: Columbia University Press, 1999), 321.

or another. The pickling tends to be heavy on salt, for vinegar is only used for a few items; also, chili, sugar, and other spices are not used as much as they are in most of Southeast Asia. Today, green grapes—not unripe, but genuinely green— are eaten in Japan and are used to make a fine muscat wine.

18. All our dishes are served covered, except for bread; it is the opposite in Japan, with only the rice being covered.

It perhaps goes without saying that a covered dish keeps food hotter, for longer, particularly when you are passing dishes around a table in the informal "French style."[36] Bread that is covered and not allowed to breathe becomes chewy and difficult to eat, particularly for those with poor teeth (common in Frois' Europe); better to allow it to go nearly stale and use it as a *manchet*.

The Japanese were (and are) as particular about their rice as Europeans were (and are) about their bread. Rice is usually served in a covered pot so it is piping hot. (In a good restaurant today soup is also carried out covered; this apparently is a later development.)

19. As fond as Europeans are of sweets; the Japanese are equally fond of salty foods.

The cultivation of sugar in America, particularly Brazil, during the sixteenth century made it possible for more and more Europeans to enjoy "dessert"—finishing a meal with tiramisu, cakes, pies, and other sweet things. Previously, Europeans had to be content with food flavored with sugar or served with sauces made from raisins, grapes, figs, almonds, and prunes.[37] Okada explains the Japanese love of things salty as a result of an abundance of salt in Japan, while sugar was an expensive import.[38] Perhaps it is true that sugar was harder to come by in Japan relative to Europe, but the paucity of interest in most ripe fruit makes one wonder whether some other factor may be involved. The European craving for sweets might be related to the consumption of bread or pasta, both of which have a sugar content that is low relative to the rice eaten in Japan (unlike the *indica* variety of rice common in the West, which is short-grained and glutinous). Moreover, Japanese sake is very sweet. Isabella Bird's translator, Ito, told her that all who abstain from sake crave sugar.

Even today, the Japanese claim to be astounded by the sweetness of Western pastries, and yet their own traditional cakes that are served with tea astound us equally, for they seem to be of solid sugar! Then there is Japanese bean jam, *an*, which is mentioned in Rodrigues' 1620 dictionary and tastes very sweet. Moreover, almost all fruit in Japan seems to be advertised as "sweet" (*amai*)—a curious

---

36 Von Drachenfels, *The Art of the Table*, 374–375.

37 Brian Cowan, "New Worlds, New Tastes, Food Fashions after the Renaissance." In *Food, The History of Taste*, ed. Paul Freedman, pp. 197–232 (Berkeley: University of California Press, 2007), 220. Marques, *Daily Life in Portugal*, 24–25, points out that the Portuguese in the late Middle Ages had numerous milk delicacies that were eaten as dessert.

38 The scarcity of sugar in Japan is suggested by the fact that it was considered medicine and handled by medicine wholesalers. Ochiai Kô, "The Shift to Domestic Sugar and the Ideology of the National Interest." In *Economic Thought In Early Modern Japan*, eds. Bettina Gramlich Oka and Gregory Smits, pp. 89–111 (Leiden: Brill, 2010), 90.

thing for people who supposedly do not care for sweet things. We who love some tartness in our fruit find it hard to get a merchant to tell us the truth, for merely requesting such fruit ("tart" and "sour" are a single word and never fail to draw a grimace in Japan) is to suggest he might have inferior merchandize. That the use of "sweet" as synonymous with "good" and "tasty" in Japan—contrary to Frois' assertion—is no modern development is proven by Issa's haiku portraying peasant children innocently learning a lie as their very first word from their siblings who are selling bad persimmons, crying out "Sweet! Sweet!"[39]

Still, to be fair to Frois, it is possible that during his time in Japan the new trade with Europe and the increased trade with China marked the beginning of significant changes in Japanese taste. He certainly was correct about the Japanese love for things salty, owing perhaps to the Japanese disinterest in other strong spices. Salt, in the guise of soy sauce, miso, and pickles, made sense for a hardworking people who sweated a lot and ate little meat.

20. Among us, servants clear the table; in Japan, the very same nobles who eat often clear their own tables.

This is not a general contrast but appears to apply to etiquette in a tea hut, a place where a male host did the preparation and serving and then cleared the tables. One reason why noblemen took such an interest in what Europeans thought of as "chores" was that doing these things is the art of the tea ceremony.[40] At the same time, the *dogu*, or tea ware, which are the supporting props, were fragile and often the host's most valuable possession—the equivalent of a vintage automobile that a corporate executive in the West might sully his hands on and then proudly offer rides in to friends and family.

21. We wash our hands at the beginning and at the end of each meal; because the Japanese do not touch their food with their hands, they have no need to wash them.

It is reassuring to read that "our" ancestors regularly washed their hands before and after eating. But then one reads Erasmus' account of a German inn that he visited where he was horrified to find people washing their hands in a filthy bowl of water.[41] The experience apparently contributed to Erasmus' *De civilitate morum puerilum* (1530), a work that sought to remake all of European society through new standards of cleanliness and "appropriate" behavior (e.g., "it is boorish to plunge your hands into sauced dishes."[42]).

With respect to the Japanese, Frois might have noted the exception of the tea ceremony, which dictated that guests wash their hands before holding and

39 As an aside, the Japanese do not call things or even people "sweet" in the complimentary sense (e.g. "sweetie-pie," "honey," "sugar buns") as we do in English (or in Chinese, for that matter). It is only used to mean "slut" (*ama'kko*) or as a predicate complement meaning "soft," "shallow" or "a sucker." Perhaps this lack of a sweet vocabulary proves Frois' point.

40 See Dennis Hirota, *Wind in the Pines* (Freemont, California: Asian Humanities Press, 1995).

41 Edward Muir, *Ritual in Early Modern Europe* (Cambridge: Cambridge University Press, 2000[1997]), 128.

42 Cowan, "New Worlds, New Tastes," 203.

admiring the host's priceless tea service (much as one washes their hands out of respect when entering some Shinto shrines).

22. We eat our thin noodles hot and cut up; they put theirs in cold water and eat them in very long pieces.

Once cooked, the Japanese immediately submerge their noodles in cold water to preserve their "hips" or what the Italians refer to as their bite (*al dente*). Long before instant ramen, Japanese noodles were quicker cooking than most pasta. Some, such as *somen*, were and are as thin as a hair. Although all Japanese noodles may be eaten cold, Frois may have had in mind *soba*, or buckwheat noodles, and possibly even *udon*, which are made from wheat and are generally slightly thicker and square-edged. Today *somen* is almost always eaten cold, *soba* about half the time, and *udon* rarely. (The Koreans have far more varieties of cold noodles, perhaps because they are heated sufficiently by chili peppers.)

23. We eat thin noodles with sugar, eggs, and cinnamon; they eat them with mustard and pepper.

Most Westerners forget or are unaware that tomatoes originated in the New World. In 1585, pasta with tomato sauce was unknown or a recent innovation (note that the tomato, potato, and maize all took time to gain wide acceptance in Europe). As Frois suggests, it was far more common for Mediterranean Europeans to serve pasta with raisins and spices such as cinnamon (reflecting Arab influence) and to eat it dry (meaning no sauce) with the fingers!

The Japanese often include some sweet sake and, less frequently, mandarin orange slices, in their sauce for *somen*. Thus, Frois' contrast seems a bit stark, unless, as suggested above, the Japanese developed something of a sweet tooth after Frois' time. Today, as in the past, the Japanese use a very potent sort of horse-radish (*karashi*) to flavor some noodle dishes. Presumably this is what Frois meant by mustard (*mostarda*).

24. Europeans enjoy chicken, partridge, pastries and blancmange*; the Japanese enjoy feral dog[43], crane, monkey, cat, and raw seaweed.[44]*

The last European item, *blancmange*[45] might be unfamiliar. Roberto de Nola's famous 1529 cookbook, *Libro de guisados, manjares, y potajes*, referred to *blanc-mange* as "the king of dishes." While recipes varied, it generally was created by boiling fatty chicken meat along with rice flour, rose-water, sugar, goat's milk, or white almond and saffron until the chicken looked like melted white cheese. The dish was topped off with a sprinkle of fine sugar.

Let us take the "strange" *potpourri* of Japanese items one at a time:

Feral dog was eaten in a dish that today is called *sutamina* (food for increasing one's stamina) by men doing fighting or heavy labor outdoors, and by people

---

43 *Adibe*, which can mean wolf or jackal and probably referred to feral dog in Japan. Antônio Houaiss, Mauro de Salles Villar, and Francisco Manoel de Mello Franco, eds., *Dicionário Houaiss da língua portuguesa* (Rio de Janiero: Objetiva, 2001).

44 *Llimos da praya.*

45 *Manjar branco*, a cold dessert similar to pudding, is today made with milk, sugar, flavorings and cornstarch.

of either sex suffering from *natsu-yase*, or "summer thinning." The Chinese character for "thin" includes the "sickness" radical, for wasting away was a real disease in Japan for both men and women. Today, Japanese of both sexes—but mostly men—eat liver and leek or fatty eel on rice for their *sutamina*, but no wolf (see #41 below).

As Frois knew, having eaten with the rulers of Japan, crane was a favorite banquet food of the nobility, in part because the bird was a symbol of longevity. Frois apparently never ate with Europe's rulers or he might have known that they also served crane, not to mention stork, plover, peacock and a few other exotic birds (the Judeo-Christian "great chain of being" cast birds, particularly high-flying birds, as appropriate for European elites).

Monkey is dubious, although one can imagine the Japanese not wanting to waste the meat of monkeys that were killed for damaging crops.

Okada quotes Japanese literature confirming all of the foods mentioned by Frois except cat. He believes Frois mistook *tanuki* ("raccoon dog," *Nyctereutus procyonides vivverinus*), weasel, or something else for cat. However, considering the fact that cat skin was used for making *shamisen* banjos (see Chapter 13) it is not unlikely that some part of the cat was eaten. The irony here is that if cat was eaten anywhere, it was in Europe.[46] Again, de Nola's cookbook includes a recipe for roasted cat that purportedly tasted like rabbit or veal, although the author advised against eating the brain "lest the diner become crazy in the head."

As regards raw seaweed, this is perfectly ordinary food, but one rarely hears about seaweed; the Japanese refer to it as sea grass (*kaiso*). Japanese people no more eat "seaweed" than we eat "land weed." The Japanese eat specific varieties of marine algae: *nori, ishinori, konbu, wakame, mozu, hijiki*, etc. Most of these are processed or cooked, but many varieties of raw "seaweed" (the names of which are only known by gourmets) are served on a *sashimi* platter. The Portuguese term *limos da praia*, or "beach slime," suggests the texture of only two of the six varieties mentioned above. The Portuguese language does not differentiate algae from seaweed, although *limo* most often refers to slimy algae, whereas *algas marinas*, or marine algae, is a term generally associated with seaweed, a cover term for a variety of different algae.

25. We eat our trout lightly broiled or cooked; they put theirs on wooden skewers and roast them until they are burnt.

In the old country hotel where one of us (Gill) spent his first few months in Japan, smoke quickly became the call to breakfast, which consisted of fish that was always burnt. As most of the part singed black is the heavily-salted skin, which is discarded anyway, burnt fish is not as crazy as it seems. From reading Frois it is apparent that the Japanese have had many centuries of practice at it. It should be noted that Frois probably was referring to either salmon or sweetfish (*ayu*) when

46 Albala, *Food in Early Modern Europe*, 66.

he referred to the *truta* ('trout') of Japan. (Since at least the eighth century the Japanese have used tame cormorants to catch the *ayu*, who swim upriver to spawn.)

26. Among us, wine is chilled; in Japan, they heat it before drinking, during almost the entire year.

Imagine coming home to a "hot one" rather than a chilled glass of *vinho verde*. Sake lovers explain how the heat brings out this or that quality of the *sake*, but the wariness the Japanese had, and still have, for all cold drinks may be more explanatory. Some thirty-five years after the *Tratado* was written, Rodrigues noted that while everybody now drinks warm wine all year round, the "true and ancient custom" was for warm wine to be drunk only from September to March (from the ninth day of the ninth moon until the third day of the third moon); the rest of year it was drunk cold.[47]

The Japanese were not alone in heating their wine; drinking wine warmed by the fireplace or diluted with warm water was popular among all classes in all seasons in France and Iberia. Many Iberians today share the Japanese distrust of chilled drinks, believing they are bad for the throat; warmed wine is still popular in certain parts of the Peninsula (e.g. Galicia) during the winter months.

27. Our wine is made from grapes; theirs is all from rice.

Southern Europeans considered wine, particularly diluted with water and enhanced by spices, the perfect drink. (Besides tasting "good," particularly during the winter months, spiced wine was thought to have medicinal properties such as aiding with digestion.) With respect to Japan, "all" is a bit of an overstatement, as some rice wine was or is flavored with fruit and turned into plum or persimmon wine. Some of the best persimmon wine is made at Zen temples, just as the Benedictine order is renowned for its Bénédictine, which is made from over two-dozen plants and spices (but no grapes).

28. We drink with one hand; they always drink with two.

There was no physical reason for using two hands.[48] To receive something with both hands shows that it is not taken lightly, and to continue holding a cup with two hands bespeaks sincerity. Frois might also have noted that the Japanese poured wine with the arm held straight out and rigid, with the second hand holding the pouring arm as well. This idea of propriety through stiffness is still understood in Japan, as is two-handed drinking, although today both are rare (today one might see two hands being used by an older married couple or the winner of a Sumo tournament).

29. When we drink, we do so seated in chairs; they do so on bent knees.

Again, Frois is concentrating on formal drinking, where men sit back on their feet with their knees pointing forward. Men did not always drink like that and seldom do so today. This distich is a further reflection of the Jesuits' concern with mastering the elaborate formalities of the Japanese nobility.

47 Rodrigues, *This Island of Japon*, 232.
48 Marques, *Daily Life in Portugal*, 31, notes that the glasses (*vasos*), grails (*grais*), and chalices (*tagras*) used by elites in late medieval Portugal often were so large that they did require two hands.

30. We drink from silver, glass or porcelain cups; the Japanese use sake cups made of wood or unglazed earthenware.

On special occasions such as New Year's, the Japanese use new, unglazed cups, which are then discarded. This custom apparently was in imitation of the Emperor, who reportedly used cups only once. Because every day is not New Year's day, this distich is misleading. Rodrigues wrote that the Japanese used five kinds of cups to serve *sake* to their guests: lacquered cups (gilded or plain); two of simple earthenware; one that was half or completely gilded or covered in silver (both inside and out); and another that was of earthenware but also gilded and silvered. Even more remarkable, these last cups were served on a three-legged tray that looked like:

"... a jagged seashore, with its entrances and exits like the bays and capes of a shore, ... painted entirely blue, or the colour of the sea, and decorated with various patterns of flowers or small trees, especially the pine which grows along the coast ..."[49]

31. Among us, no one drinks more than he wishes, and he is not persuaded by others; in Japan they insist so strongly that they cause some to throw up and others to become drunk.

While intoxication and "competitive drinking" may have been deemed sinful in Europe, it did not stop many people from drinking to excess. Long after Frois was dead and buried, Europeans were still celebrating feast days or other holidays with impromptu drinking bouts. According to Schivelbusch,[50] were it not for the widespread adoption of coffee in the eighteenth-century, countries such as Germany may never have become industrial power-houses.

Generally speaking, the Japanese do not drink *sake* during or after meals. Simply put, the Japanese generally drank to drink—and still drink to drink. Japanese men take pride in their drinking and many would not refuse a challenge to a drinking match. Frois' fellow Jesuit, Rodrigues, was dumbfounded:

It is also astonishing to note the various devices and means which the devil has taught them to encourage much wine drinking ... They not only concoct a thousand kinds of tasty *sakana* (these are appetizing things to eat which encourage a man to drink) as incentives, but they also sometimes summon women dancers and singers and other types of depraved people, who, when they drink, challenge whomsoever they wish to partake as well; ... Things

49 Rodrigues, *This Island of Japon*, 214–220. Some sake cups were truly unusual; Rodrigues mentions some that were made of gold, silver, rhinoceros horn, red sandalwood, the very large red and beautiful beaks of certain birds found in China, very fine red scented wood with delicate work on the outside and silver inlay on the inside, and still others of porcelain.
50 Wolfgang Schivelbusch, *Tastes of Paradise: a Social History of Spices, Stimulants, and Intoxicants,* trans. David Jacobson (New York: Pantheon Books, 1992).

sometimes reach such a pass ... that some of them challenge others to drink wine from hand-basins ...[51]

32. Among us, it is considered disgusting to drink from a soup, meat, or fish bowl; in Japan it is very common to empty one's soup bowl[52] and drink from it.

Another way to put this would be: We flavor our food with a little wine; they flavor their wine with a little food. Today, as in the past, the most popular variety of *sake* in Japan is *Junmai-shu*, which is highly acidic. This acidity may explain why it would taste good when drunk from the shell of a crab or a soup or fish bowl (also acidic), while wine, particularly red wine, would not.

Frois was so busy contrasting the crude materials of the Japanese *sake* cup and, worse yet, the yucky manner of drinking from "dirty dishes," that he forgot to contrast the thimble-sized *sake* cup with the huge (by Japanese standards) tankard preferred by many Europeans.

33. Our everyday drinking water has to be cold and clear; among the Japanese, it has to be hot and should have tea powder that has been beaten into the water with a straw brush.[53]

The Japanese seldom drink plain water; tea is arguably their main source of water. Frois, however, describes but one way of making tea, using the expensive bright green powder now identified with the tea ceremony. Tea ordinarily was lightly steeped.

Frois might have written a more generally applicable description of how the Japanese drank water: "The water has to be hot and served either as tea, as medicine, flavored by barley, or be the left-over water from cooking noodles."

Until recently, most Japanese of middle-age and older have worn heat wraps to keep their belly warm. Many still do. If ordinary cold water was, and still is, believed to be bad for digestion, cold spring water was considered quite capable of bringing on a stroke. In poetry, cold water came to be associated with the phrase *inochi-tori-ni naru*, a term meaning that indulging in something will cost you your life.[54]

34. Among us, the burnt rice at the bottom of the pan is thrown out or given to the dogs.[55] in Japan it is served as a dessert or it is placed in the hot water that is drunk at the end of the meal.

---

51 Rodrigues, *This Island of Japan*, 212. See also Eyal Ben-Ari, "At the interstices, drinking, management, and groups in a local Japanese organization." *In Japan at Play: The ludic and the logic of power*, eds. Joy Hendry and Massimo Raveri, 129–152 (London: Routledge, 2002).

52 *Shiru-goki*, or soup-bowl.

53 *Escova de cana*, referring to a bamboo whisk.

54 The Japanese attitude toward drinking water is not that unusual. Dysentery, typhoid, cholera, and other water-borne diseases historically convinced many Americans and Europeans that it was unwise to drink water.

55 The West has a long history of allowing and even encouraging dogs at dinner, even if people were discouraged from petting the dog or cat. Dogs not only received burnt leftovers but were allowed to sample *entrees*! It was not until the nineteenth century that throwing food onto the floor and dogs themselves were discouraged at dinner. Margaret Visser, *Rituals of Dinner, The Origins, Evolution, Eccentricities, and Meaning of Table Manners* (New York: Grove Press, 1991), 166.

Okada[56] explains that this is, in part, a reflection of Japanese respect for rice, which was considered more than a food. During Frois' time, a nobleman's fiefdom was valued and described in terms of potential rice harvest rather than acreage. Still, rice was not the sacred=imperial=Japanese object that it became later, when neo-Shinto nationalists argued that the only rice in the world worthy of the name was Japanese rice (*japonica*), which was derived from the body of the Sun Goddess *Amaterasu-omikami*. While the Japanese, facing imports, can still get excited about their rice, the stuff at the bottom of the cooker or, worse, the bowl, is no longer consumed religiously. Despite the high price of rice in Japan, a surprising amount of old rice ends up in the bowls of the *wan-chan* and *nyan-chan*, the dogs and cats of the house, respectively.

35. Among us, one begins drinking right after the meal starts; the Japanese begin serving their wine almost at the end of the meal.

Frois is here contrasting formal meals. As noted above, the Japanese do not generally drink *sake* with dinner. Avila Giron wrote: "About halfway through the meal, along comes a page with hot wine in a flask, but does not pour it unless the diner holds out his cup, which, in Japan, may be no other than the bowl which covered the rice."[57] But even formal occasions offered more diversity in methods of drinking than Frois' contrast suggests.

36. Among us, one does not drink out of the porcelain [bowl] from which one has eaten soup or rice without first washing it; the Japanese dump the soup out of the rice bowl and then drink hot water from it.

This contrast regarding water parallels the observation made in #32 above regarding *sake*, which is drunk in the same manner. One contrast naming both liquids would have been sufficient.

37. Our quills for [cleaning] our teeth are very short; the sticks used by the Japanese are sometimes eight to nine inches[58] long.

Europeans used feather quills as disposable toothpicks. During Frois' time toothpicks of gold or silver became fashionable in Europe and were worn on hats and jackets.[59] Japanese toothpicks were generally between three and fourteen inches in length. The short ones used today, called "fingernail toothpicks" (*tsuma-yoji*), first became popular during the Edo era (1608–1868). Japanese toothpicks are rectangular rather than round and are almost always made of bamboo. Arguably, anyone who has used both prefers the Japanese.

38. Among us it is a great offense and dishonor for a man to get drunk; in Japan they are proud of this, and when they ask, "What is your master doing?", the reply is, "He's drunk."

---

56 Akio Okada, trans. and ed., *Yoroppa-Bunka to Nihon-Bunka* [European Culture and Japanese Culture] (Tokyo: Iwanami Shoten, 1965).
57 Michael Cooper, *They Came to Japan* (Ann Arbor: University of Michigan Press, 1965), 195.
58 *Palmo*.
59 Visser, *Rituals of Dinner*, 324.

As noted above (#31), Christian Europe frowned on drunkenness, although as Montaigne[60] pointed out, this did not stop Europeans from imbibing. "The Chinese and Japanese," on the other hand, "do not consider drunkenness in banquets and revelries as something wrong, although they will not countenance violent intoxication, but this is rare among nobles."[61] Let us add Koreans to this happy company.

39. We esteem dairy products, cheese, butter and marrow; the Japanese abhor all of this and they think it smells very badly.

As previously noted (#2), the Japanese often spoke disparagingly of Europeans as "butter-stinking" (*bata-kusai*). Although the Japanese have acquired a taste, if not a fondness, for milk and flan (see footnote 10), they still eat relatively little sour cream or plain yogurt. Perhaps the higher incidence of lactose intolerance among Asians explains the Japanese dislike of dairy products.

40. We season our food with various spices; the Japanese use miso,[62] which is rice and rotten grains mixed with salt.

Spices were indeed central to the cuisine of Europe's rich and powerful, not to mention the Portuguese economy (the crown of Portugal reaped enormous profits from ships returning each year from India laden with pepper[63]). The famous European chef, Cristoforo da Messibugo (d. 1547), used spices such as cinnamon, cloves, ginger, pepper, nutmeg, mace, and coriander in over 80 percent of his recipes.[64] As noted, spices also were added to wine to increase its shelf life and were understood as having medicinal properties (e.g. spiced food was good for the elderly but might produce lust in others).[65]

The *miso* spoken of by Frois here refers to the same bean curd used for soup. Fish might be marinated in miso, roasted eggplant flavored with a particularly sweet variety, and so forth. To a spice lover, Japanese *miso* is too plain, probably the plainest in Asia. Korean *miso* is more like a pungent French cheese and the Chinese have many wonderful fermented seasonings. But when it comes to the most instant form of *miso*—soy sauce—the Japanese variety surpasses most others by remaining simple. Even today, Japanese cooking entails limited spices, but the Japanese, like Americans, eat a lot of mild ethnic foods from around the world.

41. We avoid dog [meat] and eat beef; they avoid beef and are quite happy to eat dogs as medicine.

The linkage to "medicine" clearly suggests that Frois knew that dog was not *usually* eaten by the Japanese, but rather was "medicine eating" (*kusurigui*) to beat

---

60 Michel de Montaigne, *The Complete Essays*, trans. M.A. Screech (London: Penguin, [1595] 2003), 296–303.
61 Rodrigues, *This Island of Japon*, 211.
62 Fermented soybean paste.
63 See Chapter 12.
64 Flandrin, "Dietary Choices," 410.
65 Jack Turner, "Spices and Christians." In *Encompassing the Globe, Portugal and the World in the 16th & 17th Centuries*, ed. Jay Levenson (Washington, D.C.: Sackler Gallery, Smithsonian Institution, 2007), 47–49; Cowan, "New Worlds, New Tastes," 201.

the summer thinning mentioned in the discussion of contrast #24 above. The best known medicine eating, however, was a males-only, late fall barbecue of "mountain whale" (wild boar) or venison, which was said to restore the body's heat.

42. Among us, rotten fish tripe is considered an abomination; the Japanese like it a great deal and have it as an appetizer.[66]

The Japanese once salted and aged many varieties of fish tripe and roe. Today, *shiokara*, or "salt tripe," almost invariably means the guts of squid (often mixed with strips of squid flesh). There is, however, a far more expensive fermented tripe, *konowata* (sea cucumber guts), which for centuries was a tribute item delivered annually to the imperial court. *Konowata* is still considered one of the top gourmet foods in Japan, although not all Japanese would eat it.

43. Among us, making loud noises while eating and completely draining a cup of wine are considered slovenly; the Japanese consider both of these things to be refined manners.

The Japanese do not pay much attention to eating and drinking noises. The correct way to eat noodles or drink soup is to slurp loudly, because it is the best way to experience or savor the combination of broth and noodle, not to mention avoid getting scalded. Quick eating generally has been considered good etiquette among this job-oriented culture. Samurai, in particular, took pride in eating and defecating quickly. Even today, a noodle shop in Japan gives fast food a new meaning. One feels like using a stopwatch at some of these "slurpers"!

As far as *sake* goes, since the usual sake cup holds only about half a shot and the alcohol content is as low as wine, men are not adverse to tossing them back, and the Japanese do often gulp aloud when they drink, simply because they are unconscious of such noises, having never been trained to avoid them. One could well imagine that this would look indecorous to a wine-sipping European.

44. We praise our hosts' wine with a happy and gracious smile; the Japanese praise their hosts' wine by making such a miserable face that they look like they are crying.

What the Japanese do, even today, is grimace. Europeans and Americans generally think a good drink should be mellow. Among the Japanese, strength is a desired characteristic of a drink. Thus a grimace showing that a drink hit the spot is the traditional way to express gratitude. (It is no wonder the Japanese are fond of American Westerns, as grimacing is precisely what cowboys do when they reach the saloon and knock down a whiskey.)

45. At our tables we converse, but we do not sing or dance; it is not until the very end of the meal that the Japanese converse, and more often, dance and sing.

This is *not* your average weekday dinner, but a party of men. After sitting for a good while on *tatami*, it feels good to move a little. Moreover, the song and dance of traditional Japan, unlike most of Europe, can easily be performed by individuals (see Chapter 13).

46. Among us, the guest expresses thanks to the host; in Japan the host expresses thanks to the guest.

---

66 Sacana = *sakana* = *hors d'oeuvres*.

In Japan, guests bring gifts and hosts thank them for taking the trouble for coming, rather than the guest thanking the host for hosting the affair. It makes sense, for the guest is the one who has to travel. But Frois may have a particular situation in mind. Okada believes that Frois was referring to ceremonial tea etiquette. The Jesuits became rightly preoccupied with this etiquette because it was important to the nobility and samurai class whose favors they courted. As noted in the critical introduction, one of the rules drawn up after the Bungo Consultation mandated that all Jesuit residences and even missions have a special room near the entrance door for ceremonial tea, and also a tea attendant (*chanoyusha*) who was to be continuously on duty.[67]

47. We like fried fish; they do not, and [instead] enjoy fried seaweed.

The Japanese roast fish or boil it; they rarely fry it. Deep-fried *konbu* (kelp) is rare today, except, paradoxically, in *tempura*, something the Japanese adopted from the Portuguese.[68] Fried seaweed of all kinds remains very popular.

48. Among us, fishing is viewed as recreation by honorable people; in Japan, it is considered lowly and an activity for base individuals.

Japan's oldest anthology of poetry, the *Manyoushu* (ca. 768), has several poems about noble poets who go fishing and meet goddesses in the guise of fishing girls. But the Japanese have nothing like the *"Compleat Angler"* tradition found in the West.[69] One reason for this is suggested by another poem in the same anthology by Okakura, which speaks of the sinful nature of cormorant fishers. Buddhism, with its strong taboo against the taking of life, was spreading throughout Japan at that time, and soon poets and other good people no longer fished, or at least they did not fish and boast about it.

In the twentieth century, however, the number of Japanese anglers multiplied as fast as good streams were ruined by developers, with the comical result seen in photo magazines: unbelievable crowding (more fishermen than fish).

49. We are diligent about cleaning our teeth after eating; the Japanese do so in the morning, before washing their faces.

Perhaps because the Japanese ate less sweets as well as meat, which was likely to get caught between the teeth, they saw little need to brush before bedtime.

50. Among us, animals eat the leaves of plants and ignore the roots; in Japan, during certain months of the year, the poor eat the roots of plants and ignore the leaves.

This unfair likening of the Japanese to livestock would seem to reflect Frois' encounter with the destitute in Japan, who relied on the last crops of the year— turnips and radishes (called *daikon*[70]) as a condiment to season their *miso* during

---

67 Josef Franz Schütte, S.J., *Valignano's Mission Principles for Japan 1573–1582*. Volume I, Part II, trans. J. Coyne (St. Louis: Institute for Jesuit Sources, 1985), 170.

68 *Tempura* is thought to have been derived from the Portuguese term *tempero* (seasoning), or more likely *temperas,* referring to holy days when you did not eat meat.

69 In 1653, Izaak Walton published *The Compleat Angler*, the first of what would be countless books that celebrated fly-fishing.

70 This plant produces terrible flatulence, something many Europeans have felt compelled to write about.

the winter. Of course, the poor in Europe, of whom there were many in Frois' time, ate just about anything, including all manner of plant roots and leaves (everything from dandelions to turnips).

51. Among us, it would be an insult to eat, or to send someone, a gift of rotten meat or fish; in Japan these things are eaten, and foul smell and all, they are sent [as gifts] without embarrassment.

Frois may have been referring in this distich to Japan's oldest form of *sushi*, called *narezushi* (fermented rice and carp). Then there is *kusaya*, which Kenyusha's Japanese-English dictionary defines as "a horse-mackerel dipped in salt water and dried in the sun, which has a very characteristic odor." As previously noted, most *sushi* in Frois' day was "aged" or allowed to ferment for four or five days in the fall or spring, or for a day or two in the summer. Like *natto* (fermented soy beans that have a slimy texture like okra), in winter one literally had to sleep on it in order to make it ferment in a house with no central heating. This may seem strange but one of us had an east-European neighbor who slept with his home-made yoghurt for the same reason!

52. In Europe it would be considered vulgar for an honorable citizen to sell wine in his house as if it were a tavern; in Japan highly respected citizens sell it and portion it out with their own hands.

Then, as now, European nobility or bourgeois pretenders left the actual sale of wine or grapes from their vineyards to hired hands or *negociants*. In Japan, a "liquor store" is seen as innocent as any other store. At the time Frois wrote, most *sake* was sold by *dosô*, money-lenders who operated out of earthen rooms or "stores" that provided protection from fire and thieves. There were up to 300 of these stores in operation in Kyoto circa 1585. The question is whether Frois' "respected citizens" means the owners of the largest of these stores, or, as Okada[71] suggests, major merchants who got into the sake business, selling sake alongside the *dosô*. That these "respected citizens" portioned out the sake with their own hands may well reflect the "hands-on way" of doing business that still character-izes Japanese commerce. In Japan as well as in China and Korea, business owners often go out of their way to meet and greet clients and customers, rather than entrust such tasks to an employee.

53. Europeans like to raise chickens, mallards,[72] [pigeons and ducks][73]; the Japanese don't enjoy any of this, except raising roosters to delight the children.

Chicken, duck, and geese were eaten by Europeans, in general. Game birds and spectacular fowl (e.g. crane, stork, peacock) often were focal points of banquets and feasts hosted by European nobility. Roosters were Japan's pride. Although elsewhere in Asia the bird's combativeness was particularly valued, the Japanese seem to have valued the rooster's long tail (for which they were bred) and their

---

71 Okada, *Yoroppa-Bunka to Nihon-Bunka*.
72 *Adens*.
73 The bracketed text is corrupted in the original. Schütte has suggested rabbits and ducks. Because Frois is talking about birds, we think pigeons (or geese) makes more sense than rabbits, although the latter certainly were raised in Portugal and other parts of Europe.

diligent time-keeping. Ducks actually were common in some rural areas and made a significant contribution to the health of rice paddies by oxygenating the water and eating insects. Although their wings were clipped, perhaps they were not managed closely enough for Frois to consider them honest-to-goodness domesticated animals, or he never lived in an area where they were bred and consumed.

54. In Europe, pastries are made with wheat flour; in Japan, they remove the pulp from an orange and stuff the peel to make a pie.

Europeans ate pastries that were both sweet and savory (i.e. meat pies). As noted, fresh as well as dried and preserved fruit were very popular in Portugal and were sometimes used as a filling in milk turnovers. In Japan, Frois probably was treated to *yûmiso*, which is made by stuffing sweet *miso* inside a hollowed-out *yuzu*, or citron (also called a "Chinese lemon"), which is lightly braised. (The scent of the citron skin is heavenly!) Although *yûmiso* is still common in Japan today, Western-style pies are more common, as are continental pastries, particularly cakes (Japanese "pastry shops" or *wagashiya* are mostly places where you buy beautifully wrapped treats to bring as gifts when visiting someone).

55. In Europe one eats wild boar roasted; in Japan it is eaten raw, in slices.

Restaurants in Portugal (e.g. Fialho in Evora!) are still renowned for their roast pork, especially from black hogs that root for acorns in the cork oak forests of the Alentejo region, to the south and east of Lisbon.

This contrast would seem to suggest that *sashimi*, in the modern sense of the word (fresh and raw slices), was a part of Japanese cuisine in the sixteenth century, although pork (cooked or raw) was not something eaten by most Japanese. When one considers the incredibly diverse swine culture of their Chinese neighbors, Japanese forbearance is nothing short of miraculous. Indeed, perhaps Japanese attitudes toward pork were at some level meant to signal their distance from the Chinese. The Jesuits in Japan initially raised pigs and goats and purchased cattle that were slaughtered on their premises, but this largely stopped once it was realized that the Jesuits were seen by the Japanese as "slobs with little upbringing" (*sucios y de poca criacion*).[74]

56. With us, not having salt for food is but a small inconvenience; the Japanese become bloated or sick if they do not have salt.

Europeans, and the Portuguese in particular, had access to and often preferred various spices over salt. They also ate a lot of pork products such as ham that were preserved with salt, perhaps explaining why a lack of table salt was a small inconvenience. Going without salt was considered such an excruciating experience in Japan that there was even a custom of fasting from salt (*shiodachi*). Even today, all Japanese children learn in school the tale of a sixteenth-century Japanese noble, Uesugi Kenshin, who decided not to cut off his rival's access to salt, famously saying, "Wars are to be won with swords and spears, not with rice and salt."

74 Alessandro Valignano, *Sumario de Las Cosas de Japon* (1583), *Adiciones del Sumario de Japon* (1592), ed. José Luis Alvarez-Taladriz (Tokyo: Sophia University, 1954[1592], 242; see also Schütte, *Valignano's Mission Principles*, Vol. 1 Part II, 242–243.

57. We usually find their xiru salty; they think our soup is bland.

This is a simple yet poignant distich, inasmuch as it reflects Frois' apparent appreciation that something so seemingly essential—one's senses—are governed by custom or habit.

58. In Portugal, rice cooked without salt is used as a treatment for diarrhea; in Japan, rice cooked without salt is their regular staple food, as bread is for us.

Now we know why Frois noted the absence of salt in Japanese rice. The Portuguese home remedy for diarrhea still makes sense as there is a good deal of soluble fiber in rice that helps ameliorate the problem of watery stools. It is worth mentioning parenthetically that our medical profession continued to eliminate salt from the diet to treat bowel disorders (malabsorption) until the advent of the Space Age, when they finally discovered that some salt in sugar water facilitated absorption of the latter.

59. Among us, mullet is prized; in Japan, it is considered repugnant and food for the poor.

As far back as antiquity, Mediterranean peoples relied on the red and grey mullet (the red mullet is still a Portuguese favorite). Mullet roe was appreciated in Japan, but mullet itself was mostly eaten by the poor.

60. Among us, belching at the table in front of guests is considered ill-mannered; in Japan it is very common and no one pays any mind to it.

Yet one more difference in manners to be added to #31, #38 and #43 above. The Japanese today are not quite so belch-positive. While a burp is not so strongly disliked as in the West because of the generally greater tolerance for body noise (as opposed to less tolerance for body odor, which Frois never mentions), it is not particularly welcome at a Japanese table.

7   Japanese offensive and defensive weapons and warfare

1. We use swords; the Japanese use cutlasses.

As one might imagine, given all the dueling and warfare that took place in the sixteenth century,[1] Europeans made use of a variety of swords, ranging from the huge German *zweihänder* to various types of rapiers or "long-swords" such as the *espada ropera*, which was favored by elites. European swords by and large were double-edged, absolutely straight, and had a sharp point. Correspondingly, swordplay was mostly a matter of stabbing and thrusting. The Japanese swordsman, by contrast, was intent on decapitation and his *katana* was what in English we would term a cutlass: approximately sixty centimeters, single-edged, slicing sharp, and slightly curved.[2] Because point and edge are covered elsewhere (Chapter 1, #21 and Chapter 7, #7), Frois may have been focusing here on straight vs. curved. Note that today most people probably find the differences between a sword and a cutlass meaningless. However, in Frois' day Europe and Japan were extremely bellicose and both societies had for centuries imparted privilege and status to aristocrats and warriors bearing swords.[3]

2. The handle of our swords fits the size of our hand; theirs is over one span[4] in length, and sometimes up to three.

Frois clearly has in mind the civilian sword or rapier that was worn by European elites (relatively light-weight; quick to unsheathe; great for dueling or fending off a thief). As Frois noted in Chapter 1 (#34a), the Japanese cutlass was gripped with both hands. Placement of the hands varied depending on one's technique and power, much as a baseball player varies his grip of a baseball bat (i.e. some like to "choke up").

---

1 Thousands literally died each year in duels during the second half of the sixteenth century. Francois Billacois, *The Duel: Its Rise and Fall in Early Modern France*, trans. Trista Selous (New Haven: Yale University Press, 1990); Tobias Capwell, *The Noble Art of the Sword* (London: The Wallace Collection, 2012), 112.

2 During the centuries preceding the arrival of Europeans, Japanese nobles favored a long sword (a foot longer than the *katana*) that was worn with the cutting edge slung down from the hip. By the sixteenth-century this *tachi* was superseded in popularity by the *katana*. Lisa J. Robertson, "Warriors and Warfare." In *Handbook to Life in Medieval and Early Modern Japan*, ed. William E. Deal, 131–185 (Oxford: Oxford University Press, 2006), 160.

3 Capwell, *The Noble Art of the Sword*; Keith Thomas, *The Ends of Life* (Oxford: Oxford University Press, 2009), 44–78; Lisa J. Robinson, "Warriors and Warfare."

4 A *palmo,* or span, equaled 8.23 inches. The average Japanese sword had a hilt at least a span, about nine inches long.

3. Our men carry their swords in baldrics; their men have a hook on their sashes.

The heavier long sword used by European military required a sling-style belt, or baldric, that hung over one shoulder. The low side of the baldric tended to be lower than the Japanese *obi*, so that European swords often hung way down the thigh. Although the Japanese *katana* originally was carried on a hook on the *obi* (as Frois suggests here), by 1585 most Japanese men were tucking their swords directly under or between the wraps of the *obi* (what Frois termed a sash).[5]

4. Our men wear a sword on one side and a dagger on the other; the Japanese always wear their sword and dagger on the left.

By the time Frois left Europe (1548) the parrying dagger was a regular accompaniment to the dueling sword or rapier. As Capwell points out, fighting with dagger and sword amounted to a new, fearsome fighting style; it also created an opportunity to indulge in yet more fashion accessorizing.[6]

The "dagger" mentioned here by Frois was, in the Japanese case, more like a small cutlass. Because the Japanese themselves sometimes referred to this smaller cutlass, or *adaga*, as a dagger (*wakizashi*), Frois is reflecting rather than creating a confusing nomenclature. Generally, the sword or *katana* was for battle and the dagger or *wakizashi* for self-defense (a warrior going into a building left his *katana* on a rack and kept his dagger with him.[7])

Apparently the Japanese did not always wear their *adaga* to one side, since Avila Giron[8] wrote that it was worn crosswise over the stomach.

5. Our daggers are short; some of theirs are more than half the length of their cutlass[9]

Again, Frois uses dagger to refer to the Japanese *adaga*, thereby creating a contrast that only makes nominal sense and which is clarified below (see #11).

6. On our swords we hang our gloves; they hang a cord that serves no purpose.

The gloves frequently worn by Europeans during swordplay otherwise hung from the sword handle. During a military campaign the Japanese "sword knot" functioned to secure a scabbard to the outside of the *obi*. As noted, by Frois' time most Japanese tucked their swords inside their *obis*, so the "sword knot" was largely a vestige of former times.

7. The people of Europe are accustomed to thrusting during swordfights; the Japanese never do so.

The most famous swordsman in Japanese history, Miyamato Musashi, who was born in 1584, included thrusting strokes in his "Water Book" or second volume of *The Book of Five Rings (Go Rin No Sho)*, a treatise on sword fighting and "the

5 Michael Cooper, *They Came to Japan, An Anthology of European Reports on Japan, 1543–1640* (Ann Arbor: University of Michigan Press, 1999[1965]), 142.
6 *The Noble Art of the Sword*, 47.
7 Bruce A. Coats, "Arms & Armor." In *Japan's Golden Age, Momoyama*, ed. Money L. Hickman, pp. 261–274. New Haven: Yale University Press.
8 Ibid., 142.
9 *Katana*.

proper way of the warrior." Still, the stabbing or thrusting that is characteristic of Western fencing[10] seemingly was never a first resort in Japan. In 1560, Hayashizaki Jinsuke Shigenobu founded a school of swordsmanship that standardized fighting techniques. Shigenobu emphasized mastery of fluid motion, self-defense and, if necessary, killing an opponent with one swift stroke of the sword.[11]

8. Among us, swords of good quality iron are given to lords as gifts; in Japan, they give them wooden swords with scabbards made of cloth.

European swordsmiths of the sixteenth century in places such as Milan crafted swords that were not only beautiful to look at—decorated with gold, silver, enamels and jewels—but wonderfully balanced and highly effective at stabbing and cutting. Such swords made great gifts for those seeking to endear themselves to a rich merchant, prince, or king.[12]

For almost a thousand years before Frois' time, the rulers of Japan received gifts of wooden swords called *tsukuridachi, kidachi* or *kodachi*. These swords were worn on mostly ceremonial occasions. As Frois points out, the swords were carried in special "cord bags" (*tsurubukuro*) that resembled quivers (one Japanese dictionary defines them as "bags that were not really bags"). The Japanese also had *bokuto*, blunt wooden swords that served for exercise and were sometimes used in matches between heads of schools. (Made of heavy oak, they could kill.) They also had the equivalent (while also opposite) of the Euro-American square-edged foil, which was post-Frois. These tubular swords, or *shinai*, are made of strips of bamboo that are bound at intervals with strips of leather. They produce an extraordinarily pleasant sound when they collide. Even today, one-on-one *shinai* matches are part of physical education (*kendo* classes for both sexes) in all public schools in Japan. Because "*xinai*" appears in the 1604 Japanese-Portuguese dictionary, they probably predate Frois.

Frois overlooked a perhaps more interesting "ceremonial weapon," the *hamaya*, which are demon-destroying arrows with no head that ordinary people still acquire at shrines as talismans to undo a bad event or year and to insure happiness in the future.

9. We place nothing more than a sword in our scabbards; the Japanese place a knife in one side of theirs, and in the other a kougai that serves no purpose.

The knife mentioned here by Frois apparently is a pocket knife of sorts called a *kogatana*. The *kougai*, which is almost as old as the wooden swords mentioned above, was almost as long as a chopstick, about twice as thick and rounded at one end. Often it was made of ivory or silver, and at least as far back as the eleventh century nobles used the *kougai* to scratch their scalp or re-arrange their hair after putting on their armor. By Frois' time the *kougai* was largely superfluous. Subsequently, women adopted it as a "hair pin." (The *kougai* worn by women

---

10 As per Camillo Agrippa's *Treatise on the Science of Arms*, published in Rome in 1553. See also Capwell, *The Noble Art of the Sword*, 44–46, 100–108.

11 Robertson, "*Warriors and Warfare*," 161.

12 See for instance, Silvio Leydi, "The Swordsmiths of Milan, c. 1525–1630." In *The Noble Art of the Sword* by Tobias Capwell, 176–188 (London: The Wallace Collection, 2012).

generally were made of gold, silver or tortoise-shell.) During the peaceful Edo period, the *kougai* was split in two and became *wari-kôgai*, portable chopsticks for samurai.

10. If our swords are of high quality, they are very costly, even when new; in Japan the new ones have no value, and it is only very old swords that are expensive.

The Japanese still revere swords "with a history," swords that have proven themselves, particularly in battle. Japanese sword technology reached its apogee in the early fourteenth century and by the sixteenth century the secrets of the old sword smiths had been lost.[13] Thus, very old swords often were worth more than new ones.

Frois may never have heard Japanese legends or stories associated with their valued swords.[14] Even still, you would think that he would have appreciated how legends and stories might have mattered, given the famous swords of European epic heroes such as Arthur, Charlemagne, or El Cid.

11. Among us, one carries at most one sword and one dagger; the Japanese sometimes wear two swords and a wakizashi on their belt.

Generally speaking, more Japanese men wore three blades than did their European counterparts. With two "swords" and a *wakizashi*, we might assume that the latter is the dagger. Actually, it is hard to say, for the *wakazashi* had a cutting blade one to two feet in length, while the small "swords" (*kogatana, tanto*) had blades sticking out less than a foot beyond their blade-guards.

12. Our knives generally have wooden handles; Japanese knives have handles made of copper or other metals.

The Japanese knives are the "small swords" already mentioned.

13. When we cut with a knife, the movement is usually either toward the body or from left to right; the Japanese always cut away from the body.

While Europeans and Americans learn *not* to point a gun at themselves or others because one never knows when it might be loaded, the Japanese have traditionally taken great care when handling sharp blades; they neither whittle toward themselves nor when examining a sword in company allow the cutting side of the blade to face others.

14. Our prayer beads, as well as our crosses, are always turned on a lathe; the Japanese frequently make theirs with a knife, and these turn out just as well as those made using a lathe.

Small lathes, often consisting of a hand-held bow that was used to spin a piece of wood that simultaneously was carved, have great antiquity in various parts of the world, including Europe. During the sixteenth century pole lathes also were common throughout Europe. The lathe amounted to a treadle-operated rope or pulley that rapidly moved a piece of wood back and forth in a reciprocating rather than a continuous, spinning movement.

---

13 Alfred Dobrée, *Japanese Sword Blades* (London: Arms and Armour Press, 1974[1905]), 3, 11.
14 Catharina Blomberg, *The Heart of the Warrior* (Sandgate, UK: Japan Library, 1994), 57–59.

The Japanese had lathes as early as at least the eight century. Between 764–770 CE they were put to work producing a million miniature pagodas containing Buddhist incantations, which the Empress Shoken distributed to ten monasteries.[15] Even so, making religious items by hand was itself a form of devotion (not unlike the *santeros* of New Mexico who are inspired to carve wooden images of particular saints). People carved everything from statues of the Goddess of Mercy to prayer beads. Because the focus of the chapter is weapons and war, Frois presumably was not deprecating Japanese technology (an absence of lathes) but praising the quality of Japanese blades and the skill of Japanese workers.

15. We generally cut our nails using scissors; the Japanese always cut theirs with a knife.

As discussed in Chapter 1–#28, the Japanese seem not to have had much use for scissors and preferred quality knives for cutting things like cloth or their nails.

16. The leaves and twigs that we gather from trees to adorn gifts, the Japanese make by hand using their kogatanas.

The Japanese did not simply whittle replicas. Their foliage, if that is what it stood for, resembles the "tinder sticks" made by Boy Scouts and Girl Scouts, but the shavings are much finer and longer, so they curl like a ribbon. This art form may have originated with the Ainu, who are perhaps the world's most prolific shaving artists.

17. Our lances have long, broad blades; the blades of their lances are short and narrow.

The lances carried by mounted European cavalry often had spear points that looked something like the ace of spades (Frois' "broad blades"). Charging in formation, such cavalrymen were very effective in shattering and breaching enemy infantry lines.

The Japanese had various lances and Frois focuses here on the most common variety (*yari*), which had a double-edged blade from twelve to twenty-nine inches in length. If thrusting through armor or simply stabbing a body is the main intent (the *yari* was not thrown), a short and narrow blade is quite efficient. The *yari* was standard issue for Japanese infantry (*ashigaru*) during the "Warring States period" (1467–1568).[16]

18. Our lances are smooth, [the shaft being] the natural color of the wood; theirs have either lacquered or gilded shafts.

Originally, Japanese spear shafts were made of natural wood, but during the sixteenth-century it was common to cover the wood with black lacquer, mother-of-pearl, or vermillion; the last was retricted to those who had distinguished themselves in battle.[17]

15 Noel Perrin, *Giving Up the Gun, Japan's Reversion to the Sword, 1543–1879* (Boston: D.R. Godine, 1979), 96, f.20.

16 Robertson, "Warriors and Warfare," 162–163.

17 Akio Okada, trans. and ed., *Yoroppa-Bunka to Nihon-Bunka* [European Culture and Japanese Culture] (Tokyo: Iwanami Shoten, 1965), 110.

19. We use halberds; they use naginata shaped like a sickle.

European halberds were ferocious looking infantry weapons: spears with a sharp point as well as an axe-like head (angled in such a way as to add some slice to the hack) that also featured a prong or hook jutting out the back, which was effective in pulling horsemen to the ground.

The *naginata* was more like a curved sword on a long shaft. Traditional varieties, which feature large blades, look a lot like sickles. During the Edo era, when the *naginata* became the official weapon of noblewomen, the blade shrunk to knife length and became even more curved. (Japanese "Easterns" often include scenes where *naginata* are whirled around like huge batons in defense of lords and castles.)

20. We use bombards; they do not have them, but they do use matchlocks.

The bombard originally was a stone thrower but came to mean a cannon or mortar, which used gunpowder to shoot cut stone balls or lead shot weighing up to 200 pounds. Cannon and artillery (more mobile cannons) proved particularly valuable in siege warfare in fifteenth century Europe and were used with great success by Portugal's King Afonso in his "conquest" of Morocco.[18] The effective use of cannon contributed to the end of the medieval castle as we know it and the appearance of "star forts," which themselves used strategically placed cannon and a system of cross firing to counter artillery bombardment and other siege tactics.[19]

Although the Japanese were very quick to adopt European firearms,[20] they were decidedly slower to manufacture and make use of cannon.[21] Perhaps this lack of interest was due, in part, to Japanese fortifications, which often were temporary constructions of brush or wood.[22] That said, in 1576 Nobunaga began construction of Azuchi Castle, which had massive stone walls and was described by Frois as comparable to the greatest buildings in Europe.[23] Subsequent castles that were

---

18 A.R. Disney, *A History of Portugal and the Portuguese Empire, Volume I* (Cambridge: Cambridge University Press, 2009), 140–141; John Francis Guilmartin, Jr., *Gunpowder & Galleys* (Annapolis, MD: Naval Institute Press, 2003), 167–170.

19 Luís de Moura Sobral, "The Expansion of the Arts." In *Portuguese Oceanic Expansion, 1400–1800*, eds. Francisco Bethencourt and Diogo Ramada Curto, pp. 390–460 (Cambridge: Cambridge University Press, 2007), 392.

20 In 1543, a year after witnessing a Portuguese demonstration of a harquebus, the feudal master of Tamegashima, Lord Tokita, had his chief swordsmith produce ten guns. Within a decade, smiths all over Japan were making guns in large quantities, and within a generation many Japanese principalities had more firepower than some European powers. Moreover, the Japanese "improved" on the actual use of the gun by developing a serial firing technique that intensified the discharge of bullets during a battle. Noel Perrin, *Giving Up the Gun: Japan's Reversion to the Sword, 1543–1879* (Boston: D.R. Godine, 1979).

21 Howe, citing Ljungsted (1836), states that Asian rulers relied on the Portuguese foundry in Macau for large armaments. Christopher Howe, *The Origins of Japanese Trade Supremacy* (Chicago: The University of Chicago Press, 1996), 10.

22 Robinson, "Warriors and Warfare, 173.

23 Carolyn Wheelwright, "A Visualization of Eitoku's Lost Paintings at Azuchi Castle." In *Warlords, Artists, and Commoners, Japan in the Sixteenth Century*, eds. George Elison and Bardwell L. Smith, pp. 87–112 (Honolulu: University of Hawaii Press, 1981), 87.

inspired by Azuchi (e.g. Osaka, Fushimi, Himeji) and erected by Nobunaga's successor, Hideyoshi, were likewise on a grand scale.[24]

21. We carry our powder flask on a shoulder belt; they carry theirs around the neck like a reliquary.

The Japanese carried gun powder in a horn called a "mouth-drug-holder" (*kuchigusuri-ire*), or in a pouch (literally "torso-rampant"). Both dangled from the neck but were secured to the chest to keep them from bouncing around.

22. Our bows are medium in size and made of wood; theirs are very large and made of bamboo.

Frois is apparently contrasting the equally destructive English long bow (developed in Wales in the twelfth-century but then embraced by armies throughout Europe because of its armor-piercing abilities) and the still longer Japanese compound bow (*shinge-to-shumi*), which was used by Japanese nobles or samurai. European long bows were up to seven feet long and were ideally made of Spanish yew, which naturally has the qualities of a composite (hard core and springy outer layers). Because it took years to learn to effectively use a long bow, it was largely replaced during the fifteenth century by the less demanding and more powerful crossbow, which, by the time Frois wrote, had been displaced by the harquebus.[25]

The Japanese *shinge-to-shumi* was a true compound bow with a wood core (generally of oak) that was sandwiched between bamboo laminates that were secured with glue and rattan bindings. The entire bow also was lacquered for water-proofing.[26]

The way Japanese archers held their bows is as interesting as the bows themselves. Unlike European and all other archers we know of who grip their bows in the middle, the Japanese gripped theirs one third of the way up from the bottom of the bow, which apparently made it easier to shoot from horseback.[27] The former cultural importance of this bow is suggested by the bow dance that is still done today by the Sumo grand champion.

23. Our arrows are of wood; theirs are made of bamboo, just as their bows are.

The bamboo fighting arrows used by the Japanese generally were a meter long and thrice fletched with bird feathers.[28] Although the Japanese used various types of arrow heads, including some for piercing armor, apparently they never copied Ainu arrows, which incorporated poison in the hollow of the bamboo shaft adjoining the tip.

24. Among us, archers remain clothed when they shoot their arrows; in Japan an archer removes half his kimono in order to leave one arm bare.

The left arm is removed from the kimono, exposing the left shoulder and some of the chest. With practice, a Japanese archer could "disrobe" in a split second. As

---

24 Money L. Hickman, "Introduction." In *Japan's Golden Age: Momoyama*, ed. Money L. Hickman, pp. 19–57 (New Haven: Yale University Press, 1996), 28–55.

25 Disney, *History of Portugal*, 140–141; Guilmartin, *Gunpowder & Galleys*, 154.

26 David Miller, *Samurai Warriors* (New York: St. Martin's Press, 2000), 70.

27 Ibid., 70.

28 Ibid., 72.

"nudity" is still a significant Western pre-occupation, many Westerners who visit Japan today would no doubt still find it strange to see people lined up at a *kyudo* gallery, all with one arm/shoulder exposed (except for the arm guard).

25. Among us, no one utters a sound when shooting a bow; the Japanese have to let out a big cry when they release an arrow.

"Our" side needs no explanation; "theirs" is remarkable. This sudden loud cry also characterizes Japanese sword fighting (see #51 below) and the modern martial arts of judo and karate. The standard explanation is that this is done to disrupt an opponent's concentration.[29] The Japanese refer to the shout or sharp cry as *kiai*, literally "spirit-meet." To put *kiai* into something (*kiai-o irete*) is "to do something with spirit."

26. Among us, we use shields, [including] gilt roundels[30] and oval leather shields; the Japanese use flat wooden shields that resemble doors.

Europeans for centuries used shields of varying sizes, including a small "buckler" when battling with swords. They might also be used by elites in a pre-arranged duel or in fencing classes, but they were too big and cumbersome to be part of elite "dress."[31]

The Japanese did in fact have small shields, but these were not ordinarily used by samurai, who, as mentioned, used both hands when wielding their long sword, or *katana*. The door-like shields that caught the attention of Europeans like Frois were deployed at the outset of battles to receive volleys of arrows from opposing archers. With the adoption of firearms, these "wall-shields," as they are known in Japanese, were replaced by bundles of bamboo, which more effectively deflected musket balls.[32] A variant of the wall-shield survives in the five- or six-foot long narrow shields used today by riot police in Japan as well as in Korea and China.

27. Our armor is very heavy; Japanese armor is very light.

The chain mail and more expensive plate armor worn by European soldiers was notoriously heavy; often soldiers and armored horses died in battle after falling and not being able to right themselves. Japanese armor was made from composite materials and was relatively light and flexible as compared with European armor.

28. Our suits of armor are all made of steel; theirs are made of plates of horn or leather laced together with braided silk.

Japanese *lamina*, or plates (to use Frois' technically correct term), overlapped like shingles or the scales of a fish. Europe had something similar to this called a coat of mail (as opposed to chain mail). Japan, however, is said to have produced more varieties of mail than the rest of the world combined. In this regard, Frois' sole mention of horn and leather is misleading. The Japanese used a variety of

29 In Tadanobu Tsunoda's best-selling book, *The Japanese Brain* (Tokyo: Taikushan Publishing Company, 1985), it was even alleged that the Japanese heard such a yell on the verbal (left) side of their brain, unlike other peoples, who heard it on the right (as noise); thus, yelling had more effect on the Japanese.

30 A small round shield.

31 Capwell, *The Noble Art of the Sword*, 35.

32 Okada, *Yoroppa-Bunka to Nihon-Bunka,* 112–113.

other materials, including iron, steel, hide, paper, brass, and shark skin, which usually were coated with thick lacquer.[33]

29. The tuft of feathers on our helmets are a very beautiful brown or white;[34] *the Japanese use the longest tail feathers from roosters.*

Based on distichs #30 and #31 below, which speak of round helmets with visors, Frois appears to be referring here to the *armet*, a closed helmet with a two-piece visor that was popular in sixteenth-century Europe. (Most of us are perhaps more familiar with the *morion* worn by Spanish conquistadors, an open helmet with a crest that ran front to back, which was sometimes decorated with feathers.) The *armet* had a small, funnel-shaped cone in the back of the helmet that held a plume of feathers.

Japanese roosters have perhaps the longest tails in the world. The Japanese, along with the Chinese and Malay, identified the cock with a martial spirit, although the Japanese were not much into cock fighting as compared with their Asian neighbors. It should be noted that besides rooster feathers, the Japanese adorned their head gear with diamond-shaped swords, stag horns, crescent moon horns (sometimes together with the stag horns), and even a strange sail-like adornment that resembled a snow shovel. Shortly after Frois wrote this, Tokugawa Ieyasu wore a helmet into battle designed after the cap of the deity of wealth, Daikokuten. The battle of Sekigahara took place in the year of the mouse/rat, a creature that is closely related to that deity.

30. Ours helmets have visors; Japanese helmets cover half the face with the visage of a devil.

Japanese foot soldiers wore a simple conical helmet (*jingasa*) made of leather or metal. Samurai wore more elaborate helmets with a face mask of lacquered iron that incorporated removable mouth and nose pieces that were intended to strike fear and awe in an opponent.[35] This was accomplished through grimacing mouths, wide eyes, flaring nostrils, and occasionally a moustache and even teeth. Ironically, this diabolical visor was partly created by the Europeans, for it was devised to protect the lower half of the face from bullets.

31. Our helmets are round; theirs have plates[36] *over the ears and neck.*

The folded-back "ears" on Japanese helmets often stick out like enormous bat ears. Besides contributing to a diabolical visage, they apparently helped protect the head and shoulders from the descending sword blows of opposing samurai. Neck guards of plate, which functioned much like the neck piece or *gorget* on European armor, protected Japanese soldiers from lateral blows and decapitation. (Note that one measure of victory in battle was the number of heads collected that belonged to opposing samurai.) As an aside, Frois probably was ignorant of the

---

33 Miller, *Samurai Warriors*, 62.
34 *Branqas ou pardas. Pardas* is brown or dark grey.
35 Miller, *Samurai Warriors*, 66.
36 Frois uses the same *laminas* here as in #28 above.

fact that many Japanese kept "dirty pictures" in their helmets.[37] Apparently there was a superstition going back to ancient China that pictures of men and women in coitus were a charm of sorts.

32. Among us, one must first don thick clothing before putting on armor; before the Japanese put on their armor, they disrobe entirely, remaining as naked as the day they were born.

The weather in Japan being what it is (hot and humid in summer), it makes sense that the Japanese undressed before donning their relatively lightweight armor. It is doubtful, however, that they were "as naked as the day they were born," i.e. that they did not wear loincloths.

33. Among us, one does not look like he is going into battle unless he is fully armed; in Japan, one only needs to don an armored collar to say that he is armed.

The Japanese concern with neck protection makes sense when one considers that war in Japan was focused on taking heads; the Japanese even had arrows with tips designed to decapitate. As noted above, the heads of samurai were collected at the end of a battle and ritually prepared for inspection by the victorious general. The Japanese word *kubi*, or "neck," refers to a decapitated rather than an attached head, or *atama*. When Americans lose their job, they get "fired"; the Japanese get "necked" (*kubi ni naru*).

34. Among us, fifes, drums, and royal trumpets are played during battle; the Japanese have nothing more than some raucous horns that sound awful.

The Japanese horn that Frois refers to is in fact a large conch-like shell (actually a large whelk) with a metal mouthpiece, which is used by mountain priests as well as the military. Okada writes that the Japanese also used drums, bells, and gongs.[38] Perhaps these were not played in parades, as in the West, so Frois never heard them.

35. Among us, each unit brandishes a square field banner, and these are carried by hand; among the Japanese, each soldier carries his own banner on a long bamboo pole fastened to his back.

European armies went into battle with men whose sole job was to carry the flags that identified individual units (e.g. infantry, cavalry), commanders (e.g. the Duke of Albuquerque), or the army as a whole (e.g. the red-white-red striped flag of the Hapsburgs).

Six-panel folding screens with paintings of famous Japanese battles evidence no shortage of flags, or rather, vertical banners (*nobori*), colorful banners, and standards, which distinguished individuals as well as field units.[39]

36. Among us there are sergeants, squad leaders, decurions and centurions; the Japanese pay absolutely no attention to such things.

37 Presumably had Frois known about this custom he would have "jumped on it," contrasting the "dirty pictures" with a purported Christian norm of taking relics, rosaries, and prayers into battle.
38 *Yoroppa-Bunka to Nihon-Bunka*, 115.
39 See, for example, "The Battle of Nagashino" and "The Summer Siege at Osaka Castle" in Money L. Hickman, ed., *Japan's Golden Age, Momoyama* (New Haven: Yale University Press, 1996), 102–103.

The Japanese seem to have had a far larger military class than Europe. Moreover, each samurai brought along peasants to serve him. There were in addition large contingents of archers, lancers and, later, rifle-carrying infantrymen (*ashigaru*). There also were "special forces" called ninja.[40] In point of fact, Japanese armies were diverse and enormous. For instance, during the brief "war of succession" from 1598–1600, over 150,000 troops fought in one battle on one day.[41] Contrary to what Frois seems to imply (that Japanese armies lacked a chain of command), the armies were organized into different elements (cavalry, foot soldiers, supply, etc.), appropriately bearing heraldry and banners that enabled generals and their aides to direct military engagements. Significantly, the vanguard of a Japanese army often consisted of followers of a daimyo who had recently capitulated.[42]

Still, for all its size and complexity, the vocabulary for a complex chain of command is not evident in Japanese, perhaps because most armies were conscripted. Thus, in the nineteenth century when the Japanese modernized their military they borrowed the West's terminology for different ranks.

The question is less why so few terms in Japanese and why so many in the West? Perhaps the institutional requirements (payroll, morale, privileges) of a full-time professional army required a chain of command as complex as that found in the West (Frois gave only a few examples). Interestingly, the long economic development of the Tokugawa era gave rise to a multiplicity of "ranks" within Japanese corporations, something that proves vexing when translating the ubiquitous Japanese business card (*meishi*) into English.

37. Among us, one fights on horseback; the Japanese dismount when they fight.

We discuss this "riding gap" in the next chapter on horses. Suffice it to say that the Japanese were not the Mongols; fighting by sword, on foot, and one on one was considered the "manly" way to fight in Japan. Note that Europeans felt much the same way until the late Middle Ages, when Muslim invaders demonstrated the advantages of "light cavalry."[43]

38. Our kings and captains provide soldiers with a salary; in Japan everyone must pay for his own food, drink, and clothing during the course of a war.

The Hapsburg rulers of Spain created a professional army that was the best in Europe, owing to the training, salaries (including a veteran's stipend) and opportunities for advancement that were afforded recruits and officers. In Japan, where conscription was more the rule, armies came and went and campaigns tended to be short. The Jesuits came to believe that lack of proper payment was one cause of the disloyalty "endemic" to Japan (see #42 below). They also recognized that the "self-responsibility" method of conscription was a clever way for Japanese lords, who often were relatively poor in terms of wealth and rent, to quickly assemble

---

40 Miller, *Samurai Warriors*, 51–52.
41 Ibid., 102–103.
42 John Whitney Hall, "Introduction." In *The Cambridge History of Japan, Volume 4, Early Modern Japan* (Cambridge: Cambridge University Press, 1991), 14.
43 Ann Hyland, *The Medieval Warhorse from Byzantium to the Crusades* (Dover, N.H: Alan Sutton Publishing Inc., 1994).

and field extraordinarily large forces. (In 1614, Tokugawa Ieyasu commanded a force of 200,000 men for his Osaka "summer campaign.") While the master-vassal relationship was exploited to the hilt, this is not to say that war had no reward. As with knights in Europe, the samurai on the winning side often received grants of land and titles with corresponding privileges. There was also a sort of patriotism, for the Japanese have been equally fierce fighters for the honor of their local "countries" (even today in Japan "returning to [one's] country" means going to one's hometown), whose existence often was threatened during war.

39. Among us, one goes into battle to take places, cities, villages and riches; in Japan, the fighting is almost always to take wheat, rice and barley.

Taking grain to supply one's own soldiers' needs while depriving the enemy of food was a common war strategy in Japan and was referred to as *kari-ta* or "reap-field." To suggest, however, that *kari-ta* was "almost always" the reason why the Japanese went to war is as misleading as suggesting that Europeans went to war to destroy foodstuffs, given the relative frequency with which European armies destroyed fields, either one's own (during a retreat) or those of the enemy.[44] In both Europe and Japan most wars were fought over arable land.

40. Among us, horses, dromedaries, camels, etc., carry the soldiers' gear; in Japan, the peasants[45] attached to each soldier carry his gear and food on their backs.

During the late Middle Ages the southern third of the Iberian peninsula was occupied by Berbers and other North Africans who introduced camels and dromedaries, which were used along with horses and mules as "pack animals." As noted above, Japanese samurai often went into battle with conscripted peasants who shouldered the samurai's gear. The contrast, while correct, is misleading if one thinks that the Japanese practice was specifically military. As discussed in the next chapter, the Japanese as a whole depended more on human than non-human animal power for transportation.

41. Among us, killing oneself is considered an extremely grave sin; during war, if the Japanese feel they cannot go on, slitting their belly is considered an act of great valor.

During the Crusades tens of thousands of Europeans sacrificed their lives in the hope of liberating Jerusalem from the infidels. Meanwhile, the Japanese evolved their own particular cult of suicide. What apparently began as a battlefield demonstration of bravery (disemboweling oneself is a particularly *difficult* way to go) and a way of denying the enemy a psychological victory, became a Japanese social institution, one that provided individuals with a means of limiting the repercussions, especially to family, of an individual's wrongdoing or shortcomings.

Suicide always has been part of the Western experience (consider the heroic captain who goes down with his ship), and yet the West is loathe to acknowledge the often-felt need to take one's own life. This might be thought of as a contrast between

---

44 During the invasion of the Americas, Native Americans often were shocked by European armies that burned or destroyed fields and foodstuffs.

45 *Hyakusho.*

individualism and collectivism, or between Christianity and Buddhism (the former says life is sacred while the latter says it is an illusion). However, from the traditional Japanese point of view, it takes someone with self-discipline and self-respect (valuing one's name over one's life) to kill him- or herself at the right time.

Today, one still reads of Japanese who commit suicide to take responsibility for scandals, but on the whole there is little to differentiate Japanese suicide from that in the West, particularly when the "West" includes Eastern European countries with double the suicide rate of Japan. Interestingly, doctor-assisted suicide has, if anything, met stronger resistance in Japan than in most of the West. (Japanese doctors, and the Japanese as a whole, are reluctant to take responsibility for someone else's life.)

42. Among us, treason is rare and is considered highly reprehensible; in Japan, it is so common it that it is almost never considered reprehensible.

Early modern Europe certainly had its fair share of treason, *à la* Macbeth. Treason was strongly censured, but also justified (Machiavelli). The extent of treachery is reflected in some of "our" current dinner rituals and dining room furniture. The credenza, for instance, initially was used as a "lab table" where servants tested the food and wine for poison before serving both.[46]

With respect to the Japanese, the main reason for treason apparently was not so much a lack of proper compensation (see #38 above); after all, as Xavier and others noted, honor meant more to the Japanese than wealth. Instead, treason appears to have resulted from the political instability of sixteenth-century Japan. During Frois' time feudal lords came and went almost with the seasons. The era revealed the arbitrary nature of authority, which made even persons *suspecting themselves to be under suspicion* break and run for a new master to save himself and his family. Ironically, the nobilities' quick recourse to capital punishment itself was due, in part, to fear that the retainer, *suspecting that he might be suspected*, might betray his master. This vicious circle of uncertainty was outlined by one of Frois' Japanese contemporaries:

> In our country, no one, not the lord nor anyone under his jurisdiction can live with peace of mind. The one constantly dreads treachery, while the other dreads unjust punishment at the hands of his mercilessly angry lord, or owing to a plot against him. So it is not at all rare that the sound of song and dance at the height of a banquette instantly becomes a bloodbath resounding the torments of hell.[47]

Retrospectively, there is irony here because the Japanese today think of themselves as a particularly loyal people, and this notion has been promulgated by

46 Margaret Visser, *Rituals of Dinner, The Origins, Evolution, Eccentricities, and Meaning of Table Manners* (New York: Grove Press, 1991), 139–141.
47 Alessandro Valignano, *De Missione Legatorum Iaponen*, Trans. Duarte de Sande (Macao [Lima Library Collection], 1590), Dialogue 12.

large corporations.[48] Frois' contrast warns us that the attractive Japanese aesthetic of transience reflected in part the real and terrifying mutability of life; vaunted Eastern stability and harmony is as much myth as it is fact.

43. Among us, it is considered a great disgrace to be an executioner; in Japan, taking another's life to serve justice is something that any noble will do, and he takes pride in doing it.

Perhaps because capital punishment in early modern Europe often was capricious or unjust, the executioner was shunned and feared and sometimes forced to wear distinctive clothing and reside outside the city or town. This was true in much of Mediterranean Europe (i.e. Iberia, Italy, France), but not Germany. (Note that while shunned, executioners often were well paid in grain or with the assets of those they executed).

It was not out of the ordinary in sixteenth-century Japan for a lord or samurai to cut down a maleficent on the spot. There also were formal executions, sometimes performed by a lord (usually to test a sword), but mostly by untouchables, a class of people who were entrusted with executing criminals as well as butchering domesticated animals. Lastly, there were *seppuku*, "seconds," who were asked by an individual intent on suicide to behead the individual just as he began disemboweling himself.[49] This assistance often was rendered by samurai or nobles and might best be called euthanasia rather than execution.

44. The cambalas[50] that are used as fans in India by the Moors and gentiles are used by the Japanese as hair to adorn the rims of their helmets.

The Japanese valued imported yak hair from China (see Chapter 2, #5) as a charm as well as adornment. Tail hair from white yaks was used on everything from spear heads to implements carried by religious leaders. As Frois notes, "fans" of yak hair (they actually look more like long-haired dusters) were used in India primarily for giving flies and mosquitoes the brush-off.

45. Our razors are thick and flat; theirs are thin and curved, with a single edge.

If Frois had possessed a greater understanding of Japanese blade technology he might have mentioned the most essential difference between Japanese blades and all others, namely that Japanese blades have a hard and keen edge and a relatively soft and resilient blade body. European blades were of a uniform consistency (relatively soft), so while they were durable, they were comparatively dull.[51]

46. We sharpen our blades using oil on a hard stone; the Japanese sharpen theirs using a soft stone and water.

---

48 In the 1980s, this corporate public relations image was challenged by one of Japan's most popular authors, Sakaya Taiichi, who used his considerable knowledge of the sixteenth century to argue in a series of books and articles that loyalty has never been something particularly Japanese.

49 Ideally, to insure that the condemned man can show his mettle, the beheading comes after actual disembowelment.

50 Although the Spanish edition of the *Tratado* produced by Ricardo de la Fuente Ballesteros (2003) notes that *kambala* is a Sanskrit word that means a cloth or sheet made of wool, we follow Okada (*Yoroppa-Bunka to Nihon-Bunka*, 117) in believing that Frois used the term as a referent for yak hair.

51 Dobrée, *Japanese Sword Blades*, 19.

The Japanese for many centuries have used sharpening stones made of sedimentary rock (the most desired stone was mined north of Kyoto in Narutaki) that is softer than the novaculite preferred by Europeans and Americans. Frois is also correct in that the Japanese use water rather than oil when sharpening their blades on the whetstone. The use of a softer stone and water means the stone does not become glazed or loaded with "swarf" as quickly, although the sharpening stone wears out faster than an oilstone. Because dull blades are useless (if not dangerous), Europeans and the Japanese prized blade sharpeners. In Europe, they went door to door in larger towns or cities, sharpening a variety of blades, including knives and scissors. During the sixteenth century Sengo Muramasa gained almost mythical status in Japan for the incredible edge he was able to produce on a sword blade.[52]

47. Among us, only barbers give shaves; in Japan, almost everyone knows how to do this.

Given the incredible sharpness of Japanese cutting devices (one could apparently shave with an *adaga* or short sword), it makes sense that nearly everyone in Japan was his own barber, particularly as Japan had professional sharpeners (*togishi*) who offered door-to-door service. Moreover, because the Japanese wrote with a brush, they may have enjoyed greater manual dexterity, enough so they could safely shave without a safety razor. The relative paucity of facial and body hair may have helped as well, but the Japanese threw away much of that advantage by also shaving part of the head.

48. Among us, if one does not go to the barber, one cannot shave his beard; many bonzos and laymen shave their beards and heads by themselves.

This contrast seems to be a repeat of #47 above, except in pointing out that not just laymen, but also Buddhist priests shaved themselves and had no need of a barber.

49. Among us, soldiers carry the fuse on their left arm; the Japanese carry it on their right.

Frois is referencing here a requirement of some of the earliest handguns used by cavalry in Europe and later introduced to Japan. These rather primitive guns were fired by a lighted fuse that was applied to a touchhole on the top of the barrel near the breech.[53] The "fuse" carried by both European and Japanese soldiers is more aptly conveyed by the Japanese term *hinawa*, or "fire-string," which was kept smoldering during battle. The *Dicionário Houaiss da Língua Portuguesa* indicates that the *morrão* generally was made of linen cord, one end of which was soaked in a solution of quicklime and potassium so that it would burn slowly. The fact that the Japanese carried the fuse on their right arm, implying that they used their left hand to ignite the charge, may reflect a previous samurai tradition of holding the bow in the left, or "bow" hand (see Chapter 8, #10). In Europe, the gun was held under the right arm and ignited by a fuse held in the right hand.[54]

52 Blomberg, *Heart of the Warrior*, 58.
53 Guilmartin, *Gunpowder & Galleys*, 159; Mick Bennett, *The Story of the Rifle* (London: Cobbett Publishing, 1944), 11–12.
54 Ibid., 12.

50. Our fuses are made of cloth fibers; theirs are made of paper or bamboo husks.

This is a difference, but hardly a striking contrast, unless European fuses burned much more slowly. For a real difference we have to wait until the seventeenth century, when Europeans embraced the flintlock.

51. Among us, one fences without speaking; the Japanese must give a shout with every blow and parry.

This shouting was discussed in #25 above. One can *hear* a high school kendo class in Japan practicing with their split bamboo swords from outside the gym. Scream! Whack! Scream! Scream! Whack!

52. Our soldiers in Switzerland[55] fire their harquebus from the shoulder; the Japanese place theirs against their face as if they are sighting in on an enemy.

The matchlock or harquebus, which did not require a hand-held "fuse" (the "fuse" was incorporated into the firing mechanism of the gun), was invented around 1500 in Spain and quickly became a favorite among European armies. Because of the substantial weight and recoil of the harquebus,[56] it often was fired while mounted on a forked rest or pole. Following their defeat of the armies of Charles the Bold in the 1470s, the Swiss were acclaimed Europe's greatest soldiers. The Swiss mercenary harquebusiers mentioned here by Frois were engaged all over Europe by anyone with money to hire them, including Pope Julius II, who in 1506 initiated the enduring Papal Swiss Guard.

In 1543, several Portuguese sailors who had travelled aboard a Chinese junk to Tanegashima Island put on a demonstration of the harquebus for the ruling daimyo, and in a few short years the Japanese were producing their own muskets (called *hinawaju*).[57] For reasons unknown, the harquebus developed by the Japanese had a relatively short butt. Presumably it produced less recoil,[58] which might explain why the Japanese were sufficiently comfortable placing it against the face. Frois says "as if," but perhaps the Japanese harquebusier *did* sight in on the enemy. Whatever the case, by 1585 numerous daimyo were using European and Japanese harquebuses to overpower competitors.[59] At the battle of Shimabara in 1584, the Jesuit supporter Ōtomo fielded an army of 25,000 men, at least 9,000 of whom carried harquebuses.[60] During the opening decades of the seventeenth century, the Tokugawa became fearful that an armed peasantry might mount a successful rebellion, and so the government disarmed the peasantry and forbade firearms.[61]

---

55 *Os nossos soldados na Suisea.*

56 Bennett, *The Story of the Rifle*, 13, tells of an harquebus in a museum in England that was nearly nine feet long and weighed eighty-seven pounds. Guilmartin, *Gunpowder & Galleys*, 160, states that the "typical" sixteenth-century arquebus weighed ten pounds or less, although Spanish muskets weighed at least eighteen pounds.

57 Robertson, "Warriors and Warfare," 164.

58 See Guilmartin, *Gunpowder & Galleys*, 160.

59 Jurgis Elisonas, "Christianity and the Daimyo," In *The Cambridge History of Japan, Volume 4, Early Modern Japan*, ed. John Whitney Hall, pp. 301–369 (Cambridge: Cambridge University Press, 1991), 302.

60 James Murdoch, *A History of Japan*. 3 Vols. (New York: Ungar Publishing, 1964), II, P.I, 99.

61 Blomberg, *The Heart of the Warrior*, 50.

8   Concerning horses

1. Our horses are very beautiful; Japanese horses are greatly inferior to ours.

Frois presumably had in mind the Spanish Andalusian horse and its Portuguese relative, the Lusitano, when he referred to "our" beautiful horses (the world-famous Lipizzaner stallions are also derived from the Andalusian). Equines of all types, including warhorses that were bred from European, Barbary, Arabian, and oriental breeds, were a big part of European culture and identity. This was particularly true of Iberians, who embraced the equestrianism of the Moors (riding *a la jineta*) to drive the latter from Iberia during the two centuries before Frois was born.[1] Note, however, that relatively few Europeans during the sixteenth century actually owned a horse and in many locales only the nobility had the right to own and ride a horse (Columbus, for instance, petitioned the Spanish crown for the right after returning from America in 1493). In Iberia in particular, commoners were more likely to own a donkey or a mule, which were generally used as beasts of burden (i.e. to plow, haul goods, or power small mills).

Contemporary and later Europeans shared Frois' negative opinion of Japanese horses. The Englishman John Saris, who wrote a few decades after Frois, is one of the few Western observers who admired Japanese horses, particularly for their mettle.[2] The Japanese horse apparently was descended from the Mongolian horse, whose ancestor was the Asiatic wild horse. Hyland describes it as a short (at 52 inches from ground to withers), stocky, heavy-boned animal, with a rather coarse, big-headed, straight-necked appearance.[3] This high-spirited horse apparently was introduced (or re-introduced) to Japan in the fourth and fifth centuries by mounted warriors from Korea who settled in the Kanto province of Japan. There they initiated what was to become a long tradition of elite warriors who fought from horseback with bow and arrow.[4]

2. Ours can be brought from running to a halt in quick order; theirs are very hard to control.

The Spanish Andalusian still has a reputation for a lightning-quick start and an equally quick halt. The unmanageability of Japanese horses was a common complaint of European visitors to Japan.[5] Dogs, too, were and still tend to be, relatively undisciplined. Arguably, neither horses nor dogs were as common or as

---

1 Robert M. Denhardt, *The Horse of the Americas* (Norman: University of Oklahoma Press, 1975); Ann Hyland, *The Medieval Warhorse: From Byzantium to the Crusades* (Dover, N.H: Alan Sutton Publishing Inc, 1994).
2 Michael Cooper, *They Came to Japan* (Ann Arbor: University of Michigan Press, 1965), 143.
3 Hyland, *The Medieval Warhorse*, 127–28.
4 Lisa J. Robertson, "Warriors and Warfare." In *Handbook to Life in Medieval and Early Modern Japan*, ed. William E. Deal, 131–185 (Oxford: Oxford University Press, 2006), 154–155.
5 Isabella Bird, *Unbeaten Tracks in Japan* (Boston: Beacon Press, 1987[1880]), 152.

central to life in Japan as they were in Europe, where horses and dogs were used for many purposes, including hunting and warfare.[6] That said, the Japanese at the time Frois wrote had a long history of valuing the horse for its mysterious ability to attract or communicate with Shinto gods and to positively affect the weather. Larger shrines often kept two live horses for this purpose and many smaller Shinto shrines had horse sculptures or encouraged offerings of horse-shaped figurines and votive tablets called *ema*.[7]

3. Ours allow riders on their backs; Japanese horses are not accustomed to this.

Europeans were not averse to putting two people on a horse; the smaller Japanese horses were not built for more than one rider. Also, horses in Japan generally were led, not ridden; mostly elites or warriors had access to horses in Japan.

4. Ours are accustomed to going along side by side; those in Japan always follow one another.

In classical Japanese poetry, horses (actually ponies) almost always race across the fields side by side (*koma narabete*), in a comic reversal of the norm, which, as Frois indicates, was for elites or dignitaries on horseback to proceed in single file, led by footmen. Roads in Europe were wider because they were frequented by greater numbers of equines, including many that pulled carts, wagons, and coaches. Thus, European horsemen, be they crusading knights or nobles on their way to Venice were apt to ride side by side.

5. We leave the tail of our horses loose for beauty's sake; theirs are bound in a knot.

As noted in Chapter one, Europeans equated long, flowing hair with power and virility; what was true for men was true for horses. The Japanese often used a Chinese-style saddle and would stuff the tail into a sack that was then bound to the tail (referred to as "China-tail," or *kara-o*).

6. The longer the mane on our horses, the prettier they are; in Japan they cut the mane and at intervals they attach pieces of wheat straw, to enhance the horse's magnificence.[8]

Okada cites literature suggesting that the Japanese had two major ways of presenting horses' manes: *nogami*, meaning "field" or "wild-hair," which is basically the same as the unfettered mane preferred by Europeans, and the *karihoshi* or "shaved-priest" style, which Frois emphasizes here.[9] The "wheat straw" inclusions actually were rice straw, which does not have the same humble connotation it has in English, and was auspicious for its association with plenty.

6 Horses and dogs were instrumental in the English domination of Ireland and the Spanish conquest of Mexico, to give just two examples. Robertson, "Warriors and Warfare," 155, suggests that the "unmanageability" of Japanese horses was actually desired by the Japanese, who also favored stallions over geldings.

7 Money L. Hickman, "Painting." In *Japan's Golden Age: Momoyama*, ed. M.L. Hickman, pp. 93–181 (New Haven: Yale University Press, 1996), 137–144.

8 *Yxei* [*isei*]. Here we follow De la Fuente's Spanish translation of the *Tratado* in his use of the term "magnificence."

9 Akio Okada, trans. and ed., *Yoroppa-Bunka to Nihon-Bunka* [European Culture and Japanese Culture] (Tokyo: Iwanami Shoten, 1965).

7. Our horses are all shod with iron horseshoes and nails; in Japan no horses are thus shod, but instead are fitted with straw shoes that last for a couple of miles.[10]

Europeans began selectively breeding larger horses for mounted combat during the Middle Ages. The demands of increased weight (armor for the horse as well as the rider) and the pounding impact of combat, often in damp soil, led to the development of metal horseshoes to protect horse hooves from splitting, cracking, deterioration, and bruising.[11] As Frois suggests, the Japanese used relatively impermanent shoes or slippers (*umagutsu*) made of twisted straw. Thus, Kaempfer[12] commented, "... this country hath more farriers, than perhaps any other, tho' in fact it hath none at all." Although the superiority of iron shoes, particularly on rocky surfaces and ice, convinced some samurai to copy the Portuguese, iron horseshoes were largely unknown in Japan a century after Frois. Indeed, the re-introduction of iron horseshoes in the nineteenth century (after Japan was re-opened to the West) caused quite a sensation. Today, Japanese horses all wear horseshoes.

8. Among us, the footman walks ahead of the horse, leading it by the halter; in Japan, depending on the condition of the road, the footman is loaded down with straw shoes for the horses.

Japanese footmen had to be "straw farriers," ready at a moment's notice to replace a worn-out horse slipper. Thus, many carried a load of straw shoes while leading their master's horse.

9. Among us, the bridle has a little tongue and rings that go inside the horse's mouth; in Japan they have nothing more than a piece of iron crossing the horse's mouth.

Europeans during the Middle Ages developed and made use of a bridle with various bits and snaffles (metal bars and rings, respectively) that allowed the rider to essentially control the horse via the horse's mouth and head. Again, horses were never central to Japanese culture and thus the Japanese did not develop a bit technology comparable to that of Europe. This may help explain why Japanese horses often were said to be out of control (see #2 above).

10. We mount with the left foot; the Japanese with the right.

Okada explains that the samurai held his bow in his left "bow hand" and the rein in his right "rein hand." Today the Japanese (no bows, of course) mount from the left.

11. Our reins are leather and are very well made; theirs are made of strips of cloth that is painted and rolled.

Although Frois' Portuguese usage speaks of Japanese reins as rolled (*emrolada*), Okada notes that "ancient" Japanese reins generally were made of white, dark blue, and pale blue hemp that was twisted into a triple braid, which kept it from unraveling.

10 "*Mea legoa*," or half a league (approximately 1.8 miles).
11 Hyland, *The Medieval Warhorse*, 57–59.
12 Engelbert Kaempfer, *The History of Japan, Together with a Description of the Kingdom of Siam, 1690–92*. 3 Vols. (Glasgow: James MacLehose and Sons, 1906[1690–92]), II, 284–285.

12. We use a saddle and full-length stirrups[13]; in Japan they ride with only short stirrups.[14]

Europeans embraced the long stirrup during the Middle Ages because it gave the rider greater control of the horse and made it possible to wield a large, heavy sword or crossbow. It also provided stability for those wearing heavy armor and wielding a heavy lance.

Japanese horsemen rode in the manner of present-day jockeys, which presupposed strong, powerful legs (otherwise encouraged by the squatting behavior common to Japanese and Asian cultures, more generally). The Japanese may have favored short stirrups because their horses were relatively short and short stirrups made it easier to see over the horse's head when shooting a bow. Recent studies of jockeys using high-speed cameras show that much of the time that a horse is galloping the jockey "floats" above the horse; short stirrups and powerful legs (both rider and horse) may have made for a fearsome combo.

13. Our stirrups are made of iron and are open in the front; theirs are made of wood, closed in the front, and very long and narrow, like Moorish slippers.

The Japanese at one time used open-loop stirrups (adopted from the Chinese) that were similar to those of the West. By the eighth century[15] these stirrups were superseded by a stirrup that had a toe bag, and at times a hard tongue, or what Westerners would call a sole that extended the length of the foot and provided added support.[16] With the exception of horses ridden on ceremonial occasions, the Japanese today use Western-style stirrups.

14. We use spurs; they do not, using instead only very short stalks of vara, which are like our reed canes.[17]

Europeans began using spurs at least as early as the eleventh century. As Frois suggests, the Japanese encouraged their horses with whips of bamboo grass (i.e. *sasa*) with the leaves left on the end.

15. The pommel on our saddles is completely closed in front; theirs has a hole that one can grab and hold onto.

Frois is apparently referring here to a handhold (*tegakari*) under the front edge of the Japanese saddle. Presumably it was grabbed on to when going uphill or over rocky terrain. If European saddles generally were in the shape of a lazy, inverted "U," Japanese saddles tended to be in the form of an inverted "V," or as Isabella Bird phrased it, "... like a saw-horse."

13 *Há bastarda.*
14 *Não se cavalga senão só a jineta.* See De la Fuente Ballesteros, 88–89.
15 Robertson, "Warriors and Warfare," 156.
16 When it was no longer than the toe bag, it was called a "short tongue." There were also half-tongue and long-tongue designs, the last of which gave support to the entire sole of the foot. This development was partly due to the soft bottoms of the footwear worn by the Japanese while riding.
17 *Somente de vara, que hé da cana de nós muito curtos.*

16. On our horses we use cruppers, caparisons and equipment adorned with brass tacks,[18] *on the horses in Japan they use none of these things, only a type of caparison made of tiger hide with the fur side out.*

Europeans once spoke readily of cruppers and caparisons the way people today speak of ABS brakes and four-wheel drive. For those unfamiliar with equitation, a crupper is a leather strap that is attached to the back of the saddle and goes under and around the horse's tail, keeping the saddle from creeping forward. Caparisons are robes; many of us have seen them in movies on horses ridden by medieval knights competing in jousting matches.

Frois' larger point here seems to be that 1) Japanese horses ordinarily were less well furnished and, 2) the tiger skins that were used by the Japanese as caparisons (mostly by the shogun and nobility) had the fur side out; presumably Frois felt the normal or logical thing was to have the fur side in, as per the following distich.[19]

17. Our saddles[20] *are made of leather and wool; theirs are made of wood and lacquer.*

Saddles in the West are still made of leather and usually placed over a "blanket" made of wool, felt, or cotton. Again, the horse was not central to Japanese culture and the wooden saddle here mentioned by Frois was designed with a mounted archer in mind rather than a Japanese elite travelling from Kyoto to Edo.[21]

18. Our stables are always behind or in the lower part of the house; in Japan they are built at the front of the house.

Okada cites a contemporary account of the residence of a Japanese magistrate, which also places the stables near the front of the house. Although in 1585 the mounted samurai warrior no longer decided battles (infantry with rifles now made the difference),[22] ownership of a horse (made apparent by a stable at the front of the house) was of great symbolic importance for samurai.

19. In the homes of European nobility guests are first welcomed in the living quarters; in Japan their first reception takes place in the stables.

For guests and horses alike the Japanese welcome is arguably both more efficient and friendlier. Because horse fanciers always will take you to their stables to show off, one might as well get it over with at once, at the same time you have your own horse "parked" and groomed down.

It is somewhat surprising that Frois did not comment on how differently horses were stabled in Japan as compared with the West.[23] This was one of the first things

---

18 *Retrancas e caparazóes e nominas.* The last, *nominas,* also translates as phylactery—wrap around leather straps, although Japanese translators write "decorative studs."

19 See also Chapter 1, #13.

20 The Portuguese original is problematic. Although Schütte has suggested *"ressas,"* *arreio* (saddle) would seem to make more sense.

21 Robertson, "Warriors and Warfare,"155–156.

22 Ibid., 155.

23 Extant Japanese screens from ca. 1560–1600 provide a sense of how Japanese horses were stabled. See Money L. Hickman, "Painting." *In Japan's Golden Age: Momoyama,* ed. Money L. Hickman, pp. 93–180 (New Haven: Yale University Press, 1996), 140–143.

that nearly every nineteenth-century visitor noted. Here is Alcock, the first British Ambassador to Japan:

> ... the horse's head was where his tail would be in an English stable, that is, facing the entrance. It certainly seems a much more rational thing, to be able to go up to your horse's head, when he has an opportunity of recognizing you, rather than to his heels, with a preliminary chance of a kick and a broken leg.[24]

Mr. Ed, the famous talking TV horse, always faced the camera, so either he was acting Japanese or sometime in the middle of the twentieth century Americans came to place the "head where the tail ought to be!" Nowadays most "box" stalls are big enough that a horse can face any way it pleases and some people feed them from an inside window and others hang a bucket from the front of the stall in what is (unbeknownst to them) the Japanese style. The world of horses, like that of humans, is becoming gray.

20. Our horses are cleaned with a currycomb; theirs are cleaned using either the hand or a tool made of cords.

The Japanese did in fact use a comb called an *akatori* or "crud-remover," but apparently relied mostly on their hands and the corded tool spoken of by Frois.

21. Our horses have mangers; Japanese horses eat from low troughs.

Okada has suggested that Frois is pointing to a contrast between the use of individual mangers or "hay-tubs" (which was the norm in Europe) and the use of a collective hay trough in Japan. Frois' use of the adjective "low" may also be speak surprise, as low troughs are what pigs ate from in Europe.

When most English speakers think of a "manger," they think of a Christmas nativity scene rather than a small bucket or hay tub. In her otherwise uninspiring book, *A Diplomat's Wife In Japan* (1899), Mrs. Hugh Frazer recounted how the term's multiple meanings posed problems for the Japanese:

> I did not realize the intense difficulty of translating our thoughts into Japanese till the day after our Christmas tree, when O'Matsu came to me looking very puzzled, and said she would like to ask a question: Why did Imai Sam (the gentlemen who made the little address about the meaning of Christmas) say such a dreadful thing about "Jesu Sama"? He had said that Jesu Sama was put into a bucket, such a thing as ponies have their food in![25]

22. In the stables of our nobles, the horses often lie down; those in Japan, day or night, are nearly always kept standing by a belt tied around the belly.

24 Rutherford Alcock, *The Capital of the Tycoon, A Narrative of a Three Years' Residence in Japan* (London: Longman, Green, and Roberts, 1863), 165.

25 Mrs. Hugh Fraser, A Diplomat's Wife in Japan. (London: Hutchinson & Company, 1899), 310.

Horses do not usually sleep for extended periods like humans. They instead take frequent short naps of several minutes duration. Adult horses mostly sleep standing up, with the front legs and one hind leg doing most of the weight bearing (the horses shift their weight and have leg bones with a "stay apparatus" that allows their muscles to relax without collapsing). Lying down is more stressful for an adult horse, although horses will lie down for a brief rest if given the opportunity.[26] In this regard, and as Frois suggests, the stables of European nobility seem perfectly suited to horse behavior.

Japanese screens, or *byôbu*, from the early seventeenth century affirm the use of a rope tied around the horse's stomach and attached to the rafters overhead.[27] Such stabling of horses, particularly the emphasis on restricting the horse's behavior while at rest, often has appeared cruel to outsiders. First, Alcock:

> When not eating, however, their head is often tied up rather above the level of the neck, without any freedom or power of moving from right to left, merely to keep them quiet, which is great cruelty, and all to save a lazy groom the trouble of cleaning them if they lie down.[28]

Although Alcock makes no mention of a belly lift, not allowing the horse to lie down is the same idea. For reasons made clear in the next contrast, a Japanese stable might not make a good bed, anyway. This was further suggested by Isabella Bird, who observed the belly sling used with ponies in Korea.

> At the inn stables they are not only chained down to the troughs by chains short enough to prevent them from raising their heads, but are partially slung at night to the heavy beams of the roof. Even under these restricted circumstances, their cordial hatred [of one another] finds vent in hyena-like yells, abortive snaps, and attempts to swing their hind legs round. They are never allowed to lie down, and very rarely to drink water and even then only when freely salted. Their nostrils are all slit in an attempt to improve upon Nature and give them better wind. They are fed three times a day on brown slush as hot as they can drink it, composed of beans, chopped millet stalks ... I know not whether the partial slinging of them to the crossbeams is to relieve their legs or to make fighting more difficult.[29]

23. Our stables have earthen floors; theirs have wood plank flooring.

Stable floors of wood planking, particularly of cedar, undoubtedly kept the unshod hooves of Japanese horses relatively free of moisture, which otherwise would have caused the hooves to deteriorate and crack. (Europeans used metal

26 Paul McGreevy, *Equine Behavior: A Guide for Veterinarians and Equine Scientists* (Edinburgh: Saunders, 2004).
27 See Hickman, "Painting," 142.
28 Alcock, *The Capital of the Tycoon*, 165.
29 *Isabella Bird, Korea & Her Neighbours*, 2 Vols. (London: John Murray, 1898), I, 138–139.

horseshoes in part to keep their horses' feet dry.) Frois noted elsewhere that in 1565 he visited a Kyoto mansion that had a stable at the entrance made of *sugi* (*Cryptomeria japonica*), a fragrant smelling Japanese cedar that is always used for constructing Shinto shrines, Buddhist temples, and other sacred or honored places. According to Frois, the only part of the stable that was not of cedar were the rush mats used by the horses' human attendants!

24. Horses in Europe urinate on the floor of the stable; in Japan they remove the horses' urine with long-handled ladles.[30]

The Japanese made use of two kinds of ladles, one for scooping up water to wash the horse and another for receiving the horse's urine. The latter had a handle that was a little over five feet long and a scoop that was nine inches across and ten inches deep. While horses can drop their dung on the run, to urinate they must "set up" by moving their legs apart. Attentive grooms who were quick to the ladle apparently were successful in keeping the stable floor reasonably clean.

25. Among us there are mules, zebras, donkeys and pack animals; there are none of these in Japan.

As noted, Europeans relied on a variety of equines for transportation and as beasts of burden. Although Frois focuses in this chapter mostly on horses (ridden by elites), mules and donkeys were more common than horses in Iberia as late as the nineteenth century. Zebras always have been rare in Iberia. During the mid fifteenth century the Portuguese began trading and raiding for slaves in West Africa and also initiated a lucrative trade in gold and a variety of exotic animals, including zebras. Frois is correct that the Japanese had no mules, zebras, donkeys, etc.

26. Among us, only mules wear a long saddlecloth; the horses of the Japanese nobles wear both round leather saddlecloths and others made of straw.

The French translators of the *Tratado* suggest that the point of this contrast was that a saddlecloth used on a beast of burden (i.e. a mule) was used on elite horses among the Japanese. If on the one hand the Japanese did not mind nudity, on the other they liked multi-layered dress. This same tendency is seen with respect to horses. Speaking practically, their wooden saddle naturally needed more padding below.

27. For us it would be ridiculous for a nobleman to go about with the halter on his horse and the lead rope in his own hand; in the Kingdom of Bungo, the sons of the king often go about in this manner.

Ridiculous? Not if you like to sit back and enjoy the ride. From the Japanese perspective, galloping across an open field was something warriors did out of necessity during battle. As for the province or "kingdom" of Bungo, on the southern island of Kyushu, it became a Christian stronghold early on, thanks to the

---

30 *Fixaqus* (*hishaku*).

conversion of the local lord or "king,"[31] who was converted by none other than Frois himself.

28. When we gallop or ride on horseback, the reins are held in one hand only; in Japan they are held in both hands.

Again, most Japanese elites were not particularly interested in galloping, but rather in sitting back, taking in the countryside and receiving the prostrations of their retainers. The first American Ambassador to Japan, Townsend Harris, was undiplomatically blunt:

> The Japanese are no horsemen; both hands are employed in holding the reins; they have no martingale[32], the horse therefore carries his head very high with his nose stuck out straight. They therefore have no command over them.[33]

29. Among us, bleeding is the only treatment used on horses; in Japan, while they are bled often, they also place large cauterizing irons under the jawbone.

As discussed in the following chapter, Europeans embraced a humoral theory of health and disease, believing that the health of human beings (as well as horses) required a proper balance of various humors that could be maintained or restored through bleeding. An Englishman, William Dade, recommended drawing blood from a horse's neck on the first day of April to help them stay healthy the whole year. Farriers (those who shoed and doctored horses) used a bloodletting tool called a fleam, which looked something like a pocketknife with different sizes of cutting blades.[34]

The Japanese did not practice phlebotomy. What Frois means by "bled" is being stuck by needles. Acupuncture was indeed practiced routinely on horses. It could draw a little blood but was hardly comparable to European bloodletting. The "fire," or *moxa*, combustion treatment, which is described in the next chapter, was primarily preventative and apparently was intended to stimulate the immune system. (It was done on a calendrical/ritual, basis.) Ambassador Harris believed that the treatment helped explain the poor behavior of Japanese horses.[35]

31 Frois uses the terms "kingdom" and "king" (*regno* and *rei*). In the prologue to the missing first volume of the *Historia*, "king" is the ninth of ten examples of Portuguese terms that Frois explains do not do justice to Japanese realities. Frois notes that, in Japan, it is commonly written that there are sixty-six realms, but their rulers' power is limited. Frois went on to note that, while there is only one "king" of Japan using the Europeans sense of the word, there were some exceptionally powerful rulers such as the "King of Bungo," Ōtomo Sōrin, who was baptized by Frois in 1578 and ruled before Nobunaga conquered most of Japan.
32 Martingales come in different forms and basically consist of a strap that is used to keep a horse from throwing his head up and back, unsettling the rider.
33 Townsend Harris, *The Complete Journal of Townsend Harris: First American Consul General and Minister to Japan*, Ed. Mario E. Cosenza, (Garden City: Doubleday and Company, 1930), 398.
34 Louise H. Curth, "English Almanacs and Animal Health Care in the Seventeenth Century." *Society and Animals* 8(2000):1:71–86.
35 Harris, *The Complete Journal*, 399.

30. In Europe the reins are loosened to make the horse run and tightened to make it halt; in Japan they are loosened to stop and tightened to run.

It might seem to be common sense to release and pull on the reins of a horse to make it go and stop, respectively. However, horses can be trained to respond to any number and variety of commands. Indeed, today it is common for well-trained dressage horses to stop when the reins are released. Some horse fanciers will tell you that you do not need to do anything with the reins to stop a "good" horse; all you need to do is shift your weight back slightly.

31. We till the earth only with oxen; in Japan they use either horses or oxen.

Europeans may have preferred to till the earth with oxen as a plow pulled by oxen turned the soil to a greater depth, often resulting in greater crop yields, over time. Still, many a field in Frois' Iberia was plowed with mules. Because Iberian farmers often became haulers once their crops were harvested, they preferred mules over oxen. Mules also were valued for their endurance, toleration of heat, and ease of feeding, to name but several advantages they had over oxen and horses.[36]

32. Packsaddles in Europe are made of cloth and straw; in Japan they are made of wood.

This is the last mention of saddles. Frois neglects to mention perhaps the most interesting contrast involving packsaddles, which is how they were ridden. On each side of the Japanese packsaddle was a side trunk (port mantle) that was used to carry something light and voluminous. Behind the rider, helping to fasten those trunks together, was a stronger back trunk, or *atozuki*, for valuables, made of "thick strong grey paper." Kaempfer continues:

> ... the middle cavity between the two trunks, fill'd up with some soft stuff, is the travelers seat, where he sits, as it were upon a flat table, otherwise commodiously enough, and either crossleg'd or with his legs extended hanging down by the Horse's neck.[37]

The "soft stuff" makes it clear that Frois is not describing the entire saddle but its frame.

33. Among us, no load is carried without a crupper; in Echizen these are not used.

It is not clear why in this contrast Frois chose one specific area of Japan to contrast with Europe. Moreover, in #16 above, Frois already indicated that the Japanese, in general, did not use cruppers. (Recall that the crupper is a strap that goes around the horse's rump and helps keep the saddle in place.)

34. Our pack horses wear bells and rattles; in Japan they wear metal disks like those on a tambourine.

36 Gomez A. Mendoza, "The Role of Horses in a Backward Economy: Spain in the Nineteenth Century." In *Horses in European Economic History*, ed. F.M.L. Thompson, pp. 143–155 (Reading, UK: The British Agricultural Historical Society, 1983).
37 Kaempfer, *The History of Japan*, II, 282.

In both Europe and Japan bells and rattles obviously warned people to stand clear. With respect to Japan, Okada surmises that Frois was referring to either *gyoyo* (literally "apricot leaf," which were trinkets that hung behind Chinese-style saddles) or *kanrei* (which were hollow, donut-like bronze bells). The Japanese continue to take driving seriously; cities like Tokyo are loud not because people are impatient (as in New York) but because it is mandatory—indeed, automatic—for drivers to use their horns whenever they back up or otherwise perform a potentially dangerous maneuver.

35. Our bulls are huge and mean; in Japan they are small and tame.

The Japanese raised cattle primarily for draft animals, presumably without interest in particularly large (thus costly to feed) and aggressive animals. Iberians raised cattle for a variety of purposes, including bullfighting. As an aside, a form of "bullfighting" where two bulls go head to head (not unlike sumo wrestling) is popular in parts of Japan (e.g. Okinawa) and also Korea.

36. In Europe, muleteers burden their beasts and carry nothing themselves; in Japan, out of sympathy for the beasts, the muleteers sometimes carry a third of the load on their own backs.

Neither Shintoism nor Buddhism are predicated on the notion of a great chain of being that implies that human beings can use other life forms as they see fit, in the manner of the Judeo-Christian worldview laid out in Genesis (I:28). Perhaps more importantly, equines were never as numerous in Japan as in Europe and thus the Japanese were accustomed to carrying loads. Because the grass in Japan is not as calcium-rich as in Europe, horses may have been more prone to leg injuries[38] and thus Japanese concern for their horses also may have been a matter of prudence.

There is also a difference between European muleteers and the Japanese who work with horses. In the Japanese language both those who care for horses and those who use horses to haul cargo or for other transportation services (usually the same person) are called simply *mago*, "horse-child" in Chinese characters, where "child" has the nuance of the American slang term "boy," meaning a person doing menial work, especially but not always service-related. Japanese-English dictionaries provide only the awkward "road-horse man," so there appears to be no simple English equivalent, as both muleteer and groom miss the mark.

37. In Europe, the load to be placed on a beast is determined visually; in many kingdoms of Japan, nothing is loaded on a beast that is not weighed first.

Who can say whether this was due to a Japanese tendency to be exacting or for the reasons of kindness or prudence noted above? Living in Japan for twenty years, Gill was always struck by a Japanese reluctance to make a "rough guess." The Japanese usually insisted on making him wait until they arrived at a precise figure or answer.

---

38 It was for this reason that Japanese racehorses broke bones at a tremendous rate in the 1980s.

38. Among us, an unsaddled horse is led by a man using a halter; in Japan the horses of noblemen, even those that are very gentle, have to be moved by one man with a rope in front and another with a rope in the back, like a roped bull.

Even a gentle horse can react when bitten by a horsefly, so it did not hurt to be careful in a country with crowded streets where dereliction of duty could, quite literally, cost a man his head.

39. Our saddles are strapped onto the horse using a girth beneath the saddle; Japanese saddles are secured with a strap over the front pommel.

This difference between strapping beneath the saddle and strapping over top of it may reflect the fact that European horses often were ridden at a gallop. It also may reflect the different manner of cinching up the girth. The Japanese have long excelled in all forms of binding and fastening. Kaempfer[39] was impressed with the way horses could be "unsaddled and unladen in an instant."

---

39 Kaempfer, *The History of Japan*, II, 282.

9   Diseases, doctors, and medicines

1. Among us, it is commonplace to suffer from swollen glands,[1] kidney stones, gout, and plague; in Japan all of these ailments are rare.

Swollen lymph nodes (they are not actually glands), particularly in the neck, are a common symptom at the outset of a variety of illnesses. Sixteenth-century Europe was repeatedly subjected to acute and chronic infectious diseases, including bubonic plague, which refused to go away after devastating Europe in the fourteenth century.[2] Frois might also have mentioned typhus and syphilis, two diseases previously unknown in Europe that ravaged the continent during Frois' lifetime.[3] Most of us are familiar with kidney stones and gout. The Portuguese term used by Frois for the latter (podagra) is still used by doctors and often refers to gout that manifests as pain in the joint at the base of the big toe. Kidney stones and gout were a particular problem for European elites, who consumed large amounts of meat and not enough diuretics (e.g. beets, peas, artichokes, cabbage).

Japan in the sixteenth century appears to have been relatively free of acute and chronic infectious diseases, despite its large and urbanized population.[4] The Japanese penchant for cleanliness and Japan's physical separation from the rest of Asia and the world might help explain why Japan went unscathed (relatively speaking) by diseases that elsewhere changed the course of history.[5]

2. We use bloodletting; the Japanese use a cauterizing iron with herbs.

Bloodletting as "preventative maintenance"[6] or to restore the body's humeral balance was common medical practice in Europe. Burning *moxa*—a wool-like material ideally taken from the leaves of a species of Chrysanthemum (*Artemesia*

---

1 *Alporcas* (referred to in English as scrofula) is a swelling or tuberculosis of the lymph nodes of the neck.

2 Brian Pullan, "The Counter-Reformation, Medical Care and Poor Relief." In *Health Care and Poor Relief in Counter-Reformation Europe,* eds. Ole P. Grell, Andrew Cunningham, and Jon Arrizabalaga, pp. 18–40 (London: Routledge, 1999), 21–22; Laurence Brockliss and Colin Jones, *The Medical World of Early Modern France* (Oxford: Clarendon Press, 1997), 37–80.

3 J.D. Oriel, *The Scars of Venus* (London: Springer-Verlag, 1994), 11–23; Daniel T. Reff, *Disease, Depopulation, and Culture Change in Northwestern New Spain, 1518–1764* (Salt Lake City: University of Utah Press, 1991), 170–172.

4 William E. Deal, *Handbook to Life in Medieval and Early Modern Japan* (Oxford: Oxford University Press, 2006), 63.

5 Ann Bowman Jannetta, *Epidemics and Mortality in Early Modern Japan* (Princeton: Princeton University Press, 1987), 28l; Linda Newsom, *Conquest and Pestilence in the Early Spanish Philippines* (Honolulu: University of Hawai'i Press, 2009), 17; William H. McNeill, *Plagues and Peoples* (Garden City: Anchor-Doubleday, 1976):124–127, 201.

6 Constitutions from late medieval monasteries in Portugal prescribed preventative bleeding every two to six months. A.H. De Oliveira Marques, *Daily Life in Portugal in the Late Middle Ages* (Madison: University of Wisconsin Press, 1971), 149.

vulgaris)—and acupuncture, were the Chinese and Japanese way of restoring or insuring bodily health. Both were similar to European practices in that they were predicated on the idea that health presupposed a balance of vital force (*ki* in Japanese, from the Chinese *qi*).[7] Maintaining or restoring *ki* entailed engaging bodily energy through acupuncture (strategic placement of very thin silver or gold needles) and/or burning very small, cone-shaped *moxa* at particular sites on the body (the heat generated by the *moxa* was thought to "unblock" or accelerate the flow of *ki*). As Kaempfer wrote in his thorough chapter on moxibustion,[8] the *moxa* burned so slowly that "... the pain is not very considerable, and falls short of that which is occasion'd by other Causticks." Although Japanese and Chinese physicians did not agree (and still disagree) about where to burn for various complaints, Kaempfer observed that the backs of the Japanese "... of both sexes are so full of scars and marks of former exulcerations, that one would imagine they had undergone a most severe whipping."[9]

Much like bloodletting, moxibustion was used to treat specific ailments (e.g. headaches, toothaches), as well as to maintain bodily health. Again, Kaempfer: "Here, these little mugwort cones [*moxa*] are to be found in most houses, and people are burned in the spring, just as in England blood-letting was formerly customary at the same season."[10]

Today, few Japanese, particularly among the younger generations, practice moxibustion, just as few Europeans embrace phlebotomy. Note, however, that there have been some impressive studies of the physiological equivalent of blood-letting, i.e. blood donation, that suggest significant increases in life expectancy. Reading about disfiguring scars caused by *moxa* and the unnecessary deaths caused by overzealous bloodletting, we laugh at our ancestors, yet our ancestors may well have the last laugh.

3. Among us, men ordinarily are bled from their arms; the Japanese use leeches or a knife to the forehead, and they bleed horses using a lancet.[11]

The ordinary procedure for bloodletting in Europe was to open a vein with a lancet or fleam and to then collect and measure the blood flowing or spurting from the patient's arm (the goal was to remove "excess" blood and restore the body's humeral balance and health). Europeans also used leeches and cupping devices to remove smaller amounts of blood from severed capillaries. (Perhaps because leeches are so painless, their frequent use led to their extinction in some parts of Europe.)

The forehead bleeding mentioned here by Frois refers to a Chinese practice carried out with a "three-corner-needle" or fleam on the crown and occipital part

7 Cheng Xinnong, *Chinese Acupuncture and Moxibustion* (Beijing: Foreign Language Press, 1999), 361.

8 Engelbert Kaempfer, *The History of Japan, Together with a Description of the Kingdom of Siam, 1690–92*. 3 Vols. (Glasgow: James MacLehose and Sons, 1906[1690–92]), II, 282.

9 Kaempfer, *The History of Japan*, II, 282.

10 Ibid.

11 *Com sanbixugas ou c[om] faca na testa, e aos cavalos com lanceta.*

of the head (because the crown usually was shaven, Frois speaks of the forehead). This bleeding to remove "bad blood" was not so common a practice as venesection and probably was used for certain maladies. Thus, Valignano (and others) wrote "They never bleed a person, ..."[12]

4. We make use of enemas or syringes; under no circumstance do the Japanese use such remedies.

For at least two-thousand years before Frois wrote this, the West made use of enemas to treat constipation and flush parasitic worms from the colon and lower intestine. Syringes of wood or carved from ivory frequently were used to propel an anti-worm drug, or vermifuge, up into the small intestine. During the sixteenth century tobacco from the New World became a popular key ingredient in vermifuges used to treat worms.

Frois' Jesuit superior, Valignano, contradicted Frois in a rare contrast not found in the *Tratado*: "... their purges are sweet-smelling and gentle—in this they certainly have an advantage over us for our purges are evil-smelling and harsh."[13] Marcelo de Ribadeniera, a Franciscan who came to Japan in 1594, wrote that, aside from the various "... simple medicines and potions made by boiling roots" (taken from books written in Chinese, i.e. *kanpoyaku*), "... they also administer purges in candied pills so that they may be taken more easily."[14]

5. Among us, doctors write prescriptions to be filled by pharmacists; doctors in Japan dispense medicines from their own homes.

By the fourteenth century the professions of physician and apothecary were distinct and proto-pharmacies could be found in many European cities, often in monasteries and religious houses (the Church of Santa Maria Novella in Florence, Italy claims to have the oldest pharmacy, dating to 1221). In sixteenth-century Portugal druggists were licensed and apothecary shops were required to have a small and specialized reference library, appropriate weights and measures, and both simple and compound medicines.[15]

Doctors in sixteenth-century Japan usually were called *kuzushi* or "medicine-masters," and true to their name, they filled their own prescriptions whenever they could (sometimes ingredients had to be ordered from a specialist). This does not mean they grew, gathered, and made it all. When Luis de Almeida (1525–1584), a merchant and surgeon turned Jesuit, took over a clinic in Bungo (Kyushu) in 1559, he quickly set up a pharmacy and put a former Buddhist monk in charge who could read Chinese and order Chinese medicines from abroad.

6. Our doctors take the pulse of both men and women first from the right arm and then from the left; the Japanese take a man's pulse first from the left, and a woman's first from the right.

12 Michael Cooper, *They Came to Japan* (Ann Arbor: University of Michigan Press, 1999), 240.
13 Ibid.
14 Ibid.
15 Marques, *Daily Life in Portugal*, 151.

This difference, writes Okada, stems from Oriental yin-yang philosophy. The pattern was not restricted to medicine; male-left, female-right also applied to "signing" documents or making oaths using a bloody fingerprint.

7. Our doctors examine one's urine to gain greater information regarding the illness; under no circumstance do the Japanese examine this.

It is hard to overestimate the importance of urine as a diagnostic tool for medieval and early modern Western medicine (the *mantula*, or urine flask, was the symbol of the medical profession during the Middle Ages).[16] Medical practitioners in sixteenth century Europe analyzed and described urine much as *sommeliers* today discuss wine. Urine was swirled and sniffed and visually examined to determine bouquet, color, sediments, thickness and other qualities that were thought to reflect bodily health. Okada notes that de Almeida checked the urine of the fief lord of the Goto islands (this according to de Almeida's letter of October 20, 1566[17]). Around this time, Japanese medical practitioners, led by Mansae Dosan (1507–94), re-worked Chinese neo-Confucian ideas (i.e. that disease was a consequence of an undisciplined, poor lifestyle) and popularized a four-fold approach to clinical care that emphasized visual observation of a patient's skin color, hair, feces and urine.[18] Frois apparently was unaware of this development. Today, Japanese hospitals seemingly collect urine samples for almost anything under the sun (perhaps because it occupies the patient during his/her long wait to see a doctor; there is insurance money for it; and the test is relatively innocuous).

8. Because the flesh of Europeans is so delicate, it heals very slowly; Japanese flesh is robust and recovers much better and faster from serious injury, burns, abscesses, and accidents.

Recall Frois' very first contrast in Chapter 1, which cast Europeans as "well built" or robust as compared with the Japanese. A contemporary of Frois', Mexia (1540–1599), likewise wrote: "When they [the Japanese] fall sick, they recover in a very short time without taking hardly any medicine."[19] This, together with statements by many European visitors about the light diet of the Japanese, may well be the first elaboration of the stereotypical oriental that is frugal, long-lived, and can survive on less than the Westerner.

9. Among us, wounds are sutured; the Japanese cover them with a little bit of paste-coated paper.

The Japanese did not suture wounds, perhaps because sword wounds healed quickly owing to the sharpness of Japanese swords. A good adhesive band-aid apparently worked perfectly well. Okada wonders if the "paste" was ointment that also functioned as an adhesive.

10. All the dressings that we make using cloth, they make with paper.

16 Ibid., 150.
17 See *Cartas que os Padres e Irmãos da Companhia de Iesus Escreuerão dos Reynos de Iapão & China aos da Mesma Companhia da India & Europa, des do Anno de 1549 Até o de 1580.* 2 Vols. Facsimile edition by José Manuel Garcia (Maia: Castoliva Editora, 1997), I, 213–224.
18 Deal, *Handbook to Life in Medieval and Early Modern Japan*, 234.
19 Cooper, *They Came to Japan*, 241.

As Frois points out in the following chapter (see #10), the Japanese had many varieties of paper, compared to a handful in Europe. The Japanese could use paper and not cloth for treating wounds because some of their paper was as soft as gauze. It would not be surprising to learn that the paper also had the advantage of breaking down in time, i.e. that it was the equivalent of today's dissolvable stitches.

11. Among us, abscesses are treated using intense heat; the Japanese would rather die than use our harsh surgical methods.

The European practice of using a red-hot iron to burn an abscess, or pouring scalding oil into a gun-shot wound, were sometimes effective, but always horrifying ways to treat a localized infection or trauma. Of course, the treatment also was likely to scar someone for life. It is perhaps no surprise that the Japanese referred to Europeans as "southern barbarians."

12. When our sick have no appetite, we work hard to make them eat; the Japanese think this cruel, and a sick person who does not want to eat is allowed to die.

Okada points out that eating, especially rich food, was thought to reduce the efficacy of Chinese medicine. Arguably, what is eaten without an appetite or even in the presence of nausea may exhaust an already stressed gastro-intestinal system, increasing putrefaction and flatulence and perhaps hastening death. Fasting may allow organs to recoup enough to make eating beneficial.

13. Our sick lie on beds or cots with mattresses, linens, and pillows; the sick among the Japanese lie on mats on the floor using a wooden pillow,[20] with their kimono over them.

This is simply the ordinary sleeping arrangement described elsewhere in separate contrasts regarding beds, bedspreads, and pillows (see Chapter 11). Perhaps Frois felt repetition was worthwhile, for the soft versus hard contrast might be more poignant in the context of the sickbed.

14. In Europe, chickens and young cocks are considered medicine for the sick; the Japanese consider them poison, and they instead feed fish and pickled radish to the sick.

It is tempting to think that Frois is referring in the first half of this distich to a light chicken broth (ironically not unlike Japanese *miso shiru*). Although Europeans at least as far back as the Middle Ages considered chicken broth healthful, Frois does not explicitly refer to soup or broth. As we saw in Chapter 6 (#7, #24), Europeans were apt to boil a fat and succulent chicken and then add rice flour, sugar, rose water, almonds, and goat's milk, producing a dish that had the consistency of melted white cheese. Serving such a dish to somebody who was sick is suggested by Valignano's comment that, "... they regard hens, chickens, sweet things and practically all the foods we would give patients as unwholesome

20 *Makura.*

for them; on their part they prescribe fresh and salted fish, sea snails and other bitter, salty things, and they find from experience that they do patients good."[21]

One reason the Japanese rejected domestic birds, as Alvarez noted, was because they were considered a taboo food ("... they never eat anything they breed"[22]), and for a sick person to eat their meat would be to tempt fate. As Valignano acknowledged, the Japanese found from experience that fish and slightly fermented pickles worked quite well.

15. We pull teeth using dental pincers, dental forceps, the parrot's beak, etc.; the Japanese use a chisel and mallet, or a bow and arrow tied to the tooth, or a blacksmith's tongs.

Dentistry in sixteenth-century Europe was practiced mostly by barbers and by itinerant tooth-pullers who extracted dental roots and broken or rotten teeth using various pliers-like tools such as the "duck bill," "goat's foot," and "pelican." Tooth-pullers advertised their experience and expertise by wearing strings of extracted teeth.[23] Although dentistry in sixteenth-century Europe bordered on torture,[24] some of the tools mentioned by Frois (or modern variants of the same), such as the parrot's beak, are still in use by dentists, albeit with anesthesia.

It is fun to imagine a tooth tied to a ten-foot string, which in turn is attached to an arrow, shot from a bow. However, as Okada suggests, Frois' mention of a bow and arrow probably is a reference to Japanese use of a bow drill.

16. Our spices and medicines are ground in a pounder or mortar; in Japan they are ground in a small copper vessel with an iron disk that is held between both [hands].

In medieval and early modern Europe, spices such as saffron, basil, and pepper were considered powerful medicine (not just seasoning), and thus Frois' mention of spices along with [other] medicines that were ground with a mortar and pestle (e.g. bezoars, relics, coral, salts).[25]

The Japanese variant of the pestle and mortar seemingly entailed an iron disk of some thickness that was rolled alternately left to right in a copper vessel.

17. Among us, pearls and seed pearls are used for personal ornamentation; in Japan they serve no other purpose than to be ground for the making of medicines.

Europeans may not have used pearls as medicine, but they did use various "stones" (i.e. bezoars) found in the stomachs of animals, not to mention ground-up

21 Cooper, *They Came to Japan*, 240.
22 Ibid., 191.
23 Andrès Pérez de Ribas, *History of the Triumphs of Our Holy Faith Amongst the Most Fierce and Barbarous Peoples of the New World*, trans. Daniel T. Reff, Maureen Ahern, and Richard Danford (Tucson: University of Arizona Press, 1999[1645]), 97.
24 James Wynbrandt, *The Excruciating History of Dentistry* (New York: St. Martin's Press, 1998).
25 Jack Turner, "Spices and Christians." In *Encompassing the Globe, Portugal and the World in the 16th & 17th Centuries*, ed. Jay Levenson (Washington, D.C.: Sackler Gallery, Smithsonian Institution, 2007), 48.

relics and mummies from Egypt![26] In Chinese-style medicine, pearl dust served to relax the spirit, settle the soul, brighten the eyes, and cure deafness.[27] That is to say, it was considered good for the nerves (pearls contain zinc, selenium, and calcium; inferior pearls are used today by pharmaceutical companies to make high-quality calcium).

18. Among us, a doctor who is not certified is punished and cannot treat patients; in Japan, anyone who wants to may take up practicing medicine as a way to make a living.

The thirteenth and later centuries in Europe witnessed the growth of cities and the establishment of hospitals and universities that awarded medical degrees. A medical degree, in the case of physicians, and practical knowledge and experience, in the case of surgeons and apothecaries, were generally required before an individual could legally practice medicine in a given locale, especially in cities.[28] Because a medical degree entailed years of study, there were relatively few university-trained physicians in sixteenth century Europe and most were employed by the rich and powerful.[29] In Frois' Portugal, a shortage of university-trained physicians led to an influx of doctors from Spain.[30] Finding a doctor was one thing; paying for it was another. At the time Frois wrote, the cost of seeing a university-trained doctor in England was a gold coin or ten shillings; in today's money this would be close to 100 pounds or 150 US dollars.[31] Professionalization was costly in another sense: while it may have reduced the number of "quacks" practicing medicine, it also drove experienced and knowledgeable midwives and other lay practitioners from the field, leaving the vast majority of Europeans to fend for themselves.

In Japan, there is an old saying that "a hundred men must die to make a good doctor." The Japanese were keenly aware of the presence of quacks, which they called *yabu-isha* or "bush-doctors."

19. Among us, it is always a dirty and shameful thing for a man to suffer from venereal disease[32]; Japanese men and women see this as a common occurrence and are not at all ashamed of it.

26 "Mummy," or ground up corpses preserved with bitumen, was in great demand in Europe ever since the days of the Crusades. When French physician Guy de la Fonteine investigated the mummy trade in Alexandria in 1564, he found that fresh corpses were being dug up to satisfy Europe's demand for this "medicine." Brian Fagan, "Mummies, Or the Restless Dead," *Horizon* XVII (1975):64–82.

27 Okada, *Yoroppa-Bunka to Nihon-Bunka*.

28 Brockliss and Jones, *The Medical World of Early Modern France*, 188–195.

29 Charles Webster, *Health, Medicine, and Mortality in the Sixteenth Century* (Cambridge: Cambridge University Press, 1979).

30 Isabel Mendes Drumond Braga, "Poor Relief in Counter-Reformation Portugal: The Case of Misericôrdias." In *Health Care and Poor Relief in Counter-Reformation Europe*, eds. Ole P. Grell, A. Cunningham, and J. Arrizabalaga, pp. 201–215 (London, Routledge, 1999), 206.

31 See Andrew Wear, *Knowledge and Practice in English Medicine, 1550–1680* (Cambridge: Cambridge University Press, 2000).

32 *Mula*, a colloquial expression in Portuguese for venereal disease

In 1493 syphilis appeared for the first time in Europe (gonorrhea, buboes, and genital ulceration had been a problem for centuries) and within two years raged throughout Europe, infecting one in five people.[33] However shameful the "French disease"[34] may have been, it became a chronic endemic disease of Europe during Frois' lifetime.

Syphilis may have reached Japan as early as 1512 and spread rapidly owing in part to the "casual" Japanese attitude toward prostitution.[35] Writing in 1576, the Jesuit Vice-Provincial of Japan, Francisco Cabral, noted that the Jesuits had treated Japanese with the "French evil" at their hospital in Funai.[36]

In this distich, Frois reveals an unspoken bias to the effect that only Christians were moral enough to feel shame (not that shame stopped many from having sex with strangers). Actually, while the Japanese may not have picked out sexually transmitted diseases for approbation, they long have been very ashamed of all incurable and visually distressing diseases. They were, until very recently, unrelenting in their attitude about leprosy, preserving a far more stringent segregation than found in the West.

33 Oriel, *The Scars of Venus*, 11.
34 The epidemic of 1493 seemingly began among the army of the French King Charles VIII. The epidemic was understood as punishment from God for the French armies' wanton destruction of Naples. Mary Elizabeth Perry, "Magdalens and Jezebels in Counter-Reformation Spain." In *Culture and Control in Counter-Reformation Spain*, eds. A.J. Cruz and M.E. Perry, pp. 124–145 (Minneapolis: University of Minnesota Press, 1992), 131.
35 Brett Walker, "Epidemic Disease, Medicine, and the Shifting Ecology of Ezo." In *Race, Ethnicity and Migration in Modern Japan*, Michel Weiner ed., pp. 397–424 (London: Routledge, 2004), 405.
36 James Murdoch, *A History of Japan*. 3 Vols. (New York: Ungar Publishing, 1964), II, Pt. I, 77. Note that there is no mention of syphilis or the "French evil"—perhaps edited out!—in the version of Cabral's letter that appears in *Cartas ... de Iapão & China*, I, 357.

10 Japanese writing and their books, paper, ink and letters

1. We write with twenty-two letters; they write with forty-eight in the kana alphabet and with infinite characters for a variety of representations.

The alphabet used by Romance languages at the time did not really have *k* or *w*, and *i* and *j* and *v* and *u*, respectively, were interchangeable, hence Frois' twenty-two rather than twenty-six letters.[1]

The letters in the Japanese syllabary, known as *kana* (as opposed to *kanji*, or Chinese characters), are uniformly short, like the Greek *mora*. In *kana*, consonants invariably come with an associated vowel sound, e.g. "ka, ke, ki, ko, ku," where each of these *open* syllables is represented in writing by a single letter. Japanese has only five vowels, and these are almost identical to those used in Latin. When a Japanese vowel appears alone in a given syllable (i.e. without a consonantal onset), it is also represented by a letter. The forty-eight letters in *kana* are the forty-seven comprising the syllabic poem on the vanity of life written by the abbot Kobo Daishi (d. C.E. 776), in which no syllable is used twice,[2] plus the controversial syllable "n," the only consonant without an associated vowel and thus the only consonant that can end a written word in Japanese. (The syllables "su" and "se" at the ends of words sometimes only get as far as their "s" sound when they are spoken, as a result of a process of reduction and elimination of the vowel nucleus.) The syllabary most commonly used today (but also in use at Frois' time) is not a poem, but is arranged instead according to the five vowel sounds. Its logic (unlike "our" somewhat illogical Roman alphabet) is reflected in its decimal-linked name: *goju-on* or "fifty-sounds."

Because Frois does not give details about *kana*, the contrast here would seem to be between a finite number of letters in European alphabets and the "infinite characters" used in Japanese.

---

1 Many of Frois' comments in this chapter receive further elaboration in what remains perhaps the best source on the Japanese language, particularly during the sixteenth-century: João Rodrigues' *Arte da Lingoa de Iapam* (1604); a facsimile edition prepared by Shima Shozo was published in 1969 by Bunka Shobo Hakubunsha. Book Three of Rodrigues' *Arte* is essentially a guide or treatise on epistolary style. See Jeroen Pieter Lamers, ed. and trans., *Treatise on Epistolary Style, João Rodriguez on the Noble Art of Writing Japanese Letters* (Ann Arbor: Center for Japanese Studies, 2002). For examples of Japanese letters, see Adriana Boscaro, *101 Letters of Hideyoshi* (Tokyo: Sophia University Press, 1975).

2 See Basil Hall Chamberlain, *Things Japanese, Being Notes on Various Subjects Connected with Japan*. Fourth revised and enlarged edition (London: John Murray, 1902), 378.

2. We study different arts and sciences through our books; they spend their entire lives coming to know the essential meaning of the characters [used in their writing system].

Frois grew up in a Europe that had been profoundly transformed during the fifteenth century by mass production of rag paper and Johannes Gutenberg's development of the printing press. The production of hundreds of thousands of books and pamphlets on innumerable subjects encouraged people from many walks of life to learn to read and to engage authors and ideas that were previously available only to the privileged elite. Movable type and the printing press made possible the Humanist education that Frois alludes to, which presupposed the ready availability of books of Latin grammar and rhetoric or books on Roman history by Livy or the works of Aristotle.

With respect to Japan, Frois accurately emphasizes the great extent to which education in Japan focused on mastering written Japanese. The children of the nobility studied at home rather than at a school, usually with a tutor.[3] Fellow Jesuit and linguist Rodrigues wrote that there were as many as 80,000 letters and characters to be learned, although it was generally enough to know about 10,000 characters or a little less, "because if these are known, many others can be understood by their composition." Note that not only the characters had to be learned, but the many ways that they may be pronounced and combined with the *kana*. As linguist and polemicist Roy Andrew Miller has noted, to say that Japanese employs a complex writing system is to risk the most sweeping understatement possible.[4]

3. We write across the page, going from left to right; they write going down the length of the page, and always from right to left.

On Jan. 14, 1549, Xavier wrote John III, King of Portugal, about this very matter:

> I am sending you a copy of the Japanese alphabet. Their way of writing is very different from ours because they write from the top of the page down to the bottom. I asked Paul why they did not write in our way and he asked me why we did not write in their way? He explained that as the head of a man is at the top and his feet are at the bottom, so too a man should write from top to bottom.[5]

Paul, who accompanied Xavier as a translator, was from Malacca, where he learned Christian doctrine. There is a Japanese saying that "writing is the man" (*bun-wa hito nari*), which makes Paul's reasoning even more poignant.

The Japanese on certain occasions also write horizontally, left to right, as well as right to left (on Buddhist plaques with the name of a temple, and perhaps most visibly, on the right side of a moving vehicle, such that the writing flows from the

3 Michael Cooper, *They Came to Japan* (Ann Arbor: University of Michigan Press 1999[1965]), 243.
4 *Japan's Modern Myth* (New York: Weatherhill, 1982).
5 Cooper, *They Came to Japan*, 180.

front to the back). Because both Chinese characters and Japanese syllables are written individually by moving the writing instrument from the upper left to the lower right in the space occupied by that character or letter, it would seem logical for the vertical lines to also go left to right, but for some reason this was reversed.

4. Where the final pages of our books end, that is where theirs begin.

If it were not for the reversal indicated in the note to #3 above this difference would not exist.

5. We hold printing in high regard; they use handwriting for nearly everything because their printing is unsuitable.

Block printing in Japan went back about 800 years before Frois' time. It is not clear why Frois found it "unsuitable." Fellow Jesuit Rodrigues seemed to be of a different opinion:

> First of all they take a sheet of paper the same size as the proposed book and carefully write on it in the desired style with the required number of lines, spaces and everything else. Then they glue this sheet face down on the block and with great skill cut away the blank paper, leaving only the block letters … They then carve these letters on the block with iron instruments … They are so dexterous in this art that they can cut a block in about the same time as we can compose a page.[6]

6. We write with quills from ducks and other birds; they use paintbrushes with hare-fur bristles and a bamboo handle.

Quill pens made from the feathers of waterfowl, particularly geese and less frequently swans, crows, hawks, eagles, and owls, were the writing instrument of choice in Europe. Although a brush may seem a crude and inefficient instrument with which to write, the physical and aesthetic satisfaction of the brush far exceeds that of the quill, an instrument that originated for the purpose of cutting as much as covering sheepskin parchment. The lifelong mastery of characters (see #2 above) is in large part not about memorizing characters, which really does not take that long, but learning to write characters in many different styles, far more different than our printing and cursive. Therefore, practicing this is an art, which is tremendously satisfying in itself.

7. Our ink is liquid; theirs is made in loaves that are ground as they write.

Ink was made in Europe from carbonized plants (e.g. the burned branches of the hawthorn tree) and minerals such as salt, which were mixed with wine, walnut oil, or other mediums.

The *sumi* ink of the Japanese usually is made by the writer, who grinds a bar on the device Frois mentions in #8 below. Sometimes servants, wives, or children did the grinding. One ink stick the size of a small candy bar, mixed with water, makes gallons and gallons of ink. Rodrigues wrote that "the best kind is made from the smoke of sesame oil … which adheres to a vessel, and from this they make paste."

---

6 Ibid., 251.

The paste was made into small loaves, "others long and others round," stamped and "decorated with various flowers, serpents and figures from legends ... they add some musk while making the best sort so that it will smell sweetly when they write with it."[7]

Today most Japanese would say they have no time to make their own ink. Still, it is not unheard of to receive as a gift an ink-stick in the form of a cicada covered with gold.

8. Our inkwells are round and made of horn; theirs are made of elongated pieces of stone.

In Europe "horners" (a respected trade) cut, sawed, carved and pressed animal horn into sheets that were used for everything from window and lantern panes to combs, chess-pieces, and inkwells.[8] In English we can even call an inkwell an "inkhorn." As one might imagine, these inkhorns ranged from simple to exquisitely carved works of art.

Frois' colleague, Rodrigues, elaborated on the Japanese inkstand, noting it was made of a slab of smooth marmoreal stone that was usually rectangular or oval in shape, or somewhere in between:

> They have a raised rim around the edge and a reservoir in the middle where the ink is ground. At one end of this there is a small well, gracefully carved, wherein they pour the water with which the ink is mixed ... This is rather like the stone or palette in which artists prepare and mix the colours that they use in painting.[9]

One of the most magnificent Japanese inkstands that we know of has an other-worldly reservoir below the cosmic, Mt. Feng-lai, with its three peaks. Today, most inkstands have no well *per se*, but a graduated slope, resembling a boat-launching ramp.

9. Our inkwells have lids and pen wipers[10]; in Japan they have neither of these.

Because the Japanese made ink as they needed it they had no need of a well to store it or a lid to keep the ink from drying out. Pen wipers (one or more little brushes for removing excess ink from the quill tip as one wrote) also were unnecessary. But the Japanese were not lacking accessories, as this contrast might seem to suggest. The Japanese had beautiful lacquered boxes in which they kept their writing supplies and equipment.

10. We have only four or five varieties of paper; in Japan they have more than fifty.

7 Michael Cooper, trans. and ed., *This Island of Japon, João Rodrigues' Account of 16th-Century Japan* (Tokyo: Kodansha, 1973[1620]), 332–333.

8 John Blair and Nigel Ramsay, *English Medieval Industries* (London: Hambledon and London, 2003), 365.

9 Cooper, *This Island of Japon*, 333.

10 *Poidouros*.

European texts during the Middle Ages were inscribed on parchment made of specially prepared animal skins, often from sheep, which have soft skins. By the thirteenth century, rag-based paper was being used throughout much of Europe. With the advent of the printing press, which required a medium with an even and absorbent surface, it became the material of choice for all manner of writing and printing.

Europeans were "paper-poor" as compared with the Japanese and Chinese. In China, Marco Polo was amazed to find that paper money (made from the bark of the mulberry tree) was used throughout the empire and for every transaction. In Japan paper was made from dozens of plants. Alcock mentioned an "infinite variety of paper" and sent sixty-seven different kinds to The International Exhibition in London in 1862.[11] Even today, the Japanese are rightly proud of their rich diversity in paper.

11. On official documents, we use the notary public's mark only; the Japanese each make their own mark on their letters, in addition to their signatures.

The notary public had its origins during the Roman Empire, when scribes or *scribae* were entrusted with drafting petitions to the emperor, recording public proceedings, transcribing state papers, and registering the decrees and judgments of magistrates.[12] The Japanese had no such office; individuals applied their own personal seal to whatever they valued, be it a contract or prints and paintings. Documents could be both signed and stamped, or just stamped, but they were seldom just signed.

12. Among us, the mark of the notary public never changes; in Japan they change marks whenever they want to.

Again, because there were no notary publics in Japan, it is hard to know who Frois was referring to with respect to the Japanese. Japanese "marks" or *kao* ("flower-stamp") were a stylized signature or monogram, which changed when an individual was promoted, as might be expected given that individuals often changed their names upon securing a new office. Because they generally had more than one *kao* at any given time, individuals sometimes used different combinations of *kao*. Okada guesses that great men had an average of about twenty "official" *kao* over the course of their lives.

13. Among us, all paper is made from old pieces of cloth; in Japan it is all made from tree bark.

The Chinese apparently were the first to make rag paper from discarded rags that were disassembled and mixed with water, making a pulp that was pressed into sheets. The technology spread across the Arab world in the ninth century, reaching Spain and the rest of Western Europe following the Crusades and by the late thirteenth century.

11 Sir Rutherford Alcock, *The Capital of the Tycoon, A Narrative of a Three Years' Residence in Japan* (London: Longman, Green, and Roberts, 1863), I, 443.
12 See Chapter 1 of Nigel Ready's *Brooke's Notary 13th edition* (Auckland: Brookers, 2009) and Serena Connolly, *Lives Behind the Laws* (Bloomington: Indiana University Press, 2010).

The Japanese knew how to make paper from rags but preferred paper made from tree bark and shrubs (e.g. hemp). Alcock found this tree-bark paper tougher than any paper in Europe. "Even the finer kinds can only be torn with difficulty, and the stronger qualities defy every effort."[13] As noted above, Alcock sent over sixty different kinds of Japanese paper to the International Exhibition in London in 1862.

14. We cannot convey complex thoughts in our letters without going on at great length; in Japan, letters are extremely short and very concise.

Frois was speaking from experience as regards the first part of this distich, as his lengthy annual reports even irritated Jesuit superiors. François Caron (1600–73), a French-born employee of the Dutch East-India Company, wrote that the terse writing style mentioned by Frois' was common to the Chinese, Japanese, and Koreans:

> A man that can contract much matter into a few lines, and [make it] intelligible, which is that which they all practice, is greatly esteemed amongst them; for such they employ to write their Letters, Petitions and the like to great persons; and truly it is admirable to see how full of substance, and with how few words these sort of writing is penned.[14]

Caron would seem to be talking about the telegraphic Chinese style of writing. Women in Japan often used what Rodrigues described as a "soft and fluent style" with a particular vocabulary, which was every bit as long as "ours."[15]

15. Among us, writing between the lines would be uncouth; in Japan they always intentionally[16] write between the lines.

Writing letters in which one shared experiences with fellow Jesuits, particularly one's superior, was an integral aspect of being a Jesuit missionary.[17] The Jesuits were part of a long tradition going back to the apostles and Greek and Roman forebears (e.g. Cicero) who understood "letter-writing" as a distinct genre. This European tradition, which conceived of the letter as an intimate conversation between friends,[18] dictated that a letter received was answered with a "fresh" response.

---

13 Alcock, *The Capital of the Tycoon*, I, 442.

14 Cooper, *They Came to Japan*, 176–177.

15 *Treatise on Epistolary Style*, 72–73.

16 *Vaza to*. It is surprising that Frois would use Japanese for an ordinary expression such as "on purpose" (*waza to*), particularly as his occasional use of Japanese is largely confined to physical objects.

17 Missionary correspondence often was collected and "edited" by superiors and then published in volumes that were read by Jesuits, particularly novices, as well as the general public back in Europe. These books of letters reinforced the Society's particular values and beliefs. Because they often recounted martyrdoms, miracles, and exotic heathen practices, they also made for exciting reading for a secular elite that had grown up reading the lives of the saints.

18 Brian W. Ogilvie, *The Science of Describing* (Chicago: University of Chicago Press, 2006), 82.

With respect to Japan, Okada[19] mentions a number of types of recognized *gyoukan-gaki* or "line-between-writing." There is *otte-gaki* or "chasing-writing," something like our postscript; *kaeshi-gaki* or "return writing," where one person's letter is returned with the reply between the lines; and *nao-nao-gaki* or "this-too-this-too-writing," which simply adds more detail.

If you did not read Okada's notes, you might conclude that this writing between the lines was phonetic syllabary written small, next to Chinese characters, thus supplying the pronunciation in the case of hard-to-read names, unique usage, or for the sake of poor readers. Such wonderful little training wheels (called *furigana*) permit one to play with Chinese characters. They have nevertheless reaped scorn from the West: "One hesitates for an epithet to describe a system of writing which is so complex that it needs the aid of another system to explain it."[20] Even the Japanese novelist turned pedagogue, Yamamoto Yuzo, has expressed exasperation at the procession of "disgusting black bugs" that crawl around our sentences.

16. Our letters are sent folded; Japanese letters are rolled up.

While the Japanese are fond of *origami* or "fold-paper" art, and at times folded their letters,[21] Frois may be correct that letters ordinarily were rolled. It is hard to say why rolls might have been preferred. One reason may have been the availability of cheap tubes in the form of bamboo. Japanese literature does offer examples of letters that were folded and stuffed into the bosom for carrying, so the difference was not absolute. When during the nineteenth century Japan began "modernizing/Westernizing" and sending mail by the packet, Morse wrote that the old style letterboxes big enough to fit a number of rolls (see #19 below) were abandoned as too bulky. Letters written on paper attached to a roll "… were torn off, … flattened by smoothing with the hand, and slid into a long, narrow envelope."[22]

16A. Among us, we indicate the year in which we are writing; the Japanese give only the day of the lunar [month] in which it is sent.

(This contrast was not numbered in the original manuscript.) The European/Christian worldview is predicated on a linear, progressive notion of the passage of time, which it is believed will culminate in Christ's return and life without end (for the saved). Therefore, marking the passage of years since Christ's birth (i.e. AD, *Anno Domini*, The Year of Our Lord) has figured in European timekeeping since the early sixth century, when a Scythian Monk, Dionysius Exiguus, introduced the qualifier *Anno Domini*.

Many of the letters of Hideyoshi, translated by Adriana Boscaro,[23] follow the pattern suggested by Frois (e.g. "6th month, 20th day," "12th month, 2nd day").

19 Akio Okada, trans. and ed., Yoroppa-Bunka to Nihon-Bunka [European Culture and Japanese Culture] (Tokyo: Iwanami Shoten, 1965).
20 G.B. Sansom, *Historical Grammar of the Japanese Language* (Oxford: Clarendon Press, 1928), 44.
21 Boscaro, *101 Letters of Hideyoshi*, xi.
22 Edward J. Morse, *Japan Day By Day, 1877, 1878–1879, 1882–1883*. 2 Vols. Boston: Houghton Mifflin, 1917), II, 410.
23 Bosacaro, *101 Letters of Hidyoshi*.

17. The Christian era never changes from the birth of Christ to the end of the world; eras in Japan change six or seven times during the lifetime of a king.

As suggested above, Shinto and Buddhism, the religious foundations of Japanese culture, make no claims to the unfolding of time in a linear, progressive fashion. The Japanese did not live out their lives reflecting on their temporal place in "God's unfolding plan." What mattered was who was emperor; the latter could change the course of a million lives. Thus, the year in Japan was reset to "Year One" whenever an emperor died and a new reign began, or when a regent made a major policy change or there was a major disaster (the change was made for the sake of better luck). In the six decades before the *Tratado* was written there were new eras beginning in 1521, '28, '32, '55, '58, '70 and '73. And just before the Meiji Reformation (1868), we find eras beginning in 1844, '48, '54, '60, '61, '64 and '65.

In 1869 the *gengo* system was modified so that the era would only change with the inauguration of a new emperor. The system continues today alongside the Western/Christian system of reckoning time. Thus Japanese newspapers generally put both year dates on the top of each page (for example, 2005 appears alongside Heisei 17).

18. Our letters are sent sealed with beeswax or sealing wax; in Japan they place a small ink seal over the signature.

The Japanese actually had more ways of sealing letters than Europeans. Okada[24] mentions "glue-sealing, twist-sealing, knot-sealing, and fold-sealing and so forth." But they did not stamp warm wax, be it bee's wax or wax made from a mixture of shellac, rosin, and turpentine. The symbolic closure Frois referred to was achieved by making an ink mark, either an initial, a diagonal line, or a diagonal line with a small line crossing it to make a sign resembling the syllable *me*, which stood for *shime* or "closed=tight=done." Today it is common to initial documents in the same way, with the mark crossing the divide to make what is, to use a printing term, a registration.

19. Our letters are sent in bundled stacks; theirs are sent in small, elongated lacquered boxes made for that purpose.

Every year, usually in March, a fleet bound for Asia sailed from Lisbon, arriving six months later in Goa, India. Another year might go by before the ships, loaded with spices, trade goods, passengers, and correspondence (collected from as far away as Japan), made the return trip to Europe. It was normal during this lengthy period between voyages for Jesuit correspondence to accumulate before it was eventually bundled and dispatched from Japan to India and then on to Europe.

As Frois indicates, the Japanese transported letters in special waterproof containers called *fubako* or *fuminohako* (letter-boxes).

20. In Europe paper is beaten flat with an iron mallet on a smooth stone; in Japan they roll it up on a round pole and beat it with two other poles.

---

24 *Yoroppa-Bunka to Nihon-Bunka.*

One of the first stages of rag-paper production entailed soaking discarded linen cloth, including underwear, in water and sometimes lime to break down the fibers. The resulting mass was subsequently placed in a trough and beaten before being subjected to further processing in vats, drying on felt, and final pressing to remove excess water. Although Frois may have observed rag-pulp being beaten by hand during his youth, by the time he left Portugal (1548) water mills were being employed in Europe for large-scale paper production.[25]

In Kochi Prefecture, which is famous for its handmade paper (*Toshi Washi*), Japanese artisans still make some of the highest-quality paper in the world, employing methods that go back to the sixteenth century, including beating the still unfinished paper with poles.

21. We clean the ink off our quills by wiping them on our black clothing; the Japanese suck them clean with their mouths.

Although the Jesuit order did not require members to wear particular garb, the Jesuits early on distinguished themselves by a preference for the simple black cassock worn by priests (thus the appellation "the black robes"). With respect to the Japanese, any sucking that is done is done after the ink has been essentially removed from the brush by brushing it dry. Arguably the sucking is to smooth out the hairs and leave the brush with a sharp point. This has more to do with arranging the point of the brush before it fully dries than with cleaning.

22. We write our letters at a table or desk; the Japanese write theirs upon the fingers of the left hand.

When the Japanese teenagers sent by the Jesuits as ambassadors to Europe met with Phillip II at the recently completed Escorial, in 1585, they gave him a gift of a writing desk made of bamboo.[26] In point of fact, the Japanese had very nice portable desks and generally used them to write. Still, prints from the seventeenth century often show letter writers holding the paper in their left hand and the brush in their right. This delicate style of writing, with its touching body language, was possible because a brush does not need to push down on paper like a pen to release ink. Writing on paper held by the hand releases a different, connected sensibility physically (and perhaps mentally) that is not there when writing on a desk or the floor, where Japanese calligraphy is usually done.

23. We seal our letters with scissors; they seal theirs with a knife.

Frois wrote "seal" in both halves of this distich; he presumably meant to write "open." The knife used by the Japanese as a letter-opener was called a *sasuga* ("stab sword") and was kept in a writing box with the inkstand, ink stick, water vessel, etc.

24. We sprinkle sand on our letters [to absorb excess ink]; theirs is absorbed quickly by their paper.

25 David Landau and Peter Parshall, *The Renaissance Print 1470–1550* (New Haven: Yale University Press, 1996), 15.

26 J.A. Abranches Pinto, Yoshimoto Okamoto, and Henri Bernard, S.J., eds. La Premiere Ambassadi du Japon en Europe. *Monumenta Nipponica Monographs* 6 (Tokyo: Sophia University, 1942), 88.

Sand has a wonderful capacity to absorb water or oil, and of course, ink, which, as noted above, often consisted in large part of one or both mediums.

25. Our handwriting is very small; theirs is larger than our uppercase letters.

Small, indeed! The British Library has one of two extant copies of Alessandro Valignano's 1601 manuscript account of the Jesuit mission to Japan (*Libro Primero del Principio ...*), and the lettering is so fine and small that a modern reader requires (or certainly benefits from) a magnifying glass. The majority of classical texts discovered and celebrated by Humanists during the Renaissance were in Carolingian miniscule,[27] which does not use all upper-case letters. Well-educated Europeans such as Frois and Valignano grew up imitating the Carolingians. For this and other reasons (e.g. paper and ink were expensive[28]), European handwriting tended to be on the small side.

Now that brushes are used only for signing art gallery registers and writing old-style New Year greetings, Japanese letters are written by ballpoint or are printed about the same size as ours, despite, in the case of characters, holding ten times the visual information.

26. The stanzas in our ballads are made up of four, six or eight lines; all Japanese songs contain only two verses, with no rhyme.

During Frois' lifetime the Italian Renaissance exerted a significant influence on Portuguese literature and many of Frois' contemporaries followed Petrarch's example of ballads that followed the octave and sextet rhyming scheme (i.e. abba, abba, aba, aba).[29] Even before the Italian Renaissance, Portugal had its own medieval tradition of poetic parallelism that resulted in ballads with even-numbered stanzas.[30]

The name for Japanese classical verse, *waka*, literally breaks down into "peace=Japanese + song." Poets were said to "sing" poetry rather than to "make" or "write" it. (The Chinese character for the verb was different than that used for singing a truly melodic song, however.) Frois' use of *cantigas* ('canticles' or poetry set to music) for Japanese poems suggests he understood the sung aspect of the verse. While Japanese poetry, unlike Chinese poetry, did not use obvious end-rhyme, it is not right to say that there was no consonance. There is considerable Dickinsonian rhyme, which is usually considered to be assonance or "vowel rhyme," which can be brought out through parsing.

---

27 Andrew Pettegree, *The Book in the Renaissance* (New Haven: Yale University Press, 2010), 7. See also Stephen Greenblatt, *The Swerve, How the World Became Modern* (New York: W.W. Norton, 2011).

28 Marques, *Daily Life in Portugal*, 231. John Correia-Afonso, S.J., *Letters from the Mughal Court* (St. Louis: Institute of Jesuit Sources, 1981), 15.

29 Joaquim de Carvalho, *Estudos sobre a Cultura Portuguesa do século XVI*, Volume II (Coimbra: University of Coimbra, 1948), 7; Luís de Sousa Rebelo, "Language and Literature." In *Portuguese Oceanic Expansion, 1400–1800*, eds. Francisco Bethencourt and Diogo Ramada Curto, pp. 358–390 (Cambridge: Cambridge University Press, 2007).

30 Manuel da Costa Fontes, "Between Ballad and Parallelistic Song: *A Condessa Traidora* in the Portuguese Oral Tradition." In *Medieval and Renaissance Spain and Portugal*, eds. Martha E. Schaffer and Antonio Corijo Ocaña, pp. 182–196 (Rochester: Tamesis, 2006).

*27. Our reading is done very quickly; when they read, they do so inserting pauses and taking little leaps [*forward in the text*].*

Most Japanese can read as quickly as Westerners, despite the fact that the pronunciation of many characters depends upon a context that is sometimes not grasped until the word has passed before the eyes. Here Frois must be describing how the Japanese read Chinese or pseudo-Chinese, called *kanbun*. This is one of the cleverest ways to read that has ever been invented, for the Japanese mark the edges of the lines with a number of signs that indicate how to change the word order and parse the grammar of the original as one reads. They are translating, then, or rather, doing simultaneous interpretation. One method of doing this does not vocalize; the other, which does, also gives native Japanese word equivalents for many of the characters.

This writing is of intellectual interest because it shows how Chinese characters (or any large vocabulary common to more than one language) allowed for communication between different languages.

28. We write on tall tables, seated on chairs; they write while seated on small stools placed on the ground or on mats.

This distich appears to be related to #22 above, where the focus is on one style of Japanese writing that does not entail use of a desk. Ironically, the traditional Japanese desk (going back to at least the sixteenth century) is one of the few examples of "furniture" in Japan. The small desk has folding legs and sometimes a writing surface on which the angle can be adjusted. Arguably, during the latter half of the twentieth century Japan could boast more desks *per capita* than any nation in the world. A Japanese child may not have their own bedroom but they invariably have their own desk.

29. In Europe books are bound by sewing the pages together along the margins; in Japan they sew the ends together but the folds remain loose.

Well into the twentieth century, particularly in Portugal and the Spanish-speaking world, the pages of books were, as Frois suggests, sewn together close to both the left and right margins. The task or honor of cutting the right edge of the pages was left to the individual who purchased the book.

It may be difficult for the reader to gather from Frois' description how Japanese books were bound. Imagine a very long piece of paper, folded back and forth on itself like the folds of an accordion. Then imagine it sewn on one side only, and not right at the edge but half an inch or so from the edge where the spine would be, if there were a spine. The other side is just left as it is. Because the leaves are not cut with these books, one can remove the thread and be left with a very long piece of paper that has print on just one side.

11 Houses, construction, gardens and fruits

1. Our houses are tall and multi-storied; in Japan they generally are low and at ground level.

European cities, including Lisbon, experienced dramatic population growth during the sixteenth century, which led to the erection of apartment buildings with upwards of four and five stories.[1] As Frois suggests, the Japanese also erected multi-story buildings but more frequently their *Shoin*-style homes were single-story structures that were virtually wall-less. Chamberlain, following Morse, noted:

> The side of the [Japanese] house, composed at night of wooden sliding doors called *amado*, is stowed away in boxes during the day-time. In the summer, everything is thus open to the outside air.[2]

Even with the floor raised a foot or so off the ground for the sake of ventilation, the *Shoin*-style house[3] had to deal with an ever-present threat of mildew and fleas (see #11 below). To block the rain and provide ventilation, the roof tended to extend well beyond the walls. This design feature also limits the amount of sunlight coming in from overhead. The potted plants that most Japanese kept (and still keep) outside, and the inner gardens of the wealthy, all would suffer from multi-story dwellings. For these reasons, Japan in recent decades passed "sunlight laws" to ensure that new development did not take away people's right to sunlight.[4]

---

1 Between 1528 and 1590, the population of Lisbon went from 70,000 to over 120,000. Vitorino Magalháes Godinho, *A Estrutura Da Antiga Sociedade Portuguesa* (Lisbon: Arcádia, 1980), 27. See also Raffaella Sarti, "The Material Conditions of Family Life." In *The History of the European Family, Volume I, Family Life in Early Modern Times*, 1500–1789, eds. David I. Kertzer and Marzio Barbagli, pp. 11–23 (New Haven: Yale University Press, 2001), 7; Damião de Góis, *Lisbon in the Renaissance, A New Translation of Urbis Olisiponis Descriptio*, trans. Jeffrey S. Ruth (Ithaca, N.Y.: Ithaca Press, 1996[1554]); A.R. Disney, *A History of Portugal and the Portuguese Empire* (Cambridge; Cambridge University Press, 2009), 148.

2 Basil Hall Chamberlain, *Things Japanese, Being Notes on Various Subjects Connected with Japan.* Fourth revised and enlarged edition (London: John Murray, 1902), 24; Edward S. Morse, *Japanese Homes and Their Surroundings* (New York: Dover Publications, 1961[1886]). The latter is still considered an excellent source on Japanese architecture.

3 See Fumio Hashimoto, *Architecture in the Shoin Style: Japanese Feudal Residences*, trans. H.M. Horton (Tokyo: Kodansha and Shibundo, 1981).

4 The contemporary situation in Japan is summarized well by Richard Ronald, "Homes and houses, senses and spaces." In *Home and Family in Japan*, eds. R. Ronald and A. Alexy, pp. 174–200 (London: Routledge, 2011).

2. Our houses are made of stone and mortar; theirs are made of wood, bamboo, straw and mud.

Stone was fairly plentiful in Mediterranean Europe and both rich and poor took advantage of it to erect houses that ranged from humble to palatial.[5] In Frois' Portugal granite was a popular building material in the north, while houses of mud and stucco were common in the south.[6] Structures of wood were more common in northern Europe (e.g. the wooden churches of Scandinavia, which are often said to appear oriental). As Frois indicates, wood was the main material for Japanese building. Frois' Jesuit contemporary, Rodrigues, elaborated:

> All the houses of the nobles are constructed of various sorts of precious woods, the usual kind being very fine cedar which is most pleasing on account of its luster; all the pillars are made of this cedar or of even more precious wood. Ordinary folk make use of pine or other inferior timber, although well-bred people build at least their guest house with cedar.

Rodrigues went on to note that wood, being light, was mobile, and "Thus they can move an entire house of this sort to another place nearby without dismantling it, apart from removing the roof from on top because of its weight, and this we have seen them do many times."[7]

3. Our houses have foundations that are deep in the ground; Japanese houses have a single stone under each hashira and these stones rest on the ground.

The *hashira* are large square, wooden pillars standing at each corner and in two walls to support the center-ridge of the roof. All but the smallest houses also have a central *hashira*, which usually retains at least part of its natural features. Some were and still are completely natural, a reassuringly powerful piece of unpainted, polished natural wood that can be seen and felt inside the house. The butt of each *hashira* rests on a stone, the bottom half of which is slightly under-ground and visible from the outside. Hashira are usually of cedar and resist rot and termites. These pillars may rest freely on their non-foundations, but they are linked together on top by transverse beams. This is another reason the houses can be moved without being dismantled, as Rodrigues pointed out.

4. Our doors generally hang on hinges; Japanese doors almost all slide on sills.

Sliding doors save space and do not push in or pull out air, which is why they increasingly are the choice for modern buildings. Japanese windows, whether door-size or occasionally small, likewise slide on sills. One exception to this rule was noted by Morse: the Japanese privy often has a hinged (butterfly joint) door.

---

5 Sarti, "The Material Conditions of Family Life," 4.
6 Orlando Ribeiro, *Geografia e Civilização: Temas Portuguesas* (Lisbon: Livros Horizontes, 1992), 31; A. H. de Oliveira Marques, *Daily Life in Portugal in the Late Middle Ages* (Madison: University of Wisconsin Press, 1971), 97.
7 Michael Cooper, *They Came to Japan* (Ann Arbor: University of Michigan Press, 1965), 216–217.

5. The partitions dividing our rooms are made of stone and mortar or brick; Japanese rooms are divided by doors made of paper.

Japanese houses generally have no internal walls *per se*. The house is divided into rooms by lightly framed sliding "doors" made of paper. The items described in this and the previous distich are referred to as "doors" in English and Portuguese. The Japanese actually use different terms. The outside front door is called a *to*, the translucent paper inner door and veranda doors are called *shoji*, and the generally opaque and lightly ornamented room partitions are called *fusuma*. The *fusuma* are grooved above as well as below in such a manner that they can easily be lifted and removed from their tracks, turning several rooms into one.

6. Our roofs are made of tile; in Japan they generally are made of wooden planks, straw, or bamboo.

The homes of Portuguese nobles may have had tile roofs, but the majority of people in Portugal lived in simple rectangular homes with roofs of thatch; even some city dwellers had roofs made of broom straw.[8]

Japanese nobles, like their European counterparts, often had tile roofs. Indeed, *raku* ware, which was invented in the 1570s for the tea ceremony, was the work of a gifted artisan who made roof tiles.[9] That said, most roofs in Japan, particularly in rural areas, were similar to those on farmhouses in Portugal or England. They appear as an extension of the landscape or even a veritable flower garden. Here is a nineteenth century description by Morse:

> In many cases the ridge is flat, and this area is made to support a luxuriant growth of iris, or the red lily (fig. 41). A most striking feature is often seen in the appearance of a brown somber-colored village, wherein all the ridges are aflame with bright-red blossoms of the lily; of farther south, near Tokio [sic], the purer colors of the blue and white iris form floral crests of exceeding beauty.[10]

Sometimes light and dark colored straws were alternatively laid so that the cleanly cut eaves (up to three feet thick) were decorative. They offered superb insulation and came in a great variety of regional styles, especially in terms of the central ridge design. Note that housing-related Chinese characters show a Far Eastern tendency to identify shelter with the roof (i.e. the house radical is a roof).

7. The wood in our rooms is highly finished and polished; the wood in the rooms where they hold their tea ceremony[11] is just as it comes from the woods, in imitation of nature.

---

8 Marques, *Daily Life in Portugal*, 117, 119 (fig. 67).

9 Nicole C. Rousmaniere, "Tea Ceremony Utensils & Ceramics." In *Japan's Golden Age, Momoyama*, ed. Money L. Hickman, pp. 203–236 (New Haven: Yale University Press, 1996), 206.

10 Edward S. Morse, *Japanese Homes and Their Surroundings* (New York: Dover, 1961[1886]), 93.

11 *Chanoyu*, which transliterates as "tea's hot-water," refers to what is commonly called the tea ceremony. In Japanese, different words are used for hot water (*yu*), water (*mizu*) and cold water (*ohiya*).

Rodrigues wrote many magical pages about the *sukiya*, the name for a tea hut.[12] Because meeting to drink cha was for "the quiet and restful contemplation of the things of nature, ... Everything employed in this ceremony is as rustic, rough, completely unrefined and simple as nature made it."[13] Such taste is understandable among *literati* (and that includes many samurai), who respected sage-poets who lived simple lives in the mountains.[14] What is perhaps more impressive is that some ordinary houses showed similar taste. Kaempfer wrote:

> The ceiling is sometimes neither planed nor smoothed, by reason of the scarcity [rare] and curious running of the veins and grain of the wood, in which case it is only cover'd with a thin slight couch of a transparent varnish, to preserve it from decaying.[15]

In the first book on China published in the West (1569), Gaspar da Cruz wrote something very similar about the houses of common folk in China: "The timber is all very smooth and very even, and very finely wrought and placed, that it seemeth to be all polished ..."[16]

8. Our rooms generally have windows that allow in a lot of light; the seating area[17] *of their tea huts are windowless and dark.*

This contrast is ironic if not misleading because the Japanese *Shoin*-style house was essentially all windows and no walls. Because glass was expensive, European houses in the sixteenth century tended to be all walls and no windows, figuratively speaking.[18] However, this contrast does not appear to concern houses *per se*, but the main seating area in a Japanese tea hut as compared with a "living room" or *cámara de paramento* in a well-to-do Portuguese home.[19] Frois' preoccupation with the tea hut reflects the fact that the tea ceremony was at the peak of its popularity in 1585. The small, enclosed tea hut, allowed for some very quiet person-to-person communion, and it was a democratic place where the usual rank-related formalities were suspended. All in all, the Jesuits appreciated these retreats, if only because these small shrines to

---

12 See especially João Rodrigues, Arte del Cha, ed. J.L. Alvarez-Taladriz. *Monumenta Nipponica Monographs 14* (Tokyo: Sophia University, [1620]1954, 81–96

13 João Rodrigues, *This Island of Japon*, trans. and ed., Michael Cooper (Tokyo: Kodansha International Limited, 1973[1620]), 264.

14 See Dennis Hirota, *Wind in the Pines, Classic Writings of the Way of Tea as a Buddhist Path* (Fremont, California: Asian Humanities Press, 1995).

15 Engelbert Kaempfer, *The History of Japan, Together With a Description of the Kingdom of Siam, 1690–92*. 3 Vols. Glasgow: James MacLehose and Sons, 1906[1690–92]), II, 319.

16 See C.R. Boxer, ed. *South China in the sixteenth century, being the narratives of Galeote Pereira, Fr. Gaspar da Cruz, O.P. [and] Fr. Martín de Rada, O.E.S.A. (1550–1575)* (London: Hakluyt Society, 1953), 99.

17 *Zaxiqis.*

18 Most window glass in Frois' Europe was made from blown glass cylinders that were opened into sheets. Such windows were generally small and relatively expensive, as compared with windows with "panes" of paper, pressed horn, or oiled canvas.

19 Marques, *Daily Life in Portugal*, 121–122.

quiet and calmness were embraced by high-ranking Japanese Christians who made *chanoyu*, or the way-of-tea, a discipline of sorts.

9. Treasure for us consists of items ornamented with gemstones and objects made of gold and silver; the Japanese treasure old cauldrons, old and broken porcelain, clay vases, etc.

Europe during the first half of the sixteenth century, especially Spain and Portugal, was awash in gold, silver, and precious stones, mostly from colonial ventures in Africa, Mexico, Peru, and Asia. Kings, nobles, merchants, and church officials (encouraged by the Council of Trent) commissioned all manner of gilt and jewel-encrusted art and religious objects to decorate their homes, churches, and chapels.[20]

The Japanese "treasures" referenced here are all items related to *chanoyu* (See also Chapter 14, #21). Rodrigues explains:

> The vessels and dishes used in this gathering are not of gold, silver, or any other precious metal, nor are they richly and finely wrought; instead they are made of clay or iron without any polish, embellishment or anything which might incite the appetite to desire them for their beauty and luster ... there are utensils, albeit of earthenware, which come to be worth ten, twenty or thirty thousand cruzados or even more—something which will appear as madness and barbarity to other nations that come to hear of it.[21]

As an aside, the Portuguese and Spaniards actually made handsome profits importing old pottery from the Philippines, especially caddies reputed to be especially good at keeping tea fresh in the humid season.

10. We decorate our rooms[22] with tapestries, godomecis,[23] and drapes from Flanders;[24] the Japanese have folding screens of paper[25] that are decorated in gold or with black ink.

Portugal's elite and indeed the wealthy throughout Europe were fond of wall coverings, particularly from Flanders and Italy.[26] Tapestries were not only

20 Dias, "The Manueline," 32–34.
21 Rodrigues, *This Island of Japon*, 264–265.
22 The Portuguese original is corrupted. Although Schütte suggests 'houses,' it seems that 'rooms' (from '*camaras*') is more probable, given that this is the term Frois uses in both 7 and 8 above. It appears that "rooms" is also the referent in 11 and 12 below.
23 Ricardo de la Fuente Ballesteros, ed. and trans., *Tratado sobre las contradicciones y diferencias de costumbres entre los europeos y japoneses por Luis Frois* (Salamanca: Ediciones Universidad de Salamanca, 2003[1585]), 103, suggests that the term is from the Arabic *gadaamesii*, which, according to Corominas and Pascal, refers to the Libyan city of Gadames, where this famous item was made. The word is documented as early as the twelfth century, in the poem *El Cid*. In Spanish the word is rendered as *guadamecíes* (plural of guadamecí).
24 *Panos de Frandes.*
25 *Beobus* [*byôbu*], or in Portuguese, *biombo.*
26 Pedro Dias, "Manueline Art." In *Museum With No Frontiers Exhibition The Manueline, Portuguese Art During the Great Discoveries*, pp. 22–38 (Lisbon: Programa de Incremento do Turismo Cultural, 2002), 34.

decorative but helped insulate large, otherwise drafty rooms. Unlike frescoes and paintings, tapestries also were highly portable.[27] So too were *godomecis*, which were rectangular pieces (ca. 66 × 45 centimeters) of worked leather that were adorned with paint or raised artwork and used as a decorative covering on walls, chests, or as bed canopies.[28]

Japanese folding screens (*byôbu*) nearly always had six panels.[29] Both gold dust and black ink were commonly used to paint scenes or poetry on them. This is, in a sense, an extension of the last two contrasts, for paper is less substantial than tapestry. *Byôbu* are still used in Japanese-style homes and especially restaurants.

11. We decorate our [rooms] with carpets and rugs; they use straw cushions.

Carpets from the Middle East and Ottoman Turkey were a symbol of taste and wealth in Frois' Europe.[30] This much is apparent from Renaissance art, which often depicts the homes of Europe's elite; the homes are decorated with "oriental" rugs on walls and floors and draped over tables ("prayer rugs"). Ambassadors from Venice who visited Portugal in 1580 were amazed at the money (40,000 *cruzados*) spent by the Portuguese on tapestries.[31]

The cushions favored by the Japanese were/are a good four to six inches thick, like a mattress. Japanese houses were built so as to conform to what was a standard mattress measurement (called *ma*; approximately three feet by six feet). Even today the size of a dwelling for rent is advertised in terms of this cushion-size measurement. A *roku-ma*, or six-cushion apartment, would be understood to have 108 square feet of floor space (a figure that would not include the kitchen and bathroom). This standardization of mats extends to other areas as well, since the length of the mat (180 centimeters) is also the height of "paper doors" of all types and the length of all closets and many beds.

Tatami, while beautiful, soft, light and easier to keep clean than carpet, have one Achilles heel: they are loved by fleas. If you are wealthy enough to get new mats every few years, have a well-ventilated floor (all Japanese houses are supposed to be built up from the ground, but not all actually are) and do not allow your cats to rove, *tatami* will do you no wrong. Otherwise, you will get fleas. One wonders if most Japanese learn to appreciate them as much as the eighteenth-century Japanese poet, Kobayashi Issa, whose one hundred-plus flea haiku[32] include:

27 Lisa Jardine, *Worldly Goods: a New History of The Renaissance* (New York: Nan A. Talese, 1996).

28 Marques, *Daily Life in Portugal*, 131–132.

29 For some examples of these screens, which depict Japanese interaction with Europeans, see Money L. Hickman, ed., *Japan's Golden Age: Momoyama* (New Haven: Yale University Press, 1996); Yukio Lippit, "Os Biombos Dos Bárbaros Do Sul." In *Portugal E O Mundo Nos Séculos XVI E XVII*, 343–354 (Lisbon: Museu Nacional de Arte Antíga, 2009). See also *Naban Art: A Loan Exhibition from Japanese Collections*, eds. Shin'ichi Tani and Tadashi Sugase (International Exhibitions Foundation, 1973).

30 Rosamond Mack, *Bazaar to Piazza: Islamic Trade and Italian Art, 1300–1600* (Berkeley: University of California Press, 2001).

31 Dias, "Manueline Art, 34.

32 Shinano Kyoiku-kai, ed., *Issa Zenshuu*, Vol. 1, Hokku. (Nagano: Shinano Mainichi Shinbunsha, 1979), 377.

beauty is as beauty does [title]

the fleas in my hut
are cute as can be:
because, because
they sleep with me![33]

12. We [decorate] our [rooms] with leather trunks and chests[34] from Flanders or with cedar chests; the Japanese [decorate] theirs with black baskets made from cow hides.

Marques notes that the chest was second only to the bed as the most important piece of furniture in a Portuguese home of the late Middle Ages.[35] In Frois' day the homes of Europe's elite still proudly displayed large, elaborately decorated chests of carved wood or leather, including a bride's coffer or chest. The Flemish were particularly known for their chests, including those covered with leather (*cuir bonilli*). The leather was first steeped in melted wax and boiled; once hardened it was embossed, painted, gilded, or inlaid with velvet.[36]

On the Japanese side, it is surprising to find even this black basket, which, according to Okada, was probably woven with a wisteria warp and hide weave, then lightly lacquered. Japanese rooms generally have a large closet (*oshi-ire*, literally "stuff-in") that includes a shelved area and boxes for storage. Valuables, however, went under the floors, or in the case of the wealthy, into special storerooms. Quality space could thus be saved for people rather than furniture, which was regarded as so much clutter.

Today, most Japanese have more things to fit in fewer and smaller *oshi-ire* closets, especially in the cheaply designed apartments called "mansions" that many Japanese call home. The result is clutter, and more interesting still is the fact that this development was observed as early as 1891 by Eliza Scidmore:

> The very use of foreign furnishings or utensils seems to abate the national rage for cleanliness, and in any tea-house that aspires to be conducted in the

---

33 *Iori no nomi kawai ya ware to inurunari* (shack's flea/s cute! me-with sleep-become).
34 Frois used the word *arca* for both leather and cedar furniture. (In Portuguese, the word encompasses chest, large box, treasure and the ark). Another interesting note is that Frois spells Flanders as "Frandes" rather than "Flandres." One might assume that the loss of 'r' in the final syllable and the substitution of 'r' for 'l' in the initial syllable are a reflection of Frois' lengthy contact with the Japanese language, particularly given the well-known phenomenon of Japanese speakers who confuse the liquid consonants 'r' and 'l' when they speak European languages. Such an assumption would be mistaken, however, as this substitution of 'r' for 'l' is a common feature in the historical development of Portuguese. There are many such examples, so while Latin *fluitare* 'to flow' is the root of Modern Portuguese *flutuar* 'to float,' we also find examples such as *frota* 'fleet (of ships)' from the Old French *flote*, as well as *branco* 'white' from the Old Germanic *blank*.
35 Marques, *Daily Life in Portugal*, 127.
36 Esther Singleton, *Furniture* (New York: Duffield and Company, 1911), 102.

foreign fashion, one discovers a dust, disorder, shabbiness, and want of care that is wholly un-Japanese.[37]

13. People in Europe sleep up off the floor on beds or cots; in Japan they sleep down low on the mats with which the house is floored.

Frois may overstate the extent to which Europeans slept in cots and beds, as many a peasant was happy to have dry straw to sleep on.[38] Certainly those who could afford a bed were likely to share it with other family members or servants.[39] Well into the eighteenth century concerned clergy complained that a shortage of beds encouraged incest ("How many sins are committed for lack of bread, and how many for want of a bed?")[40] Marques suggests that it was largely the wealthy in Portugal who enjoyed beds. These often were made of heavy, carved wood and had as many as three mattresses (straw, wool or cotton, feathers), not to mention fine linens and a canopy with curtains.[41]

Many Japanese still prefer sleeping on a futon or "heavily wadded comforter," to use Morse's description. After explaining that the ordinary Japanese house had a minimum of furniture, Alice Mabel Bacon waxed enthusiastically about the futon:

> Certainly, the independence of furniture displayed by the Japanese is most enviable, and frees their lives of many cares. Babies never fall out of bed, because there are no beds; they never tip themselves over in chairs for a similar reason. There is nothing in the house to dust, nothing to move when you sweep ... the chief worries of a housekeeper's life are non-existent.[42]

14. Our bedclothes are always spread out over the bed; in Japan, during the day they are always rolled up and hidden from view.

Generally futon are not rolled up but folded in three and put away in the *oshi-ire* closet. With the beds stashed away, one need only remove the *fusuma* and one's living-room is doubled. In good weather, the futons are hung over balconies and thoroughly beaten. This is still true: every modern apartment must have a place for futons to be aired and beaten.

15. Our pillows are made of feathers, canha,[43] or cotton, and they are soft and wide; in Japan, they are made of wood, and they use only a single pillow, one palm in width.

---

37 *Jinriksha Days in Japan*, 375.
38 Thomas, *The Ends of Life*, 117.
39 Sarti, "The Material Conditions of Family Life," 5–6.
40 Brian Pullan,"The Counter–Reformation, Medical Care and Poor Relief," In *Health Care and Poor Relief in Counter-Reformation Europe*, eds. Ole P. Grell, Andrew Cunningham, and Jon Arrizabalaga, pp. 18–40 (London; Routledge, 1999), 19.
41 Marques, *Daily Life in Portugal*, 123–127.
42 Alice Mabel Bacon, *A Japanese Interior* (Boston: Houghton, Mifflin & Company, 1893), 42.
43 Although Schütte has suggested that Frois intended *"canga,"* *cana*, which can be translated as reeds or rushes, seems to make more sense in the context of stuffing for a bed pillow.

Hard, narrow, and as high as a double pillow, Westerners found Japanese pillows a literal pain in the neck. Why did the Japanese use such pillows? According to Morse:

> The pillow was evolved to meet the peculiar method of arranging the hair. The elaborate coiffure of the women and the rigid queue of the men, waxed and arranged to last for a number of days, required a head-rest where these conditions would not be disturbed. In hot weather the air circulates about the neck, and this is very agreeable.[44]

Okada has suggested that Frois mentioned wooden pillows to maximize his contrast. There also were lacquered, woven-bamboo pillows that still can be found in some old inns. Although more giving than solid wood, they are still far too hard for most Westerners and young Japanese. Golownin also reported that "the higher or richer classes make use of a very neat box, about eleven inches high, to the lid of which an oval cushion is affixed, from six to eight inches in length, and from two to three in breadth. This box contains articles which they make use of at the toilette, such as razors, scissors, pomatum, tooth-brushes, powder, &c."

Today, the top part of the traditional pillow, the conical cushion, without the wood, survives.

16. In Europe we use draperies, bed hangings and curtains made of damask and silk; in Japan during the summer they use very thin mosquito netting[45] made of cotton[46] or paper.

Frois is contrasting the decorative curtains and bed enclosures used by European elites year-round with the open beds of the Japanese, which in summer had a very insubstantial yet altogether functional mosquito net. To borrow from a haiku of Issa that is only slightly more popular than the one on the flea/s (#11 above), a summer vesper in Japan is an announcement that one has crossed the border and entered mosquito country (*kane naru ya ka-no kuni-ni koyo-koyo-to*).

Alcock, who minced no words concerning his hatred for "these Poisoners of the human race, and Destroyers of all peace," cited the mosquito net as a happy example of Japanese ingenuity. At the various inns where he spent the night when traveling, he attests:

> We should have been devoured by the musquitoes had the landlords not come to our rescue by the simplest of all contrivances, a musquito curtain, open at the bottom, made up in the shape of a parallelogram, is let down over the mat (6 feet by 3) selected by the sleeper, a cord is run from each of the four upper corners (into which a sort of eyelet hole has been worked), and four nails

44 *Japan Day By Day*, I, 62.
45 *Cayas* [*kaya*].
46 *Nuno*.

driven in to enable a servant to suspend it. Under this, the persecuted martyr creeps, tucking in the sides and ends under his cotton quilt or mat ...[47]

17. Among us, it would be unseemly for a nobleman to sweep his room; Japanese lords[48] regularly do so and are proud of it.[49]

Manual labor of any kind was beneath European nobility;[50] even a gifted surgeon, because he worked with his hands, was valued less than a college-educated physician (someone who relied solely on "intellect" to treat the sick).[51]

The Chinese character for a wife has a woman with a broom over her head, so you might think that men in the Sinosphere were opposed to sweeping, yet many Japanese men seem to have delighted in creating wave patterns in the gravel at Zen temples or in their tea gardens. Golownin also offered this bit of insight:

> It is a whimsical rule that the guests must leave the apartments as clean as when they entered them; so that no person ever quits an inn, until he has seen his apartment put into proper order, well swept, and washed if necessary. In short, it would be considered an act, not only of impoliteness, but even of ingratitude, if the smallest speck of dirt was to be left behind. So precise are the Japanese in this respect, that even the Dutch,[52] when permitted to traffic there were deemed deficient in neatness.[53]

Note that Frois might also be referring to the annual Beat-out-the-Dust Day (*susu-barai*). Every year television news in Japan shows battalions of dust-masked priests and volunteers from the congregation doing what looks like a search-and-destroy mission against enormous temples using brooms and dusters with handles as long as those found on pool-cleaning implements. These annual offensives are led and dominated by men.

18. We cleanse our faces with thin towels; they purposefully[54] use coarse cloths that are very thick.[55]

Apparently "hand towels" in Japan were more likely to be thick and coarse rather than thin and soft.

47 Alcock, *Capital of the Tycoon*, II, 423.
48 *Senhores.*
49 *Tem antre si por primor.*
50 Thomas, *The Ends of Life*, 83.
51 Laurence Brockliss and Colin Jones, *The Medical World of Early Modern France* (Oxford: Clarendon Press, 1997), 188–189.
52 Cleanliness was so celebrated in Holland that Dutch warships had brooms atop their masts, signaling that they would sweep the sea of their enemies.
53 Captain Vasilïi Mikhǎilovich Golownin, *Memoirs of a Captivity in Japan during the years 1811, 1812, and 1813* (London: Henry Colburn & Company, 1824), III, 135.
54 *Vaza to.* We noted with surprise in the previous chapter Frois' use of this Japanese expression that means "on purpose" (see Chapter 10, #15).
55 *Liteiros ou tomentos muito grossos.* The term *liteiro* refers to a wool-blend fabric typical of the Alentejo region of Portugal, and *tomento* refers to the coarsest fibers taken from the flax plant.

19. Our latrines must always be hidden behind the house; theirs are out front, in plain view to all.

The West always has had an "out of sight, out of mind" approach to human excrement. Accordingly, the outhouse typically was and is "out back," far enough away from the house so that no one else has to see, hear, or smell anything, if possible. In the urban residences of European elites the latrine often amounted to a small "house-of-office" or "stool house," or a niche with a curtain where individuals could relieve themselves.

The outhouse in Japan generally was in the front garden but hardly right by the door, as this contrast might lead one to believe. The gentry generally had inside toilets as well, in the far rear or on the far north side of the house. The nobility's toilets were located inside an interior garden, with one for the lord and very favored guests and another for the women of the house. With a number of lavatories and lavatory practices to choose from, there are many more contrasts Frois could have made:

> We use water; they use sand.
> We do not take particular measures to reduce noise; they spread leaves in the urinal.
> We face out to defecate; they face in.

Why, then, was Frois struck by this particular contrast in the location of toilets? It may reflect his long stay in Miyako (Kyoto), the city that made the greatest efforts to recycle human waste, even boasting public toilets in front of shops on the main avenue and at many crossroads. The Kyoto area was and still is known for its many fine leafy vegetables (they even have a type of cabbage large enough to feed a small village), and this meant that urine, with its phosphate, was in particularly high demand, with people even directly bartering it for vegetables.

People from Edo (Tokyo) were as astounded as foreigners to see urinals out in front of the outhouses proper in Kyoto, in full view of passersby. What shocked them even more was the fact that women also used them, standing with their kimonos hiked up, buttocks bent out slightly over the troughs. And these were not only servants; the wives of wealthy merchants also joined in. Over a hundred years after Frois, *senryu* poets, largely from Edo, could not resist taking a dig at Kyoto and its women, who were otherwise considered the ideal of womanhood.

20. We sit; they squat.

This refers to what the Japanese call doing the "big" one, or what Americans refer to as "number two." Sixteenth-century Europeans went to the bathroom by sitting on "closed stools" or chairs with holes in the seat that allowed the urine and excrement to fall into a chamber pot, cesspool, running water, or the ground. At night, when it was often too cold to venture far, Europeans might forgo a trip to the privy and squat in their bedroom over a chamber pot that was dumped in the morning.

When somebody from Europe or the United States who is not used to squatting squats, they often need to grab on to something so as to not tip over. The Japanese, for their part, can read a book while squatting in the toilet. The trick is getting the upper part of your foot to come closer to your shin so that you may squat flat on your heels.

21. We pay someone to carry our excrement away; in Japan they buy it and give rice and money in exchange for it.

European cities in Frois' day generally lacked what we think of as sanitation systems; most people simply tossed their excrement into a nearby cesspool or river or dumped it into the street at night (with the next significant rainfall gravity might take it to a nearby stream or river). Portugal's João II, who reigned from 1481–1495, became so offended with the citizens of Lisbon and their cavalier "overturning of chamberpots" that he proposed the construction of a city-wide sewer system. Such a system was still a dream in 1585.[56] More affluent Europeans paid people to remove their bodily wastes. As one might imagine, "scavengers" and "goungfermours" were poorly paid for collecting waste and cleaning streets, cesspools, and privies. Social approbation went hand-in-hand with low wages.

As previously suggested, the Japanese attitude toward human waste was much more practical. A straight exchange of rice or some other commodity was common for buckets of urine, while ordure was usually purchased, and food, if offered, was a bonus. In Osaka and Kyoto, according to Aramata,[57] waste products comprised a not-to-be-laughed-about portion of the family income. Even store clerks were reimbursed for their contribution. In parts of Japan, four people renting a small room could pay their entire rent with their waste, which is to say, they could stay for free. Kaempfer gives the situation in the seventeenth-century countryside:

... care is taken, that the filth of travelers be not lost, and there are in several places, near country people's houses, or in the fields, houses of office for them to do their needs. Old shoes of horses and men, which are thrown away as useless, are gather'd in the same houses, and burnt to ashes, along with the filth, for common dung, which they manure all their fields withal. Provisions of this nasty composition are kept in large tubs, or *tuns*, which are buried even with the ground, in their villages and fields, and being not cover'd, afford full as ungrateful and putrid a smell of radishes (which is the common food of country people) to tender noses, as the neatness and beauty of the road is agreeable to the eyes.[58]

Most Japanese apparently were inured to the stench, and even toward the end of the twentieth century they put up with the incredibly pungent smell of raw human waste coming from their *kumitori* toilet. Ironically, this foul-smelling "scoop-take" toilet is a modern invention, which, according to Aramata, is based on the "septic toilet" system minus the septic tank. Instead of waste being

56 Marques, *Daily Life in Portugal*, 141.
57 Hiroshi Aramata, *Nihon Gyôten Kigen* [Japan-shocking-origins] (Shûeisha, 1994), 80.
58 Englelbert Kaempfer, *The History of Japan, Together with a Description of the Kingdom of Siam, 1690–92*. 3 Vols. (Glasgow: James MacLehose and Sons, 1906[1690–92]), II, 293–294.

channeled away to a distant cistern, it collects in a concrete cistern directly below the toilet, from which it is collected once a year or so.[59]

Stench aside, the Japanese arrangement made far more sense than ours. Morse alone, in 1877, recognized it as more hygienic than our practices:

> Somewhat astonished at learning that the death-rate of Tokyo was lower than that of Boston, I made some inquiries about health matters. I learned that dysentery and cholera infantum are never known here ... But those diseases which at home are attributed to bad drainage, imperfect closets [toilet systems], and the like seem to be unknown or rare, and this freedom from such complaints is probably due to the fact that all excrementitious matter is carried out of the city by men who utilize it for their farms and rice fields. With us, this sewage is allowed to flow into our coves and harbors, polluting the water and killing all aquatic life; and the stenches arising from the decomposition and filth are swept over the community to the misery of all ... It seems incredible that in a vast city like Tokyo this service should be performed by hundreds of men who have their regular routes. The buckets are suspended on carrying sticks and the weight of these full buckets would tax a giant.[60]

22. In Europe horse manure is spread on vegetable gardens and human excrement is thrown on dunghills; in Japan horse dung is thrown on dunghills and human excrement goes onto vegetable gardens.

It is not likely that horse manure was thrown away. It may not have been sold in the city but it was surely used by someone for something. Moreover, it is debatable to what extent the Japanese actually had dunghills in the sense that we understand them. Haiku often mention sweep piles (*hakidome*) and specific piles of shellfish shells, disposable chopsticks or flower petals, but all of these were small and temporary. Honest-to-goodness dumps were hard to find, as noted by Morse in the late nineteenth century:

> In country village and city alike the houses of the rich and poor are never rendered unsightly by garbage, ash piles, and rubbish; one never sees those large communal piles of ashes, clam shells and the like that are often encountered in the outskirts of our quiet country villages. In refined Cambridge ... This land was so disfigured by a certain type of rubbish that for years it was facetiously called the "tin canyon"! The Japanese in some mysterious way manage to bury, burn, or utilize their waste and rubbish so that it is never in existence.[61]

A century after Frois, Kaempfer noted that horse dung does not "lie long upon the ground but it is soon taken up by poor country children and serves to manure the

---

59 Aramata, *Nihon Gyôten Kigen*, 102.
60 Morse, *Japan Day By Day*, I, 23. Note that in his later book, *Japanese Homes and Their Surroundings*, Morse qualified his remarks, admitting that the runoff from the fertilizer might sometimes cause cholera in the southern part of Japan.
61 Ibid., 42.

fields." Obviously, horse dung, and also cow dung, was not as abundant as human offal, while cow urine apparently was not used at all, for an old Japanese proverb equates "the lectures of parents to a cow urinating: long and good for nothing."

23. *We lock our trunks with iron locks; they close their baskets with cords, paper seals, or padlocks from China.*

Trunks during the Middle Ages often had sliding-bolt locks or padlocks. During the sixteenth century they were increasingly fitted with various new types of locks that were manufactured in southern Germany.

Here Frois would seem to be contrasting solid protection with something far less secure. The Chinese padlock in question would not be of more than nominal value on a weak basket. Locks are not a key part of Japanese culture to begin with. As noted previously, when Japanese doors were locked, it was generally by bolt from the inside only and not by lock and key.

24. *We make our chests with compartments inside; they make boxes that fit one inside the other*[62] *in their baskets.*

This contrast suggests a more general one that Frois missed, which Lee O-Young focused on in his book *Furoshiki Bunka no Posuto-Modan*:

> We Europeans put things into solid containers or fill up soft ones of a predetermined size; they wrap up things in *furoshiki* [attractive square cloth] to fit the size of the thing.

In China, Korea and Japan a cloth rather than a container of fixed size is used to store or carry things. Objects are first set on the cloth or *furoshiki* and then the opposing corners are tied diagonally, two at a time. Professor Lee claims that this "primary opposition" of cultural codes, i.e. "putting in" (the box principle) versus "wrapping up" (the cloth principle), goes back to primeval times. Lee boasts that the greater versatility of the *furoshiki*, which bring to mind morphing robot toys (largely a Japanese invention), make the Far East more fit for the postmodern world. The box or Ark, suggests Lee, will no longer save us.

25. *Our carpenters work standing up; theirs generally always remain seated.*

For "us" sitting supposedly impedes all physical work except pushing papers. However, for most cultures (not just Japan's) sitting allows more work to be done. Not only does it save energy wasted on standing; it also frees up the feet to join in the work. As Percival Lowell put it, "from the tips of his fingers to the tips of his toes, in whose use he is surprisingly proficient, he (the Far Oriental) is the artist all over."[63] People all over the globe used to use their feet in this way, but in Europe and the United States "we" only encourage people without functioning arms to use their feet. Today, most carpenters in Japan feed their table saws from a standing position, but people working on sheet metal and other materials not

---

62 *Caquegos* [*kakego*].
63 *The Soul of the Far East* (Boston: Houghton Mifflin, 1888), 111.

requiring large tables can still be seen seated on their tatami, with their feet out, fast at work.

26. Our gimlets make holes using the strength of our arms; those of the Japanese are turned by striking them repeatedly with a mallet.

A gimlet is a T-shaped twist drill that works much like a simple corkscrew, which was once called a gimlet. Because the spiral starts close to the tip, "our" drill or gimlet can start screwing from the outset by simply applying a bit of downward pressure and torque.

The Japanese drill was not a spiral. Indeed, the first screws had just arrived in Japan (in the harquebus) and would not find other uses for quite a while. The Japanese drill used a different method to bore, namely three or four very sharp edges (the *mitsume-giri* had three edges and the *yotsume-giri*, four). While both Japanese drills work well for boring and enlarging holes, getting them started (the first half-inch or so) is difficult and requires a hammer to gain "purchase." This is apparently what Frois was struck by (no pun intended).

27. In Europe one does not feed carpenters or their helpers; in Japan they are fed wherever they work, as are their assistants, who do nothing.

This is still true in Japan. Carpenters may bring some snacks of their own or go out for a soft drink, but the lady of the house usually brings out trays of food and tea. Alice Mabel Bacon was of the opinion that:

> So rigid are the requirements of Japanese hospitality that no guest is ever allowed to leave a house without having been pressed to partake of food, if it be only tea and cake. Even tradesmen or messengers who come to the house must be offered tea, and if carpenters, gardeners or workmen of any kind are employed about the house, tea must be served in the middle of the afternoon with a light lunch, and tea sent out to them often during their day's work.[64]

Another factor may be considered together with this hospitality, and Bacon herself gave much of her chapter on "domestic service" to it. To wit, the Japanese were fundamentally more egalitarian than Westerners when it came to their attitude toward servants and other people doing menial work.

> ... in Europe and America a servant is expected never to show any interest in, or knowledge of, the conversation of his betters, never to speak unless addressed, and never to smile under any circumstances.[65]

28. Our adze is large and wide and can perform many tasks; Japanese adzes look like a toy.

---

64 *Japanese Girls and Women* (London: Kegan Paul, 2001[1892]), 79.
65 Ibid, 250.

Today houses in the United States and Europe often are built with a frame of 2×4 or 2×6 lumber, which carpenters simply order from a lumberyard. In the sixteenth century carpenters had to essentially fashion their own framing timber, and the adze, which had a short handle and a relatively long and wide blade, was the tool of choice for transforming rough-sawn lumber (supplied by a sawyer) into squared beams. (Adzes with smaller blades were used to carve joints or mortises in the beams, which "snapped" together, so to speak.)

The Japanese adze was made from a single piece of iron and had a long, thin handle and a short and narrow blade (relative to the adze used in Europe). Presumably the blade on the Japanese adze was incredibly sharp (as with their other cutting blades), in which case it may not have required the larger mass or size of the Western adze(s). Japanese use of bamboo and soft woods such as cedar may also help explain the smaller size of their adze.

29. In Europe a house is built at the pace the lumber is prepared; in Japan they first prepare all the lumber for the house and then erect it in very short order.

The Japanese actually took just three or four days to erect a house, and this is still true today. A carpenter spends most of his days at home planing, marking, cutting and otherwise preparing parts for assembly. If you are a friend of the carpenter and visit him, you can see he is very busy. Otherwise, you get a very different impression of construction in Japan. Because the foundation is usually laid long before the home itself is ready, an observer might wonder "when are they going to get started." However, a few days later the house is finished. This approach to construction may make sense in a country with earthquakes, typhoons, and monsoon rainfall, which do not respect half-built buildings.

30. Among us, the more figures in a painting, the better; in Japan, the fewer the better.

Renaissance art such as Quentin Massys' "Adoration of the Magi," Tintoretto's "Last Supper," or the Manueline artist Nuno Golçalves' polypytch of São Vicente de Fora,[66] are known for their detail and crowded spacing.[67] Perhaps this is what Frois meant by "the more figures in a painting the better." Although Okada has pointed out that genre pictures (*fûzoku-e*) full of people were painted on screens (*byôbu*) in sixteenth-century Japan, perhaps the most highly respected genre of painting was *sumi-e*, or black-ink painting, which was decidedly minimalist. (Frois and Valignano both were amazed that the Japanese ruler, Hydeoshi, spent a fortune on a black ink painting "of a withered tree with a bird in it.") As Rodrigues explained:

... although they copy nature in their paintings, they do not like a multitude and crowd of things in their pictures, but prefer to portray, even in a

66 See the "Prince's Panel" in particular, In *Museum With No Frontiers Exhibition "The Manueline: Portuguese Art During the Great Discoveries,"* pp. 48–49 (Lisbon: Programa de Incremento do Turismo Cultural, 2002), 30–31.
67 Anne Fitzpatrick, *The Renaissance* (Mankato, MN: Creative Education, 2006), 38.

sumptuous and lovely palace, just a few solitary things with due proportion between them ...[68]

There is one caveat to this "less is more" esthetic: Kano Eitoku (1543–1590) transformed Japanese painting in 1576 when he was commissioned by Nobunaga to execute huge, wall paintings (*shôhekiga*) for Azuchi castle; the paintings purportedly featured clouds of gold dust and flowers and birds in brilliant colors, and rather than a few solitary things, left little to the imagination.[69]

31. We purposefully plant trees in our gardens that will bear fruit; the Japanese place greater esteem on planting trees in their gardens[70] *that bear only flowers.*

The Moorish occupation of Iberia during the latter part of the Middle Ages turned the southern third of the peninsula into a veritable garden. The Japanese ambassadors to Europe reported that a single orchard in Lisbon had no less than seventy-six varieties of pears.[71] (No wonder Columbus described the shape of the earth as a pear.)

Japan was practically fruitless. What surprised the Jesuits, however, was not so much the absence of fruit and the abundance of flowers in Japanese gardens, but the fact that the very trees Europeans cultivated for fruit were, in Japan, feted for their bloom. If we do not specify that we are talking about a tree, the words "cherry" and "plum" are assumed to refer to the fruit. In Japan, on the other hand, these trees became synonymous with their blooms, so much so that people use the generic term *hana* (flowers/bloom) all by itself to refer to what we call a tree.[72]

The premier garden tree was and is the plum (some say it is actually a variety of apricot). It blooms right on the broken back of winter, at what was the New Year in Japan, attracting the bush warbler (rightly translated as a nightingale to preserve its trope), whose first call was eagerly awaited. Moreover, a big deal is made of the plum's scent, which is said to slip inside the house and permeate all the cold corners of the room. Because the plum tree's Chinese rendering combines a tree radical with a mother, the very name has a warm, motherly character, further enhanced by a homophonic affinity with birth.

32. We use fireplaces; the Japanese use a covered cotaccus[73] *in the center of the house.*

The main source of heat in a sixteenth-century home in Portugal and other parts of Europe was the kitchen hearth. European elites might have homes with fireplaces in halls or bedrooms. In Frois' day, and still today, Iberians also made

---

68 Cooper, *They Came to Japan*, 254.

69 Carolyn Wheelwright, "A Visualization of Eitoku's Lost Paintings at Azuchi Castle." In *Warlords, Artists, & Commoners*, eds. George Elison and Bardwell Smith, pp. 87–112. (Honolulu: University of Hawaii Press, 1981), 96.

70 *Nivas* [*niwa*].

71 Valignano, *De Missione Legatorum Iaponen*, Dialogue 17.

72 See Emiko Ohnuki-Tierney, "Cherry Blossoms and Their Viewing." In *The Culture of Japan as Seen Through Its Leisure*, eds. Sepp Linhart and Sabine Fruhstuck, pp. 213–237 (Albany: SUNY Press, 1998).

73 *Kotatsu*.

use of "space heaters" in the form of braziers.[74] (The brazier typically amounted to a metal box with heated coals, which is placed under a bed or under a table draped with a heavy cloth that reaches to the floor.)

As noted in Chapter 6, Japanese homes during the sixteenth century generally had an *irori*, a centrally located, square sunken hearth that functioned much like the kitchen hearth in European homes (i.e. a place to cook and source of heat). The *kotatsu* essentially is an *irori* with a wooden frame raised up over it, which in turn is covered with a large quilt. The great traveler, Isabela Bird, who had been around the British Isles and the American West before visiting Japan, put the *kotatsu* into international perspective. With "the whole" of a Japanese house "being merely a porous screen from the inclemency of the weather," ... "the invitation to creep under the *kotatsu* is as welcome as the "sit-in" of the Scotch Highlands or the "put your feet in the stove" of Colorado."[75]

Okada points out that the *kotatsu* is a Chinese invention. Still, it is the Japanese who have championed it (haiku is full of *kotatsu*) and developed it into a splendid heater. Along these lines, there is a *hori-kotatsu* (which is what Frois seems to be referring to here), consisting of a recessed pit in the floor that contains coals. There is also a modern version, the *denki-kotatsu*, which amounts to a small electrical heater attached to the bottom of a table.

33. In Europe one pays for the sawyer but not the saw; in Japan you pay the same per day for the saw as you do for the sawyer.

Sawyers in Europe and other skilled laborers in the building trades had modest financial resources and often preferred "simple" as opposed to "ambitious" contracts, that is, many preferred to hire out their labor for a set period at a set wage rather than contract for a job that required them to invest in equipment or assistants who might not be needed once a particular project was finished.[76]

Perhaps because Japan was home to feudal lords with "deep pockets" who could employ workers on huge construction projects,[77] many sawyers and other craftsmen favored ambitious contracts that entailed both their labor and equipment.

34. The lawns in our courtyards[78] *are valued as a place for sitting; in Japan they purposefully*[79] *remove all grass from the grounds.*

All grass is considered a weed by the Japanese, except for bamboo, mungo grass (called *ryu-no-hige* or dragon-whisker) and grass for walking on. The word for grass is the same as the word for weed, and what we call "weed-pulling" the Japanese call *kusa-tori* or "grass-taking." This lack of sympathy toward all

74 Marques, *Daily Life in Portugal*, 134–135.
75 *Unbeaten Tracks in Japan* (Boston: Beacon Press, 1987[1880]), 254.
76 Richard A. Goldthwaite, *The Building of Renaissance Florence: An Economic and Social History* (Baltimore: The John Hopkins University Press, 1982), 126.
77 Oda Nobunaga employed thousands of laborers for three years (1576–1579) on the construction of "Azuchi castle," which included not simply a magnificent residence for himself, but an entire castle town.
78 In Iberian homes *patios* refers to a walled space within the structure of the residence itself, separated from the street.
79 *Vazato*.

things not growing in pots, gardens, or farm fields is said to derive from a farmer's control-oriented mentality. As Tetsuro Watsuji pointed out in his 1935 classic *Fudo: ningengakuteki kōsatsu* (wind-earth = natural feature = theory), Japanese crops, unlike those in Europe, were in perpetual danger of being overtaken by the weeds that grow in Japan's warm, humid summers. Today if you ask, most Japanese are likely to say that their grass taking is to prevent mosquitoes and other harmful bugs (*gaichu*) from "boiling up" (*waki-deru*) during the humid season and to allow more air to circulate, preventing houses from rotting. Some Japanese, however, add, "We Japanese like mud, it makes us nostalgic for our paddy fields."

35. In Europe the streets run to the center, thus allowing the water to drain; in Japan, the streets are high in the center and low next to the houses so that the water can run alongside them.

Here is a clear case of where "we" have changed our ways, as streets that are slightly higher in the center (i.e. crowned) are the norm in the United States and Europe. Today the only streets with a gulley going down the center is likely to be of cobblestone in the "old town" or late medieval section of European cities. Okada cites a Japanese source indicating that Kyoto streets were especially high in the middle. Frois explains immediately below how the Japanese handled water that ran down the sides of the road and in front of their doors.

36. In Europe, the entrance to a house is flush with the ground; in Japan, they build bridges using some wood or stones to enter the house.

European practice makes sense, inasmuch as water was forced to the center rather than the sides of the street (recall #21 above and the dumping of chamber pots late at night or at dawn). The small bridges used by the Japanese likewise allowed the water to flow down the street unobstructed while keeping the entrance high and dry. Needless to say, they also provided an aesthetic opportunity.

37. In Europe, the front door of a home opens directly onto the street; in Japan, they open into their yard or garden,[80] and they make an effort to have them not open directly onto the street.

Frois is obviously talking about townhouses in European cities such as his own Lisbon. In Japan, the gate and the door are still generally separate, even for small houses with miniscule yards. One can think of the space between as a buffer because the doors themselves are not very strong, the house itself has few walls, and the front door, like the rest of the house, is left wide open all day in the summer.

But Frois' contrast only concerns the houses of the gentry. Many if not most of the homes of townsmen and almost all boarding houses in most parts of Japan had no front garden. A note by Golownin's editor describes the Japan of the "common folk:"

---

80 *Nivas* [*niwa*].

In their houses, the street door always stands open; but there is a jealousy or blind put up at the entrance, formed of small network, which prevents the inmates from being seen, without impeding their sight.[81]

The biggest difference with Europe would seem to be that the door in Japan remains open. In addition to the blind, which is usually completely open for the bottom three feet, the Japanese take additional measures to prevent dust and heat from blowing in from the street, such as regularly dashing or sprinkling water in front of their homes.

38. In Europe, we build fountains coming out of a wall that are squared and clean; in Japan, they dig small ponds or basins in the ground, with nooks and small inlets and with rocks and little islands in the middle.

There is a world of difference in aesthetic taste expressed here: geometrical perfection (Europe) versus natural scenic beauty (Japan). Arguably, it is the Japanese and not Europeans who long for the Garden of Eden. Today in the West, the Far-Eastern-looking pond (for the credit hardly belongs to Japan alone) may well be more common than rectangular ones. Still, one might only wish that Eliza Scidmore's prediction came true, namely, "a Japanese gardener will doubtless come to be considered as necessary a part of a great American establishment as a French maid or an English coachman."[82]

In all fairness to the West, quite a few homes and estates of wealthy Europeans in the sixteenth century featured gardens and fountains that anticipated Disney World in their hydraulic engineering and "playfulness." The Japanese teenagers who acted as ambassadors to Europe at the time Frois wrote the *Tratado* went on for pages (Dialogue 21) about the fabulous gardens they visited, particularly in Italy, which had fountains that squirted "spears of water" such that there was not a single place in the garden where you were safe from a water attack.[83]

39. We work to get our trees to grow straight upward; in Japan, they purposefully[84] hang stones from the branches so that they will grow crooked.

Watsuji claimed that the mild climate of the Mediterranean produced straight trees that seemed artificial to the Japanese, who were used to the windblown, gnarled trees of their own country. While wind may have created the irregularity of Japanese pines in the mountains, Watsuji might have given his countrymen a bit more credit for their work to make domestic trees look "natural." Alcock was impressed:

> It is perfectly astonishing to see the amount of industry and perseverance which the Japanese must have devoted to the production of these plants. There were some little fir trees, not more than a foot in height, and yet I counted

81 Golownin, *Memoirs of a Captivity in Japan, III*, 157.
82 *Jinrikisha Days in Japan* (New York: Harper & Brothers, 1897), 12.
83 Alessandro Valignano, *De Missione Legatorum Iaponen*, trans. Duarte de Sande (Macao [Lima Library Collection], 1590).
84 *Vazato* [*waza to*].

upward of fifty ties, by means of which the shoots were bent backward and forward in a zigzag way.[85]

Some Westerners say the result is stunted and ugly; Frois used the word *tortas* (meaning "bent" or "crooked"), which shares its root with the English word tortured. Such is the life of a pine tree that has endured for more than a century on the side of a mountain in the face of a brisk wind.

40. We wash our hands and face in silver or porcelain hand basins; in Japan they wash in a wooden tub,[86] which at most is lacquered.

The wooden tub or *tarai* is usually made like a barrel, out of slats reinforced with soft metal bands. These small tubs are used not only for washing one's face and hands, but also to scoop water out of the bath to wash oneself. Frois caught a small contrast but missed a large one:

We wash with soap inside the bath; they wash and rinse off outside the bath before climbing in.

41. We pour water for our hands through the spouts of our pitchers so that they produce a slow, thin stream; they pour water out of wooden pails, unleashing a very strong stream.

This is a fairly arcane contrast, although Frois seems to depict the washing of hands in Europe as controlled and economical and perhaps more aesthetically pleasing (imagine a pitcher that was probably made of metal or porcelain, versus a wooden bucket). Frois would no doubt be impressed with contemporary Japanese flush toilets, which, when activated, send a little stream of water through the air (you can stick your fingers into the stream and clean them) and then into the tank to refill it.

42. In Europe ordinarily our roofs are clean; in Japan they are loaded down with stones, wood, and bamboo to protect them from the wind.

Much of Japan is like Chicago, and the same gusts of wind that lead to crooked trees can also blow the straw off a poor man's roof. Big stones are still found on houses that have roofs made of straw or the more popular corrugated tin. Not all are there for wind protection, however, as Okada notes that stones and lumber sometimes were (and are) stored on the roof. The main roof of finely laid straw was usually too sharply sloped for stones to rest upon, and it was heavy enough by itself, so the roofs referred to here by Frois were likely on tiny shacks or were a type of awning-like extension sometimes found on larger roofs.

43. Our pine trees generally bear fruit; in Japan, even though there is an infinite number of pine trees and they bear nuts the size of walnuts, they are worthless.

The Italian stone pine is the most common fruit-bearing pine tree found in Spain, Portugal, and Italy. For centuries the tree's pignolia nuts have

---

85 *Capital of the Tycoon*, 324.
86 *Taray* [tarai].

figured prominently in Mediterranean cuisine (e.g. toasted and tossed with pasta, sun-dried tomato, olive oil, garlic, and feta cheese).

The Japanese white pine is as common in Japan as the stone pine is in Mediterranean Europe. Presumably, this is the tree Frois had in mind when he noted it produced inedible fruit. However, "worthless" is a bit extreme, as Kaempfer noted that pine nuts were gathered for use as fuel.

44. Our cherry trees bear very tasty and beautiful cherries; those in Japan bear cherries that are very small and bitter, but also very beautiful flowers that the Japanese value.

In the twenty years that one of us (Gill) lived in Japan he never noticed Japanese cherries, much less heard of anyone tasting them. These develop after the blossoms fall, and nobody goes to view the cherries, but instead focuses on the pretty, dappled shade of the cherry trees. Until something the Japanese call the "cherry-peach" (*sakura-momo*) was imported in the nineteenth century, there were no real fruit-bearing cherries in Japan. On the other hand, Japanese flowering cherries now bring delight to people by the Reflecting Pool in Washington D.C. and elsewhere.

45. Among us, when one picks a fragrant rose or carnation, we first smell it and then examine it visually; the Japanese pay no attention to the smell and take pleasure only in the visual experience.

Japanese native plants that are the closest equivalents of the "rose" and "carnation" (a briar rose and a pink) are practically without scent, and the cherry blossom is also scentless. Nevertheless, the Japanese pay almost as much attention to the scent of the official bloom of the New Year, the plum flower, as "we" pay to the rose. The difference is that the rose literally is brought to the nose (or *vice-versa*), while plum blossoms fill the air (all the way to the hazy moon, if haiku are to be believed).

46. We have many roses, flowers, carnations and herbs that are fragrant and quite aromatic; in Japan, very few of these things have a fragrance.

Frois is correct, although he might have noted that the violet is an exception to his rule, at least according to poets such as Issa. The violet's scent is famous for its effervescence; soon after you have smelled it, you no longer do, so it would hardly work for perfume.

47. Europeans find the fragrant water from roses, angelicas, etc. very pleasing; the Japanese do not find any of these scents pleasing.

Rose water was made by distilling rose petals or by simply letting the petals soak in water for two or three weeks (the more economical route). As far back as the Romans rosewater was something of an aphrodisiac and a means of treating depression. Angelica, including *Angelica heterocarpa*, a native of Iberia, is an aromatic flower (yellow or greenish in color) that was thought to be especially efficacious against spells and enchantments.

If the Japanese were not wild about rosewater or angelicas this was because they were not used to such scents, which were much sweeter than their own plum blossom or incense. Even today the Japanese feel that Westerners use perfumes that are too powerful. However, it would be remiss not to mention one scent the Japanese do appreciate: thick peels from oranges that are placed in bathwater.

48. We greatly esteem the scent from balsamic resins, calendulas, etc.; the Japanese think they are strong and cannot tolerate them, nor do they find them pleasing.

Calendulas or marigolds are said to have a scent that resembles the smell of hops, which might help explain why they were esteemed by Europeans.[87] The Japanese also found balsamic resins or benzoin offensive or "too strong." One wonders if the occasional bathing of Europeans, as opposed to the daily bathing of the Japanese, had something to do with the differences in their attitudes toward scents.

---

87 Beer, which is made with hops, apparently became more popular than ale (made without hops) over the course of the sixteenth century. Richard Unger, *Beer in the Middle Ages and the Renaissance* (Philadelphia: University of Pennsylvania Press, 2004).

12 Ships, seafaring and *dogus*[1]

1. Among us, there are naos, galleons, caravels, galleys, fustas, catures, brigantines, etc.; in Japan they have absolutely none of these.

Frois was a proud son of Portugal and had difficulty acknowledging Japanese ships and seafaring, which admittedly were not on a par with the Portuguese maritime tradition. At the time Frois wrote, his native land boasted more than a century of excellence at sea (Henry the Navigator died in 1460). By leading the way in the age of exploration, Portugal and Spain not only gained the prestige that the United States received for making it to the moon, but enormous wealth that made them the envy of Europe.[2] Well over 1,000 ships sailed to and from Portugal and Asia during the sixteenth century.[3]

Frois here mentions a handful of the many types of Portuguese ships that plied the seas during his lifetime.[4] The *nao* (today spelled *nau*) was the Airbus A-380 or Boeing 747 of sixteenth century shipping. This three or four-mast ship had three or four decks and a capacity ranging from an ideal of 450 to over 1,000 tons. The *nao* was Portugal's mainstay ferrying people and goods back and forth between Portugal and Asia. The Nossa Senhora dos Mártires that sailed from India and sank in sight of Lisbon in 1606 was carrying 450 people and 250 tons of peppercorns, not to mention a host of other commodities.[5] From the Japanese perspective, the *nao* was the typical "southern barbarian boat." It was lightly armed compared to its look-like, the galleon, but still outgunned anything in the East (see #9 below). The closest Japanese analog to the *nao* was the *bezaisen* or *kitamae-bune*—a cargo ship with a capacity of only ninety-eight tons that had a

---

1 Frois presumably used the Japanese word *dogu* (meaning tool, equipment, implement, apparatus, etc.) to refer here to a ship's outfitting because he was struck by the distinctiveness of Japanese anchors, ropes, sails, etc.

2 Francis Dutra, "The Social and Economic World of Portugal's Elite Seafarers, 1481–1600," *Mediterranean Studies* XIV (2005): 95–105; K.M Mathew, *The History of Portuguese Navigation in India, 1497–1600* (Delhi, India: Mittal Publications, 1988), 275–278; John Francis Guilmartin, *Gunpowder and Galleys: Changing Technology and Mediterranean Warfare at Sea in the 16th Century*. Rev ed. (Annapolis, MD: Naval Institute Press, 2003); Roger C. Smith, *Vanguard of Empire, Ships of Exploration in the Age of Columbus* (New York: Oxford University Press, 1993); Filipe Vieira de Castro, *The Pepper Wreck: A Portuguese Indiaman at The Mouth of the Tagus River* (College Station: Texas A&M Press, 2005).

3 T. Bentley Duncan, "Navigation Between Portugal and Asia in the Sixteenth and Seventeenth Centuries." In *Asia and the West: Encounters and Exchanges from the Age of Explorations, Essays in Honor of Donald F. Lach*, ed. C.K. Pullapilly and E.J. Van Kley, pp. 3–26 (Notre Dame: Notre Dame Press, 1986), 22.

4 Mathew, *History of Portuguese Navigation*, 276–277.

5 Vieira de Castro, *The Pepper Wreck*. See also T.R. de Souza, "Goa-based Portuguese Seaborne Trade in the Early Seventeenth Century." In *The Indian Economic and Social History Review* 12(1975): 433–443.

flat keel and a single mast (hardly an ocean-going vessel) that plied the Inland Sea and occasionally the Sea of Japan.[6]

A galleon's guns were legend. In *De Missione Legatorum Iaponen* (Dialogue 14) one of the Japanese ambassadors to Europe commented that it had "one large cannon for every day of the year." Another of the ambassadors noted that the Republic of Venice could boast a galleon with 500 large cannon. By contrast, the Japanese warship, or *atake-bune*, was relatively small (20–65 feet in length), propelled by two-dozen oarsmen, and featured a wooden tower at the stern, whence bowman and later harquebusiers fired volleys of arrows and shot, respectively.

The lateen-sail caravel was what got the West around the world. Lateen sails were found on small boats in the Mediterranean for centuries (maybe a millennium).[7] Triangular, they let a boat tack into the wind. The three-mast caravel was light, strongly built, and streamlined because the cabins were put fore and aft and the central deck was low and clear. In 1520 King Manuel of Portugal made it a crime to sell a caravel to a foreign country or to go abroad for the purposes of building a caravel.[8]

During the second half of the fourteenth century the Portuguese Crown made a significant investment in building, equipping, and maintaining squadrons of galleys,[9] which were powered by multiple rows of oarsman (mostly slaves, criminals, or prisoners of war), who sat on benches and worked oars of varying length (from thirty to fifty feet). Galleys were mostly used in the Mediterranean, not infrequently for ramming in war, but equipped with sails, they also served for North Africa trade. Over 400 galleys took part in the famous naval battle of Lepanto (1571), when a combined European force under Don Juan of Austria defeated an Ottoman armada lead by Ali Pasha.[10]

Fustas and *caturs* were smaller vessels built by the Portuguese in India, principally at their shipyard in Goa. Both were powered by oars and sails. The brigantine was likewise a smaller, two-masted ship that got its name (brigand's ship) from the fact that it was a favorite of pirates in the Mediterranean.

2. Our ships have ribs and decks; Japanese ships do not.

Then what, one wonders, did Japanese boats have if not ribs and decks? Okada, citing Ishii Kenji's *Nihon-no Fune* ("the Japanese boat") goes into great technical detail, but suffice it to say that Japanese boats were more like an insect—all shell—while more seaworthy European vessels had shell-based hulls reinforced with posts and frames.[11] For this reason, the size of Japanese ships was severely

6 William E. Deal, *Handbook to Life in Medieval and Early Modern Japan* (Oxford: Oxford University Press, 2006), 333–338.

7 George D. Winius, *Studies On Portuguese Asia, 1495–1689* (Burlington, VT: Ashgate, 2001), XVII, 8.

8 Mathew, *History of Portuguese Navigation*, 283.

9 A.R. Disney, *A History of Portugal and the Portuguese Empire* (Cambridge: Cambridge University Press, 2009), 142.

10 Angus Kostam, *Lepanto 1571: The Greatest Naval Battle of the Renaissance* (Oxford: Osprey Publishing, 2003), 18–20; Guilmartin, *Gunpowder and Galleys*, 209–268.

11 See Vieira de Castro, *The Pepper Wreck*, 34–35.

limited. However, lest "we" get uppity, it should be pointed out that the Chinese seagoing junks of the fifteenth century—the largest of which were over 400 feet in length and 165 feet wide—dwarfed Western ships from the age of exploration.[12] The ships, which regularly sailed to east Africa and possibly around the world, were not only large, but were also technical marvels, with water-tight bulwark compartments (something the West "invented" in the late eighteenth century), prows that handled heavy seas, and a balanced rudder.[13]

3. Many of our vessels are powered only by sail; all Japanese boats are powered with oars.

Generally speaking, the Japanese did not rely on sails as much as Europeans. Japanese boats, while they may have had a sail, were relatively small and poor at going into the wind. Moreover, the Japanese often operated near convoluted, rocky coasts and islands, with fickle winds; most of the time they very wisely relied on manpower.

4. Ours ships are treated on the outside with tar or pitch to keep them from taking on water; the Japanese use no pitch at all, relying solely on the tight fit of their wooden boards.

When Commodore Perry's four ships sailed into Tokyo Bay in 1853, insisting that Japan have relations with the West for the first time in two centuries, the Japanese disparagingly hailed the arrival of "the black ships" (*kurofune*). As was the case in Frois' day, the ships' hulls were black with tar; at least two of the four ships, which were steamers, also belched black smoke.

According to Okada, the Japanese *did* use caulking to stop a leak; they just did not treat the whole bottom of the boat with tar or pitch. If anything, the Japanese were likely to have imitated the Chinese in accentuating the natural look of the wood by applying dammar or some other oil.[14] As Frois indicates, the precision of Japanese workmanship ruled out significant shrinkage and a need for filling cracks with thick coatings. The straight lines of Japanese naval architecture also helped:

The body of the ship is not built roundish, as our European ones, but that part which stands below the surface of the water, runs almost in a straight line towards the keel.[15]

5. Our small vessels are high in the stern and low in the bow; those of the Japanese are high in the bow and low in the stern.

12 Louise Levathes, *When China Ruled the Seas, The Treasure Fleet of the Dragon Throne, 1405–1433* (Oxford: Oxford University Press, 1997).
13 During the fifteenth-century Chinese rulers did an "about-face" and decided their ocean-going fleet was not only unnecessary, but a potential source of trouble. See Jared Diamond for a more essentialist argument: *Guns, Germs and Steel: The Fates of Human Societies* (New York: W. W. Norton & Company, 1997).
14 H. Warington Smyth, *Mast and Sail in Europe and Asia* (London: John Murray, 1906), 396–425.
15 Englebert Kaempfer, *The History of Japan, Together with a Description of the Kingdom of Siam, 1690–92*. 3 Vols. (Glasgow: James MacLehose and Sons, 1906[1690–92]), II, 300.

The high stern (or poop) on European boats of all sizes from the sixteenth century is striking (consider the traditional Venetian gondola or Columbus' ship the Santa Maria). Large Japanese vessels also had high sterns, although their poop deck was more of an extension out over the stern (in the traditional Chinese manner) than the top of a multi-deck aft cabin, as was the case with European sailing ships.

A high bow on a small ship or boat (e.g. a "Boston whaler") is ideal for navigating choppy, coastal waters as it allows the boat to slice through waves without taking on excessive water. And, lacking true decks and bilges, the Japanese would want to keep water completely out, rather than taking it on and having it run out the scruppers (deck-level drains on the side or rear of a boat).

6. Ours ships have cloth sails; all theirs have straw sails.

Frois apparently is still referring to small vessels, which, in the case of the Japanese, probably still relied in 1585 on straw-mat sails. According to Okada, at this time many or most Japanese ships (i.e. *bezaisen*) were using sails of cotton cloth.

7. Our ship's rigging is made from hemp, palm fiber, or coconut fiber; theirs is made from straw.

Frois is comparing the most common type of rope used for rigging. The Japanese may have relied heavily on straw, but they also used rope made from *ichibii* (Indian mallow, for which one of the Chinese characters is 'hemp'), bark from the hinoki tree (a type of cypress), and an unknown plant that was denoted with the Chinese characters for silk grass and hemp.

8. Our anchors are made of iron; theirs of wood.

Wooden anchors may sound strange, but they sank because they had stones tied to them and a cross-bar that helped keep the single barb pointing down. There were probably some four-fluke (Chinese-style) iron anchors, too. A hundred years after Frois, Kaempfer wrote that "the anchors are of iron, and the cables twisted of straw, and stronger than one would imagine." So wood turned to metal but straw remained king.

9. Our ships' prows have either a ram or a bowsprit; the Japanese funes[16] have open bows and are not very well suited for battle.

Going to sea and going to war went hand in hand for Europeans.[17] And if real naval battles were not enough, Europeans enjoyed making believe. As part of his wedding festivities in 1589, Grand Duke Ferdinando I de' Medici flooded the courtyard of the Palazzo Pitti in Florence to stage a spectacular mock sea battle.

European ships were built with a bowsprit (a pole-like projection that served as a bridge for boarding other ships) and sometimes—particularly in the case of the galley—a ram for puncturing and then sinking enemy vessels (the ram was at the waterline or slightly lower). Prior to the loss of the Spanish armada in 1588—a loss

16 This is the first time the term *fune* is used in this chapter; it is the generic Japanese term for ship, similar to the Frois' Portuguese term *navio*.
17 Guilmartin, *Gunpowder and Galleys.*

attributed in significant part to British use of long-range culverins—conventional naval warfare was a matter of ramming, boarding, and hand-to-hand combat.[18]

The unsuitability of Japanese ships for any kind of warfare is legend. Japan had one famous ancient naval battle (*Da no-ura*) in 1185 that sent the whole Heikei clan to the bottom of the sea, where legend has it the warriors left their faces on the shell of the crab called *heikei-gani*. Otherwise, the Sea of Japan generally was for fishing and trade, not fighting.

Frois in his *Historia* recounts an occasion in 1586 when the mighty Hideyoshi asked the Jesuit Vice Provincial Gaspar Coelho for help securing two Portuguese warships to lead Hideyoshi's own Japanese fleet in an invasion of Korea. Although nothing came of the request, it is doubtful that two ships would have made a difference. In 1592 Korean Admiral Yi Sun, in one of the greatest feats of naval warfare, sank the Japanese fleet with a squadron of his newly invented, heavily-armored "turtle-boats"—a whole fleet of ships that anticipated the Monitors and Merrimacs of the American Civil War.

10. Our sailors, as they row, remain seated and quiet; Japanese sailors row standing and almost always singing.

Frois obviously was *not* thinking of the *gondolieri* of Venice who still today row while standing (and some sing as well). Frois presumably had in mind the "ordinary" European galley (*gallia sotil*), which was propelled by upwards of 100 or more seated oarsmen who were divided into groups of four men per oar; usually only one of the four was a free man and the other three were slaves.[19] It is no wonder these galleys were without song.

With respect to Japan, it already has been noted that Japanese boats generally were smaller than European watercraft. Captain Sarris, in 1613, observed something that perhaps only a captain might observe, namely that by performing "their worke standing as ours doe sitting ... they take lesse roome."[20] Kaempfer seconded Frois on the singing aspect of Japanese rowing: "They row according to the air of a song, or the tune of some words, or other noise, which serves at the same time to direct and regulate their work and to encourage one another." Japanese seamen were not the only ones who "sang," as both Elizabeth Bird and Eliza Scidmore were struck by the singing of the men who pulled carts. Eliza Scidmore wrote, rather unsympathetically:

> Those coolies who pull and push heavily loaded carts or drays keep up a hoarse chant, which corresponds to the chorus of sailors when hauling ropes. "Hilda! Hoida!" they seem to be crying, as they brace their feet for a hard pull, and the very sound of it exhausts the listener. In the old days, people

18 Ibid., 75–101. Note that Guilmartin, *Gunpowder & Galleys*, 73–100, persuasively has argued that Mediterranean warfare "at sea" was in reality "amphibious warfare."

19 Konstam, *Lepanto 1571*, 19; Guilmartin, *Gunpowder & Galleys*, 78.

20 Quoted in Douglas Sladen and Norma Lorimer, *More Queer Things About Japan* (London: Anthony Treherne & Company, 1905), 287.

were nearly deafened with these street choruses, but their use is another of the hereditary customs that is fast dying out.[21]

11. Our oars are made as a single piece of wood; Japanese oars are made as two pieces.

The long oars used on European galleys and *galleasses* (galleys with sails) were mostly made from ash, beech, and pine; these are all relatively strong, light-weight woods. According to Kaempfer, the long oars used on Japanese ships were "... not at all streight, like our European oars, but somewhat bent, with a moveable joint in the middle, which yielding to the violent pression of the water, facilitates the taking of them up. The timber pieces and boards are fasten'd together in their joints and extremities, with hooks and bands of copper."[22] Eliza Scidmore gave us a picture in words of these oars in action:

> ... voluble boatmen keep up a steady bzz, bzz, whizz, whizz, to the strokes of their crooked, wobbling oars as they scull in and out.[23]

12. Our oars have a wide, detachable blade; Japanese oars are made of a single piece of wood and the blade is narrow.

The shape of an oar's blade, including its width, affects an oar's performance (i.e. a sea-going oar blade is narrower than an oar blade used on a river). Detachable blades also were an answer to the problem of frequently damaged or broken oar blades. If you chose to use one oar and most of your rowing is in the coastal waters of Japan, a narrow oar makes sense (an oar with a wide blade would be tiring in choppy water).

13. When our sailors row, they lift their oars out of the water; the Japanese row with their oars continually under the water.

Chamberlain[24] devoted almost two pages to debating the pros and cons of the different ways of rowing. He noted that the constant use of the entire body, and the fact that the oars were always submerged, meant that the Japanese oarsman never got to rest. However, rowing with such a large stroke—like using a low gear on a bicycle—can be more efficient and easier than sculling very fast (in the "Western way").[25] Morse wrote: "Our man ... began sculling at ten o'clock at night and kept it up with one or two intermissions until four o'clock the next afternoon, with no sleep and apparently no fatigue."[26]

21 *Jinrikisha Days in Japan* (New York: Harper & Brothers, 1897), 10.
22 Kaempfer, *The History of Japan*, II, 302.
23 *Jinrikisha Days in Japan*, 4.
24 Basil Hall Chamberlain, *Things Japanese, Being Notes on Various Subjects Connected With Japan.* Fourth edition (London: John Murray, 1902), 408.
25 The "Western way" of rowing, which emphasizes great bursts of speed, may have a lot to do with the realities of Mediterranean warfare using galleys. See Guilmartin, *Gunpowder & Galleys*, 209–215.
26 Edward Sylvester Morse, *Japan Day By Day, 1877, 1878–1879, 1882–1883.* 2 Vols. (Boston: Houghton Mifflin, 1917), I, 113.

14. On our boats, we are very cautious about fire; even though Japanese boats are all straw, there is no precaution taken for fire.

Sailors who were with Columbus apparently introduced snuff (ground tobacco that was snorted) to Europe during the closing decade of the sixteenth century. We might now understand why snuff became so popular, so quickly: Sailors obviously were discouraged from smoking aboard ship. (Apparently the "smoking lamp" came into being during the early sixteenth century to essentially restrict smoking to the area near the galley.)[27]

The Japanese were less concerned with fire and even had a boat (*yu-bune*) that was a floating public bath, which was supplied with warm water from a wood-burning fire aboard ship.[28] Perhaps because the Japanese tended to stay near shore, they felt comparatively safe with fire.

15. Among us, respected individuals always ride astern; in Japan the nobility ride on the bow, where at times they get soaked.

One reason for the high poop in Western vessels is for the steersman (or watch) to better see over the bow. Here we learn of another good reason: The smoothest and driest ride generally is at the back of a ship, up high. Unlike Japanese nobles, however, European nobles were not the first to arrive where they were going.

16. Our boats have rounded masts; the masts on the funes are squared.

A square mast is perhaps yet another reflection that the Japanese rowed more than they sailed, as suggested by other distiches in this chapter.

17. We never lower the sails on our boats; they do so the minute they start rowing.

"Never" is a bit of an exaggeration, because in bad storms Europeans not only lowered their sails but sometimes cut down the mast, as the violent swaying of a heavy mast can cause a ship to capsize.

18. Our boats have topsails, mizzen-sails, and foresails; Japanese fune have none of these.

As noted, European ocean-going vessels (e.g. the *nao*, the galleon and the caravel) generally had three masts. The mizzen mast was at the rear or aft of the ship and usually had a lateen-shaped sail, which not only helped propel the ship forward but acted as a giant wind rudder. At the front of the ship was a square foresail, which, in combination with the main sail (also square), generated more propulsion than the sum of each sail on its own. Often above the main sail was yet another, smaller topsail, which also was square.

Japanese ships, including the largest vessels (*bezaisen* or *kitamae-bune*), had one mast with a square sail.

19. Our boats can travel by day or night; Japanese ships put into port at night and travel only by day.

At the time Frois wrote Japanese ships were trading as far away as the Philippines. This shipping, as well as illegal trade with China, clearly required nights spent at sea. One wonders if most of this long-distance sea travel by the

27 Charles Gibowicz, *Mess Night Traditions* (Bloomington: AuthorHouse, 2007), 174–175.
28 Deal, *Handbook to Life in Medieval and Early Modern Japan*, 338.

Japanese actually was done in Chinese ships or ships modeled after the very seaworthy Chinese junk. Kwan-wai So cites a sixteenth-century document to the effect that most of the alleged Wako pirates were using ships with a "sharp bottom" that was introduced by "traitorous people of the Fukien seaboard."[29] The same document notes that the seagoing vessels of Japan had flat bottoms and sails that required favorable winds; it purportedly took Japanese ships a month to cross seas that Chinese boats crossed in days.

Whatever the reality with respect to Japanese long-distance trade, the vast majority of Japanese ships were seemingly built for fishing or coastal shipping, which apparently was conducted strictly by day. (At night, ships put into the nearest harbor.) The irony here is that a half-century after Frois wrote this (beginning in 1633 with the *sakoku* or isolation policy of the Togukawa shogunate), it became illegal for the Japanese to construct any seaworthy ships[30]

20. Our ships often sail regardless of rain; Japanese ships are not to sail unless the weather is clear.

According to Kaempfer, the deck on a Japanese ship "… is built so loose that it will let the [rain] water run through before the mast hath been taken down and the ship cover'd, partly with mats, partly with sails." Knowing this, Kaempfer writes, "We can't accuse the Japanese captains of 'fear and cowardice' for the manner in which they repair to the nearest harbour—available on every inhabited island, and there were many—at the slightest pretext."[31] So, if Frois exaggerates the contrast, he doesn't exaggerate much.

21. Among us, when you hire a small boat, the cost of the crew is included; in Japan, you must pay the same for the fune as you do for a sailor.

This contrast would seem to reflect nothing more than the Japanese having made explicit what is true to both contractual arrangements: When you rent a boat you are also renting its crew (in neither culture did you simply rent a boat and supply your own crew).

22. Among us, a ship's capacity is determined by the size of its hull; in Japan, it is determined by the number of sections in the sail.

Frois is evidently talking about classes of ship rather than capacity per se, which was measured in tonnage in the West and in "stones" of rice in Japan (thought of as a numerical quantity, rather than a weight). Estates were also ranked for prestige and taxes according to this same unit, representing the output of the harvest. Japanese sails were not measured in their equivalent to our square feet or yards, but in units of a given area, namely woven mats, so you have the ten-mat sail class, the twenty-mat sail class, and so on.

29 Kwan-wai So, *Japanese Piracy in Ming China during the Sixteenth Century* (East Lansing: Michigan State University Press, 1975); Jurgis Elisonas, "The inseparable trinity: Japan's relations with China and Korea." In *The Cambridge History of Japan, Volume 4, Early Modern Japan*, ed. John W. Hall, pp. 235–301 (Cambridge: Cambridge University Press, 1991), 250. See also Nancy Yaw Davis, *The Zuni Enigma* (New York: W.W. Norton & Company, 2000), 97.

30 Kaempfer, *The History of Japan*, II, 300–301.

31 Ibid., 298.

23. Among us, each ship has a designated carpenter; the officers aboard Japanese funes are nearly all carpenters.

The *naus* that sailed to and from Lisbon and India had crews of over 100 (mostly sailors and cabin boys) that included various officers charged with maintaining the ship: a carpenter and his assistant; a caulker and his assistant, and a cooper, who was expected to make or repair just about everything aboard ship.[32] As Okada has pointed out, Rodrigues' Japanese-Portuguese dictionary, which appeared less than twenty years after Frois wrote the *Tratado*, includes *funa-daiku* (ship's carpenter), suggesting that there were in fact Japanese specialists in shipbuilding. As often is the case, perhaps Frois exaggerated to make a larger point, namely that an officer aboard a Japanese ship was expected to know how to keep it afloat, whereas officers on a European ship were more specialized.

24. Among us, the person who receives cargo onto a boat provides a bill of lading to the owner, who remains on land; in Japan, the man handing over the cargo also provides a bill of lading to the carrier.

At the time Frois wrote Hideyoshi was using his military forces as well as control of trade to successfully reign in many of Japan's regional elites. A Japanese ship's captain had to be careful about what he carried and where he carried it. Having a bill of lading on board made sense.

25. Our ships' flags are squared; theirs are a long strip of cloth strung on a bamboo pole.

Square nautical flags with different designs and symbols were flown by European ships to identify themselves as well as communicate between ships. Japanese ship "flags" served the same purposes and came in two basic types. The one Frois mentions might better be called a banner and is identical to what one often sees in American cities and towns on light poles on main thoroughfares, announcing local events of interest. This type of Japanese ship flag may have fluttered but it did not move in the breeze, so they served well for purposes of identification. The other major variety of Japanese nautical flag was shaped like a pennant, but tended to have longer tails. Fastened at one end, they dangled in the doldrums or moved about dragon-like when the wind blew.

26. Nothing taken aboard our boats is considered to be an omen;[33] the Japanese have a great fear of transporting bells from Buddhist temples.[34]

Frois wrote at the height of the counter-Reformation when Protestants were damning Catholics as superstitious idolaters. He may therefore have found it difficult to acknowledge that Iberians ships sailed with one or more devotional images as well as rosaries, belonging to the crew. Europeans in general embraced superstitions such as the idea that having women on board was bad luck.

32 Vieira De Castro, *The Pepper Wreck*, 62–63. See also Pablo E. Pérez-Mallaína, *Spain's Men of the Sea*, trans. Carla Rahn Phillips (Baltimore: Johns Hopkins University Press, 1998), 80.

33 *Augúrio*, a terms that does not necessarily mean bad luck. In fact, in his Spanish edition of Frois, De la Fuente Ballesteros translates this term as good luck. The more general sense, however, is that of an omen.

34 *Das varelas*. In Indochina, China and Japan, a Buddhist pagoda and monastery.

According to Okada, large bells were considered dangerous cargo in the Far East because they were popular with the Dragon King living at the bottom of the sea, who would capsize boats to get the bells.

27. We consider all stories regarding mermaids and mermen to be nonsense; the Japanese believe there is an undersea kingdom of lizards that are rational and defend themselves.

Frois again casts Europeans as entirely rational, yet a decade or so before he was born, in 1520, the Bishop of Nidros in Norway wrote a letter to Pope Leo X in which he recounted how he said mass on the back of a sea monster, in apparent imitation of Saint Brendan. The late Middle Ages and early modern period are replete with reports of "bishop-fish," "monk-fish," the "sea-knight," and a host of other anthropomorphic sea creatures, which many Europeans took seriously.[35]

At the time Frois wrote many Japanese fishermen continued to supplicate their age-old sea gods, which were a Dragon King and a Dragon Princess who were indeed "rational" in the sense that they were benign unless angered, in which case they were a likely source of a typhoon.

28. On our boats we always carry a supply of water sufficient for an extended period of time; the Japanese funes re-supply their water stores almost every two days.

This contrast is a variation on #19 above. Again, the Japanese were more "day sailors" than "cruisers."

29. If one of our sails is ripped, it is repaired immediately; in Japan they leave their sails ripped or unrepaired and this is not a matter for concern.

Japanese straw sails were made in sections of the size mentioned in #22 above, so a stitch in time would not make much difference. Moreover, it is probable that some of the "rips" or openings were (unknown to Frois) deliberate. After changing to cotton, it was common for the sails on Japanese ships to be made of long, narrow strips of thin cloth laced together, leaving a space of three or four inches in between. According to Morse, these openings in the sail worked like "reefing" to help keep Japanese sailboats from capsizing in a strong wind.[36]

30. On our fustas and catures, you embark and disembark at the bow; on Japanese vessels, the stern is quickly swung around toward land and one embarks and disembarks from there.

Fustas and *caturs* were smaller vessels with no deck, more like a boat than a ship (see #1 above). Chamberlain offers a similar observation of this contrast: In Japan, "Boats are hauled up on the beach stern first."[37] This also is what "proper people" do with their shoes when they remove them at the portico in Japan: They leave them facing outwards so as to be ready for the next trip.

35 Fletcher S. Bassett, *Legends and Superstitions of the Sea and of Sailors in All Lands* (Chicago: Belford, Clarke and Company, 1885), 209.

36 *Japan Day By Day*, I, 113.

37 *Things Japanese*, 476.

13 Japanese plays, farces, dances, singing and musical instruments

1. Our autos ordinarily are performed at night; the Japanese almost always perform theirs during the day.

During Frois' lifetime the term *auto* came to refer to any relatively brief, one-act play, including a large number of secular dramas written for the Portuguese court by the goldsmith-turned-dramatist Gil Vicente (1465–1537), considered the father of Portuguese theater.[1] The secular variety of the *auto* developed out of the *auto sacramental*, a one-act drama that generally was performed on holy days, particularly the Feast of Corpus Christi. Commissioned by Church or public officials, *autos sacramentales* reiterated religious "truths" or stories from the Bible, lives of the saints, or Christian oral tradition. By the mid-sixteenth century *autos sacramentales* often were accompanied by skits, dialogues, and singing and dancing that often were laced with satire and romance, all of which, according to critics, undermined the religious message of the *auto* itself.[2]

As Frois suggests, secular autos were performed at night, more often than not in the palaces of the nobility and royalty. (*Autos sacremantales* ordinarily were held during the day and frequently outdoors, as per #6 below.)

The Japanese analogue to the *auto* alluded to by Frois almost certainly is *Noh*, which was superficially similar to European drama (e.g. both involved almost exclusively male actors wearing masks, an audience, and a stage). *Noh* is distinctive, however, in that it consists of dialogue or prose as well as singing (by the actors individually and by a chorus off to the side of the stage), dancing (principally by the *shite* or protagonist) and instrumental music provided by three drums and a fife in the "orchestra section" at the rear of the stage. Moreover, whereas European drama sought mostly to mimic reality (e.g. realistic-looking sets, costumes and masks; moving dialogue and the linear unfolding of plot), *Noh* is seemingly more abstract. Many *Noh* are of the *mugen* variety and feature a masked principal actor who portrays a supernatural protagonist (*shite*). The *shite* comes and goes, taking various forms and interacting with supporting, non-masked characters (waki), often an antagonist in the form of a travelling monk, a warrior, or a farmer. A successful *Noh* performance is one in which the actors and audience find

---

1 A complete collection of Vicente's works first appeared in 1562. Gil Vicente, *Auto Da Barca Da Glória, Nao D'Amores*, ed. Maria Idalina Resina Rodrigues (Madrid: Clásicos Castalia, 1995), 61–62.
2 Melveena McKendrick, *Theatre in Spain 1490–1700* (Cambridge: Cambridge University Press, 1992), 39; Jonathan Thacker, *A Companion to Golden Age Theatre* (Woodbridge: Tamesis, 2007), 162.

themselves lost in almost ineffable emotions and spiritual states.[3] In this regard, *Noh* is not unlike *chanoyu*, which also captured the interest of warlords during the sixteenth century.[4]

As Okakura[5] observed, *Noh* was performed on a stage of hard, unpainted wood, with a single pine tree somewhat conventionally portrayed on the background, thus suggesting "a grand monotony" to heighten the "infinite suggestiveness" of this short epic drama. Although one-act *Noh* are not unusual (e.g. *Hagoromo* or "Robe of Feathers"), the majority of *Noh* have at least two acts and many have three or more. One-act seldom went more than an hour without a comic interlude or *kyôgen*. Thus, a *Noh* performance could go on for a whole afternoon or evening (i.e. for five or six hours).

2. Among us, one actor wearing a mask slowly makes his way onto the stage; in Japan two or three actors without masks rush out onto the stage and face each other in the manner of cocks ready to fight.

The sixteenth century witnessed profound innovation in European theatre, fueled by a proliferation of great dramatists, formal acting companies, and the building of public theaters such as the Globe in London and the Corral de la Cruz in Madrid. And yet for all the dynamism, European theater remained true to Greek and Roman drama, including use of the prologue—an extended moment before a play when a masked actor appeared on stage to briefly explain or introduce the comedy or tragedy (signaled, respectively, by a smiling or sorrowful mask).

Frois' comment in this distich about Japanese drama corresponds to the opening sequence in many *Noh*, in which the supporting actor and entourage come out and line up as described. The fact, however, that the actors are said to rush out on to the stage has prompted Okada to suggest that Frois is contrasting a European prologue to a *kyôgen* interlude, which typically separate acts of a *Noh* drama. *Kyôgen* are comic or light-hearted skits that often feature popular song and focus on simple truths or adventures such as travel to the city, or, in the case of city-dwellers, a trip out to the countryside.[6] Most *kyôgen* feature a principal actor

3 Shelly Fenno Quinn, *Developing Zeami: The Noh Actor's Attunement in Practice* (Honolulu: University of Hawai'i Press, 2005), 3–18; Donald Keene and Thomas Rimer, "The Vocabulary of Japanese Aesthetics II," In *Sources of Japanese Tradition, Second Edition, Volume One: From Earliest Times to 1600*, eds. Wm. Theodore de Bary, D. Keene, G. Tanabe, and P. Varley, pp. 364–387 (New York: Columbia University Press, 2001), 369; Andrew J. Perarik, "Noh Masks." In *Japan's Golden Age: Momoyama*, ed. Money L. Hickman, pp. 291–30 (New Haven: Yale University Press, 1996), 291; Shio Sakanashi, *Kyôgen: Comic Interludes of Japan* (Boston: Marshall Jones Company, 1938); Kunio Komparu, *The Noh Theater, Principles and Perspectives* (New York: Weatherhill, 1983).

4 *Noh* reached the peak of its popularity during the reign of Toyotomi Hideyoshi (1536–1598), who was himself fond of performing. George Elison, "Hideyoshi, The Bountiful Minister," In *Warlords, Artists, and Commoners*, eds. George Elison and Bardwell L. Smth, pp. 223–245 (Honolulu: University of Hawai'i Press, 1981), 242; Perarik,"Noh Masks," 291.

5 Kakuzo Okakura, *The Ideals of the East, with Special Reference to the Art of Japan* (New York: IGG Muse Inc., 2000[1904]), 183.

6 Frank Hoff. "City and Country: Song and the Performing Arts in the Sixteenth Century." In *Warlords, Artists, and Commoners, Japan in the Sixteenth Century*, eds. George Elison and Bardwell Smith, pp. 133–163 (Honolulu: The University of Hawai'i Press, 1981), 134–137.

(*shite*) and two associates (*ado*); their comic intent is immediately made known either verbally or by exaggerated observance of rigid stage conventions.[7] Eliza Scidmore[8] described a *kyôgen* entrance as follows:

> The actors enter at a gait that out—struts the most exaggerated stage stride ever seen, the body held rigid as a statue, and the foot, never wholly lifted, sliding slowly along the polished floor.

3. Our autos are in verse; theirs are all in prose.

Speakers of Romance languages found rhyming fairly easy because their languages had fewer phonemes to match and used a wide range of versification. Consider the following stanza from Gil Vicente's *Nao D'Amores*, first performed for Portugal's João III in 1527:

Señora, yo vengo acá	**My lady, I come here**
con fatiga y passion tanta	**tired but filled with a passion**
cual nunca fue ni Será[9]	**as never there was, nor ever will be**

Japanese lacks the proper syntax for end rhyme, as Frois points out in Chapter 10 (#26). Moreover, as noted, Noh performances consist of more than dialogue or prose.

4. Ours often vary and others are reworked; theirs are predetermined in all aspects from the outset and do not vary.

This contrast bears some similarity to Frois' comment about changing fashions in Europe and the lack therof in Japan (see Chapter 1, #3). With respect to Europe, certainly the sixteenth century was a time of significant change. Even though most works of drama, particularly *autos*, were formulaic and reiterated "old" themes (e.g. human frailty and God's power and mercy), theatrical genres were constantly subverted and re-invented such that spectators both knew what to expect, and yet expected to be surprised.[10]

In Japan, Zeami, *Noh's* Shakespeare, died ca.1443, a hundred years before the first Portuguese reached Japan.[11] By then, *Noh* had become *the* drama of Japan and most Japanese acting schools took their cue from Zeami, the actor, the playwright, and the theorist. Although critics and scholars often blame the Tokugawas for enforcing Hideyoshi's law of 1591, which essentially fixed theatrical repertoires,[12]

---

7 Sakanashi, *Kyôgen*, 19.

8 *Jinrikisha Days in Japan* (New York: Harper & Brothers, 1897), 98.

9 Vicente, *Auto Da Barca Da Glória*, 107. As this quote indicates, Vicente wrote in Spanish as well as Portuguese.

10 Thacker, *A Companion to Golden Age Theatre*, 145.

11 Quinn, *Developing Zeami*; Eta Harich-Schneider, *A History of Japanese Music* (London: Oxford University Press, 1973), 420–422.

12 Akira Tamba, *The Musical Structutre of Noh*, trans. Patricia Matoré (Tokyo: Tokyo University Press, 1981), 17.

Frois' comment here would seem to suggest that Noh drama had become prescriptive over a decade before that much-maligned era began.

5. Ours, being autos rather than tragedies, are not divided into acts; theirs are always divided into first, second, third, etc.

Autos were one-act plays that lasted anywhere from thirty to ninety minutes; generally they have only one setting or scene. For instance, Gil Vicente's auto "The Boat to Hell" all takes place in the chamber of one Queen Maria. The queen's chamber is the scene for a trial-like encounter between the devil and a host of sinful elites who enter the chamber only to be successively assigned a seat on the devil's boat leaving for hell.[13]

Zeami argued that *Noh* should follow the principle of *Jo, Ha* and *Kyû*, which translate respectively as introduction or slow beginning, development or a build-up in dramatic tension, and then a rapid finish. In keeping with this principle, each act of *Noh* is divisible into smaller units (*dan*) with particular instrumental music, dialogue, poetry, and/or chorus.[14] Thus, a two-act *Noh* would have at least six *dan* and, as noted, each act would be separated by a *kyôgen* interlude.

6. Our performers emerge onto the stage from a separate structure in which they cannot be seen; Japanese performers are near the theatre behind sail-like curtains.

Frois seems to be referring here specifically to *autos sacramentales*, which had their origins in the Feast of Corpus Christi (instituted in 1264 by Pope Urban IV). These *autos* often were the culmination of a procession that featured wagons (*carros*) with elaborate superstructures and tableaux that graphically and dramatically depicted religious truths or allegories. Usually the procession eventuated at an important or central plaza, where a pair of wagons was pulled up next to a temporary stage where the *auto* was performed.[15] This may be what Frois is referring to when he speaks of performers emerging on stage from a "separate structure."[16]

The stage for a *Noh* performance typically has a bridge (visible to the audience) leading from the back of the stage to a "green room" off to the left. Here the actors wait behind what Sakanishi describes as a "curtain of five colors."[17] Okada guesses that Frois' odd expression "sail-like curtains" (*cortinas de fune*) meant an entrance curtain that was hoisted in the manner of a sail. Indeed, such a curtain is still used in *Noh* today. The curtain is raised from the bottom hem and has the visual effect of a billowing sail. As Komparu[18] notes, before the curtain

---

13 Vicente, *The Boat Plays*, 24–45.
14 Tamba, *The Musical Structutre of Noh*, 22–27; Harich-Schneider, *History of Japanese Music*, 436.
15 Brown, *History of Theatre*, 162–163.
16 *Autos sacramentales* also were performed indoors in the palaces and homes of the nobility. Gil Vicente, for instance, staged plays in the palace of João II and his wife Queen Leonor, as did Juan del Encina for the Duke of Alba in his palace near Salamanca. It is not clear what the "separate structure" would be in this case, although Frois' larger point seems to be that the audience, in any case, cannot see actors waiting to take the stage.
17 See Sakanishi, *Kyôgen*, xiv–xv.
18 *The Noh Theater*, 140.

is raised the principal actor or *shite* actually begins his performance (apparently as a shadow behind the curtain), perhaps explaining Frois' preoccupation in this distich with performers "off stage" who are visible (as opposed to those who are hidden, in the European case).

7. Our autos are performed through speaking; theirs are nearly always sung— or danced.

As Frois indicates, European drama was by and large a matter of spoken dialogue and soliloquy. In 1585 opera was still an emerging art form in Italy, spawned by experiments at recovering "authentic" Greek drama, which humanist scholars argued was primarily sung rather than spoken.

Although the first recognized performance of *ka-bu-ki*, or sing-dance-technique, did not take place until 1594, song and dance long had been a part of Japanese drama. In this regard, what perhaps distinguishes *Noh* from earlier drama is that is has more "telling" than dialogue *per se* and this "telling" is conveyed through "song" and dance. With regard to the "song," Okakura found it full of what we now call sound effects, such as "the soughing of the wind amongst the pine boughs, the dropping of water, or the tolling of distant bells, the stifling of sobs, the clash and clang of war, echoes of the weavers beating the new web against the wooden beam, the cry of crickets, and all the manifold voices of night and nature, where pause is more significant than pitch."[19] During these extended moments of "semi-articulate sound," actors could rest their voices and allow dance to tell, or rather suggest, the story.

8. We consider it disruptive and insulting to make noise during an auto; in Japan a performance is honored and praised if there are some people on the outside giving loud hoots and hollers.

Autos of both the secular (i.e. palace performances) and religious variety were pretty staid affairs. *Autos sacramentales* often were a dramatic portrayal of a theological statement about God's enduring presence in the lives of Christians, realized especially through the Eucharist. Certainly for Catholics it was rude (if not "sinful") to make noise or otherwise act disrespectfully during these particular *autos*.[20] However, theatergoers attending one of Cervantes' plays, or spectators in Italy who crowded around street performers who pioneered the *commedia dell' Arte*, were hardly quiet. Indeed, with the exception of the *autos sacramentales*, theatrical performance in sixteenth century Europe was all about the playwright and actors engaging the audience and making them part of the performance.[21]

At climactic moments of *Kabuki*, it is not unusual for audience members to yell out and cheer on actors, much as fans at an American baseball game yell insults or

---

19 Kakuzo Okakura, *The Ideals of the East, with Special Reference to the Art of Japan* (New York: IGG Muse Inc., 2000[1903]), 184.

20 This was especially true given that Catholics and Protestants were literally killing each other over the Catholic belief that the consecrated host was truly God incarnate.

21 Steven Mullaney, *The Place of the Stage, License, Play, and Power in Renaissance England* (Chicago: University of Chicago Press, 1988), 48–49.

cheer for their favorite players when they are at bat.[22] It is conceivable that in Frois' time some *Noh* or *Kyôgen* interludes encouraged the audience to voice their approval of actors during a performance. Because *Noh* involve relatively little dialogue, audience participation was not likely to compete with the actors' infrequent, slowly drawn out speech. In Japanese folk (festival and farm) singing, a sporadic musical accompaniment or a shrill chorus of voices, usually female, is often used to spice up the melody. Especially in festivals, this "sassy" sound works wonderfully to increase the total energy level of the performance, much in the way that "call backs" enrich the total sound effect of a Southern black Baptist congregation in America.

9. Our masks cover the entire jaw and beard; in Japan the masks are so tiny that if an actor is playing the role of a woman, his beard is always sticking out from under it.

Imagine the role of Juliet in *Romeo and Juliet* being played by a man with a beard! Sounds strange, but in much of Europe (Italy, Spain and France witnessed more exceptions) it was still common in 1585 (or 1594, when Shakespeare wrote) for men or boys to play female roles.[23] The Church and Europeans more generally frowned on women taking to the stage. Thus, Frois' focus here on masks that succeeded or failed to hide the beards of male actors.

In *Noh* men also played both male and female roles and wore small masks carved from cypress wood.[24] Because Frois noted that it was unusual for any Japanese man to have a beard (see Chapter 1, #5), he is probably referring in this distich to the fact that *Noh* masks were not "full-face" masks intended to actually cover and disguise the actor's face, and thus if a Japanese man *were* to have a beard, the beard would be apparent. *Noh* masks generally bespeak an archetypal figure (*shite*), whose emotional/spiritual state is conveyed by the actor through dialogue, song, dance, and gesture. Japanese three-dimensional "art" could be very realistic (e.g. statues showing each pore of the skin, with carefully implanted real hair). The *Noh* mask bespeaks an aesthetic choice for an icon with more typological rather than explicit meaning.[25] European drama, much like Renaissance art, aimed for mimetic credulity, using backdrops and other props that were realistic and often cost a small fortune.

10. Our comedies or tragedies feature gentle musical instruments; in Japan they use small kettledrums shaped like goblets, a larger kettledrum played with two sticks, and a bamboo flute.

Frois is generally correct that European drama featured music that served as aural background rather than conveying significant meaning and thus being integral to a performance. Arguably, the Japanese used their instruments (two different

---

22 Mira Felner, *The World of Theater, Tradition and Innovation* (Boston: Allyn and Bacon, 2006), 32.

23 During the second half of the sixteenth century (Frois left Europe in 1548) women increasingly appeared on stage in Spanish theaters, perhaps as result of the example set by Italian touring companies.

24 Perarik, "Noh Masks," 291.

25 Ibid., 292. Perarik suggests that the masks are not altogether typological in that an experienced actor can convey different feelings or emotions by lifting a mask or tilting it in various directions.

drums and a flute) to create what is analogous to a modern-day movie soundtrack: the music could get very intense and often conveyed as much or more meaning than the dialogue or movements of the actors.

The first drum mentioned by Frois is called a *ko tsuzumi*, and it is played by hand. It looks like a long hourglass, with percussive membranes on each end that are laced together with chords that can be squeezed as one strikes the drum membranes. Striking the membranes while squeezing the chords results in what is essentially a "talking-drum."

The second type of drum (*taiko*) is just a drum; when hit on the head it gives a good solid drum sound. Note that the sticks that Frois mentions spend most of their time hitting the wood on the side of the drum. Both drums were used to emphasize and harmonize with the telling and the action of the play, mostly in a temporal rather than tonal way.

The bamboo flute is more like a "fife." The naturally shrill quality of the instrument, which makes it a favorite for military bands in the West, achieves a new level in the sound world of the Japanese. While the Japanese fife is capable of a soft and gentle sound in the low range, it more frequently is used to produce a blasting sound. This blasting has two characteristics not often found in Western music. First, it is not always worked up to in the Western manner where sounds crescendo, but often begins in its full fury. That is to say, it is explosive. It hits as strong gusts of wind often do. Second, the fifer does not stop when the sound threatens to break, but enjoys blasting it up and over its limits. This critical break is played upon like a surfer riding a wave, and the thrill to the initiated—or those with an ear for it—is pretty much the same.

11. In our dances, the dancers move to the sound of the tambourine, but they do not sing; Japanese dancers must always sing to the sound of the drum.

Frois' mention here of the tambourine suggests he had in mind folk dances or even courtly dances (*danzas de sarao*) that were performed by local dancers in conjunction with *autos* or religious feasts.[26]

It is difficult to know the Japanese referent in this distich. The hourglass-shaped drum (*ko tsuzumi*) that is part of the *Noh* ensemble (see #10 above) was very popular in Japan at the time Frois wrote. It served as accompaniment for all manner of performers and party-goers, including samurai on picnics or flower-viewing outings.[27] Music was a regular feature of daily life in Japan and one can well imagine that Frois might also have witnessed Japanese peasants singing (and dancing) while sowing rice to the accompaniment of a drum and perhaps the fife mentioned above.[28]

26 Lynn Matluck Brooks, *The Art of Dancing in Seventeenth-Century Spain* (Lewisburg, PA: Bucknell University Press, 2003), 24–26.
27 See Kanō Hideyori's screen painting "Maple Viewing at Mount Takao" (Ca. 1577). Money L. Hickman, "Painting." In *Japan's Golden Age, Momoyama*, ed. Money L. Hickman, pp. 93–181 New Haven: Yale University Press, 1996), 114–115.
28 William P. Malm, "Music Cultures of Momoyama Japan." In *Warlords, Artists, and Commoners, Japan in the Sixteenth Century.eds.* George Elison and Bardwell L. Smith, pp. 163–186 (Honolulu: The University of Hawaii Press, 1981), 166, 175–176.

234 Japanese plays, farces, dances, singing and musical instruments

12. Our performers move about upright, with rattles; in Japan they carry fans and always move about [stooped over][29] or like people looking down at the ground in search of something they have lost.

Rattles figure prominently in the *folia*, a traditional dance of Portuguese peasants that underwent "refinement" in Iberian royal courts during the sixteenth and seventeenth centuries. The name for the dance derived from *folle*, which means crazy, apparently suggested by the seemingly chaotic sound produced by the dancers wielding their rattles.[30]

For Japan, Frois presumably was referring to the popular Buddhist dances (*odori*), such as the present day *bon odori*, which is performed in late July through September as part of a joyous festival of the dead (ultimately rooted in Chinese Buddhism). The *bon odori* is a circle dance of sorts, except that individuals do not hold hands (as in Europe), but rather progress individually in a counter-clockwise fashion, with everyone synchronously moving forward and back, and then left and right, making a bent over or swooping movement. Japanese performers do indeed look like they might be searching the ground for a lost item.

13. Our dances are performed during the day; theirs, nearly always at night.

Most Iberian folk dancing took place during weddings, feast days, harvest festivals, etc., which mostly took place outdoors and in the afternoon (or before dark).[31] Such dances are commensurate with the Japanese *bon odori*,[32] which, as noted above, is a festive dance held each year in late summer or early fall.

14. European dance involves many [different] movements by the feet; Japanese dance is more solemn and for the most part is done with the hands.

This is one of the few distichs where Frois explicitly speaks of Europe as opposed to the more ambiguous "ours" or "we." Europeans, be they from the north or the south, Catholics or Protestants, let their feet and legs do the talking when it came to dance.[33] The *galliard*, which was popular throughout Europe in the sixteenth century, typically had five steps to a measure and featured leaps and jumps.

From the Japanese perspective people who are possessed or otherwise experiencing an altered state of consciousness whirl about and leap wildly, as Europeans were wont to do. An actor performing the lion dance (*shishimai*) might also become exuberant. However, generally speaking, Japanese dance is restrained and stylized, as is the case with Japanese music, where silence between notes is as

---

29 The Portuguese original is missing a word or two; "stooped over" would seem to be implied by the remainder of the distich.

30 Rui Vieira Nery, *História da Música* (Lisbon: Imprensa Nacional-Casa da Moeda, 1991); Brooks, *The Art of Dancing*, 138–139.

31 Gayle Kassing, *History of Dance: An Interactive Arts Approach* (Champaign, IL.: Human Kinetics, 2007),77–79; Rodney Gallop, "The Folk Music of Portugal: I." *Music & Letters* 14(1933):220–230.

32 In their Japanese-language edition of the *Tratado*, Matsuda and Jorissen have taken issue with this contrast, citing numerous instances of night dancing in Europe. However, it seems that Frois is talking about formal as opposed to social dancing.

33 Not that all European dance featured leaps and jumps; for instance, during circle dances such as the *ballo Sardo* (Sardinian dance) the feet stay close to the ground.

meaningful as the notes themselves. "Doing nothing" or non-movement is integral to Japanese dance.[34]

15. Our music, with its multi-part harmonies, is gentle and full; in Japan, since they all screech, singing a one-part melody, it is the most horrendous music possible.

The European music that Frois knew, presumably polyphonic masses, motets, and some of the secular *cantigas* of the period,[35] made a big deal of harmony (multiple layers of sound that formed a complex background to a primary melody).

As Tamba explains, Japanese singing as encountered in *Noh* reflects a different esthetic (as compared with Western singing) and a whole host of vocal skills and techniques, including, for instance, pronounced use of the pharynx (the very back of the mouth, just above the vocal chords) rather than the nasal or oral cavity.[36] Most Westerners seemingly lack the ear to comprehend the complex Japanese voice and hear it instead as primitive cacophony. Isabella Bird was perhaps an exception. Despite finding a Japanese vocal performance "most excruciating" and even complaining that the minor scale was "a source of pain" (an ebullient Christian, she was no doubt into major keys), Bird gamely kept her ears uncovered long enough to offer one of the better descriptions of Japanese traditional singing, one that includes what Frois' contrast misses:

> It seemed to me to consist of a hyena-like howl, long and high (a high voice being equivalent to a good voice), varied by frequent guttural, half-suppressed sounds, a bleat, or more respectfully, "an impure shake," which is very delicious to a musically educated Japanese audience which is both scientific and highly critical, but eminently distressing to European ears.[37]

16. Vibrato exists in all the nations of Europe; among the Japanese there is no one who uses vibrato.

Frois is apparently still talking about singing (as opposed to instrumental music), in which case his observation about *vibrato* (a tremulous effect imparted by slight and rapid variations in pitch) is interesting, inasmuch as music scholars disagree about the prevalence of *vibrato* in sixteenth century vocal music. Although Frois seems to imply that *vibrato* was widely used in Europe, the question remains as to whether it was used with discretion or as an incessant "disfigurement" of musical performance.[38]

---

34 William E. Deal, *Handbook of Life In Medieval And Early Modern Japan* (Oxford: Oxford University Press, 2007), 268.

35 Marques, *Daily Life in Portugal*, 259–260, states that there is no evidence of the use of polyphony in Portugal before the fifteenth century. There are a number of extant collections of Portuguese *cantigas* or songbooks from the sixteenth century, including the *Cancioneiro de Elvas*, which was compiled around 1560. The Elvas songbook has sixty-five songs written in three-part harmony. Manuel Morais, *Cancioneiro Musical d'Elvas* (Lisbon, Fundacão Calouste Gulbenkian, 1977).

36 Tamba, *The Musical Structure of Noh*, 35–37.

37 *Unbeaten Tracks in Japan* (Boston: Beacon Press, 1987[1880]), II, 210.

38 James Stark, *Bel Canto: A History of Vocal Pedagogy* (Toronto: University of Toronto Press, 1999), 123–124,

Westerners such as Frois apparently have difficulty recognizing Japanese *vibrato* because the fluctuation in pitch that characterizes *vibrato* in *Noh* strays beyond the narrow frequency implied by a Western definition of vibrato.[39]

17. Among us, music played on the clavichord,[40] *viola, flute, organ, doçaina,*[41] *etc. is considered extremely gentle; the Japanese find all our instruments harsh and unpleasant.*

While the Japanese generally disliked European music, and *vice versa*, some very prominent Japanese found European music engaging. Oda Nobunaga (1534–1582) and Toyotomi Hideyoshi (1536–1598), the top rulers of Japan, reportedly listened with pleasure to performances of Western music.[42] Also, Frois' friend and fellow Jesuit, Organtino, wrote to the Jesuit Father General in Rome that if he had organs and other musical instruments and plenty of missionaries he could convert all of Miyako [Kyoto] and Sakai in a year.[43] Reading this, and knowing that many Japanese and Japanese-Americans perform today in symphony orchestras around the world, one cannot help but wonder if Western music would have made significant inroads in Japan had Japan not isolated itself from the West during the Tokugawa period. Sadly, it seems less certain that European attitudes toward Japanese instruments and music would have changed given more exposure. Writing in 1890, Chamberlain dismissed the idea of Japanese music:

> Music, if that beautiful word may be allowed to fall so low as to denote the strummings and squeals of Orientals, is supposed to have existed in Japan ever since mythological times.[44]

18. We hold the harmony and symmetry of polyphonic[45] *music in high esteem; the Japanese find it noisy and clamorous*[46] *and do not enjoy it at all.*

Not all Europeans, educated or otherwise, were excited about polyphonic music; some felt that it was a "big noise" that paled in comparison with the beauty of a

---

39 Tamba, *The Musical Structure of Noh*, 37–39.
40 *Cravo*. The perhaps more familiar harpsichord (*espineta* in Portuguese) is older and smaller than the *cravo*. Portuguese also has the word *clavicórdio*, which refers to an instrument that is similar to the cravo, yet somehow different. Antônio Houaiss, Mauro de Salles Villar, and Francisco Manoel de Mello Franco, eds., *Dicionário Houaiss Da Língua Portuguesa*. (Rio de Janiero: Objetiva, 2001).
41 The *doçaina* was a reed instrument belonging to the oboe family that was very popular in Europe from the fourteenth to seventeenth centuries. Houaiss et al., *Dicionário Houaiss*, 1068.
42 Michael Cooper, *The Japanese Mission to Europe, 1582–1590* (Kent UK: Global Oriental, 2005), 158. See also Harich-Schneider, *History of Japanese Music*, 445–486.
43 Josef Franz Schütte, S.J., *Valignano's Mission Principles for Japan*, Volume I, Part II, trans. John J. Coyne, S.J. (St. Louis: Institute for Jesuit Sources, 1985), 117.
44 *Things Japanese: Being Notes on Various Subjects Connected With Japan*. Fourth edition (London: John Murray, 1902), 248.
45 *Canto d'orgão*. Houaiss et. al., *Dicionário Houaiss Da Língua Portuguesa*, 614.
46 *Caxi maxi* (*kashimashi*), a word that refers to noise made by the inclusion of too many elements. To use modern idiom, "cacophonous." It is often written with a Chinese character (despised by Japanese feminists) for three women.

solo voice.[47] Japan had never known polyphonic music, so one could well imagine that many Japanese had difficulty appreciating polyphony. However, the Japanese did have one type of inadvertent or unconscious harmony created by Buddhist sutra chanting. In a large temple with fifty or more people sing-songing the sutra in their natural tone of voice-each pausing to take his or her breath whenever they naturally run out and perhaps partially synchronizing this subconsciously to the periodic chime-an effect is incidentally or accidentally achieved that is similar to the staggered singing of "Row, Row, Row Your Boat."

19. Ordinarily among us the music of the nobility is gentler than that of the common folk; we cannot stand to listen to the music of the Japanese nobles, but we find their sailors' music acceptable.

As is apparent from the two previous contrasts, Europe's nobility generally took pride in supporting choral and chamber music. In 1585, the nobility in Japan was basically the military class, which embraced the relatively stark music found in *Noh*. The "sailors' music" that Frois and other Europeans found acceptable was probably the working chants mentioned in Chapter 12 (#10). Frois may also have heard honest-to-goodness folk-songs or sea chanteys:

> The sailors in rowing their boats back and forth in the harbour have a peculiar song entirely unlike the sailors' songs further south [i.e. Yokohama, Kobe and other mainland ports in Japan]. It is musical and catchy … the curious chant as it comes over the water is very pleasant.[48]

Morse wrote this in Hakodate, at the southern tip of the northernmost island now known as Hokkaido. In a footnote he added something that suggests exactly what Frois heard:

> In the extreme southern part of Japan I heard the identical song sung by the sailors of Kagoshima Gulf, and on my return to America a Russian troupe which visited Salem sang a piece called a Volga sailor's song strongly suggesting the Hakodate song. Such an air might easily spread through northern Russia to Kamchatka and find its way to Yezo [Hokaido] through the Kurile Islands.

Because Frois likely predates Russian influence, a more likely source is the Koreans, who have many lullabies that are considered sweet to the ears.[49]

47 Jeanice Brooks, *Courtly Song in Late Sixteenth Century France* (Chicago: University of Chicago Press, 2000), 129.

48 Edward S. Morse, *Japan Day By Day, 1877, 1878–1879, 1882–1883*. 2 Vols. Boston: Houghton Mifflin, 1917), I, 422.

49 Peter H. Lee, *The Columbia Anthology of Traditional Korean Poetry*, edited by Peter H. Lee (New York: Columbia University Press, 2002); Hoff, "City and Country."

20. In Europe boys sing an octave higher than men; in Japan they all screech out the same note, the one on which the treble clef rests [on the staff].[50]

European Children at a very early age used song to memorize prayers (e.g. *Ave Maria, Pater noster*), litanies, hymns, and Church teachings/canons, which often were performed in distinctive registers at school, church, or during processions.[51] The sixteenth century also was a time when cathedrals across Europe combined boys' and mens' choirs to perform polyphonic music (with pre-pubescent boys and some men assigned the alto parts).[52]

As noted, the Japanese do not harmonize but rather sing a single melody, in a single key. Frois' usage (screech) once again reveals his inability to "walk the walk" of cultural relativism.

21. Our violas have six strings, except the double-stringed ones,[53] *and they are plucked using the fingers; the Japanese viola has four strings and is played with a kind of comb.*

The violas mentioned here by Frois are unlike the four-stringed bowed instrument that today forms a regular part of string sections or quartets (accompanying two violins and a cello). The six-stringed instrument is a *viola da gamba*, which looks somewhat like a modern cello (or miniature base) and is played with a bow, although the bow hairs are relatively loose and the bow itself is held with the palm up, rather than down, as with a modern cello bow. The plucked, "double-stringed" *viola* mentioned by Frois is the *viola braguesa*,[54] which was descended from the Spanish *vihuela* (a guitar-like instrument).

The four-stringed Japanese instrument is a *biwa*, a beautiful, teardrop-shaped lute with a round back and flat front, sound-holes modeled after heavenly bodies, and a neck that bends obliquely back at the top. Like the folk samisen, it is powerfully plucked, or perhaps better said, struck, for a *biwa* player is called a *biwa-uchi* or "*biwa*-striker." This is accomplished with an enormous plectrum, usually made of ivory, with the size and shape of a thin hatchet head. (Frois wrote "comb" because combs used to be very high-backed and the over-all shape resembles the plectrum.) A large and heavy pick is indeed about as far as one can get from

---

50 The second half or Japanese part of this contrast has stumped many of Frois' translators, particularly "… *em que o tipre estaa descansado*." The Portuguese word is, in fact, *tiple*, which means treble or soprano. Treble is the name assigned to one of the clefs in which music can be composed, the other most common one being bass clef. 'Treble clef' in Portuguese is *clave de soprano* (= *tiple*), or *clave de sol na segunda linha*, which means that the clef symbol rests on the second line of the musical staff, representing the note *sol* or G. Frois' text says *em que o tipre esta descansado*, meaning 'the note on which the treble rests,' which means the line on the staff around which the curl of the treble clef is centered, hence our translation as rendered.

51 Kate van Orden, "Children's Voices: Singing and Literacy in Sixteenth-Century France." *Early Music History* 25(2006):209–256.

52 Marques, *Daily Life in Portugal*, 221–222.

53 *Dobradas*.

54 Houaiss et. al., *Dicionário Houaiss*, 2865, note that the *viola braguesa* (from the Braga region in northwestern Portugal) was plucked rather than bowed and had five or six pairs of strings, which were tuned in the same manner as a guitar.

delicate fingertips. It sounds astounding, but it actually has three clear advantages over a smaller one or simply using the fingertips. First, it prevents almost any acoustic leakage: the vibration that would be lost with a lighter pick is all saved to produce a higher volume. Second, its length translates a small movement of the wrist into a large one at the end of the pick. And third, it can serve as a defensive weapon—against a snowball in a haiku by Issa, but more commonly (at least in pulp literature and "Easterns"!) to cut the throat of another or oneself in defense of virtue. Apparently the large plectrum is a purely Japanese invention, for the Chinese, from whom the *biwa* was adopted, pluck with their fingers.

22. Among us, the nobility take pride in playing the viola; in Japan, it is an occupation for the blind, like concertina[55] players in Europe.

If Japanese noblemen and samurai were expected to be proficient at composing poetry, the tea-ceremony and swordsmanship, Portuguese nobility were expected to master the troubadour's art of singing one's own poems or *romanceiros* (ballads) while plucking the viola [*braguesa*].[56] The popularity of ballads in Portugal is suggested by their publication as inexpensive broadsides and in booksized collections, beginning around 1548.[57] In his *Book of the Courtier* (1528) Castiglione remarked, "… singing poetry accompanied by the viola seems especially pleasurable, for the instrument gives the words a really marvelous charm and effectiveness."[58]

As regards blind concertina players, today in Portugal or Spain one is likely to encounter gypsies playing the concertina; the blind often sell lottery tickets.

In Japan, the lute was indeed identified with blind musicians, who were called *biwa-houji* or priests of the *biwa-h shi*, and they seem to have been particularly active in and around Kyoto. Although they were rarely actual Buddhist priests, they assumed a religious guise (i.e. costume and shaved head). Unlike the Portuguese nobility, the specialty of the *biwa* players was not love songs or hymns, but legend, and mostly the *Heike-monogatari*, which tells of the tragic downfall of a beloved, highly aesthetic noble clan.[59] However, it is apparent that the *biwa* was played by more than the *biwa-houji*. When Saris visited Nagasaki twenty-eight years after Frois penned the *Tratado*, he was paid a courtesy call by the "King of Hirado" who brought some women with him who played the *biwa* in a manner of a *samisen* (a three-string banjo introduced to Japan from the Philippines a century later):

55 *Sanfonineiros.*

56 Marques, *Daily Life in Portugal*, 259. In his *A History of Song* (New York: W.W. Norton, 1970), 20, Denis Stevens seemingly takes issue with Frois, suggesting that many or most troubadours were from the upper class.

57 Manuel da Costa Fontes, "Between Ballad and Parallelistic Song: A *Condessa Traidora* in the Portuguese Oral Tradition." In *Medieval and Renaissance Spain and Portugal*, eds. Martha E. Schaffer and Antonio Corijo Ocaña, pp.182–196 (Rochester: Tamesis, 2006), 182.

58 Baldesar Castiglione, *The Book of the Courtier*, trans. George Bull (London: Penguin Books, 1967[1528]), 120.

59 Shelley Fenno Quinn, "Oral and Vocal Traditions of Japan," In *Teaching Oral Traditions*, ed. John M. Foley, pp. 258–266 (New York: Modern Language Association, 1998), 262; Helen Craig McCullough, trans., *The Tale of the Heike*, (Stanford: Stanford University Press, 1988).

The kings women seemed to be somewhat bashful, but he willed them to bee frolicke. They sang diuers songs, and played vpon certain instruments (whereof one did much resemble our lute) being bellyed like it, but longer in the necke, and fretted like ours, but had only foure gut strings. Their fingring with the left hand like ours, very nimbly, but the right hand striketh with an iuory bone, as we vse to playe upon a citterne with a quill. They delighted themselues much with their musicke, keeping time with their hands.[60]

23. Our clavichords have four strings and are played with keys; the Japanese ones have twelve strings and are played with wooden picks made for this purpose.

The clavichord was a small (less than four feet long), free-standing or tabletop keyboard that was very popular with middle class families in Europe as well as lesser nobles. It also was a favorite of music schools attached to monasteries and cathedrals.[61] Around the time Frois was growing up, his hometown of Lisbon had twelve clavichord makers.[62] While four strings may not seem like a lot, fretted clavichords had multiple keys and associated tangents that struck each string in a different location. Also, unlike the piano, which produces a relatively finite sound when the keys are depressed, the clavichord is more like a guitar in that one can depress the keys with differential force and correspondingly engage the strings in such a way as to allow for variation in sound.

The Japanese *koto* is a long zither that is invariably played using a tubular pick that fits completely over the end of the finger. (The verb *hamaru*, used to indicate donning a pick, is also used for putting on a ring.) By the mid-nineteenth century the *koto* had thirteen rather than twelve strings. Arguably it was the one instrument that most attracted Westerners, for it makes a sweet tinkling or harp-like sound far sweeter than Japanese lutes and softer than Japanese flutes. Despite the considerable strength needed to depress the strings and carry the *koto*, traditionally it has been the instrument of "proper" young women. During the Edo era that followed Frois, *senryû* joked about the *koto* being an instrument played and appreciated by women who grew up as guarded young virgins. Yet this cloying quality is not intrinsic to the instrument, which some Japanese and Korean women play with the fervor of a blues guitarist.

24. Among us the blind are very pacific; in Japan they like to fight and they go about with canes and daggers[63] and are very amorous.

Europeans viewed blindness as punishment from God, particularly for lustful behavior.[64] Thus it is not surprising that the blind were pacific, accepting alms or playing the concertina for passersby.

60 Quoted in Henry Davenport Northrop and John Ruseell Young, eds., *The Flowery Kingdom and the Land of the Mikado or China, Japan and Chorea* (J.H Moore and Company, 1894), 486.
61 Bernard Brauchli, *The Clavichord* (Cambridge: Cambridge University Press, 1998), 54.
62 Ibid., 54.
63 *Vaqizaxis* [*wakizashi* = dagger(s)].
64 Irina Metzler, *Disability in Medieval Europe* (London: Routledge, 2006), 78.

The Japanese had a somewhat similar attitude toward the blind, believing that blindness was karmic or an expression of a prior sinful existence. Blind singer-prostitutes, the *goze*, are usually beaten in *senryû*. Superstition said it was good luck to hit the *goze* that one slept with!

And yet the blind also were understood as privileged *vis-à-vis* the unseen world, particularly the world of the dead.[65] The blind in Japan have a long history of working as musicians, masseurs, pimps and money-lenders. Many became extremely wealthy in the latter capacity. During the Edo era some even bought—that is to say, freed—high-level courtesans, something that cost the equivalent of millions of dollars today. But perhaps the most striking thing about the blind was how they organized themselves during the centuries prior to the arrival of the Jesuits. In 1548, there were two blind "sects," and like most Buddhist sects, each sect did not hesitate to guard its turf. And if sect violence was not enough, the blind had a reputation for being sharply tempered and for nursing a grudge. With all their money and women to protect, their canes came in handy, especially in the dark when they were the only one who could "see" what was happening.

25. Noblemen in Europe sleep at night and have their entertainments during the day; Japanese noblemen sleep by day and have their parties and amusements at night.

In the following chapter (14) Frois implies that only women and children in Europe were afraid of the night. Arguably, most sensible Europeans stayed home after sundown, owing to thieves and sociopaths.[66] Elites entertained themselves during the day at cock matches, horse races, gambling houses, taverns, pleasure gardens, banquets,[67] and occasionally by mixing it up with commoners at fairs, where people occasionally delighted in such things as cat burning.[68]

In ancient times, Japanese noblemen used to play the roving tom at night. This contrast suggests the upper class still had a generally nocturnal lifestyle.

26. In Europe, it is not customary to eat and drink during [theatrical] soirées,[69] plays and tragedies; in Japan they never have such events without wine and appetizers.[70]

65 In Korea, too, the blind were not thought of as handicapped and a burden for others. Specifically, in Korea shamanism (fortune-telling, exorcism and benediction all in one) was "big business" and one of the two principle classes of shamans was blind. In China as well, blind men often found work turning power-wheels for mills, while blind women became prostitutes (as was often the case in Japan).

66 Roger Ekrich, *At Day's End: Night in Times Past* (New York: W.W. Norton, 2005).

67 George Irving Hale, "Games and Social Pastimes in the Spanish Drama of the Golden Age." *Hispanic Review*: 8(1940):219–241. See also Alessandro Arcangeli, *Recreation in the Renaissance* (London: Palgrave, 2003).

68 Norbert Elias, *The History of Manners* (New York: Pantheon, 1978 [1939]), 203–204; Norman Davies, *Europe: A History* (Oxford: Oxford University Press, 1996), 543.

69 *Serões*, which does indeed translate as '*soirées*.' However, most contemporary English speakers think of a *soirée* as an evening party that does not involve a theatrical presentation. We believe Frois had the latter in mind and thus our qualifying bracket [theatrical].

70 *Sacana* (*sakana*).

Nowadays in towns and cities across the United States (e.g. New York's Central Park) or in Europe (e.g. Verona) people bring a picnic to operas and classical music performances. You might say "we" have developed a Japanese sensibility for mixing food with performance, particularly during the summer.

27. Among us, it is customary for there to be jumping about and tambourines raised in the air during merrymaking[71]; they find this very strange and consider us mad or barbaric.

As one of the Japanese ambassadors to Europe noted, Japanese dancers jumped and whirled about to depict someone possessed of a demon or spirit (see #14 above). The Japanese infrequently "jumped for joy," except perhaps when drinking (and singing) or in response to certain festival music. Reading this distich one wonders who put on such a show for the Japanese. Presumably Portuguese sailors rather than Jesuits did the merrymaking.[72]

28. Among us it would be considered mad and barbaric for a great nobleman to ride bareback and with his head uncovered; in Japan it is customary for them to go about in this manner.

This distich would seem better suited to Chapter 1 on men or Chapter 8, on horses, as it has no obvious tie to drama, dance, etc. Apparently having discussed how European merrymaking looked foolish to the Japanese, Frois felt compelled to concoct a contrast that said, "Hey, you Japanese do things that are foolish too." In a Europe that was preoccupied with civility,[73] the thought of a nobleman riding a horse without a hat or a saddle was shocking. As regards the Japanese, Morse remarked:

> An illustration of the tolerance of the people and the good manners of the children is shown in the fact that no matter how grotesque or odd some of the people appear in dress, no one shouts at them, laughs at them, or disturbs them in any way. I saw a man wearing for a hat the carapace of the gigantic Japanese crab. This is an enormous crab found in the seas of Japan, whose body measures a foot or more in length and whose claws stretch on each side four or five feet. Many looked at this man as he passed and smiled. It was certainly an odd thing to wear upon the head when most of the people go bareheaded.[74]

29. In Europe, plowing is done by one man with a pair of oxen; in Japan, plowing is done by one ox with two men.

---

71 *Nas fulias.* Note the plural rather than the singular, which is why we have rendered it as 'merrymaking,' rather than as the old Portuguese dance known as the *fulia.* It is actually this former sense that has come to be associated with the singular *fulia* in Portuguese today.

72 According to James Murdoch, *A History of Japan.* 3 Vols. (New York: Ungar Publishing, 1964), II, P.I, 79, the Jesuits bitterly complained about the scandalous behavior of Portuguese seamen and merchants who began arriving in Japan after c. 1585; previously they had been well behaved.

73 Dilwyn Knox, "*Disciplina*: The Monastic and Clerical Origins of European Civility," In *Renaissance Society and Culture*, John Monfasani and Ronald G. Musto, eds., pp. 107–137 (New York: Italica Press, 1991).

74 Edward S. Morse, *Japan Day By Day, 1877, 1878–1879, 1882–1883.* 2 Vols. (Boston: Houghton Mifflin, 1917), I, 128.

No drama or dance here either. Evidently, after proceeding from "foolish in dance to foolish with horse," Frois recalled how surprised he was to observe two men plowing with an ox in Japan. The Japanese did not generally goad their oxen (poking them forward with a stick) but rather led them using a nose ring. One could well imagine a Japanese farmer and his son plowing a field with one in front and the other in back. Actually, one could imagine a similar scene in Europe, particularly as an Anglo-Saxon manuscript from England shows two men plowing with two oxen (one goads the oxen forward and the other guides the plow)![75] The Japanese apparently used both shallow and deep tillage plows,[76] depending on the land being farmed (cows and even people might pull a shallow tillage plow in "soft" soil; one or more oxen might be used to pull a deep tillage plow or to break hard-packed soil).

75 See Paul Lacroix, *Manners, Customs and Dress During the Middle Ages and Renaissance* (Ebook 10940, 2004; http://en.wikipedia.org/wiki/File:Ploughmen_Fac_simile_of_a_Miniature_ in_a_very_ancient_Anglo_Saxon_Manuscript_published_by_Shaw_with_legend_God_Spede_ ye_Plough_and_send_us_Korne_enow.png).
76 Morse, *Japan Day by Day*, I, 139. See also Jiro Iinuma, "The Meiji System: The Revolution of Rice Cultivation Technology in Japan." Agricultural History: 43 (1969): 289–296.

14 Various and extraordinary things that do not fit neatly in the preceding chapters

1. We strike a fire using the right hand, with the left hand holding the flint; they strike with the left, holding the flint in the right.

This chapter certainly lives up to its billing as *miscellanea*, as Frois contrasts everything from picking your nose to matters of crime and punishment. Frois nevertheless understood that "simple things" like gift wrapping or assisting others could have profound consequences in Japan. To give an example, back home in Europe a teenager or adult who got in trouble with the law was apt to call for a priest. A Jesuit priest in Japan, where "mandatory sentencing" was more the rule (see #7 and #8 below), did not have the power and authority that he might have enjoyed in Europe. It was important for a Jesuit not to offend a *daimyo* or samurai by asserting himself in situations where, from a Japanese perspective, a priest did not belong.

Frois got this very first contrast half right, for while the Japanese held the flint with their right hand, they also struck with it. The left hand held a piece of wood shaped like a blackboard-eraser with a runner of metal embedded in it (often a piece of sickle blade). Because it was larger and heavier than the flint, it remained stationary while the flint or firestone did the moving/striking. Note that this Japanese method of spark-generation, called *kiribi*, also was used for healing, exorcism, and in Edo at least, for what might be called "charming departures." In the last case, the eraser-shaped wood with the metal blade was held up by the host, above and behind the shoulder of a departing guest. Just before the guest stepped away, the steel was struck with the stone, sending a small shower of sparks out in front of the guest.

2. We show great emotion when we lose our fortunes and our houses burn down; the Japanese, as far as outward appearances go, take all this very lightly.

The same thing Frois observed has been observed over and over: to wit, the Japanese are incredibly stoical. Henry Heusken, the brilliant interpreter for the first American consul to Japan, Townsend Harris, was astonished by the Japanese reaction to a typhoon that destroyed a third of the town of Shimoda in 1856: "Not a cry was heard. Despair? What! Not even sorrow was visible on their faces." Western media outlets recently highlighted this Japanese stoicism after the tsunami of 2011.

Although Frois implicitly seems to suggest that Japanese composure was feigned or "abnormal," Westerners constantly remind themselves that it is pointless "crying over spilt milk" and that "people matter, not things." It would seem the Japanese do a better job of convincing themselves of these truths.

3. We battle house fires with water and by dismantling neighboring houses; the Japanese climb up on neighboring rooftops and fan [the flames] with winnows,[1] shouting at the wind to go away.

The growth of cities with structures made of wood or framed with wood, including buildings that were two or three stories tall and separated by narrow alleys, made for terrible fires in early modern Europe.[2] Although some cities in the sixteenth century began battling fires with primitive fire trucks (picture a carriage with a huge syringe-like device or a lever-activated pump that shot a stream of water into a building), most relied on concerned neighbors toting buckets of water. Fires that began to spread or the simple fear of a fire prompted cities to hire carpenters to remove timbers and entire wooden structures that posed a fire threat.[3]

With respect to Japan, Okada[4] wonders if Frois was misled by paintings of large, fan-like devices that were used to block flying sparks, rather than fan flames. Frois' contrast is further misleading because the Japanese long have been world leaders in deconstruction. Removing fuel was the main method of fire-fighting in Japan from time immemorial. Morse, who first found the weak Japanese water pumps ridiculous and thought Western methods of fire-fighting better, changed his mind when he became more familiar with the realities of fire-fighting in Japan:

> Mats, screen partitions, and even the board ceilings can be quickly packed up and carried away. The roof is rapidly denuded of its tiles and boards, and the skeleton framework left makes but slow fuel for the flames. The efforts of the firemen in checking the progress of the conflagration consist mainly in tearing down these adjustable structures; and in this connection it may be interesting to record the curious fact that oftentimes at a fire the streams are turned, not upon the flames, but upon the men engaged in tearing down the building![5]

Nevertheless, fires on dry, windy, winter days often were unstoppable. One of the worst, in 1657, destroyed half of Edo and killed over a hundred thousand

---

1 *Supis* [*supi*: winnow/s].

2 A good part of Lisbon was destroyed by fire in 1369 and the "great fire of London" in 1666 destroyed as much as eighty percent of the city and some 13,000 homes. A.H. de Oliveira Marques, *Daily Life in Portugal in the Late Middle Ages* (Madison: University of Wisconsin Press, 1971), 100–101; Adrian Tinniswood, *By Permission of Heaven* (New York: Riverhead Books, 2004).

3 Tinniswood, *By Permission of Heaven*, 43–45; Penny Roberts, "Agencies Human and Divine: Fire in French Cities, 1520–1570". In *Fear in Early Modern Society*, eds. William G. Naphy and Penny Roberts, pp. 9–27 (Manchester: Manchester University Press, 1997), 13–14.

4 Akiom Okada, trans. and ed., *Yoroppa-Bunka to Nihon-Bunka* [European Culture and Japanese Culture] (Tokyo: Iwanami Shoten, 1965).

5 Edward S. Morse, *Japanese Homes and Their Surroundings* (New York: Dover Publications, 1961:[1886]),13.

people.[6] Not surprisingly, the Japanese over time developed a vocabulary to match their terrible experience with fire:

> So completely did this destructive agency establish itself as a national institution that a whole vocabulary grew up to express every shade of meaning in matters fiery. The Japanese language has special terms for an incendiary fire, an accidental fire, fire starting from one's own house, a fire caught from next door, a fire which one shares with others, a fire which is burning to an end … We have not given half.[7]

4. Among us, it is a great offense to call someone a liar to his face; the Japanese laugh at this and consider it polite behavior.

Although both Machiavelli and Castiglione championed dissimulation in the service of politics and politeness, respectively, Europeans were impatient with "bold-face" lies. During the Middle Ages Europeans stuffed suspected liars into sacks and hurled them into a moat or pond to have God affirm their guilt or innocence (if they sank they were deemed innocent and hurriedly rescued; if they floated they were guilty and promptly yanked from the sack and hanged).

Even today the Japanese lightly say "*uso-tsuki!*" or "liar!" when someone tells them something interesting (this a version of the more common "*uso!*" or "[it must be a] lie!"). We are talking about an idiom comparable to the Anglo-American expression "you don't say." But the issue probably runs deeper than idiom. Europeans and Americans, with their tendency to take oaths on the Bible or to "swear to God," may have a far more black and white attitude about lying than other people. The Japanese, on the other hand, seem to place a remarkable premium on being secretive. Regardless of whether this secrecy derives from the insecurity of the long warring era or the positive valuation (a sign of maturity) of hiding emotions, the Japanese prefer to remain silent about many things. In this situation it is not the liar but the person who insists upon asking questions that force one to lie who is resented. It may well be that foreigners hear more lies because they unwittingly force the Japanese to lie.

5. Among us, no one kills another except those who have jurisdiction and authority to do so; in Japan anyone can kill in his own house.

Technically speaking, the public executioner was the only person in Europe who could take another life. However, duels, *vendettas*, and killing for reasons of honor were fairly common in Mediterranean Europe.[8] Honor-vengeance dramas, in which wives were routinely murdered on stage by their husbands, also were

---

6 Basil Hall Chamberlain, *Things Japanese, Being Notes on Various Subjects Connected with Japan.* Fourth revised and enlarged edition (London: John Murray, 1902), 164.

7 Ibid.

8 Edward Muir, *Mad Blood Stirring: Vendetta in Renaissance Italy* (Baltimore: Johns Hopkins University Press, 1998).

popular in sixteenth and seventeenth-century Spain.[9] Presumably art, to some degree, mimicked life and *vice versa*.

The absolute power enjoyed by Japanese men, particularly of the samurai or *bushi* class, was one of the first things Xavier commented on when he arrived in Japan. Despite the turmoil of the warring-states era, the Japanese legal system still was based in 1585 on the samurai code of ethics (*Joei Shikimoku*) codified in 1232.[10] The code established a clear-cut chain of command that precluded a Japanese noble from exercising his fiat over everyone. This was probably good if one's master was a better man than one's master's *master*; but when the opposite was true, one had no right of appeal. One could appeal but it would likely cost your life, even if the appeal won. Moreover, because of the notion of collective responsibility, the appealer's family, and perhaps even his neighbors, might have to die for a crime against hierarchy! (See #8 below).

6. We are terrified to kill a man, but think nothing of killing cows, chickens and dogs; the Japanese are terrified to see animals killed but killing men is commonplace.

At the time Frois wrote Europe was beginning to experience a significant downward trend in the incidence of murder.[11] Still, homicide rates in sixteenth century Europe appear to have been much higher than they are today.[12] So not all Europeans were, in fact, terrified to kill another human being, particularly if the human being was sufficiently different (i.e. Jews, sodomites, Native Americans, Muslims) and stood in the way of a fortune or pleasing God. But perhaps Frois' "larger point" was that the Japanese of the warring-states era had become more comfortable than Europeans with killing *each other* (as opposed to "others"). Indeed, Valignano, who was anxious to recruit young Japanese nobles into the Jesuit order, worried that the Jesuits could not find enough recruits because so many otherwise qualified Japanese were murderers.[13] Buddhism, with its emphasis on preserving all life, often is cited as the reason why the Japanese made it taboo to kill cows, chickens, dogs, and other animals. That Buddhism could exercise such influence seems plausible, although one has to wonder why Buddhist precepts were ignored when it came to killing people (just as one has to wonder why Christians frequently ignored their own commandment against killing).

9 Georgina Dopico Black, *Perfect Wives, Other Women: Adultery and the Inquisition in early Modern Spain* (Durham: Duke University Press, 2001), 12.

10 William E. Deal, *Handbook To Life in Medieval and Early Modern Japan* (Oxford: Oxford University Press, 2006), 101; Paul Varley, "Law and Precepts for the Warrior Houses." In *Sources of Japanese Tradition, Second Edition, Volume One: From Earliest Times to 1600*, eds. Wm. Theodore de Bary, D. Keene, G. Tanabe, and P. Varley, pp. 413–433 (New York: Columbia University Press, 2001).

11 Wolhelm Heitmeyer and John Hagan, eds. *International Handbook of Violence Research* (Dordrecht, Netherlands: Kluwer Academic Publishers, 2003), 48.

12 Julius Ralph Ruff, *Violence in Early Modern Europe* (Cambridge: Cambridge University Press, 2001), 120–121.

13 Valignano actually wrote to the Father General in Rome inquiring about a dispensation from the Church's prohibition on admitting individuals to religious orders that had killed another human being. Josef Franz Schütte, S.J. *Valignano's Mission Principles for Japan 1573–1582*. Volume I, Part II, trans. J. Coyne (St. Louis: Institute for Jesuit Sources, 1985), 62.

7. Among us, no one is killed for stealing, unless they steal above a certain sum; in Japan they are killed no matter how trifling the sum.

In 1585 Europeans were re-thinking their centuries-old attitudes and practices of capital punishment, which had been imposed on petty thieves, heretics, and everybody in between. During the Middle Ages killing and torture of "criminals" were not only justice but popular entertainment.[14] Influenced by writers such as Thomas More,[15] who remarked in his *Utopia* (1516) on the brutality and injustice of petty thieves who were hanged for stealing bread, many European legal codes were changed by Frois' time such that capital punishment was confined to a relatively small number of crimes. However, "variety rather than monotony"[16] characterized punishment in early modern Europe. On a good day a thief might be rescued by a priest and taken to confession; on a bad day he could be hanged.

All accounts of Japan from the time of Xavier (1549) well into the nineteenth century mention Japan's "draconian" laws against stealing. What is fascinating is that in Japan, at least, the draconian laws (and large rewards posted for murderers) evidently worked. Europeans who expressed surprise at the severity of Japanese laws also marveled at how safe it was to walk the streets of Japanese cities. Isabella Bird traveled throughout Japan with no more than an eighteen-year old translator. Morse, who was amazed at the lack of rowdiness in Japan, gives some interesting statistics. If you think the great disparity in our murder rates is a late twentieth-century phenomenon, think again:

> Among vital statistics [for Michigan in the year 1879] I found that eighty-seven murders had been committed in that year. As the population of the State of Michigan at that time was only slightly lower than the population of Tokyo, I asked Mr. Sugi how many murders had been committed in Tokyo for the year. He said none, indeed, only eleven murders and two cases of political assassination had been committed in Tokyo in the last ten years.[17]

8. Among us, if we kill another with just cause or in self-defense, we are spared; in Japan, he who kills another must die, and if he does not appear, another is killed in his place.

The early Church deemed killing unacceptable *for any reason*. During the Middle Ages this position was "softened" by the likes of Augustine, Thomas Aquinas, and later theologians and jurists who argued that there were occasions

---

14 Norbert Elias, *The History of Manners* (New York: Pantheon, 1978[1939]), 191–205.

15 Edward Muir, *Ritual in Early Modern Europe* (Cambridge: Cambridge University Press, 2000[1997]), 147.

16 John Briggs et. al., *Crime and Punishment in England: An Introductory History* (London: Routledge, 1996), 73–74. See also Pieter Spierenburg, "The Body and State, Early Modern Europe." In *The Oxford History of the Prison: The Practice of Punishment in Western Society*, 44–71, eds. Norval Morris and David J. Rothman (New York: Oxford University Press, 1995).

17 Edward S. Morse, *Japan Day By Day, 1877, 1878–1879, 1882–1883*. 2 Vols. (Boston: Houghton Mifflin, 1917), II, 426.

(e.g. just wars) when an individual or a society might kill without offending God.[18] As Frois indicates, taking another life was acceptable in Europe provided it was a consequence of protecting yourself and your lawful interests (i.e. family or property). Not a few murderers, particularly nobles or wealthy magnates who committed crimes of passion ("hot anger"), also were spared as a result of pardons from European royalty.[19]

With respect to Japan, the apparent discrepancy between seemingly getting away with murder, per #5 above, and the suggestion here of automatic death for killing another is explained thus: the former concerns the right to kill someone who is your charge, while the latter mainly concerns those who kill a superior, an equal (except during war) or an inferior who is the charge of another. With regard to "substitute punishment," Okada has suggested that Frois was referring to Japanese medieval law, which allowed a corporate entity like a family to substitute one member for another sentenced to death. This was considered merciful because it allowed the family to safeguard its most important members or "bread winners." However, during the chaotic sixteenth century this medieval practice was abandoned by many local daimyo who formulated "house codes" (*kahō*) that embraced what amounted to "mandatory sentencing" (#7 above).[20]

It is possible that Frois also meant to highlight in this distich the absence in Europe, and the presence in Japan, of a type of "collective responsibility" known as *kenka rysoeibai*, which dictated that the relatives, neighbors, or employer of a convicted criminal were punished (and sometimes executed) along with the criminal.[21] Here is Kaempfer's apt description of this late medieval tradition, which was still operative in Japan at the end of the seventeenth century:

> If quarrels, or disputes, arise in the street, whether it be between the inhabitants or strangers, the next neighbours are oblig'd forthwith to part the fray, for if one should happen to be kill'd, tho' it be the aggressor, the other must inevitably suffer death, ... All he can do, to prevent the shame of public execution, is to make away with himself, ripping open his belly. Nor is the death of such an unhappy person thought satisfactory, in their laws, to attone for the deceased's blood. Three of those families, who live next to the place where the accident happen'd, are lock'd up in their houses for three, four or more months, and rough wooden boards nail'd a-cross their doors and windows, after they have duly prepar'd themselves for this imprisonment, by getting the necessary provisions. The rest of the inhabitants of the same street, have also their share in the punishment, being sentenc'd to some days, or months, hard labour at publick works ... The like penalty, and in a higher degree, is inflicted on the Kumi Gasijra [gashira], or heads of the Corporations of that street, where the crime was committed. It highly aggravates their guilt,

18 Natalie Zemon Davis, *Fiction in the Archives* (Stanford: Stanford University Press, 1987), 36.
19 Davis, *Fiction in the Archives*, 74–75.
20 Varley, "Law and Precepts," 421.
21 Deal, *Handbook*, 102–103.

and the punishment is increas'd in proportion, if they knew beforehand, that the delinquents had been of a quarreling humour ... The landlords also and masters of the delinquents partake in the punishment for the misdemeanors of their lodgers, or servants.[22]

As with so many Japanese customs, the principle of collective responsibility appears to have been borrowed from China, although in China the emphasis was on reporting on your neighbors rather than the responsibility of the group to work out their troubles by themselves. That said, during the Tokuagawa period the Japanese developed their own "impressive" internal spy system, which horrified Westerners ("Everybody is watched. No man knows who are the secret spies around him ... This wretched system is even extended to the humblest of the citizens."[23])

9. Among us, people are not crucified; this is very common in Japan.

It is true, Europeans did not crucify. However, this probably had more to do with respecting Jesus than shunning cruelty. Sixteenth century Europe was home to some very public forms of torture and execution, everything from breaking on the wheel to burning, quartering, mutilation, and exposure on the scaffold or pillory.[24]

Okada gives a list of ten forms of Japanese punishment that were extant in Frois' time, including one as gruesome as "our" skinning and quartering: the "saw-pull," where—if Japanese TV "Easterns" are to be believed—passersby were actually required to take a pull at a saw that slowly cut through a man in a stock by the side of the road!

According to Okada, before the arrival of Europeans (pre 1540s), the Japanese often crucified individuals, head down. Apparently, by Frois' time it was mostly done head up. Writing in 1610, Careletti noted that the Japanese, unlike the Romans, provided some support between the legs and under the feet. Victims were tied to the cross with ropes or "with iron straps hammered into the wood." The cross was then lifted and the base was slid into a prepared hole. Then, at a judge's order—this is where the last minute reprieve arrives in Japanese TV "Easterns"— lances were simultaneously thrust up and through the body, from the right and left, with the intention of piercing vital organs and hastening death. It was not always as merciful, since skillful executioners could pierce the body as many as sixteen times, avoiding vital organs.[25] Carletti saw people left alive on crosses, and "they similarly crucify women with babies still nursing at their breasts, so that both the one and the other die of privation." Carletti describes hellish scenes:

---

22 Engelbert Kaempfer, *The History of Japan, Together with a Description of the Kingdom of Siam, 1690–92*. 3 Vols. (Glasgow: James MacLehose and Sons. 1906[1690–92]), II, 119–120.

23 Sir Rutherford Alcock, *The Capital of the Tycoon: A Narrative of a Three Years' Residence in Japan* (London: Longman, Green, and Roberts, 1863), I, 64–65.

24 Spierenburg, "The Body and the State," 46–50.

25 Michael Cooper, *They Came to Japan* (Ann Arbor: University of Michigan Press, 1995[1965]), 166–167.

along all the streets and roads .... one sees nothing .... but crosses full of men, of women, or of children ....''[26]

This last quote pertains to the martyrdom of twenty six Christians at Nagasaki in February of 1597. They were left up as a warning to other Japanese contemplating conversion to Christianity. Of course, Europeans engaged in similar extremes of [in]human behavior. In Aubrey's *Brief Lives*, which was written toward the end of the seventeenth century, he recounted a story about the head of Sir Thomas More, which had been placed on a pole atop London Bridge:

> There goes this story in the family, viz. that one day as one of his daughters was passing under the Bridge, looking on her father's head, sayd she, That head haz layn many a time in my Lapp, would to God it would fall into my Lap as I passe under. She had her wish, and it did fall into her Lappe, and is now preserved in a vault in the Cathedral Church at Canterbury.[27]

10. Among us, servants are reprimanded and serfs are punished by whipping; in Japan the reprimand and punishment is beheading.

This is an extension of #5 above. As noted, during the politically unsettled sixteenth century some *daimyo* took the already severe samurai code and made it stricter with "amendments" or the *daimyo's* own house code. These local regulations severely limited individual rights. For instance, commoners were prohibited (often on pain of death) from travelling or farming without first securing permission from the local lord.[28] However, there is a paradox here. Judging from what Valignano wrote in his *Sumario* (1583),[29] samurai or *daimyo* undoubtedly thought twice before punishing or abusing their servants, for servants had high self-esteem and might avenge an insult by killing their master and committing suicide.[30] Thus, stories of the famously sadistic shogun Nobunaga, who reputedly decapitated a servant girl for leaving the stem of a fruit on the *tatami*, may overstate the cruelty of Japanese elites. On the whole (see Chapter 11, #27), they probably were no better or worse than European elites.

11. Among us there are prisons, judicial authorities, civil servants in the justice system, and prison superintendents[31]; the Japanese have none of these, nor do they make use of whipping, cutting off ears, or hanging.

26 Carletti, Francesco, *My Voyage Around the World*. Trans. Herbert Weinstock (New York: Pantheon Books, 1964[1610]).

27 *Aubrey, John Brief Lives*, Volume II (I-Y). Andrew Clark ed.(Oxford, Clarendon Press, 1898), 84.

28 Deal, *Handbook*, 103.

29 *Sumario de Las Cosas de Japon (1583), Adiciones del Sumario de Japon (1592)*. Ed. José Luis Alvarez-Taladriz (Tokyo: Sophia University), 29.

30 Varley, "Law and Precepts," 423.

31 Frois speaks of *troncos*, which can be rendered as the stake or stocks but also as prison or jail; *alcaides* (judicial authorities), *meirinhos* (civil servants in the justice system) and *belenguins* (seconds-in-command to the *alcaides*, responsible for prisons).

As noted above, European justice frequently entailed some form of corporal punishment (e.g. death, mutilation, whipping) administered in public and with great theatricality (e.g. use of scaffolds, processions, masked executioners). Jail or "prison" was where you waited until your sentence was administered; they were not punishment *per se*. This all changed during Frois' lifetime, when more and more judges sentenced criminals to imprisonment (often with forced labor) or penal servitude (e.g. oarsmen on a Mediterranean galley, as per chapter 12, #10).[32]

Apparently during the unsettled, warring-states era the Japanese closed or otherwise made little use of prisons or jails.

12. Among us, when stolen goods are found they are returned by law to the owner; in Japan stolen goods that are found are confiscated by the court as lost.

Few if any European towns or cities in the sixteenth century had a "police force" that systematically retrieved stolen property, which, ironically, was more likely to be returned to the victim not by the police or a magistrate but by the thief, for a fee.[33] Throughout Iberia and other parts of Europe voluntary associations or brotherhoods "policed" roads, markets, and neighborhoods (these associations were not unlike the volunteer fire departments found today in many smaller American communities).

As politically turbulent Japan rapidly unified, there was evidently a lot of confiscation going on under one pretext or another (Okada cites a document showing that, by law, stolen goods were supposed to be returned to their owners in Japan).

13. Among us, men, women and children are afraid of the night; in Japan, to the contrary, neither young nor old have any fear of it.

Europeans had good reason to fear the night, given the crime and murder rates that obtained in sixteenth-century European cities. Many Europeans also worried about witches, the devil, and even the moon. In his influential treatise "On the diseases that rob man of reason," Paracelsus (1493–1541) wrote that the phases of the moon were responsible in part for various expressions of mania, such as frantic behavior and mischievousness.[34]

Most Japanese probably felt relatively safe in the light of the full moon, for it was identified with the cleansing mercy of Buddha. While "our" moon spawned werewolves and maniacs, the Japanese moon made even savage boars take a break from ravaging farms. Gazing up at the night sky, the Japanese equated the Milky Way with the home of souls; every year they celebrated a star festival for the "loving stars" (the Herder and the Weaver). Still, as far as pitch-black nights go, one has

32 Spierenburg, "The Body and the State;" Edward M. Peters, "Prison before Prison: The Ancient and Medieval Worlds." In *The Oxford History of the Prison: The Practice of Punishment in Western Society*, 3–43, eds. Norval Morris and David J. Rothman (New York: Oxford University Press, 1995).

33 See Natasha Korda, "The Case of Moll Firth: Women's Work and the 'All-Male Stage.'" In *Women Players in England, 1500–1660, Beyond the 'All-Male Stage,'* eds. Pamela A. Brown and Peter Parolin, 71–88. (Burlington VT: Ashgate, 2005).

34 H.C. Erik Midelfort, *History of Madness in Sixteenth Century Germany* (Stanford: Stanford University Press, 1999), 117.

to wonder if the Japanese were all that comfortable with the darkness. Arguably the Japanese always have had a greater variety of ghosts than Westerners, and it is hard to believe parents never used them to get children to go to sleep. During the Tokugawa era, when these ghosts evidently had their heyday, it would seem that fear got the upper hand, for here is Scidmore writing in 1897:

> The outer veranda is closed at night and in bad weather by *amados*, solid wooden screens or shutters that rumble and bang their way back and forth in their grooves. These *amados* are without windows or air holes, and the servants will not willingly leave a gap for ventilation. "But thieves may get in, or the *kappa*! they cry, the kappa being a mythical animal always ready to fly away with them. In every room is placed an *andon* or night lamp.[35]

The Japanese today usually close these shutters, not to keep out the *kappa*, but because of a fear of catching night chills. Okada believes that Frois was referring specifically in this contrast to the children of the samurai, who were trained to be brave by making night-time excursions alone to cemeteries and so forth.

14. We, generally speaking, are afraid of snakes and are disgusted by touching them; the Japanese easily and fearlessly pick them up, and some eat them.

Although it has been suggested that fear of snakes is "natural" and was inscribed in the DNA of our bush-loving Hominid ancestors, human beings can love snakes just as easily as they fear them. If Westerners dislike snakes it is mostly because the poor reptile has been implicated in humankinds' "fall;" snakes also are commonplace in Western literary and artistic depictions of hell.[36]

Vipers, in particular, were thought by the Japanese to be especially good for virility. Even today one can find airline-portion bottles of whiskey with viper extract on the counter of almost every liquor store in Japan. Many snakes were considered edible, but white ones were taboo, for Shinto held them to be sacrosanct messengers from the Earth. Still, the Japanese did not usually get as close to snakes as Indians with their cobra cults, unless one is to believe *senryu* of the eighteenth century, which mention doctors using frogs to lure snakes out of human cavities. Supposedly, in the seedy part of Edo, women who were powdered and rouged to look like *Benten*, goddess of prosperity and a synonym for beauty, trained snakes to crawl into their privies (as part of a strip-show) and sometimes had trouble getting them out. Eventually (this much seems to be fact), authorities cracked down on these shows for "cruelty to animals."

15. Sneezing is a natural thing for us and we think nothing of it; on the islands of Goto it is thought to be an omen and anyone who sneezes cannot speak that same day to their lord.[37]

35 Eliza R. Scidmore, *Jinrikisha Days in Japan* (New York: Harper & Brothers, 1897), 144.
36 Piero Camporesi, *The Fear of Hell: Images of Damnation and Salvation in Early Modern Europe* (University Park: Pennsylvania State University Press, 1991).
37 *Tono.*

Here, as elsewhere, Frois conveniently ignores European customs that smacked of magic, including imploring God to bless someone who has just sneezed. "God Bless you" apparently was a common refrain during the fourteenth, fifteenth, and sixteenth centuries, when the plague repeatedly devastated European cities.

Sneezes may have gotten a bit more attention in Japan than in Europe, for there is ample literature on masking sneezes with words and *vice versa*. Even the old word for sneeze (*kusame*) may have originally meant "That I don't rot!," or was derived from "Eat shit!"(*kuso kurae*), both charms against bad spirits. But note that Frois does not refer to Japan, but rather the Goto Islands, which are about forty kilometers closer to China than Hirado, Japan. Shortly after Frois came to Japan he spent at least several months on these islands, and he devoted three delightful pages to the islanders' "superstitions" in his *Historia*.[38] The islanders closely abided by a calendar of auspicious and inauspicious days.[39] According to Frois they lived in great fear of and constantly propitiated the Devil. His main example of such "superstitious customs" is far more fascinating to us than the sneezing, for it seems to exemplify what we now think of as responsible stewardship of the earth. In the last sentence of the following quote, Frois indirectly recognized the benefit of "superstition":

> Wherever they are, whatever type of place it is, when they cut the wood to fuel their salt pots [apparently salt was one of their export items], in order that their pot not be cursed by the gods, they leave untouched, for the gods, an especially verdant and pleasant place, be it an entire hill or a part of the forest that is covered with particularly tall and valuable trees. No pagans take so much as a twig from these trees though it only be for medicinal purposes. If someone were to cut even a little from those trees, it would end up costing him a lot. This is not only because of some sort of disaster or curse of the gods, but because that person must make amends in the form of ceremonies and money to fulfill his duty for the sin of cutting off tree limbs [on such a mountain] by planting a fixed number of trees. Because of that, and because when times are hard the people pledge to the gods [not to cut certain areas], the many places they have dedicated to the gods are covered with green and there is beautiful scenery for the people.[40]

Today, the Japanese are still particularly attentive to and averse to sneezing. Many Japanese men and almost all Japanese women stifle or completely kill their sneezes.

38 *Historia de Japam*, ed. Jose Wicki, S.J. 5 vols. Lisbon: Biblioteca Nacional de Lisboa. 1976–1984 [1597]) I, 120–123.
39 Frois neglects to mention that this calendar also was common in Japan; it was only the degree to which the Islanders heeded it that was unique.
40 Ibid., I, 121.

16. We use coins made of gold and silver; in Japan they circulate pieces whose value depends on their weight.[41]

In both Europe and Japan the period from around 1200–1500 CE witnessed the rise of towns and cities with ever-expanding market economies that necessitated a shift from a reliance on bartering to the use of money, particularly coins fashioned solely of one precious metal or combinations of gold and silver or silver and copper. Although Frois seems to imply that European coins were standardized or invariable, this was mostly true of higher denomination, "stable" gold and silver coins (e.g. Portugal's silver *cruzado*, France's gold *écu au soleil* or Spain's gold *escudo* or silver "piece of eight").[42] Fluctuations in supplies of precious metals (e.g. massive imports of silver from the Americas beginning around 1530) led to fluctuations in gold-silver ratios and silver-copper ratios, which in turn, led to speculation and monetary uncertainty.[43] There also were occasions when rulers devalued their currency to raise capital. During the late fourteenth century, for instance, the crown of Portugal devalued the silver *real* to the point where it was almost entirely copper; the silver that otherwise would have gone into the *real* was used to fight a war with Castile and to finance the search for African gold.[44]

During the tumultuous sixteenth century Japanese *daimyo* and nobility engaged in mining operations for gold and silver, which were made into gold and silver coins that went to finance armies and purchase weapons. Because *daimyo* often were at war with each other, few efforts were made to standardize coinage. The earliest and perhaps the most widely accepted gold coins were issued by the *daimyo* of the Kai region (an area famous for its gold mines) and were called *koshu kin*. Each *koshu kin* was stamped with its weight and an indication of its corresponding value. This system was adopted by the Tokugawa shogunate at the beginning of the seventeenth century.[45]

17. We in Europe always use a balance; the Japanese use a dachen.[46]

The Portuguese empire (and thus a Jesuit enterprise in Japan) was made possible by profits from the pepper trade and the duties that the Portuguese crown

---

41 *Correm em pedacos sempre a peso.*

42 Vitorino Magálhes Godinho, *Os Descobrimentos E A Economia Mundial* (Lisbon: Editora Arcádia, 1963), I, 373.

43 Herman van der Wee, "Money, Credit, and Banking Systems," In The Cambridge Economic History of Europe, Volume 5, *The Economic Organization of Early Modern Europe*, eds. Edwin Ernest Rich, C. H. Wilson, Michael Moïssey Postan, Peter Mathias, pp. 290–394 (Cambridge: Cambridge University Press, 1977), 290–303.

44 Diogo Ramada Curto, "Portuguese Navigations, The Pitfalls of National Histories." In *Encompassing the Globe, Portugal and the World in the 16th and 17th Centuries*, ed. J. Levinson, pp. 37–44. Sackler Gallery, Smithsonian Institution, Washington, D.C., 2007), 43.

45 See Ethan Segal, *Coins, Trade, and the State: Economic Growth in Early Modern Japan* (Cambridge: Harvard University Press, 2011).

46 *Dachen*, which is written in contemporary Portuguese as *dachém*. From the Malay *daching*, which in turn comes from the Chinese *tá-ching*, a large Chinese scale made of steel. Ricardo de la Fuente Ballesteros, ed. and trans., *Tratado sobre las contradicciones y diferencias de costumbres entre los europeos y japoneses por Luis Frois* (Salamanca: Ediciones Universidad de Salamanca 2003[1585]).123, f.2.

collected at its forts and customs houses (*alfándegas*) that were strategically located in the Atlantic, Indian, and Pacific Oceans.[47] The weight of many items dictated their value and tax assessment and so something as simple as a scale was of great importance in the sixteenth century.[48]

The European "balance" mentioned here by Frois should be familiar to those who have been to a courthouse and seen a statue or plaque of "Lady Justice," who wears a blindfold and holds a sword in her left hand and an uplifted balance scale in her right hand.

The *dachen* is a "beam" scale, originally from China, which functioned a lot like the scale once common in a doctor's office (where a patient's weight was determined by sliding weights out on a beam, so to speak). The Chinese made beam scales in a variety of sizes, including small scales with a notched fish-bone for a beam, which merchants carried in their pockets. The scales often were used to weigh *sycee*—silver ingots used as currency—or coins that looked suspicious (i.e. counterfeit).

[17A]. Our copper coins are solid; in Japan they have holes through the center.

This is another of Frois' unnumbered contrasts. During the early sixteenth century copper production in central Europe increased significantly and solid copper coins, particularly in small denominations, were widely used for everyday transactions (e.g. buying a loaf of bread).[49] From circa 1500 through 1550 Portugal imported roughly a half-million kilograms of copper each year from Antwerp.[50]

The Japanese used copper coins for various purposes (e.g. estate rents, temple donations, prayers,[51] merchandise), although those mentioned by Frois were probably not Japanese but rather Chinese. The *kobusen* was a round copper coin with a square hole that was minted in five different denominations in China during the Ming dynasty (1368–1644).[52] The *kobusen* as well as a still earlier Chinese copper coin (*sosen*) circulated widely in Japan. One reason for the popularity of the *kobusen* was that it bore an auspicious inscription that promised its owner good luck. During the sixteenth century some regions of Japan began issuing their own copper coin (*bitasen*), modeled after the *kobusen*.

18. In Europe copper coins are widely accepted; in Japan only selected ones are, and they must be old and have the right color and markings.

47 Disney, *A History of Portugal*, 140.
48 Olivia Remie Constable, *Housing the Stranger in the Mediterranean World* (Cambridge: Cambridge University Press, 2003), 287
49 Herman van der Wee, "Money and Credit in the Local Economy." In *The Cambridge Economic History of Europe, Volume 5, The Economic Organization of Early Modern Europe*, ed. Ernest Rich, pp. 290–394 (Cambridge: Cambridge University Press, 1977), 298–299.
50 Godinho, *Os Descobrimentos*, I, 323
51 Ethan Segal, "Money and the State: Medieval Precursors of the Early Modern Economy." In *Economic Thought In Early Modern Japan*, eds. Bettina Gramlich Oka and Gregory Smits, pp. 21–46 (Leiden: Brill, 2010), 24.
52 Deal, *Handbook*, 125.

Apparently counterfeit copper coins were not a major concern in Europe during Frois' lifetime, unlike the seventeenth century, when they created a major monetary crisis in Spain and elsewhere.[53]

As early as the fifteenth century counterfeit coins had become a serious problem in Japan.[54] The *bitasen* minted in different parts of Japan were made of copper as well as varying amounts of lead. It therefore made sense for the Japanese to check out color and markings and to prefer older coins such as the Chinese *sosen* or *kobusen*.

19. In Europe one does not ordinarily give copper coins as a gift; in Japan they present caxas[55] as a formal gift[56] to lords.

Copper coins obviously were not worth as much as gold and silver coins and in some parts of Europe (e.g. England) they were not even minted. That the Japanese gave them as gifts reflects the fact that they were considered lucky (as per #17a). Today, they are sometimes given to children or as prizes in neighborhood lotteries, in their reincarnation as freshly minted five-yen coins. They do not have the aforementioned lucky words printed on them, but their denomination has an intrinsically auspicious value: *go-en* (five yen) happens to be a homophone for "good fortune!"

20. We bestow honor through titles; the Japanese bestow it all through the use of honorifics.

With far more grammatical inflections for etiquette (levels of politeness) than for verb tenses, it is true that speakers of Japanese can do more with their verbs than can speakers of English or Romance languages. The Japanese language even has different verbs with identical meanings, where usage depends on who one is speaking to or what is being discussed. But the Japanese do not rely *only* on the verb, as Frois' Portuguese original implies. For some words they also have different levels of nouns, and they have honorific prefixes and suffixes that can be added to nouns or even adjectives. Moreover, it would have been more accurate for Frois to have spoken of "honor and humility," because one can talk *up* another and talk oneself *down* with equal ease in Japanese.

The subject of honorifics admittedly is difficult to discuss in a Western language, because it is hard for "us" to imagine that the verb "be" may have various forms depending on levels of formality, politeness and whatnot (the term honorifics does not really cover the half of it!). If we were Frois, we might have written:

We demonstrate politeness and respect through our choice of words; in Japanese, the grammar of the language itself incorporates markers of politeness and respect that can be used at the appropriate time.

---

53 Martin Heijdra, "The Socio-Economic Development of Rural China during the Ming." In *The Cambridge History of China, Volume 8, The Ming Dynasty 1368–1644*, eds. Frederick W. Mote and Denis Twitchett, pp. 415–579 (Cambridge: Cambridge University Press, 1998), 412.

54 Deal, *Handbook*, 125; Segal, *Coins: Trade and the State*, 201–202.

55 *Caxa* is derived from Sanskrit and means a coin of little value.

56 *Rei.* Schütte has rendered this term as "greetings."

Today, when equality is idealized around the world, including Japan, some people have mixed feelings about language that invokes notions of rank (in the sixteenth century neither Europeans nor Japanese were concerned because few people believed that everyone was equal). Moreover, the complexity of such a language (strictly speaking, the redundant ways of "saying the same thing" that take time to learn) is thought of as a barrier to global understanding.

21. We wash our hands before touching something precious; the Japanese wash them to examine the implements of their tea ceremony.

It is not clear what Frois intended with this contrast. Was he highlighting the fact that it was surprising—from a European perspective—that the Japanese would bother to wash their hands before picking up their rustic implements of the tea ceremony? In Chapter 11 (#9), Frois wrote that, as gems are precious to "us," the tea service (*dogu*) is precious to the Japanese. With this second contrast Frois seems to abandon his cultural relativism. Whatever his intent, Frois' fellow Jesuit, Rodrigues, provided a "thicker description" (*à la* Geertz) of the "hand washing" associated with the tea ceremony:

> Then as they walk along the path through the wood up to the cha house, they quietly contemplate everything there—the wood itself, individual trees in their natural state and setting, the paving stones and the rough stone trough for washing the hands. There is crystal clear water there which they take with a vessel and pour onto their hands, and the guests may wash their hands if they so wish ...[57]

This prelude to the tea ceremony bears much resemblance to visiting a Shinto shrine or a Buddhist temple, for they often resemble shrines in this respect: one takes a nature walk and cleans one's hands in spring water ladled from a trough bored into a boulder, or better yet, a natural concavity in the boulder. The main difference is that the tea practitioners are conscious of the masterfully arranged, generally small (if not miniature) natural elements and savor them and their choreography, whereas the shrine-goers are just enjoying their walk to the shrine and may or may not enjoy incidental moments of natural epiphany in the face of a grander nature of cedar, boulder, mountain peaks and perhaps a glimpse of the sea.

Although it is true that *dogu* will be handled and drunk from, we hear nothing of soap here; the intent is, again, analogous to that which is sought by shrine- or temple-goer: spiritual purification. As previously suggested, in both sacred grounds and the tea hut there was a spirit of equality not present in the extremely rank-conscious outside world. The washing was also, then, a temporary removal of the trappings of difference.

22. Europeans kill wild boars with spears, guns, and hounds; the Japanese often beat the woods to drive them out so that they can kill them with swords.

57 João Rodrigues, *This Island of Japon*. Trans. and ed. Michael Cooper (Tokyo: Kodansha International Limited, 1973[1620]), 288.

As noted in Chapter 6, the Portuguese are still particularly fond of boar. While tasty, the wild relative of domesticated pig can be ferocious, particularly when cornered. As Frois indicates, by 1585 Europeans were hunting boar with guns (matchlock) as well as spears and greyhounds; the latter figure prominently in Francesco Salviati's sixteenth-century watercolor "Boar Hunt."

According to Blackmore, Japanese prints of deer and boar hunts show the hunters wearing "the traditional samurai sword," presumably the *katana* as opposed to the longer *tachi*.[58] Of course, doing battle with a wild boar using only a sword is incredibly dangerous, but consistent with the *macho* mindset of the samurai of the warring-states era.

23. Among us, to kill a fly with your hand is considered filthy; in Japan princes and lords do it, pulling their wings off and throwing them outside.

Avoidance of pollution was foundational to Erasmus' sixteenth-century bestseller, *Manners for Children* (1530),[59] which aimed to remake not only children, but all of European society.

In Japan, to be "so old you can only chase a fly with your chin" was a common conceit, so it seems that fly-catching by hand was a national pastime.[60] One can imagine that guilt, occasioned by Buddhism, was behind the practice, for there are thousands of haiku on the subject; indeed, the very category of "(summer) fly" is sometimes called, or at least subtitled, *hae-o utsu*, or "hitting flies."

24. Most monkeys in Europe have tails; in Japan, even though there are so many monkeys, none of them have tails, and the fact that there are monkeys with tails is novel to them.

Portuguese raiding and commerce along the west coast of Africa during the fifteenth century increased the flow of *exotica* from Asia and Africa into Europe, including various species of Old World monkeys (Cercopithecoidea) that were kept as pets or curiosities by European nobility. Albrecht Dürer kept a collection of monkeys apparently for study purposes. By the sixteenth century many European cities also were home to street performers who wore orientalized costumes and entertained passerby with trained monkeys.[61]

Then, as now, Europeans found monkeys and apes intriguing because of their human-like qualities (primates behave foolishly just like people). The Japanese were similarly taken with the Japanese macaque—a native of Japan that has a human-like face and lives in troops of anywhere from several dozen on up to one hundred individuals, led by an alpha male. Macaques appear tailless, having a stump that can be as short as two centimeters. Japanese folk tradition held that monkeys could cure equine illness and often monkeys were kept at Japanese

---

58 Howard Blackmore, *Hunting Weapons from the Middle Ages to the Twentieth Century* (Mineola NY: Dover Publications, 2000), 47.

59 Edward Muir, *Ritual in Early Modern Europe* (Cambridge: Cambridge University Press, 2000[1997]), 136.

60 See Robin D. Gill, *Fly-Ku!* (Key Biscayne, FL: Paraverse Press, 2005).

61 Donald Lach, *Asia in the Making of Europe: A Century of Wonder*, Volume 2, Book I (Chicago: University of Chicago Press, 1970), 176–178.

stables as "guardians."[62] Presumably, Portuguese sailors introduced the guenons or other Old World monkeys with long tails that the Japanese found so novel.

25. We do accounting by writing numbers down using a quill or marks; the Japanese do so with a soroban calculator.[63]

The Chinese abacus—a wooden, square-shaped device consisting of rows of beads on wooden rods that are slid back and forth—was first introduced to Japan sometime during the early sixteenth century and before the Jesuits arrived on the scene.[64] As with so many introduced items, the Japanese modified the abacus, now called a *soroban*, making it smaller and streamlining mathematical computation. People still use it in small stores and sometimes post offices in Japan.

26. Among us, giving someone a greater number of gifts signifies greater love; in Japan, the fewer the gifts, the greater the show of esteem.

In the absence of department stores and mass-produced goods, gift-giving in early modern Europe entailed mostly items of food, particularly game or fish or sweet things, or handcrafted items like socks or maybe a new spoon.[65] As is the case today in the West, the principle governing gifting was: the naughty get little, the nice get a lot.

In Japan gift giving was and to a degree still is *very* formalized.[66] Every gift, no matter how small, must be matched at some time or another. If the Japanese were not big on gifting, as Frois indicates, it probably was because giving a gift could set off a dangerous cycle of exchange every bit as hard on the pocketbook as a potlatch. Indeed, like a potlatch, it could be used to embarrass and thus undermine the authority of a rival.

Westerners residing in Japan today find it hard to simply give people things because it inevitably becomes stressful, particularly for the recipient, who usually feels compelled to buy an equally expensive return gift. Indeed, one of a wife's traditional duties is keeping tabs on the value of every present and matching it with a return gift. Wealthy professionals who are showered with gifts by clients have special recycling arrangements worked out with a specialized business, which might be called a gift broker, who takes back some gifts and recycles or resells others.

27. We never give gifts of medicine; in Japan it is a common thing to give medicine in clam shells.

Japanese and Korean clams (young ones less than four inches in diameter) are among the most beautifully marked shells in the world. One might say they

---

62 Emiko Ohnuki-Tierney, *The Monkey as Mirror: Symbolic Transformations in Japanese History and Ritual* (Princeton: Princeton University Press, 1987), 48–50; Money L. Hickman, "Painting." In *Japan's Golden Age: Momoyama*, ed. Money L. Hickman, pp. 93–180 (New Haven: Yale University Press, 1996), 140–141.

63 *Jina.*

64 Deal, *Handbook to Life In Medieval and Early Modern Japan*, 239.

65 Natalie Z. Davis, *The Gift in Sixteenth-Century France* (Madison: University of Wisconsin Press, 2000), 34–35; Thomas, *The Ends of Life*, 118.

66 Millie Creighton, "Two Wests Meet Japan." In *Dismantling the East-West Dichotomy*, eds. Joy Hendry and Heung Wah Wong, pp. 103–110 (London: Routledge, 2006), 105–106.

completely live up to their scientific name: *Meretrix meretrix*, or painted woman. However, in sixteenth-century Japan most of the clams that were used as gift containers for herbal medicines were actually painted and essentially standardized. Today the Japanese no longer make presents of medicine, except occasionally a medicinal wine similar to our Campari; they also no longer use shells for packaging gifts.

It is surprising that Frois did not highlight how the Japanese give what might be called honoraria for almost all services rendered, whereas Europeans "paid" for things like getting a tooth pulled. As Ms. Bacon pointed out, contracts and exact charges for professional services were considered disgustingly crass by both sides.

In Japan a present of money is more honorable than pay, whereas in America pay is more honorable than a present.[67]

Today, the Japanese still pay more o-rei than "we" do. But they also seem to have a thing for cash. A truly modern contrast would be:

> We give clothing and toys and other carefully chosen things to people;
> They give gifts of cash for everything, from children's New Year's presents to weddings and funerals.

But note that the cash must be enclosed in a traditionally-decorated, formal money-giving envelope (sold in any convenience store). Finally, perhaps the most interesting contrast for gift-giving today does not involve seashells or money:

> Among us, men give women flowers or chocolates on Valentine's Day;
> In Japan, the women always give chocolates to the men.

The Japanese have *giri-choko* or "dutiful-chocolate" day, when female employees give chocolate to their male colleagues (just about everyone gets chocolate on his desk). This can then be repaid on *huaito-dei*, "white-day," when men are supposed to dutifully give white chocolate to the women.

28. Among us, guests normally bring nothing when they visit; in Japan visitors usually are expected to bring something.

This is still true today; the visitor to Japan should go fully loaded with little gifts. Audubon birdcalls, if you can find them, are a good recommendation. Or buy the usual pastry, fruit or alcohol on the way to someone's house.

29. Among us, a host never serves what a guest has presented as a gift on that visit; in Japan, as a sign of affection, both the giver and the receiver must sample the gift on the spot.

In the previous distich Frois indicated that Europeans normally did not bring a gift. Now he says a European host never serves what his or her guest brings! Apparently guests *sometimes* brought a gift of something to drink or eat, as is the case today in Europe and the United States. In Japan the gift is usually food, and

---

67 Elizabeth Mabel Bacon, *Japanese Girls and Women* (London: Kegan Paul, 2001 [1892]).

because the gift can be consumed, it is wise to bring something you like so that you can enjoy giving your cake and eating it, too.

30. We embrace when we take our leave or come back from somewhere; the Japanese do not embrace at all, and they laugh when they see it done.

The Japanese are one of the least touching people in the world. In the past, any embracing they did was done by adults in private. Even children were not generally hugged. Passing someone in a crowd, the Japanese avoided touching anyone. If someone was in the way, they always said something or, if the other person was looking, they might have used a slight karate-chop-like gesture. Men and women did not generally go about with their arms over each other's shoulders or holding hands, as is found in many cultures. Hygienic types have suggested that even a handshake is too much contact and that we should copy the Japanese. Psychologists, on the other hand, may find this pathological. Still, today Japanese train passengers tolerate being packed together far tighter than Western people can bear. It is an interesting paradox.

31. We play ball using our hands; the Japanese play with their feet.

Ballgames, including various types of handball, were played throughout Europe during the late Middle Ages and early modern period.[68] Frois is presumably focusing in this distich on Basque or Valencian *pelota*, which involved hitting a ball with bare hands against a wall or back and forth in "courtfields" (similar to a tennis court). At the time Frois wrote, the city of Valencia had close to a dozen or more handball courtfields.[69]

The Japanese game *kemari*, literally kickball, may have come to Japan from China during the Heian Period (794–1192), when everyone, including the Emperor, supposedly played the game. As Rodrigues explains, the game is a lot like today's "hacky sack," only it involves a ball rather than a bean bag:

> The balls are inflated and are the size of a man's head. This is played a great deal by the nobles and *kuge* [peers: imperial line, as opposed to shogunate or fief-related nobility], and many of them gather in a circle wearing on the right foot a certain shoe with a blunt point; it is a fine sight to see them kick forward the point of the foot and hit the ball upwards, and then do various tricks and clever feats with it without letting it touch the ground.[70]

32. When we hit the ball, we hit it up high against the wall; in Japan when they hit the ball, they keep it closer to the ground and always strike it from the underside.

Apparently church walls were a favorite place for handball. The balls must not have been soft or resilient, as priests during the seventeenth century condemned

68 Steven J. Overman, "Sporting and Recreational Activities of Students in the Medieval Universities," *Physical Education* I (1999): 25–33.

69 Carmelo Urza, "History of Basque Pelota in the Americas," pp. 1–14. www.docstoc.com/docs/22459359/The-History-of-Basque-Pelota-in-the-Americas-Carmelo

70 Rodrigues, *This Island of Japon*, 281–282.

the sport of handball because it was responsible for large numbers of broken stained-glass windows.[71]

According to Cooper, during the tenth century a group of Japanese courtiers set a record of 260 consecutive kicks without letting the ball touch the ground.[72] In recent years the Japanese game of *kemari* has been revived (it apparently was eclipsed by Sumo wrestling not long after Frois wrote).

33. We have windmills, watermills, and beast-driven mills; in Japan all grinding is done with a hand-mill, using manual force.

By 1585 Europeans were harnessing the wind, water, and animals such as mules, oxen, and dogs to power all sorts of mills as well as butter churns, saws, looms, etc.[73] A comprehensive census in one small valley in the Austrian Alps in 1550 revealed 135 mills—most of which were grist mills powered by water.[74] Many Europeans and Americans are familiar with the expression "every dog has his day." Many may not know that in Frois' day there was a breed of small dogs (turnspits) in England that were harnessed to a rotating spit on which large pieces of meat were cooked over a fire. A royal or noble household had several such dogs that took turns providing "rotisserie power," hence the saying.[75]

As noted, the Japanese of the sixteenth century did not rely heavily on beasts of burden and probably would have been appalled at the idea of a turnspit. Somewhat surprisingly (given their metallurgy and other "industrial" arts), they made relatively little use of wind or water mills. This all changed during the ensuing Tokugawa era (1603–1868), when the Japanese developed many types of mechanical devices and complex *automata*.

34. In Europe people socialize and recreate with others in plazas and streets; in Japan they do so only in their houses and use the streets solely for walking.

Cities and towns of Mediterranean Europe are relatively compact and generally consist of contiguous neighborhoods, each with an important or central plaza (*rossios* in Portuguese) and a parish church. Particularly in the evening, the plazas and streets that connect neighborhoods are full of life.[76]

Frois was right: Japan had no such public "squares" where people socialized, except for temples and shrines (as per Chapter 3, #15). This does not mean that the Japanese did little socializing; rather, their socializing was less spontaneous. In Japan, socializing was more a matter of colleagues agreeing to meet at a temple or someone's house. The Japanese are still like this. They tend to socialize with

71 Robert Crego, *Sports and Games of the 18th and 19th Centuries* (Westport CT: Greenwood Press, 2003), 83–84.

72 Rodrigues, *This Island of Japon*, 283, f.267.

73 Alfred Crosby, *The Measure of Reality* (Cambridge: Cambridge University Press, 1997), 53.

74 Felix F. Strauss, "Mills without Wheels' in the 16th-Century Alps," *Technology and Culture*: 12 (1971): 23–42.

75 Stanley Coren, *The Paw Prints of History: Dogs and the Course of Human Events* (New York: The Free Press, 2002), 170–171.

76 Luís de Moura Sobral, "The Expansion and the Arts." In *Portuguese Oceanic Expansion, 1400–1800*, eds. Francisco Bethencourt & Diogo Ramada Curto, pp. 390–459 (Cambridge: Cambridge University Press, 2007), 394.

their own cliques, and aside from the *mama-sans* at bars, who often are witty and easy conversationalists, most Japanese are not comfortable striking up a conversation with a new acquaintance or stranger. Note, however, that the Japanese today (and since at least the mid-nineteenth century) have what has been described as an aversion to bringing guests home. The reason given by Japanese and foreign language newspapers in Japan is usually the lack of room, pride ("our home is so inadequate"), and a desire not to mix family and business (most socialization away from the home is with others who work for the same company).

35. Among us, a fake smile is considered frivolous; in Japan it is thought to be dignified and a sign of elevated status.

The Sinosphere (China, Japan, Korea) generally appreciates self-control and equanimity, which is to say, not looking troubled. It bears noting that the Japanese are no more aware of their "fake" or slight smile than Westerners are of their tendency to stare into the eyes of other people (something Asians find curious or annoying).

36. In Europe clarity is sought in words, and ambiguity is avoided; in Japan ambiguous words are considered the best language and are the most highly esteemed.

In the timeless classic by Salvador de Madariaga, *Englishman, Frenchmen, Spaniards,*[77] the ambiguity of the English language was held to be the mainstay of British diplomacy and well suited for the national temperament. Nevertheless, even in England one does not find such an explicit defense of ambiguity as found in modern Japan.

Okada opines that Frois is talking about "the honorifics that reached their most complex state of development at the time," which "took a form that avoided clear ways of saying things and favored expressions that were indirect and inconclusive." Ambiguity also was couched in the double and triple negatives that might accompany, but are not the same as, honorifics.

37. Among us, a respected man would be thought insane to hang the pelt of a fox or a jackal from the back of his belt; in Japan, whenever noblemen are performing works, they, as well as their pages, always carry such pelts in this fashion, to be used for sitting upon.

It was fashionable in sixteenth century Europe for women—not men—to go about holding or wearing a sable or marten pelt, which were sometimes bedecked with jeweled eyes or gold paws.[78]

As noted, the Japanese did not sit on couches or chairs, but rather *tatami*; having a fur pelt at the ready made it possible to sit comfortably wherever one went.

38. In Europe, the open crown for mass is only worn by priests; in the region of Gokinai [central Japan, around Kyoto], it is worn by servants[79] *who carry the shoes of their masters.*

77 Oxford: Oxford University Press, 1929.
78 Blanche Payne, *History of Costume from the Ancient Egyptians to the Twentieth Century* (New York: Harper & Row, 1965), 294.
79 *Komono.*

Frois appears to be referring here to the *biretta*—a square hat with three or four peaks on the top, worn by Catholic clergy, excepting the pope. The barnacle-shaped *eboshi* cap worn by petty servants was not as highly decorated, but perhaps too similar for Frois to resist this seemingly innocuous contrast. (Or was he advising European Jesuits not to mistake a Japanese servant for an elite?)

39. In board games in Europe the pieces are moved forward; in Japan their movement is always in a backward direction across the board.

Frois would seem to be comparing "our" chess or checkers to a parcheesi-like game called *sugoroku*. He must have known little about board games or he would have offered more interesting contrasts, such as:

> Our chess pieces are discriminated by shape; *shôgi* pieces are identified by Chinese characters meaning "castle, elephant," etc.
> In chess we try to checkmate the king; in *shôgi* they try to capture territory.

40. In Europe, hawks and falcons almost always have hoods over their eyes; in Japan their eyes are always uncovered.

Raising raptors to hunt rabbits, quail, and other small game goes back at least 1000 years in many parts of the world, including Europe and Japan. Falconry and hawking were time-consuming and expensive and were mostly embraced by the nobility. In Japan, in particular, hawking came to be surrounded with pageantry, beautiful costumes and elaborate equipment, all of which still characterize the sport today.[80]

The "hooding" of falcons and hawks supposedly keeps them quiet and composed. Although perhaps more difficult, one could imagine raising hawks and falcons such that they were relatively comfortable around people and thus required no "hooding." Okada gives a citation for a hood on a Japanese hawk, but it is almost three decades after Frois wrote; the citation could well reflect Japanese borrowing from the West. The most touching animal-related poem in the overwhelmingly human-centered *Manyoshu* (Japan's oldest anthology of poetry) is a eulogy for a hunting hawk that the poet raised. Parts of it are reminiscent of one of the West's most touching animal eulogies, John Skelton's (1460–1529) "Phillip Sparrowe."[81]

41. We wash turnips by hand; Japanese women wash them with their feet.

This distich is reminiscent of the implicit contrast Herodotus (a Greek) drew in the fifth century BC comparing Greeks and Egyptians: the Egyptians "… knead dough with their feet but lift up mud and even dung with their hands."[82]

80 E.W. Jameson, *The Hawking of Japan: The History and Development of Japanese Falconry* (Davis, CA: The Printer, 1976).

81 "From Phyllyp Sparowe: 'Whan I remembre agayn'," In *The New Penguin Book of English Verse*, Paul Keegan ed., pp. 50–54 (London: Penguin Books, 2001[1500]).

82 Robert B. Strassler, ed., *The Landmark Herodotus: The Histories* (New York Anchor Books, 2007), 134.

As previously noted (Chapter 11, #25), in Japan and other parts of Asia both men and women often make far more use of their feet than Westerners.

42. Our sacks for wheat and barley are made of cloth; in Japan they are made of straw.

Sackcloth in Europe was largely made from hemp, flax, cotton and, to a lesser extent, goat hair; the latter material was made into undergarments that were irritating and unpleasant and thus favored by penitents who sought to mortify their flesh. In Japan, nobody grew hay for sacks. Rice straw, wheat straw, etc. all are "hay" and all kindly helped to carry themselves to market.

43. When we warm our hands, we turn the palm of the hand toward the fire; the Japanese turn the back of the hand to the fire.

In Chapter 1 (#45) Frois pointed out that Europeans were reluctant to bare so much as a leg when warming themselves, while the Japanese did not hesitate to expose their entire posteriors to a fire. Backside, back of the hands—perhaps this "backward" approach to warming oneself is "real" and meaningful, but we are not sure about either.

44. Among us, when one delivers a long message, the messenger is either standing or kneeling; in Japan this is done with both knees on the ground and almost prone, with one hand on the mat and the sleeve rolled up on that arm, and with the other hand lightly rubbing the exposed arm.

It is still common practice in Europe for commoners and lesser nobility to kneel before a religious or secular authority such as a bishop or king.

The fly-like rubbing mentioned here by Frois with respect to the Japanese may be a custom borrowed from the Chinese. While in China Cruz observed, "The common courtesy is, the left hand closed, they enclose it within the right hand, and they move both hands repeatedly up and down towards the breast, showing that they have one another enclosed in their heart."[83] In Japan, only the merchant—the most Chinese trade—seems to have done a lot of this rubbing. And in Japan, it is not a point of etiquette that most Japanese seem able to explain, as with the Chinese and their heart metaphor. Like the practice of hissing between the teeth still found among old Japanese men, it would, rather, seem to be a way of showing that one is as tense as one should be in a formal situation, facing one's superior. As we have seen, the Japanese seem to feel, however unconsciously, that being tense is the most important element of being respectful.

45. Among us, when men are speaking, they stand up straight with one foot in front of the other; in Japan, when two men talk, the inferior must have his feet together, his arms crossed at the waist, his body bent forward and, depending on what the other is saying, he must make little reverences like women do in Europe.

There are actually two contrasts here, one of which has to do with the relative importance of body language in Japan as compared with Europe. In the West,

---

83 C.R. Boxer, ed., *South China in the sixteenth century, being the narratives of Galeote Pereira, Fr. Gaspar da Cruz, O.P. [and] Fr. Martín de Rada, O.E.S.A. (1550–1575)* (London: Hakluyt Society, 1953).

an inferior need not advertise subordination so much with body language; in most parts of sixteenth century Europe there were sartorial codes; what you wore, including your hair, signaled your place in society. The other of Frois' contrasts reflects a Western tendency to speak in monologues, while the Japanese mostly converse in bite-sized chunks of sentence, punctuated by the listener's "yeahs" and grunts, each of which is accompanied by a bob of the head and a slight bow (more emphatic on the part of the inferior). If the listening party forgets to, or does not know enough to grunt, the Japanese speaker stops talking.

46. Among us, we use a different towel for cleaning the face than the one we use for the feet; when the Japanese bathe, they use the same towel for everything.

Marques notes that wills from sixteenth-century Portugal testify to the fact that people of means made daily use of napkins and towels, some "for wiping the hands" and others "for wiping the mouth."[84] A separate towel for the feet, as Frois indicates, might make sense given that the majority of homes in sixteenth century Portugal had floors of beaten earth. By contrast, the floors in Japanese homes consisted of mats or *tatami*.

47. We clear our noses with the thumb or index finger; because they have small nostrils, they use their little finger.

Frois must have liked this contrast, as he used it earlier (Chapter 1, #4). It is doubtful that nostril size was the main reason the Japanese used the "pinky" finger. Because the Japanese already used their pinky for cleaning their ears, it perhaps made sense to use the same digit for cleaning the nose. And speaking of ears, we might mention that the Japanese have tiny wooden scoops, which mothers and wives often use to remove wax from the ears of their children and husbands, respectively.

48. We carry out formal courtesies with a calm and serious face; the Japanese always, and without fail, do so with their little artificial smiles.

This is essentially a repetition of #35 above. As we have seen, Europeans in the sixteenth century—and perhaps more precisely, the expanding business class that sought the privileges of the hereditary aristocracy—were preoccupied with what Greenblatt has called "Renaissance self-fashioning." The Jesuits, in particular, became champions of self-fashioning; moderation and composure were central to the "rules of civility" taught in their schools throughout Catholic Europe.[85]

Arguably it is easier to hold a grin than to maintain a grave demeanor, so a "little artificial smile" is no stranger than feigned indifference. What is curious about Frois' characterization of the Japanese is that it is at odds with the stereotypical image of the Japanese from the nineteenth-century, who appear as glum-looking as your glummest Puritans.

49. We store our wine in tightly sealed barrels on boards up off the ground; the Japanese keep their wine in large-mouthed vessels with no lid, buried in the ground up to the rim.

---

84 Marques, *Daily Life in Portugal*, 138.
85 Richard Brookhiser, ed., *Rules of Civility* (New York: The Free Press, 1997[1595]), 9–11.

The bottom of the Mediterranean is littered with a seemingly endless supply of ceramic jars *(amphorae)* that were used by the Phoenicians, Greeks, and Romans to transport wine from one end of the Mediterranean to the other. The Romans are credited with discovering that wine stored in oak barrels often took on a delightful complexity and was a lot smoother. The Romans also were quick to realize that storing the oak barrels in caves, below ground (but up off the ground) kept the wine from spoiling too quickly.[86] Note that storing wine in bottles with corks did not become widespread in Europe until the eighteenth century with the large-scale production of standardized glass bottles.

With respect to the Japanese side of this contrast, Frois seems to be describing what was at the time a centuries-old Japanese tradition of making "black" vinegar from sake. The vinegar was made by mixing brown rice sake with water and "seed vinegar" (vinegar from a previous batch) and then pouring it into large (378 liter) earthenware crocks that were buried partially in the ground. The top third of the jar was exposed and was warmed each day by sunlight, which itself was moderated by grass that was allowed to grow up between the jars. *Kuro-so* or "black vinegar" is still produced in this traditional way on the island of Kyushu,[87] where Frois lived for years.

50. Our pelts are colored with dyes; the Japanese color theirs very well using only the smoke from burning straw.

Tannins extracted from the boiled bark, leaves, and fruit of various plants and trees (e.g. oak, chestnut, walnut) were commonly used to dye animal pelts in Europe. According to Okada, one of the main "straws" used by the Japanese to dye pelts was pine needles.

51. Our cane is of little use, except for making distaffs for spinning; in Japan it [bamboo] is a delicacy added to their soup[88] and is used for bows, arrow shafts, flooring, roofing, ladders, containers for oil, vessels for wine, woven mats, tea whisks, and many other things.

A distaff was a simple stick or piece of cane about three feet long that held the unspun flax or wool fibers that were fed onto a spindle or spinning wheel. As Frois indicates, the Japanese found innumerable uses for their "cane" or bamboo. Only recently have Westerners begun to appreciate this largest member of the grass family (e.g. bamboo is now wildly popular as flooring).

52. Our gifts that are sent in little boxes have no string to keep them closed; in Japan they are tied with string or bound in paper, and in Ximo the containers are bound with women's sashes.

Small wooden gift boxes, which were used to convey and protect such things as a prayer book, date back to the Middle Ages in Europe.[89] Wrapping gifts with a

---

86 Patrick E. McGovern, *Ancient Wine: The Search for the Origins of Viniculture* (Princeton: Princeton University Press, 2007).

87 John Beleme and Jan Beleme, *Japanese Foods that Heal* (North Clarendon, VT: Tuttle Publishing, 2007), 77–78.

88 *Xiru.*

89 Victor Chinnery, *Oak Furniture; the British Tradition* (Woodbridge, UK: The Antique Collectors Club, 1979).

sash, as they apparently did in *Ximo* (western Kyushu), was and is an exceptional practice. But one thing is certain: The Japanese, who are famous for transforming a single sheet of paper into a work of art (*origami*), are the most avid wrappers on earth. To shop in Japan is to be amazed at the variety of packaging. Every culture has areas where creativity runs wild. In Japan gift-wrapping is one of those areas.[90]

53. We cool our foreheads with rosewater; the Japanese use a handful of wine.

Marques notes that rosewater was very popular in Moslem lands during the thirteenth century and apparently was introduced to Portugal and Spain around this time.[91] Here as elsewhere Frois used the word "*vinho*" when referring to *sake*, which is made from fermented rice. *Sake* and rosewater (recall that the latter is made from distilled roses) both contain alcohol, which as it evaporates adds to the refreshing feel of a liquid applied to the skin.

54. Among us, when someone drinks a cup of water, we give them a spoonful of a confection or a slice of preserved fruit; in Japan when someone drinks rice wine, all one needs to give him is a single confection or something of similar size.

Having a small piece of dried fruit or a spoonful of quince jelly with your cup of water no doubt took your mind off the fact that the water smelled, tasted terrible, and was likely to make you sick (as noted, Europeans drank a lot of low-alcohol wine and beer because the water was unsavory). In Japan, sake often is accompanied by salty tidbits, not sweet ones. In this contrast, however, Frois seems to be focusing not on sweet vs. salty but how Europeans drank what amounted to a sizeable cup of water (*púcaro*) with their "tasty bit," while the Japanese had what amounted to only a sip of sake with their equally minimal food.

55. We in Europe show friendship by presenting a friend with a handful of roses; the Japanese give only a single rose or carnation.[92]

Frois highlights a real difference in the two cultures. However, it is difficult to say whether the difference arises from different aesthetics (less is more, for the Japanese) or the simple absence of a tradition in Japan of cut flowers, other than those used for artistic creations, i.e. *ikebana*.

> The vases which hang so gracefully on the polished posts each contain a single peony, a single iris, a single azalea, stalk, leaves and corolla, all displayed in their full beauty. Can anything be more grotesque than our "florist's bouquets," a series of concentric rings of flowers of divers colours, bordered by maidenhair and a piece of stiff lace paper in which stems, leaves, and even petals are

90 Joy Hendry, *An Anthropologist in Japan* (London: Routledge, 1999), 143.
91 Marques, *Daily Life in Portugal*, 88–89.
92 In the Portuguese original the flower mentioned alongside the rose is the *cravo*, or "carnation." There were no carnations in Japan at the time. Japanese translators of the *Tratado* believe Frois had in mind the pink *Dianthus chinensis*. This flower is lacey about the edges, like a carnation, but only has a single layer of five petals. As it turns out, the carnation was imported to Japan from Holland a short time after Frois wrote and was called, in Japanese, a "Dutch pink," or *oranda-chikuseki*. (The Portuguese name for Holland is *Holanda* (with a silent 'h'), and the Japanese name shows the expected liquid consonant substitution, 'r' for 'l.')

brutally crushed, and the grace and individuality of each flower systematically destroyed.[93]

Reading Isabella Bird's strong statement it is possible to suggest a symbolic explanation for the gift of a single flower—it suggests the person receiving it is likewise the only one in the giver's mind. There was one notable exception to the single flower versus bouquet contrast that Frois neglects to mention. Tree blossoms were presented by the branch. A finely shaped and considerably large-sized branch would be the best present.

56. We place a large amount of beijoim [incense] directly on the fire; the Japanese put a few pieces of águila [agar wood incense] the size of two or three kernels of wheat on a very thin plate of silver set upon hot coals.

The benzoin and aquilaria trees of Southeast Asia produce a resinous sap and heartwood, respectively, which have been prized as incense for millennia by European and other civilizations. The Chinese characters for benzoin read "ease-breath-scent." It was correspondingly nicknamed in English "friar's balsam" and used for respiratory ailments. Okada writes that the Japanese only used benzoin in combination with other aromatics, and more interestingly, that the idea was to hear—not just smell—the tiny kernel of scent, which was sometimes even smaller than a grain of rice. What Frois describes as a thin plate of silver was a Chinese invention or "tray" that was called a "silver leaf." The profligacy of European perfuming was partly due to the fact that vast quantities were used to smoke out disease-causing "bad airs." The Japanese only used that much smoke for mosquito smudge.

57. We are very free with our anger and have little control over our impatience; they are singularly in control of themselves and are very restrained and discreet.

It is too bad that Frois did not say more about Japanese self-control and why Europeans seemed to boil over so quickly. There are parts of Japan where people fly off the handle quickly, as well as splendidly uptight parts of the West; but the contrast, on the whole, still holds. Even the Jesuits tended to be "immature" compared to the Japanese and Chinese, who judged maturity on the basis of one's self-control.

58. In Europe, if by some stroke of luck a married or single woman finds refuge in a gentleman's house, there she is protected and aided and kept safe; in Japan, if women seek refuge in the house of any lord, they lose their freedom and become his captives.

The Council of Europe estimates that one-fifth to one-quarter of all European women have experienced physical violence at least once during their adult lives. Today between a third and half of all women in the United States can expect at some point in their lives to be victims of domestic violence. The situation may have been worse in early modern Europe.[94] It was not uncommon for mothers and daughters to suffer at the hands of husbands and fathers, prompting the battered women to seek refuge in a monastery, church, or the household of what was

---

93 Isabella L. Bird, *Unbeaten Tracks in Japan* (Boston: Beacon Press, 1987[1880]), 75.
94 Ruff, *Violence in Early Modern Europe*, 2.

hoped was a sympathetic noble. It is comforting, but perhaps naïve, to believe that European nobles were mostly gentleman, as Frois suggests.[95]

It so happens that what Frois describes for Japan is common on television "Easterns" in Japan today: a woman goes in search of a noble or *tono*, to right things for her wronged husband, or for a loan to pay for a sick child's medicine, only to be sexually assaulted, after which, or during which, she commits suicide! The coincidence with Frois' observation makes one wonder, although clearly not all *tonos* were monstrous.

*59. Among us, those who make up [*after a disagreement*] ask forgiveness of each other or embrace; in Japan, the guilty one rubs his hands in front of the other and drinks from his sake cup.*

Hand rubbing is a sign of being contrite and *sake* is offered to say "I forgive you."

60. Among us, the blade of a hoe is short and broad; in Japan, they are very long, narrow, and curved inward.

Actually European farmers made use of a variety of hoes, depending on the soil being worked and the crops cultivated. The short, broad-bladed hoe mentioned by Frois is what is commonly sold today in hardware stores and might be described as an all-purpose or "standard" hoe.

After the eighth century the Japanese increasingly shifted to dry farming, with occasional flooding of rice paddies, as opposed to a "constant deep-irrigation system" of rice cultivation. This shift meant less reliance on the Chinese plow (a shallow draft plow) and more reliance on hoes that were capable of deep tillage. As Morse suggested, the Japanese hoe may have looked "clumsy," but it's long, slightly curved blade (with sharp cutting edges) made it excellent for reaching down into the soil and cutting and extracting roots.[96]

*61. Flutes in Europe are made of wood and have orifices that are fingered; in Japan they are made of cane [*bamboo*] and are open on both ends.*

European flutes were made from a dense wood such as boxwood and fell into one of two general categories: a somewhat shrill "military" instrument that had a limited range and was used to direct troops on the battlefield, and a softer-sounding chamber instrument that played in the upper range and came in many different sizes and with different pitches.[97]

The Japanese flute works like the South American *cana*; one blows across the end of it, rather than across a hole, as in the case of the European "transverse" (side-blown) flute. Playing a Japanese flute is somewhat like producing sound by blowing across the top of a pop bottle; your breath has to strike the acoustic edge at a perfect angle to produce any sound. As a result, many people cannot even make a noise come from Japanese flutes (especially the large *shakuhachi*).

---

95 Marques, *Daily Life in Portugal*, 176, notes that nobles seemingly assaulted virgins and widows at will during the Middle Ages

96 Morse, *Japan Day By Day*, I, 65,307; Jiro Iinuma, "The Meiji System: The Revolution of Rice Cultivation Technology in Japan,"*Agricultural History* 43 (1969): 289–296.

97 Ardal Powell, *The Flute* (New Haven: Yale University Press, 2002).

Once mastered, however, the great freedom of attack, coupled with different fingerings, permits remarkable nuance or tone color.

62. Among us, the hair of young servants is kept short and the manes of horses are allowed to grow; in Japan, they cut the horses' manes and let the hair of the komonos [servants] grow.

In Chapter 1 we noted that in Europe long flowing hair was a sign of power and virility; short hair was a sign of subordination (the heads of slaves and some vassals were completely shaven).

63. We find the grapes and figs of Portugal to be pleasing and very delicious; the Japanese abhor figs and do not particularly enjoy grapes.

During the long Arab occupation of Iberia (710–1492) the invaders shared with the locals their love of fountains, gardens, and orchards (the *Qur'an* repeatedly speaks of heaven as "gardens graced with flowing streams"). By the time Frois wrote, figs were grown and consumed throughout southern Spain and Portugal; grapes had been cultivated for at least two thousand years (even before the wine-loving Phoenicians showed up in 1100 BC).

As Frois suggests, the Japanese did not have fig trees and they were not wild about the dried figs introduced by the Portuguese.

64. Among us, it is not customary for domestic servants to invite their masters and mistresses into their homes; in Japan this is done frequently, sometimes out of obligation and sometimes not.

More house parties (see #34 above)! Again, Frois' description of Japanese practice is absolutely different from what is now the norm in Japan. Today people do not ordinarily invite others, particularly their superiors, into their homes.

65. In Europe, a servant does not wear his master's clothes when he accompanies him; the lords in Japan lend their servants their clothing and gilded katanas to increase their own pomp and authority.[98]

In Frois' Europe it was common for servants to wear "liveries"—simple garments or uniforms that often signaled through particular color combinations or emblems the noble family to which the servants were "attached." That being said, apparently it was not uncommon for domestic servants to be given their employer's hand-me-down clothing. Although servants often sold this clothing to second-hand clothes dealers,[99] Roberto de Nola complained in 1529 of maidservants who, "forgetting the humility of old Portugal," wore the same good clothing of their mistresses.[100]

Frois exaggerates when he suggests that Japanese nobles "lent" their fancy clothes and swords to their servants. More commonly Japanese nobles lavishly outfitted their servants to better reflect the wealth and authority of the master's household or lineage.

---

98 *Yxei.*

99 Marybeth Carlson, "A Trojan Horse of Worldliness? Maidservants in the Burgher Household in Rotterdam at the End of the Seventeenth Century." In *Women of the Golden Age*, eds. Els Kloek et al., pp. 87–96 (Hilversum, The Netherlands: Verloren, 1994).

100 Roberto de Nola, *Libro de guisados, manjares, y potajes* (Madrid: Espasa-Calpe, 1971[1529]).

References cited

Abranches Pinto, J.A., Yoshimoto Okamoto, and Henri Bernard, S.J., eds. 1942 *La Premiere Ambassade du Japon en Europe. Monumenta Nipponica Monographs* 6. Tokyo: Sophia University.

Abulafia, David 2008 *The Discovery of Mankind: Atlantic Encounters in the Age of Columbus.* New Haven: Yale University Press.

Acosta, José de 2002 [1590] *Natural and Moral History of the Indies.* Ed. Jane Mangan, Trans. Frances M. López-Morillas. With an introduction and commentary by Walter D. Mignolo. Durham: Duke University Press.

Adáo de Fonseca, Luís 1997 *Vasco de Gama; o homem, a viagem, a epoca.* Lisbon: Comissáo de Coordenacáo da Regiáo Alentejo.

Agamben, Giorgio 2013 *The Highest Poverty: Monastic Rules and Forms-of-Life.* Stanford: Stanford University Press.

Ahern, Maureen 1999 "Visual and Verbal Sites: The construction of Jesuit martyrdom in Andrés Pérez de Ribas' Historia de los Triumphos de nuestra Santa Fee (1645)." *Colonial Latin American Review* 8:1:7–33.

Albala, Ken 2003 *Food in Early Modern Europe.* Westport, CT: Greenwood Press.

Alcock, Rutherford, Sir 1863 *The Capital of the Tycoon: A Narrative of a Three Years' Residence in Japan.* London: Longman, Green, and Roberts.

Alden, Dauril 1996 *The Making of an Enterprise: The Society of Jesus in Portugal, Its Empire, and Beyond, 1540–1750.* Stanford: Stanford University Press.

Alexy, Allison 2011 "The Door My Wife Closed; Houses, Families, and Divorce in Contemporary Japan." In *Home and Family in Japan.* Richard Ronald and Allison Alexy, eds. pp. 236–254. London: Routledge.

Alisal, Maria Rodriguez del, Peter Ackerman, and Dolores P. Martinez, eds. 2007 *Pilgrimages and Spiritual Quests in Japan.* London: Routledge.

Allison, Anne 1996 "Producing Mothers." In *Re-Imagining Japanese Women.* Ann E. Inamura, ed. pp. 135–155. Berkeley: University of California Press.

Amos, N. Scott, Andrew Pettegree, and Henk Van Nierop, eds. 1999 *The Education of a Christian Society.* Aldershot: Ashgate.

Anonymous 2001 [1554] *Lazarillo de Tormes.* Trans. Stanley Applebaum. Mineola, NY: Dover.

Aramata, Hiroshi 1994 *Nihon Gyôten Kigen* [Japan-shocking-origins]. Tokyo: Shûeisha.

Arcangeli, Alessandro 2003 *Recreation in the Renaissance.* London: Palgrave.

Ariès, Philippe 1962 *Centuries of Childhood: A Social History of Family Life.* Trans. Bobert Bladlick. New York: Vintage Books.

Aubrey, John 1898 Brief Lives, Volume II (I-Y). Andrew Clark ed. Oxford: Clarendon Press.

Bacon, Alice Mabel 1893 *A Japanese Interior.* Boston: Houghton, Mifflin & Company.

Bacon, Alice Mabel 2001 [1892] *Japanese Girls and Women*. London: Kegan Paul.

Bailey, Gauvin Alexander 2005 "Italian Renaissance and Baroque Painting Under the Jesuits and Its Legacy Throughout Catholic Europe, 1565–1773." In *The Jesuits and the Arts*. John W. O'Malley, S.J., Gauvin A. Bailey, and Giovanni Sale, S.J., eds. pp. 125–201. Philadelphia: Saint Joseph's University Press.

Ballesteros, Ricardo de la Fuente, ed. and trans. 2003 [1585] *Tratado sobre las contradicciones y diferencias de costumbres entre los europeos y japoneses por Luis Frois*. Salamanca: Ediciones Universidad de Salamanca.

Bashô, Matsuo 1966 [1684–94] *Bashô: The Narrow Road To The Deep North and Other Travel Sketches*. Trans. Nobuyuki Yuasa. New York: Penguin Books.

Bassett, Fletcher S. 1885 *Legends and Superstitions of the Sea and of Sailors in All Lands*. Chicago: Belford, Clarke and Company.

Beekman, Daniel 1977 *The Mechanical Baby*. Westport, CT: Lawrence Hill and Company.

Beleme, John, and Jan Beleme 2007 *Japanese Foods that Heal*. North Clarendon VT: Tuttle Publishing.

Ben-Ari, Eyal 2002 "At the Interstices: Drinking, Management, and Temporary Groups in a Local Japanese Organization." In *Japan at Play, The Ludic and the Logic of Power*. Joy Hendry and Massimo Raveri, eds. pp. 129–152. London: Routledge.

Benedict, Ruth 1946 *The Chrysanthemum and the Sword*. New York: Houghton Mifflin.

Bennett, Mick 1944 *The Story of the Rifle*. London: Cobbett Publishing.

Bernstein, Gail Lee, ed. 1991 *Recreating Japanese Women, 1600–1945*. Berkeley: University of California Press.

Berry, Mary Elizabeth. 1982 *Hideyoshi*. Cambridge: Harvard University Press.

Bethencourt, Francisco and Diogo Ramada Curto, eds. 2007 *Portuguese Oceanic Expansion, 1400–1800*. Cambridge: Cambridge University Press.

Billacois, Francois 1990 *The Duel: Its Rise and Fall in Early Modern France*. Trans. Trista Selous. New Haven: Yale University Press.

Bird, Isabella L.1898 *Korea & Her Neighbours*. 2 Vols. London: John Murray.

Bird, Isabella L.1987 [1880] *Unbeaten Tracks in Japan*. Boston: Beacon Press.

Blair, John and Nigel Ramsay 2003 *English Medieval Industries*. London: Hambledon and London.

Blackmore, Howard 2000 *Hunting Weapons from the Middle Ages to the Twentieth Century*. Mineola NY: Dover Publications.

Blomberg, Catharina 1994 *The Heart of the Warrior: Origins and Religious Background of the Samurai System in Feudal Japan*. Sandgate, UK: Japan Library.

Boscaro, Adriana, ed. and trans. 1975 *101 Letters of Hideyoshi: The Private Correspondence of Toytotomi Hideyoshi*. Tokyo: Sophia University.

Boswell, John 1980 *Christianity, Social Tolerance and Homosexuality*. Chicago: University of Chicago Press.

Bouchard, Constance Brittain 2003 *Every Valley Shall Be Exalted: The Discourse of Opposites in Twelfth-Century Thought*. Ithaca: Cornell University Press.

Bowen, James 1975 *A History of Western Education, Volume Two, Civilization of Europe: Sixth to Sixteenth Century*. New York: St. Martin's Press.

Boxer, Charles R. 1953 *South China in the Sixteenth Century: Being the Narratives of Galeote Pereira, Fr. Gaspar da Cruz, O.P. [and] Fr. Martín de Rada, O.E.S.A. (1550–1575)*. London: Hakluyt Society.

Boxer, Charles R. 1963 *The Great Ship from Amacon: Annals of Macao and the Old Japan Trade, 1555–1640*. Lisbon: Centro de Estudos Históricos Ultramarinos.

Boxer, Charles R. 1967 *The Christian Century in Japan, 1549–1650*. Berkeley: University of California Press.

Braga, Isabel M.R. Drummond 1999 "Poor Relief in Counter-Reformation Portugal: The Case of Misericôrdias." In *Health Care and Poor Relief in Counter-Reformation Europe*. Ole P. Grell, Andrew Cunningham, and Jon Arrizabalaga, eds. pp.201–215. London, Routledge.

Braga, Isabel M.R. Drummond 2008 "Foreigners, Sodomy, and the Portuguese Inquisition." In *Pelo Vaso Traseiro*. Harold Johnson and Francis Dutra, eds. pp. 145–165. Tucson: Fenestra Books.

Brauchi, Bernard 1998 *The Clavichord*. Cambridge: Cambridge University Press.

Braudel, Fernand 1973 [1967] *Capitalism and Material Life 1400–1800*. New York: Harper Colophon.

Briggs, John, Christopher Harrison, Angus McInnes, and David Vincent 1996 *Crime and Punishment in England: An Introductory History*. London: Routledge.

Brockey, Liam Matthew 2007 *Journey to the East, The Jesuit Mission to China, 1579–1724*. Cambridge: Belknap Press.

Brockless, Laurence and Colin Jones 1997 *The Medical World of Early Modern France*. Oxford: Clarendon Press.

Brookhiser, Richard, ed. 1997 [1595] *Rules of Civility*. New York: The Free Press.

Brooks, Jeanice 2000 *Courtly Song in Late Sixteenth Century France*. Chicago: University of Chicago Press.

Brooks, Lynn Matluck 2003 *The Art of Dancing in Seventeenth-Century Spain*. Lewisburg, PA: Bucknell University Press.

Brown, Catherine 1998 *Contrary Things: Exegesis, Dialectic, and the Poetics of Didacticism*. Stanford: Stanford University Press.

Brown, John Russell 1995 *The Oxford Illustrated History of Theatre*. Oxford: Oxford University Press.

Brown, Judith C. 1986 "A Woman's Place Was in the Home: Women's Work in Renaissance Tuscany." In *Rewriting the Renaissance:The Discourses of Sexual Difference in Early Modern Europe*. Margaret W. Ferguson, Maureen Quilligan, and Nancy J. Vickers, eds. pp. 206–224. Chicago: The University of Chicago Press.

Brown, Judith C. 1994 "Courtiers and Christians: The First Japanese Emissaries to Europe." *Renaissance Quarterly* 47:872–906.

Brown, Phillip 2011 *Cultivating Commons: Joint Ownership of Arable Land in Early Modern Japan*. Honolulu: University of Hawai'i Press.

Camões, Luís de 1973 [1570] *Os Lusiadas*. Ed. Frank Pierce. Oxford: Clarendon Press.

Camporesi, Piero 1991 *The Fear of Hell: Images of Damnation and Salvation in Early Modern Europe*. University Park: Pennsylvania State University Press.

Campos, João 2008 "Some notes on Portuguese military architecture in the Persian Gulf." In *Revisiting Hormuz: Portuguese Interactions in the Persian Gulf Region in the Early Modern Period*. Dejanirah Couto and Rui M. Loureiro, eds. pp. 149–163. Weisbaden: Harrassowitz Verlag.

Capwell, Tobias 2012 *The Noble Art of the Sword: Fashion and Fencing in Renaissance Europe, 1520–1630*. London: The Wallace Collection.

Carletti, Francesco 1964 [1610] *My Voyage Around the World*. Trans. Herbert Weinstock. New York: Pantheon Books.

Cartas 1575 *Cartas que los padres y hermanos de la Compañia de Iesus que andan en los Reynos de Iapon escriuieron alos dela misma Compañia, desde el año de mil y quinientos y quarẽta y nueue, hasta el de mil y quinientos y fetenta y vno, en las qvales se da noticia de las varias costumbres y idolatrias de aquella gentilidad y se cuenta el principio y successo y bondad de los Christianos de aquellas partes*. Alcala : En casa de Iuan Iñiguez de Lequerica.

Cartas 1997 [1598] *Cartas que os Padres e Irmãos da Companhia de Iesus Escreuerão dos Reynos de Iapão & China aos da Mesma Companhia da India & Europa, des do Anno de 1549 Até o de 1580.* 2 Vols. Fascsimile edited by José Manuel Garcia. Maia: Castoliva Editora.

Carter, Henry H., ed. 1941 *Cancioneiro Da Ajuda: A Diplomatic Edition.* London: Oxford University Press.

Carvajal, Federico Garza 2003 *Butterflies Will Burn.* Austin: University of Texas Press.

Carvalho, Joaquim de 1947–48 *Estudos sobre a Cultura Portuguesa do século XVI.* 2 Vols. Coimbra: University of Coimbra.

Castiglione, Baldesar 1967 [1528] *The Book of the Courtier.* Trans. George Bull. London: Penguin Books.

Castro, Xavier de, and Robert Scrhimpf, trans. 1993 *Traite de Luis Frois, S.J.(1585) sur les contradictions de moeurs entre Europeens & Japonais.* Paris: Chandeigne.

Cesareo, Francesco C. 1993 "Quest for Identity: The Ideals of Jesuit Education in the Sixteenth Century." In *The Jesuit Tradition in Education and Missions, A 450-Year Perspective.* Christopher Chapple, ed. pp. 17–34. Scranton: University of Scranton Press.

Chamberlain, Basil Hall 1902 *Things Japanese: Being Notes on Various Subjects Connected with Japan.* Fourth edition. London: John Murray.

Chase, Wayland Johnson, trans. 1922 "The Distichs of Cato, A Famous Medieval Textbook." *The University of Wisconsin Studies in the Social Sciences and History, #7.*

Chen, Shing-Jen 1996 "Positive Childishness: Images of Childhood in Japan." In *Images of Childhood.* C. Philip Hwange, Michael E. Lamb, and Irving E. Siegel, eds. pp.113–128. Mahwah, NJ: Lawrence Erlbaum Associates.

Chinnery, Victor 1979 *Oak Furniture; the British Tradition.* Woodbridge, UK: The Antique Collectors Club.

Christian, William A., Jr. 1981 *Local Religion in Sixteenth-Century Spain.* Princeton: Princeton University Press.

Cieslik, Hubert 1963 "The Training of a Japanese Clergy in Seventeenth Century." In *Studies of Japanese Culture.* Joseph Roggendorf, ed. pp. 41–78. Tokyo: Sophia University.

Clifford, James, and George Marcus, eds. 1986. *Writing Culture: The Poetics and Politics of Ethnography.* Berkeley: University of California Press.

Coats, Bruce A. 1996 "Arms & Armor." In *Japan's Golden Age: Momoyama.* Money L. Hickman, ed. pp. 261–274. New Haven: Yale University Press.

Cohn, Bernard S. 1996 *Colonialism and Its Forms of Knowledge.* Princeton: Princeton University Press.

Coleridge, Henry James 1881 *The Life and Letters of St. Francis Xavier.* 2 Vols. London: Burns and Oates.

Connolly, Serena 2010 *Lives Behind the Laws.* Bloomington: Indiana University Press.

Constable, Olivia Remie 2003 *Housing the Stranger in the Mediterranean World.* Cambridge: Cambridge University Press.

Cooper, Michael, S.J. 1973 *This Island of Japon: João Rodrigues' Account of 16th-Century Japan.* Tokyo: Kodansha International Ltd.

Cooper, Michael, S.J.1994 *Rodrigues The Interpreter: An Early Jesuit in Japan and China.* New York: Weatherhill.

Cooper, Michael, S.J.1999 [1965] *They Came to Japan: An Anthology of European Reports on Japan, 1543–1640.* Ann Arbor: University of Michigan Press.

Cooper, Michael, S.J.2005 *The Japanese Mission to Europe, 1582–1590.* Kent, UK: Global Oriental.

Coren, Stanley 2002 *The Pawprints of History: Dogs and the Course of Human Events.* New York: The Free Press.

Cornell, Laurel L. 1996 "Infanticide in Early Modern Japan?: Demography, Culture, Population Growth." *Journal of Asian Studies* 55:22–50.

Cornwallis, Kinahan 2002 [1856–57] *Two Journeys to Japan, 1856–57.* Bristol, UK: Genesha Publishing Ltd.

Correia, Pedro Lage Reis 2001 "Alessandro Valignano's Attitude Towards Jesuit and Franciscan Concepts of Evangelization in Japan (1587–1597)." *Bulletin of Portuguese Japanese Studies* 2:79–108.

Correia-Afonso, John, S.J. 1981 *Letters from the Mughal Court.* St. Louis: Institute of Jesuit Sources.

Corson, Richard 2001 *Fashions in Hair: The First Five Thousand Years.* London: Peter Owen.

Costa Fontes, Manuel da 2006 "Between Ballad and Parallelistic Song: A Condessa Traidora in the Portuguese Oral Tradition." In *Medieval and Renaissance Spain and Portugal.* Martha E. Schaffer and Antonio Corijo Ocaña, eds. pp.182–196. Rochester: Tamesis.

Coudert, Allison P. 1989 "The Myth of the Improved Status of Protestant Women: The Case of the Witchcraze." In *The Politics of Gender in Early Modern Europe.* Jean R. Brink, Allison P. Coudert, and Maryanne C. Horowitz, eds. pp. 61–89. Kirksville, MO: Sixteenth Century Journal Publishers.

Cowan, Brian 2007 "New Worlds, New Tastes, Food Fashions after the Renaissance." In *Food: The History of Taste.* Paul Freedman, ed. pp. 197–232. Berkeley: University of California Press.

Creighton, Millie 2006 "Two Wests Meet Japan." In *Dismantling the East-West Dichotomy.* Joy Hendry and Heung Wah Wong, eds. pp.103–110. London: Routledge.

Crego, Robert 2003 *Sports and Games of the 18th and 19th Centuries.* Westport, CT: Greenwood Press.

Crosby, Alfred W. 1997 *The Measure of Reality.* Cambridge: Cambridge University Press.

Crossan, John Dominic 1994 *Jesus: A Revolutionary Biography.* San Francisco: Harper Collins.

Cruz, Anne J., and Mary Elizabeth Perry 1992 "Introduction." In *Culture and Control in Counter-Reformation Spain.* Anne J. Cruz and Mary Elizabeth Perry, eds. pp. ix-xxiv. Minneapolis: University of Minnesota Press.

Cullen, Louis Michael 2003 *A History of Japan, 1582–1914.* Cambridge: Cambridge University Press.

Cummins, James S. 1986 *Jesuit and Friar in the Spanish Expansion to the East.* London: Variorum Reprints.

Curth, Louise H. 2000 "English Almanacs and Animal Health Care in the Seventeenth Century." *Society and Animals* 8:1:71–86.

Cushner, Nicholas 2006 *Why Have You Come Here.* New York: Oxford University Press.

Davies, Norman 1996 *Europe: A History.* Oxford: Oxford University Press.

Davis, Audrey, and Toby Appel 1979 Bloodletting Instruments in the National Museum of History and Technology. *Smithsonian Studies in History and Technology* 41. Washington, DC: Smithsonian Institution Press.

Davis, Nancy Yaw 2000 *The Zuni Enigma: A Native American People's Possible Japanese Connection.* New York: W.W. Norton & Company.

Davis, Natalie Zemon 1987 *Fiction in the Archives.* Stanford: Stanford University Press.

Davis, Natalie Zemon 1995 *Women on the Margins: Three Seventeenth-Century Lives*. Cambridge: Harvard University Press.

Davis, Natalie Zemon 2000 *The Gift in Sixteenth-Century France*. Madison: University of Wisconsin Press.

Davis, Ralph Henry Carless 1983 "The Medieval Warhorse." In *Horses in European Economic History*. Francis Michael Longstreth Thompson, ed. pp. 4–20. Reading, UK: The British Agricultural Historical Society.

De Bary, Wm. Theodore, General Editor 2001 *Sources of Japanese Traditions, Second Edition, Volume I: From Earliest Times to 1600*. New York: Columbia University Press.

De Bary, Wm. Theodore, Carol Gluck, and Arthur E. Tiedemann, eds. 2001 *Sources of Japanese Traditions, Second Edition, Volume 2: 1600 to 2000*. New York: Columbia University Press.

De Bonneville, Francois 1998 *The Book of the Bath*. New York: Rizzoli International Publications.

de Guibert, Joseph 1964 *The Jesuits: Their Spiritual Doctrine and Pratice; A Historical Study*. Chicago: Loyola University Press.

De Leon, Fray Luis 1943 [1583] *The Perfect Wife*. Denton, Texas: The College Press, Texas State College for Women.

De Nola, Roberto 1529 [1971] *Libro de guisados, manjares, y potaje : intitulado Libro de cozina*. Madrid: Espasa-Calpe.

de Souza, T.R. 1975 "Goa-based Portuguese Seaborne Trade in the Early Seventeenth Century." *The Indian Economic and Social History Review* 12:433–443.

Deal, William E. 2006 *Handbook to Life in Medieval and Early Modern Japan*. Oxford: Clarendon Press.

Defourneaux, Marcelin 1979 *Daily Life in Spain in the Golden Age*. Stanford: Stanford University Press.

Denhardt, Robert M. 1975 *The Horse of the Americas*. Norman: University of Oklahoma Press.

Dias, José Sebastião da Silva 1973 *Os descobrimentos e a problematica cultural do século XVI*. Coimbra: University of Coimbra.

Dias, Pedro 1986 O Manuelino. *História da Arte em Portugal*, Vol. 5. Lisbon: Alfa.

Dias, Pedro 2002 "D. Manuel I And The Overseas Discoveries," In *The Manueline: Portuguese Art During the Great Discoveries*, ed. Museum With No Frontiers, pp. 15–38. Lisbon: Programa de Incremento do Turismo Cultural.

Díaz, Mónica 2010 *Indigenous Writings from the Convent*. Tucson: University of Arizona Press.

Disney, A.R. 2009 *A History of Portugal and the Portuguese Empire, From Beginnings to 1807 Volume I: Portugal*. Cambridge: Cambridge University Press.

Dobrée, Alfred 1974 [1905] *Japanese Sword Blades*. London: Arms and Armour Press.

Dobson, Mary 1997 *Tudor Odours*. New York: Oxford University Press.

Dominguez, Beatriz Helena 2007 *Tão Longe, Tão Perto*. Rio de Janiero: Editora Museu da República.

Dopico Black, Georgina 2001 *Perfect Wives, Other Women: Adultery and the Inquisition in early Modern Spain*. Durham: Duke University Press.

Dower, John W. 1986 *War Without Mercy: Race and Power in the Pacific War*. New York: Pantheon Books.

Duncan, T. Bentley 1986 "Navigation Between Portugal and Asia in the Sixteenth and Seventeenth Centuries." In *Asia and the West: Encounters and Exchanges from the Age of Explorations, Essays in Honor of Donald F. Lach*. Cyriac K. Pullapilly and Edwin J. Van Kley, eds. pp. 3–26. Notre Dame: Notre Dame Press.

Dutra, Francis 2005 "The Social and Economic World of Portugal's Elite Seafarers, 1481–1600." *Mediterranean Studies* 14:95–105.

Eagleton, Terry 2000 *The Idea of Culture*. London: Blackwell.

Edwards, H.J., trans. 1966 [1917]. *Caesar: The Gallic War*. London: William Heinemann Ltd.

Eire, Carlos M.N. 1995 *From Madrid to Purgatory: The Art and Craft of Dying in Sixteenth-Century Spain*. New York: Cambridge University Press.

Ekrich, Roger 2005 *At Day's End: Night in Times Past*. New York: W.W. Norton.

Elias, Norbert 1978 [1939] *The History of Manners*. New York: Pantheon.

Elison, George and Bardwell L. Smith 1981. *Warlords, Artists, and Commoners: Japan in the Sixteenth Century*. Honolulu: The University of Hawaii Press.

Elisonas, Jurgis [Elison, George] 1973 *Deus Destroyed: The Image of Christianity in Early Modern Japan*. Cambridge: Harvard University Press.

Elisonas, Jurgis [Elison, George] 1981 "Hideyoshi, The Bountiful Minister." In *Warlords, Artists, and Commoners*. George Elison and Bardwell L. Smth, eds. pp. 223–245. Honolulu: University of Hawai'i Press.

Elisonas, Jurgis [Elison, George] 1991 "The Inseparable trinity: Japan's relations with China and Korea." In *The Cambridge History of Japan, Volume 4: Early Modern Japan*. John W. Hall, ed. pp. 235–301. Cambridge: Cambridge University Press.

Elisonas, Jurgis [Elison, George] 2001 "The Evangelic Furnace: Japan's First Encounter with the West." In *Sources of Japanese Traditions, Second Edition, Volume Two: 1600 to 2000*. Wm. T. de Bary, Carol Gluck, and Arthur Tiedemann, eds. pp. 143–185. New York: Columbia University Press.

Elisonas, Jurgis [Elison, George] 2001a "The Jesuits, The Devil, And Pollution In Japan." *Bulletin of Portuguese Japanese Studies* 1:3–27.

Ericson, Joan E. 1996 "The Origins of the Concept of "Women's Literature." In *The Woman's Hand: Gender and Theory in Japanese Women's Writing*. Paul G Schalow and Janet A. Walker, eds. pp. 74–116. Stanford: Stanford University Press.

Ettlinger, Nancy 2011 "Governmentality as Epistemology." *Annals of the Association of American Geographers* 101:3:537–560.

Fagan, Brian 1975 "Mummies, Or the Restless Dead," *Horizon* 17:64–82.

Fagan, Garrett G. 1999 *Bathing in Public in the Roman World*. Ann Arbor: The University of Michigan Press.

Farge, William J. 2002 *The Japanese Translations of the Jesuit Mission Press, 1590–1614*. Lewiston: Edwin Mellen Press.

Farris, William Wayne 2006 *Japan's Medieval Population: Famine, Fertility, and Warfare in a Transformative Age*. Honolulu: University of Hawai'i Press.

Felner, Mira 2006 *The World of Theater: Tradition and Innovation*. Boston: Allyn and Bacon.

Ferguson, Margaret W., Maureen Quilligan, and Nancy J. Vickers 1986 "Introduction." In *Rewriting the Renaissance: The Discourses of Sexual Difference in Early Modern Europe*. Margaret W. Ferguson, Maureen Quilligan, and Nancy J. Vickers, eds. pp. xv–xxi. Chicago: The University of Chicago Press.

Finucane, Ronald C. 1997 *The Rescue of Innocents: Endangered Children in Medieval Miracles*. New York: St. Martin's Press.

Fitzpatrick, Anne 2006 *The Renaissance*. Mankato, MN: Creative Education.

Flandrin, Jean-Louis 1999 "Dietary Choices and Culinary Technique, 1500–1800." In *Food: A Culinary History from Antiquity to the Present*. Jean-Louis Flandrin and Massimo Montanari, eds. pp.403–418. New York: Columbia University Press.

Flandrin, Jean-Louis, and Massimo Montanari, eds. 1997 *Food: A Culinary History from Antiquity to the Present*. New York: Columbia University Press.

Flint, Valerie 1991 *The Rise of Magic in the Early Middle Ages*. Princeton: Princeton University Press.

Flugel, John Carl 1950 *The Psychology of Clothes*. London: The Hogarth Press.

Foucault, Michel 1984 "What is Critique?" In *The Politics of Truth*. Ed S. Lotringer, Trans. L. Hochroth and C. Porter. Los Angeles: Semiotext(e), 41–95. (Originally published in *The Foucault Reader*, ed. P. Rabinow, Pantheon).

Foucault, Michel 1991 "Govermentality." In *The Foucault Effect: Studies in Governmentality*. Graham Burchell, Colin Gordon, and Peter Miller, eds. pp. 87–107. Chicago: University of Chicago Press.

Foucault, Michel 1994 *Power*. Ed. James D. Faubion, Trans. Robert Hurley and Others. New York: The New Press.

Foucault, Michel 1999 *Religion and Culture*, Michel Foucault. Jeremy R. Carrette, ed. New York: Routledge.

Foucault, Michel 2007 *Security, Territory, Population*. London: Macmillan.

Foucault, Michel 2008 *The Birth of Biopolitics: Lectures at the College de France, 1978–1979*. London: Palgrave Macmillan.

Fraser, Mrs. Hugh 1899 *A Diplomat's Wife In Japan*. London: Hutchinson & Company.

Frederic, Louis 1972 *Daily Life in Japan at the Time of the Samurai, 1185–1603*. New York: Praeger.

Freedman, Paul, ed. 2007 *Food: The History of Taste*. Berkeley: University of California Press.

Fróis, Luís, S.J. 1585 *Tratado em que se contem muito susinta e abreviadamente algumas contradisóes e diferenças de custumes antre a gente de Europa e esta provincia de Japaõ*. Real Academia de la Historia, Madrid, Jesuitas 11–10–3/21.

Fróis, Luís, S.J.1976–1984 [1583–97] *Historia de Japam*, ed. José Wicki, S.J. 5 Vols. Lisbon: Biblioteca Nacional de Lisboa.

Fujita, Neil 1991 *Japan's Encounter with Christianity*. New York: Paulist Press.

Gallop, Rodney 1933 "The Folk Music of Portugal: I." *Music & Letters* 14:222–230.

García-Ballester, Luis 2001 *Medicine in a Multicultural Society*. Aldershot: Ashgate.

Gauvin, Alexander B. 1999 *Art on the Jesuit Missions in Asia and Latin America, 1542–1773*. Toronto: University of Toronto Press.

Gélis, Jacques 1991 *History of Childbirth: Fertility, Pregnancy and Birth in Early Modern Europe*. Cambridge, UK: Polity Press.

Gerstle, C. Andrew 1986 *Circles of Fantasy: Convention in the Plays of Chikamatsu*. Cambridge: Harvard University Press.

Gibowicz, Charles 2007 *Mess Night Traditions*. Bloomington: AuthorHouse.

Gil, Juan 1991 *Hidalgos y Samurais: España y Japón en los siglos XVI y XVII*. Madrid: Alianza Editorial.

Gill, Robin D. 2005 *Fly-ku!* Key Biscayne, FL: Paraverse Press.

Godinho, Vitorino Magálhaes 1980 *A Estrutura Da Antiga Sociedade Portuguesa*. Lisboa: Editora Arcadia.

Godinho, Vitorino Magálhaes 1981–83 *Os Descobrimentos E A Economia Mundial*. 4 Vols. Second Edition. Lisbon: Editorial Presença.

Godinho, Vitorino Magálhes 1963 *Os Descobrimentos E A Economia Mundial*. Lisbon: Editora Arcádia.

Góis, Damião de 1996 [1554] *Lisbon in the Renaissance: A New Translation of Urbis Olisiponis Descriptio*. Trans. Jeffrey S. Ruth. Ithaca, NY: Ithaca Press.

Golownin, Captain (Vasilĭi Mikhăilovich) 1824 *Memoirs of a Captivity in Japan, During the Years 1811, 1812, and 1813: With Observations*. London: Henry Colburn & Company.

Graham, Patricia J. 2007 *Faith and Power in Japanese Buddhist Art, 1600–2005*. Honolulu: University of Hawai'i Press.

Greenblatt, Stephen 1980 *Renaissance Self-Fashioning: From More to Shakespeare*. Chicago: The University of Chicago Press.

Greenblatt, Stephen 1991 *Marvelous Possessions: The Wonder of the New World*. Chicago: The University of Chicago Press.

Greenblatt, Stephen 2011 *The Swerve: How the World Became Modern*. New York: W.W. Norton.

Grendler, Pauls F. 1989 *Schooling in Renaissance Italy*. Baltimore: Johns Hopkins University Press.

Grieco, Allen J. 1999 "Food and Social Classes in Late Medieval and Renaissance Italy." In *Food: A Culinary History from Antiquity to the Present*. Jean-Louis Flandrin and Massimo Montanari, eds. pp. 302–313. New York: Columbia University Press.

Griffin, Nigel 1995 "Italy, Portugal, and the Early Years of the Society of Jesus." In *Portuguese, Brazilian, and African Studies*. Thomas F. Earle and Nigel Griffin, eds. pp. 133–149. Warminster, England: Aris & Phillips.

Griffiths, Jane 2006 *John Skelton and Poetic Authority: Defining the Liberty to Speak*. Oxford: Oxford University Press.

Gualtieri, Guido 1586 *Relationi della venuta de gli ambasciatori Giaponesi a Roma, sino alla partita di Lisbona, ...* Venetia: Appresso I Gioliti.

Guilmartin, John Francis, Jr. 2003 *Gunpowder and Galleys: Changing Technology and Mediterranean Warfare at Sea in the 16th Century*. Revised Edition. Annapolis, MD: Naval Institute Press.

Guzman, Luis de 1891 [1601] *Historia de las Misiones de la Compañía de Jesus en La India Oriental, en la China y Japon desde 1540 hasta 1600*. Bilbao: El Mensajero del Corazon de Jesus.

Hale, George Irving 1940 "Games and Social Pastimes in the Spanish Drama of the Golden Age." *Hispanic Review* 8:219–241.

Hall, John Whitney, ed. 1991 *The Cambridge History of Japan, Volume 4: Early Modern Japan*. Cambridge: Cambridge University Press.

Hanley, Susan 1997 *Everyday Things In Premodern Japan: The Hidden Legacy of Material Culture*. Berkeley: University of California Press.

Harich-Schneider, Eta 1973 *A History of Japanese Music*. London: Oxford University Press.

Harris, Townsend 1930 *The Complete Journal of Townsend Harris: First American Consul General and Minister to Japan*. Mario E. Consenza, ed. Garden City: Doubleday and Company.

Hashimoto, Fumio 1981 *Architecture in the Shoin Style: Japanese Feudal Residences*. Trans. H.Mack Horton. Tokyo: Kodansha and Shibundo.

Hazelton, Richard 1960 "Chaucer and Cato." *Speculum* 35:357–380.

Hearn, Lafcadio 1900 *Shadowings*. Boston: Little, Brown, and Company.

Heitmeyer, Wilhelm, and John Hagan, eds. 2003 *International Handbook of Violence Research*. Dordrecht, Netherlands: Kluwer Academic Publishers.

Henderson, John 1999 "Charity and Welfare in Early Modern Tuscany." In *Health Care and Poor Relief in Counter-Reformation Europe*. Ole Peter Grell, Andrew Cunningham, and Jon Arrizabalaga, eds. pp. 56–87. London: Routledge.

Hendry, Joy 1986 *Becoming Japanese: The World of the Pre-School Child*. Manchester: Manchester University Press.

Hendry, Joy 1994 "Drinking and Gender in Japan." In *Gender, Drink and Drugs*. Maryon McDonald, ed. pp.175–191. Oxford: Berg.

Hendry, Joy 1999 *An Anthropologist in Japan*. London: Routledge.

Hendry, Joy, and Heung Wah Wong, eds. 2006 *Dismantling the East-West Dichotomy: Essays in Honour of Jan Van Bremen*. London: Routledge.

Heng, Geraldine 2003 *Empire of Magic: Medieval Romance and the Politics of Cultural Fantasy*. New York: Columbia University Press.

Hertog, Ekaterina 2011 "I did not know how to tell my parents, so I thought I would have to have an abortion." In *Home and Family in Japan*. Richard Ronald and Allison Alexy, eds. pp. 91–112. London: Routledge,

Hesselink, Reiner H. 2002 *Prisoners from Nambu*. Honolulu: University of Hawai'i Press.

Heusken, Henry 1964 *Japan Journal: 1855–1861*. Eds. And Trans. J.C. Van der Corput and R.A. Wilson. New Brunswick: Rutgers University Press.

Hickman, Money L. 1996 "Painting." In *Japan's Golden Age: Momoyama*. Money L. Hickman, ed. pp. 93–180. New Haven: Yale University Press.

Higashibaba, Ikuo 2001 *Christianity in Early Modern Japan*. Leiden: Brill.

Hirota, Dennis 1995 *Wind in the Pines: Classic Writings of the Way of Tea as a Buddhist Path*. Fremont, CA: Asian Humanities Press.

Hirota, Dennis 1997 *No Abode: The Record of Ippen*. Revised Edition . Honolulu: University of Hawai'i Press.

Hirota, Dennis 2006 *Asura's Harp: Engagement with Language as Buddhist Path*. Heidelberg: Universitätsverlag.

Hoff, Frank 1981 "City and Country: Song and the Performing Arts in the Sixteenth Century." In *Warlords, Artists, and Commoners: Japan in the Sixteenth Century*. George Elison and Bardwell Smith, eds. pp.133–163. Honolulu: The University of Hawaii Press.

Hogden, Margaret 1964 *Early Anthropology in the Sixteenth and Seventeenth Centuries*. Philadelphia: University of Pennsylvania Press.

Hori, Ichiro 1968 *Folk Religion in Japan: Continuity and Change*. Chicago: University of Chicago Press.

Houaiss, Antônio, Mauro de Salles Villar, and Francisco Manoel de Mello Franco, eds. 2001 *Dicionário Houaiss Da Língua Portuguesa*. Rio de Janiero: Objetiva.

Howe, Christopher 1996 *The Origins of Japanese Trade Supremacy*. Chicago: The University of Chicago Press.

Hyland, Ann 1994 *The Medieval Warhorse from Byzantium to the Crusades*. Dover, NH: Alan Sutton Publishing Inc.

Hyland, Sabine 2011 *Gods of the Andes: An Early Jesuit Account of Incan Religion and Andean Christianity*. University Park: Penn State Press.

Iinuma, Jiro 1969 "The Meiji System: The Revolution of Rice Cultivation Technology in Japan." *Agricultural History* 43:289–296.

Imamaura, Ann E., ed. 1996 *Re-Imagining Japanese Women*. Berkeley: University of California Press.

Imanishi, Kinji 2002 [1941] *A Japanese View of Nature: The World of Living Things*. Pamela J. Asquith, Heita Kawakatsu, Shusuke Yagi, and Hiroyuki Takasaki, trans. Edited and introduced by Pamela J. Asquith. London: Routledge.

Immel, Andrea and Michael Witmore 2006 "Introduction, Little Differences: Children, Their Books, and Culture in the Study of Early Modern Europe." In *Childhood and Children's Books in Early Modern Europe, 1550–1800*. Andrea Immel and Michael Witmore, eds. pp. 1–18. New York: Routledge.

Inoue Hisashi 1999 *Waga Tomo Furoisu* [My Friend Frois]. Bungeishunju: Nesco.

Islam, Syed Manzurul 1996 *The Ethics of Travel: From Marco Polo to Kafka*. Manchester: Mancherster University Press.

Jameson, Everett W. 1976 *The Hawking of Japan: The History and Development of Japanese Falconry*. Davis, CA: The Printer.

Jannetta, Ann Bowman 1994 *Epidemics and Mortality in Early Modern Japan*. Princeton: Princeton University Press.

Jannetta, Ann Bowman 2007 *The Vaccinators: Smallpox, Medical Knowledge, and the "Opening" of Japan*. Stanford: Stanford University Press.

Jardine, Lisa 1996 *Worldly Goods: A New History of the Renaissance*. New York: Nan A. Talese.

Jensen, Lionel M. 1997 *Manufacturing Confucianism*. Durham: Duke University Press.

Jerome, Saint 1963 *The Letters of Saint Jerome*. Trans. Charles C. Mierow. Westminster, MD: The Newman Press.

Johnston, David, trans. 1997 *The Boat Plays by Gil Vicente*. London: Absolute Classics.

Johnson, Harold 2007 "A Pedophile in the Palace." In *Pelo Vaso Traseiro: Sodomy and Sodomites in Luso-Brazilian History*. Harold Johnson and Francis A. Dutra, eds. pp. 195–229. Tucson: Fenestra Books.

Jones, Ann Rosalind, and Peter Stallybrass 2000 *Renaissance Clothing and the Materials of Memory*. Cambridge: Cambridge University Press.

Jones, Eric 2003 *The European Miracle*. Third Edition. Cambridge: Cambridge University Press.

Jorißen, Englebert 1988 *Das Japanbild im "Traktat" (1585) des Luis Frois*. Munchen: Aschendorffsche Verlagsbuchhandlung Gmbh & Co.

Jorißen, Englebert 2002 "Exotic and 'Strange' Images of Japan in European Texts of the Early 17th Century." *Bulletin of Portuguese Japanese Studies* 4:37–61.

Kaempher, Engelbert 1906 [1690–92] *The History of Japan: Together With a Description of the Kingdom of Siam, 1690–92*. 3 Vols. Glasgow: James MacLehose and Sons.

Kasahara, Kazuo 2002 *A History of Japanese Religion*. Tokyo: Kosei Publishing.

Kassing, Gayle 2007 *History of Dance: An Interactive Arts Approach*. Champaign, IL: Human Kinetics.

Keene, Donald, and Thomas Rimer 2001 "The Vocabulary of Japanese Aesthetics II." In *Sources of Japanese Tradition, (Second Edition) Volume One: From Earliest Times to 1600*. Wm. Theodore de Bary, Donald Keene, George Tanabe, and Paul Varley, eds. pp. 364–387. New York: Columbia University Press.

Kelso, Ruth 1956 *Doctrine for the Lady of the Renaissance*. Urbana: University of Illinois Press.

Kertzer, David, and Marzio Barbagli, eds. 2001 *Family Life in Early Modern Times, 1500–1789: The History of the European Family, Volume I*. New Haven: Yale University Press.

Kim, Sangkeun 2004 *Strange Names of God: The Missionary Translation of the Divine Name and the Chinese Responses to Matteo Ricci's Shangti in Late Ming China, 1583–1644*. New York: Peter Lang.

Kirk, Stephanie 2007 *Convent Life in Colonial Mexico: A Tale of Two Communities*. Gainesville: University Press of Florida.

Knox, Dilwyn 1991 "Disciplina: The Monastic and Clerical Origins of European Civility." In *Renaissance Society and Culture*. John Monfasani and Ronald G. Musto, eds. pp. 107–137. New York: Italica Press.

Kô, Ochiai 2010 "The Shift to Domestic Sugar and the Ideology of the National Interest." In *Economic Thought In Early Modern Japan*. Bettina Gramlich Oka and Gregory Smits, eds. pp. 89–111. Leiden: Brill.

Komparu, Kunio 1983 *The Noh Theater: Principles and Perspectives*. New York: Weatherhill.

Korda, Natasha 2005 "The Case of Moll Firth: Women's Work and the 'All-Male Stage.'" In *Women Players in England, 1500–1660: Beyond the 'All-Male Stage.'* Pamela A. Brown and Peter Parolin, eds. pp. 71–88. Burlington, VT: Ashgate.

Kostam, Angus 2003 *Lepanto 1571: The Greatest Naval Battle of the Renaissance*. Oxford: Osprey Publishing.

Lach, Donald F. 1965 *Asia in the Making of Europe*. 2 Vols. Chicago: University of Chicago Press.

LaFleur, William R. 1983 *The Karma of Words: Buddhism and the Literary Arts in Medieval Japan*. Berkeley: University of California Press.

Lamers, Jeroen Pieter, ed. and trans. 2002 *Treatise on Epistolary Style: João Rodriguez on the Noble Art of Writing Japanese Letters*. Ann Arbor: Center for Japanese Studies.

Laures, Johannes, S.J. 1957 *Kirishitan Bunko: A Manual of Books and Documents on the Early Christian Mission*. Tokyo: Sophia University.

Lavrin, Asuncion 2008 *Brides of Christ: Conventual Life in Colonial Mexico*. Stanford: Stanford University Press.

Lebra, Takie Sugiyama 1984 "Nonconfrontational strategies for management of interpersonal conflicts." In *Conflict in Japan*. Ellis S. Krauss, ed. pp. 41–60. Honolulu: University of Hawai'i Press.

Lebra, Takie Sugiyama 1994 "Migawari: The Cultural Idiom of Self-Other Exchange." In *Self as Person in Asian Theory and Practice*. Roger T. Ames, Wimal Dissanayake, and Thomas P. Kasulis, eds. pp. 107–125. Albany: SUNY Press.

Lee, Christina H. 2008 "The Perception of the Japanese in Early Modern Spain: Not Quite 'The Best People Yet Discovered.'" *eHumanista* 11:345–381.

Levathes, Louise 1995 *When China Ruled the Seas: The Treasure Fleet of the Dragon Throne, 1405–1433*. Oxford: Oxford University Press.

Levenson, Jay, ed. 2007 *Encompassing the Globe: Portugal and the World in the 16th & 17th Centuries*. Washington, DC: Sackler Gallery, Smithsonian Institution.

Leydi, Silvio 2012 "The Swordsmiths of Milan, c. 1525–1630." In *The Noble Art of the Sword*, by Tobias Capwell, pp. 176–188. London: The Wallace Collection.

Linschoten, J.H. van 1885 [1598] *The Voyage of John Huyghen van Linschoten to the East Indies*. 2 Vols. William Philip, trans. Arthur C. Burnell and Pieter A. Tiele, eds. London: Haklyut Society.

Long, Susan Orpett 1996 "Nurturing and Femininity" In *Re-Imagining Japanese Women*. Ann E. Inamura, ed. pp. 156–176. Berkeley: University of California Press.

Loureiro, Rui Manuel 2004 "Jesuit Textual Strategies in Japan Between 1549 and 1582." *Bulletin of Portuguese/Japanese Studies* 8:39–63.

Lowell, Percival 1888 *The Soul of the Far East*. Boston: Houghton Mifflin.

MacCormack, Sabine 1991 *Religion in the Andes*. Princeton: Princeton University Press.

Mack, Rosamond 2001 *Bazaar to Piazza: Islamic Trade and Italian Art, 1300–1600*. Berkeley: University of California Press.

Malm, William P. 1981 "Music Cultures of Momoyama Japan." In *Warlords, Artists, and Commoners: Japan in the Sixteenth Century*. George Elison and Bardwell L. Smith, eds. pp. 163–186. Honolulu: The University of Hawaii Press.

Mancall, Peter C., ed. 2006 *Travel Narratives from the Age of Discovery: An Anthology*. Oxford: Oxford University Press.

Maravall, José Antonio 1986 *Culture of the Baroque: Analysis of a Historical Structure*. Trans. Terry Cochran, Minneapolis: University of Minnesota Press.

Markley, Robert 2004 "Gulliver and the Japanese: The Limits of the Postcolonial Past." *Modern Language Quarterly* 65:457–479.

Marques, António Henrique de Oliveira 1971 *Daily Life in Portugal in the Late Middle Ages*. Madison: University of Wisconsin Press.

Martino of Como, Maestro 2005 [1500] *The Art of Cooking*. Luigi Ballerina, ed. Jeremy Parzen, trans. Berkeley: University of California Press.

Martins, Mário 1968 "Os 'Dísticos de Catão' na base da formação universitária" *Revista Portuguesa de Filosofia* 24:103–113.

Masahide, Bitō 1991 "Thought and Religion, 1550–1700." Kate W. Nakai, trans. In *The Cambridge History of Japan, Volume 4: Early Modern Japan*. John hitney Hall, ed. pp. 373–424. Cambridge: Cambridge University Press.

Mathew, K.M. 1988 *The History of Portuguese Navigation in India, 1497–1600*. Delhi, India: Mittal Publications.

Matsuda, Kiichi, and Engelbert Jorißsen, trans. and eds. 1983 *Furoisu No Nihon Oboegaki Nihon to Yoroppa No Fushu No Chigai*. Tokyo: Chuô-shinshô.

McCullough, Helen Craig, trans. 1988 *The Tale of the Heike*. Stanford: Stanford University Press.

McGovern, Patrick E. 2007 *Ancient Wine: The Search for the Origins of Viniculture*. Princeton: Princeton University Press.

McGreevy, Paul 2004 *Equine Behavior: A Guide for Veterninatians and Equine Scientists*. Edinburgh: Saunders.

McHoul, Alec, and Wendy Grace 1996 *A Foucault Primer: Discourse, Power and the Subject*. New York: New York University Press.

McKendrick, Melveena 1974 *Women and Society in the Spanish Drama of the Golden Age: A Study of the 'Muger varonil'*. Cambridge: Cambridge University Press

McKendrick, Melveena 1992 *Theatre in Spain, 1490–1700*. Cambridge: Cambridge University Press.

McMulin, Neil 1984 *Buddhism and the State in Sixteenth-Century Japan*. Princeton: Princeton University Press.

McNeill, William 1976 *Plagues and Peoples*. Garden City: Anchor-Doubleday.

Mendoza, A. Gomez 1982 "The Role of Horses in a Backward Economy: Spain in the Nineteenth Century." In *Horses in European Economic History*. Francis Michael Longstreth Thompson, ed. pp. 143–155. Reading, UK: The British Agricultural Historical Society.

Metzler, Irina 2006 *Disability in Medieval Europe*. London: Routledge.

Midelfort, H.C. Erik 1999 *History of Madness in Sixteenth Century Germany*. Stanford: Stanford University Press.

Miller, David 2000 *Samurai Warriors*. New York: St. Martin's Press.

Miller, Roy Andrew 1982 *Japan's Modern Myth*. New York: Weatherhill.

Mochizuki, Mia 2010 "The Movable Center: The Netherlandish Map in Japan." In *Artistic and Cultural Exchanges between Europe and Asia, 1400–1900*. Michael North, ed. pp. 109–133. Burlington, VT: Ashgate.

Modras, Ronald 2004 *Ignation Humanism: A Dynamic Spirituality for the 21st Century*. Chicago: Loyola Press.

Moffett, Samuel Hugh 2005 *A History of Christianity In Asia, Volume II: 1500–1900*. Maryknoll, NY: Orbis Books.

Montaigne, Michel de 1958 *Essays*. Trans. John Michael Cohen. London: Penguin.

Montaigne, Michel de 2003 [1595] *The Complete Essays*. Trans. Michael Andrew Screech. London: Penguin.

Moore, James T. 1982 *Indian and Jesuit*. Chicago: Loyola University Press.

Morais, Manuel 1977 *Cancioneiro Musical d'Elvas*. Lisbon, Fundacão Calouste Gulbenkian.

Moran, John Francis 1993 *The Japanese and the Jesuits: Alessandro Valignano in Sixteenth-Century Japan*. London: Routledge.

Morin, Egar 1990 *Penser L'Europe*. Paris: Gallimard.

Morris, Joan 1973 *The Lady Was A Bishop:The Hidden History of Women with Clerical Ordination and the Jurisdiction of Bishops*. New York: The MacMillan Company.

Morse, Edward S. 1917 *Japan Day By Day: 1877, 1878–1879, 1882–1883*. 2 Vols. Boston: Houghton Mifflin.

Morse, Edward S. 1961 [1886] *Japanese Homes and Their Surroundings*. New York: Dover Publications.

Mott, Luis 2008 "Justitia et Misericórdia: The Portuguese Inquisition and Repression of the Nefarious Sin of Sodomy." In *Pelo Vaso Traseiro, Sodomy and Sodomites in Luso-Brazilian History*. Harold Johnson and Francis A. Dutra, eds. pp. 63–104. Tucson: Fenestra Books.

Mott, Luis 2008a "My Pretty Boy: Love Letters from a Sodomite Friar, Lisbon (1690)." *In Pelo Vaso Traseiro, Sodomy and Sodomites in Luso-Brazilian History*. Harold Johnson and Francis Dutra, eds. pp.231–262. Tucson: Fenestra Books.

Muir, Edward 1996 *Rituals in Early Modern Europe*. Cambridge: Cambridge University Press.

Muir, Edward 1998 *Mad Blood Stirring: Vendetta in Renaissance Italy*. Baltimore: Johns Hopkins University Press.

Mulhern, Chikeo Irie 1979 "Cinderella and the Jesuits." *Monumenta Nipponica* 34:409–447.

Mullaney, Steven 1988 *The Place of the Stage: License, Play, and Power in Renaissance England*. Chicago: University of Chicago Press.

Mungello, David E. 1989 *Jesuit Accommodation and the Origins of Sinology*. Honolulu: University of Hawai'i Press.

Murdoch, James 1964 *A History of Japan*. 3 Vols. New York: Ungar Publishing.

Museum With No Frontiers 2002 Museum With No Frontiers Exhibition *"The Manueline, Portuguese Art During the Great Discoveries."* Lisbon: Programa de Incremento do Turismo Cultural.

Myers, Kathleen, and Amanda Powell, eds. 1991 *A Wild Country Out in the Garden: The Spiritual Journals of a Colonial Mexican Nun*. Bloomington: Indiana University Press.

Nakamaki, Hirochika 2003 Japanese Religions at Home and Abroad. London: Routledge.

Nery, Rui Vieira 1991 *História da Música*. Lisbon: Imprensa Nacional-Casa da Moeda.

Newson, Linda A. 2009 *Conquest and Pestilence in the Early Spanish Philipines*. Honolulu: University of Hawai'i Press.

Norman, Larry F. 2001 "The Theatrical Baroque." In *The Theatrical Baroque*. Larry Norman, ed. pp. 1–13. Chicago: The University of Chicago.

Nuttall, Zelia 1906–07 "The Earliest Historical Relations Between Mexico and Japan." *University of California Publications in American Archaeology and Ethonology* 4:1–47. Berkeley: University of California Press.

Obenchain, Diane 1994 "Spiritual Quests of Twentieth-Century Women: A Theory of Self-Discovery and a Japanese Case Study." In *Self as Person in Asian Theory and Practice*. Roger T. Ames, Wimal Dissanayake, and Thomas P. Kasulis, eds. pp. 125–170. Albany: SUNY Press.

Ogilvie, Brian W. 2006 *The Science of Describing*. Chicago: University of Chicago Press.

Ohnuki-Tierney, Emiko 1987 *The Monkey as Mirror: Symbolic Transformations in Japanese History and Ritual*. Princeton: Princeton University Press.

Ohnuki-Tierney, Emiko 1996 "McDonald's in Japan," In *Golden Arches East, McDonald's in East Asia*. James L. Watson, ed. pp. 161–183. Stanford: Stanford University Press.

Ohnuki-Tierney, Emiko 1998 "Cherry Blossoms and Their Viewing." In *The Culture of Japan as Seen Through Its Leisure*. Sepp Linhart and Sabine Frûhstûck, eds. pp.213–237. Albany: SUNY Press.

Okada, Akio, trans. and ed. 1965 *Yoroppa-Bunka to Nihon-Bunka* [European Culture and Japanese Culture]. Tokyo: Iwanami Shoten.

Okakura, Kakuzo 2000 [1904] *The Ideals of the East, with Special Reference to the Art of Japan*. New York: IGG Muse Inc.

Okamato, Yoshitomo 1972 *Namban Art of Japan*. New York: Weatherhill.

Oliveira e Costa, João Paulo, ed. 1998 *Da Cruz de Cristo ao Sol Nascente: Um Encontro do Passado e do Presente*. Lisbon: Instituto dos Arquivos Nacionais/Torre do Tombo.

O'Malley, John W., S.J. 1993 *The First Jesuits*. Cambridge: Belknap Press.

O'Malley, John W., S.J., Gauvin Bailey, Steven J. Harris, and T. Frank Kennedy, eds. 2006 *The Jesuits, Cultures, Sciences, and the Arts, 1540–1773*. Toronto: University of Toronto Press.

Oriel, John David 1994 *The Scars of Venus*. London: Springer-Verlag.

Orobator, Agbonkhianmeghe E. 2008 *Theology Brewed in an Africa Pot*. New York: Maryknoll.

Ostovich, Helen, and Elizabeth Sauer, eds. 2004 *Reading Early Modern Women, An Anthology of Texts in Manuscript and Print, 1500–1700*. New York: Routledge.

Overman, Steven J. 1999 "Sporting and Recreational Activities of Students in the Medieval Universities." *Physical Education* I: 25–33.

Owen, Hilary 1996 "Introduction." In *The Boat Plays by Gil Vicente*. Trans. David Johnston. pp. 4–14. London: Absolute Classics.

Parker, Geoffrey 1988 *The Military Revolution: Military Innovation and the Rise of the West, 1500–1800*. Cambridge: Cambridge University Press.

Pascal, Blaise 2003 *Blaise Pascal: The Mind on Fire*. James M Houston, ed. Vancouver: Regent College.

Payne, Blanche 1965 *History of Costume from the Ancient Egyptians to the Twentieth Century*. New York: Harper & Row.

Pearson, Lu Emily 1957 *Elizabetheans at Home*. Stanford: Stanford University Press.

Perarik, Andrew 1996 "Noh Masks." In *Japan's Golden Age: Momoyama*. Money L. Hickman, ed. pp. 291–302. New Haven: Yale University Press.

Pérez de Ribas, Andrès 1999 [1645] *History of the Triumphs of Our Holy Faith Amongst the Most Fierce and Barbarous Peoples of the New World*. Trans. Daniel T. Reff, Maureen Ahern, and Richard Danford. Tucson: University of Arizona Press.

Pérez-Mallaína, Pablo E. 1998 *Spain's Men of the Sea*. Trans. Carla Rahn Phillips. Baltimore: Johns Hopkins University Press.

Perrin, Noel 1979 *Giving Up the Gun: Japan's Reversion to the Sword, 1543–1879*. Boston: D.R. Godine.

Perry, Mary Elizabeth 1992 "Magdalens and Jezebels in Counter-Reformation Spain." In *Culture and Control in Counter-Reformation Spain*. Anne J. Cruz and Mary Elizabeth Perry, eds. pp. 124–145. Minneapolis: University of Minnesota Press.

Peterkin, Allan D. 2001 *One Thousand Beards: A Cultural History of Facial Hair*. Vancouver: Arsenal Pulp Press.

Pettegree, Andrew 2002 *Europe in the Sixteenth Century*. London: Blackwell Publishing Company.

Pettegree, Andrew 2010 *The Book in the Renaissance*. New Haven: Yale University Press.

Piers, Maria W. 1978 *Infanticide*. New York: W.W. Norton & Company.

Pina, Isabel 2001 "Cultural Adaptation and the Assimilation of Natives." *Bulletin of Portuguese Japanese Studies* 2:59–76.

Pinto, Ana Fernandes 2001 "Japanese Elites As Seen By Jesuit Missionaries." *Bulletin of Portuguese Japanese Studies* 1:29–43.

Pinto, Ana Fernandes 2001a "Bibliography of Luso-Japanese Studies." *Bulletin of Portuguese/Japanese Studies* 3:129–152.

Pollock, Linda A. 2001 "Parent-Child Relations." In *The History of the European Family, Volume I: Family Life in Early Modern Times, 1500–1789.* David Kertzer and Marzio Barbagli, eds. pp. 191–220. New Haven: Yale University Press.

Polo, Marco 1958 *The Travels of Marco Polo.* New York: The Orion Press.

Powell, Ardal 2002 *The Flute.* New Haven: Yale University Press.

Proust, Jacques 2002 *Europe Through the Prism of Japan.* Notre Dame: Notre Dame Press.

Pullan, Brian 1999 "The Counter-Reformation, Medical Care and Poor Relief." In *Health Care and Poor Relief in Counter-Reformation Europe.* Ole P. Grell, Andrew Cunningham, and Jon Arrizabalaga, eds. pp. 18–40. London: Routledge.

Quinn, Shelley Fenno 1998 "Oral and Vocal Traditions of Japan." In *Teaching Oral Traditions.* J.M. Foley, ed. pp. 258–266. New York: The Modern Language Association.

Quinn, Shelley Fenno 2005 *Developing Zeami: The NOH Actor's Attunment In Practice.* Honolulu: University of Hawai'i Press.

Racaut, Luc 2002 *Hatred in Print.* Burlington: Ashgate.

Rainey, Ronald 1991 "Dressing Down the Dressed Up: Reproving Feminine Attire in Renaissance Florence." In *Renaissance Society and Culture.* John Monfasani and Ronald G. Musto, eds. pp. 217–239. New York: Ithaca Press.

Ready, Nigel 2009 *Brooke's Notary.* Thirteen Edition. Auckland: Brookers.

Rebelo, Luís de Sousa 2007 "Language and Literature." In *Portuguese Oceanic Espansion, 1400–1800.* Francisco Bethencourt and Diogo Ramada Curto, eds. pp. 358–390. Cambridge: Cambridge University Press.

Reff, Daniel T. 1991 *Disease, Depopulation, and Culture Change in Northwestern New Spain, 1518–1764.* Salt Lake City: University of Utah Press.

Reff, Daniel T. 1998 "The Jesuit Mission Frontier in Comparative Perspective: The Reductions of the Rio de la Plata and the Missions of Northwestern New Spain, 1588–1700." In *Contested Ground.* Thomas Sheridan and Donna Guy, eds. pp. 16–32. Tucson: University of Arizona Press.

Reff, Daniel T. 2005 *Plagues, Priests, and Demons.* Cambridge: Cambridge University Press.

Reff, Daniel T., and Courtney Kelly 2009 "Saints, Witches and Go-betweens" The Depiction of Women in Missionary Accounts from the Northern Frontier of New Spain." *Colonial Latin American Review* 18:237–260.

Rego, Antonio da Silva 1949 *História das Missoes do Padroado português do Oriente, vol. 1, India, 1500–1542.* Lisbon: Agencia Geral das Colonias divisao de Publicacoes e Biblioteca.

Ribeiro, Orlando 1992 *Geografia e Civilização: Temas Portuguesas.* Lisbon: Livros Horizontes.

Riera-Melis, Antoni 1999 "Society, Food, and Feudalism." In *Food, A Culinary History from Antiquity to the Present.* Jean-Louis Flandrin and Massimo Montanari, eds. pp. 251–268. New York: Columbia University Press.

Roberts, Penny 1997 "Agencies Human and Divine: Fire in French Cities, 1520–1570". In *Fear in Early Modern Society.* William G. Naphy and Penny Roberts, eds. pp. 9–27. Manchester: Manchester University Press.

Robertson, Lisa J. 2006 "Warriors and Warfare." In *Handbook to Life in Medieval and Early Modern Japan*. William E. Deal, ed. pp. 131–185. Oxford: Oxford University Press.

Rodrigues, Francisco 1931–50 *História da Companhia de Jesus na assistência de Portugal*. 7 Vols. Porto: Apostolado da Impresna.

Rodrigues, João 1603 *Vocabulario da Lingoa de Iapam*. Nagasaki: Jesuit College [note: Rodrigues undoubtedly authored or helped author this anonymous volume]

Rodrigues, João 1604 *Arte da Lingoa de Iapam*. Nagasaki: Jesuit College. [Facsimile edition prepared by Shima Shôzô and published in 1969 by Bunka Shobô Hakubunsha.]

Rodrigues, João 1620 *Arte Breve de Lingoa Iapoa*. Macao: Jesuit College. [Facsimile edition prepared by Hino Hiroshi (*Nihon Shōbunten*) and published in 1993 by Shin-Jinbutsu-Ôrai-Sha.]

Rodrigues, João 1954 [1620] "Arte del Cha," ed. J.L. Alvarez-Taladriz. *Monumenta Nipponica Monographs 14* Tokyo: Sophia University.

Rodrigues, João 1973 [1620] *This Island of Japon*. Michael Cooper, trans. and ed. Tokyo: Kodansha International Limited.

Ronald, Richard 2011 "Homes and houses, senses and spaces." In *Home and Family in Japan*. Richard Ronald and Allison Alexy, eds. pp. 174–200. London: Routledge.

Rose, Nikolas 1989 *Governing the Soul: The Shaping of the Private Self*. London: Routledge.

Rousmaniere, Nicole C. 1996 "Tea Ceremony Utensils & Ceramics." In *Japan's Golden Age: Momoyama*. Money L. Hickman, ed. pp. 203–236. New Haven: Yale University Press.

Ruff, Julius Ralph 2001 *Violence in Early Modern Europe*. Cambridge: Cambridge University Press.

Rummel, Erika, ed. 1990 *The Erasmus Reader*. Toronto: University of Toronto Press.

Russell-Wood, Anthony John R. 2007 "Patterns of Settlement in the Portuguese Empire, 1400–1800." In *Portuguese Oceanic Expansion, 1400–1800*. Francisco Bethencourt and Diogo Ramada Curto, eds. pp. 161–197. Cambridge: Cambridge University Press.

Said, Edward W. 1979 *Orientalism*. New York: Vintage Books.

Sakanishi, Shio 1938 *Kyôgen: Comic Interludes of Japan*. Boston: Marshall Jones Company.

Saldanha, Arun 2011 "The Itineraries of Geography: Jan Huygen van Linschoten's Itinerario and Dutch Expeditions to the Indian Ocean, 1594–1602." *Annals of the Association of American Geographers* 101:149–178.

Sand, Jordan 2003 *House and Home in Modern Japan*. Cambridge: Harvard University Press.

Sansom, George B. 1928 *Historical Grammar of the Japanese Language*. Oxford: Clarendon Press.

Schiebinger, Londa 1993 *Nature's Body*. Boston: Beacon Press.

Schiebinger, Londa 2004 *Plants and Empire, Colonial Bioprospecting in the Atlantic World*. Cambridge: Harvard University Press.

Schivelbusch, Wolfgang 1992 *Tastes of Paradise : A Social History of Spices, Stimulants, and Intoxicants*. Trans. David Jacobson. New York: Pantheon Books.

Schrimpf, Monika 2008 "The Pro-and Anti-Christian Writings of Fukan Fabian (1565–1621)." *Japanese Religions* 33:35–55.

Schurhammer, Georg, S.J. 1977 *Francis Xavier: His Life and Times*. 4 Vols. Rome: Jesuit Historical Institute.

Schütte, Josef Franz, S.J. 1955 *Kulturgensate Europa-Japan (1585)*. Tokyo: Sophia University.

Schütte, Josef Franz, S.J. 1980 *Valignano's Mission Principles for Japan, 1573–1582*. Volume I, Part I. Trans. J. Coyne. St. Louis: Institute for Jesuit Sources.

Schütte, Josef Franz, S.J. 1985 *Valignano's Mission Principles for Japan, 1573–1582*. Volume I, Part II. Trans. John J. Coyne. St. Louis: Institute for Jesuit Sources.

Schurhammer, Georg and Ernst A. Voretzsch 1926 *Die Geschichte Japans (1549–1578) von P. Luis Frois, S.J.* Leipzig: Verlag Der Asia Major.

Scidmore, Eliza R. 1897 *Jinrikisha Days in Japan.* New York: Harper & Brothers.

Segal, Ethan Isaac 2010 "Money and the State: Medieval Precursors of the Early Modern Economy." In *Economic Thought In Early Modern Japan.* Bettina Gramlich Oka and Gregory Smits, eds. pp. 21–46. Leiden: Brill.

Segal, Ethan Isaac 2011 *Coins, Trade, and the State: Economic Growth in Early Modern Japan.* Cambridge: Harvard University Press.

Sherrow, Victoria 2006 *Encyclopedia of Hair: A Cultural History.* Westport, CT: Greenwood Press.

Shikibu, Murasaki 1960 [1008] *The Tale of Genji.* Trans. Arthur Waley. New York: The Modern Library.

Shônagon, Sei 1991 [1000] *The Pillow Book of Sei Shônagon.* Trans. Ivan Morris. New York: Columbia University Press.

Singleton, Esther 1911 *Furniture.* New York: Duffield and Company.

Skelton, John 2001 [1500] "From Phyllyp Sparowe: 'Whan I remembre agayn'," In *The New Penguin Book of English Verse.* Paul Keegan, ed. pp. 50–54. London: Penguin Books.

Sladen, Douglas B. 1968 [1913] *Queer Things About Japan.* Detroit: Singing Tree Press.

Sladen, Douglas, and Norma Lorimer 1905 *More Queer Things About Japan.* London: Anthony Treherne & Company.

Smith, Bardwell 1992 "Buddhism and Abortion in Contemporary Japan: Mizuko Kuyo and the Confrontation with Death." In *Buddhism, Sexuality, and Gender.* José I. Cabezón, ed. pp. 65–90. Albany: SUNY Press.

Smith, Roger Chester 1968 *The Art of Portugal.* New York: Meredith Press.

Smith, Roger Craig 1993 *Vanguard of Empire: Ships of Exploration in the Age of Columbus.* New York: Oxford University Press.

Smyth, H. Warrington 1906 *Mast and Sail in Europe and Asia.* London: John Murray.

So, Kwan-wai 1975 *Japanese Piracy in Ming China during the Sixteenth Century.* East Lansing: Michigan State University Press.

Sobral, Luís de Moura 2007 "The Expansion of the Arts." In *Portuguese Oceanic Espansion, 1400–1800.* Francisco Bethencourt and Diogo Ramada Curto, eds. pp. 390–460. Cambridge: Cambridge University Press,

Southey, Robert, ed, 1831 *Select Works of the British Poets From Chaucer to Johnson.* London: Longman, Rees, Orme, Brown and Greene.

Souyri, Pierre-François 2001 *The World Turned Upside Down : Medieval Japanese Society.* Trans. Käthe Roth. New York: Columbia University Press.

Spence, Jonathan D. 1984 *The Memory Palace of Matteo Ricci.* New York: Viking Penguin.

Spierenburg, Pieter 1995 "The Body and State, Early Modern Europe." In *The Oxford History of the Prison: The Practice of Punishment in Western Society.* Norval Morris and David J. Rothman, eds. pp. 44–71. New York: Oxford University Press.

Steichen, M. Stephen 1909 *The Christian Daimyos: A Century of Religious and Political History in Japan (1540–1650).* Tokyo: Rikkyo Gakuin Press.

Stone, Jacqueline I., and Mariko Namba Walker, eds. 2008 *Death and the Afterlife in Japanese Buddhism.* Honolulu: University of Hawai'i Press.

Stouff, Louis 1995 *La Table Provençale: Boire et manger en Provence à la fin du Moyen Âge.* Avignon: A. Barthelemy.

Strassler, Robert, ed. 2007 *The Landmark Herodotus: The Histories.* New York: Anchor Books.

Sugiura, Kôhei 1999 *"Futo—" no geijutsu kōgaku.* Tokyo: Kōsakusha.

Suzuki, Hikaru, ed. 2013 *Death and Dying in Contemporary Japan.* London: Routledge.

Tamba, Akira 1981 *The Musical Structure of Noh*. Trans. Patricia Matoré. Originally published as *La Structure Musicale Du Noh* (Paris, 1974). Tokyo: Tokyo University Press.

Tamura, Yoshiro 2001 *Japanese Buddhism: A Cultural History*. Tokyo: Kosei Publishing.

Tani, Shin'ichi 1973 "East Asia and Europe." In *Namban Art: A Loan Exhibition from Japanese Collections*. Shin'ichi Tania and Sugase Tadashi, eds. pp. 13–18. New York: International Exhibitions Foundation.

Tani, Shin'ichi, and Tadashi Sugase, eds. 1973 *Namban Art: A Loan Exhibition from Japanese Collections*. New York: International Exhibitions Foundation.

Thacker, Jonathan 2007 *A Companion to Golden Age Theatre*. Woodbridge: Tamesis.

Thirsk, Joan 2007 Food in Early Modern England. Hambledon Continuum.

Thomas, Keith 1971 *Religion and the Decline of Magic*. New York: Charles Scribner's Sons.

Thomas, Keith 2009 *The Ends of Life: Roads to Fulfillment*. Oxford: Oxford University Press.

Tinniswood, Adrian 2004 *By Permission of Heaven*. New York: Riverhead Books.

Trigger, Bruce 2003 *Understanding Early Civilizations*. Cambridge: Cambridge University Press.

Tsunoda, Tadanobu 1985 *The Japanese Brain*. Trans. Yoshinori Oiwa. Tokyo: Taikushan Publishing Company.

Ücerler, M. Antoni J, S.J. 2004 "Alessandro Valignano: Man, Missionary, and Writer." In *Asian Travel in the Renaissance*. Daniel Carey, ed. pp.12–42. London: Blackwell Publishing.

Unger, Richard 2004 *Beer in the Middle Ages and the Renaissance*. Philadelphia: University of Pennsylvania Press.

Uno, Kathleen S. 1991 "Women and Changes in the Household Division of Labor." In *Recreating Japanese Women, 1600–1945*. Gail L. Bernstein, ed. pp. 17–42. Berkeley: University of California Press.

Valignano, Alessandro 1590 *De Missione Legatorum Iaponen*. Trans. Duarte de Sande. Macao [Lima Library Collection].

Valignano, Alessandro 1601 Libro Primero del Principio y progresso de la religion christiana en japon [Ms. British Museum Add. Mss. 9857].

Valignano, Alessandro 1944 [1601] *Historia del Principio y Progresso de la Compañia de Jesus en las Indias Orientales*. Josef Wicki, S.J., ed. Rome: Jesuit Historical Institute.

Valignano, Alessandro 1946 *Il cerimoniale per I missionary del Giappone*. Josef Franz Schütte, S.J., ed. Rome: Edizioni Di Storia e Lettteratura.

Valignano, Alessandro 1954 *Sumario de Las Cosas de Japon (1583), Adiciones del Sumario de Japon* (1592). José Luis Alvarez-Taladriz, ed. Tokyo: Sophia University

Van der Wee, Herman 1977 "Money, Credit, and Banking Systems." In *The Cambridge Economic History of Europe, Volume 5:The Economic Organization of Early Modern Europe*. Edwin Ernest Rich, Charles Henry Wilson, Michael Moïssey Postan, Peter Mathias, eds. pp. 290–394. Cambridge: Cambridge University Press.

Varley, H. Paul 2001 "Law and Precepts for the Warrior Houses." In *Sources of Japanese Tradition, Second Edition, Volume One: From Earliest Times to 1600*. Wm. Theodore de Bary, Donald Keene, George Tanabe, and Paul Varley, eds. pp. 413–433. New York: Columbia University Press.

Varley, H. Paul, and George Elison 1981 "The Culture of Tea: From its Origins to Sen no Rikyû." In *Warlords, Artists, and Commoners: Japan in the Sixteenth Century*. George Elison and Bardwell L. Smith, eds. pp. 187–223. Honolulu: The University of Hawaii Press.

Vicente, Gil 1995 [1562] *Auto da Barca da Glória, Nao d'Amores*. Maria I. Resina Rodrigues, ed. Madrid: Clásicos Castalia.

Vieira de Castro, Filipe 2005 *The Pepper Wreck: A Portuguese Indiaman at the Mouth of the Tagus River*. College Station: Texas A&M University Press.

Visser, Margaret 1991 *Rituals of Dinner: The Origins, Evolution, Eccentricities, and Meaning of Table Manners*. New York: Grove Press.

Vogel, Ezra 1980 *Japan As Number One: Lessons for America*. New York: HarperCollins.

Von Drachenfels, Suzanne 2000 *The Art of the Table*. New York: Simon & Schuster.

Von Siebold, Phillip Franz 1973 [1841] *Manners and Customs of the Japanese in the Nineteenth Century*. Rutland, VT: Charles E. Tuttle Company.

Waley-Cohen, Joanna 2007 "The Quest for Perfect Balance, Taste and Gastronomy in Imprial China." In *Food: The History of Taste*. Paul Freedman, ed. pp. 99–132. Berkeley: University of California Press.

Walker, Brett 2004 "Epidemic Disease, Medicine, and the Shifting Ecology of Ezo." In *Race, Ethnicity and Migration in Modern Japan*. Michel Weiner, ed. pp. 397–424. London: Routledge.

Walthall, Anne 1991 "The Life Cycle of Farm Women in Tokugawa Japan." In *Recreating Japanese Women, 1600–1945*. Gail Lee Bernstein, ed. pp. 42–70. Berkeley: University of California Press.

Watanabe, Tsuneo and Jun'ichi Iwata 1989 *The Love of the Samurai: A Thousand Years of Japanese Homosexuality*. Trans. D.R. Roberts. London: Gay Men's Press.

Watsuji Tetsurô 1963 [1935] *Fūdo : ningengakuteki kōsatsu*. Tôkyô: Iwanami Shoten.

Wear, Andrew 2000 *Knowledge and Practice in English Medicine, 1550–1680*. Cambridge: Cambridge University Press.

Weber, Alison 1990 *Teresa of Avila and the Rhetoric of Femininity*. Princeton: Princeton University Press.

Webster, Charles 1979 *Health, Medicine, and Mortality in the Sixteenth Century*. Cambridge: Cambridge University Press.

Wheaton, Barbara K. 1983 Savoring the Past, The French Kitchen and Table from 1300 to 1789. Philadelphia: University of Pennsylvania Press.

Wicki, Joseph, S.J. 1956 *Documenta Indica IV (1557–1560)*. Rome: Monumenta Historica Soc. Iesu.

Wiesner-Hanks, Merry E. 2008 *Women and Gender in Early Modern Europe*. Cambridge: Cambridge University Press.

Wilson, Bronwen 2005 *The World in Venice: Print, the City, and Early Modern Identity*. Toronto: University of Toronto Press.

Winius, George D. 2001 *Studies On Portuguese Asia, 1495–1689*. Burlington, VT: Ashgate.

Wiss, J., and Sons Co. 1948 *A Story of Shears and Scissors*. Newark: J. Wiss & Company.

Wolff, Larry 2007 "Discovering Cultural Perspective: The Intellectual History of Anthropological Thought in the Age of Enlightenment." In *The Anthropology of the Enlightenment*. Larry Wolf and Marco Cipolloni, eds. pp. 3–33. Stanford: Stanford University Press.

Woods-Marsden, Joanna 1998 *Renaissance Self-Portraiture: The Visual Construction of Identity and the Social Status of the Artist*. New Haven: Yale University Press.

Wynbrandt, James 1998 *The Excruciating History of Dentistry*. New York: St. Martin's Press.

Xinnong, Cheng, ed. 1999 *Chinese Acupuncture and Moxibustion*. Beijing: Foreign Language Press.

Yonemoto, Marcia 2003 *Mapping Early Modern Japan*. Berkeley: University of California Press.

Zupanov, Ines G. 1999 *Disputed Mission: Jesuit Experiments and Brahmanical Knowledge in Seventeenth-Century India*. Oxford: Oxford University Press.

Index

halberds, 152; helmets, 155–6; knife, 149, 150; long bow, 148; lances, 151; *naginata*, 152; military divisions, 157; military ranks, 156–7; military salaries, 157; military service, 87; military, and musical instruments, 156; shields, 154; *shinge-to-shumi*, 153; *tsukuridachi*, 149; *wakizashi*, 148; warfare and crops, 158; warfare and pack animals, 158; warfare on horseback, 157; *wari-kôgai*, 150; *yari*, 151. *See also* swords
waste, 205–6. *See also* defecation
Watsuji, Tetsurō, 212, 213
witch craze, 108

whittling, 151
women. *See* gender, feminine; clothing, women's
writing, 183–93; between the lines, 188; instruments, 185–6, 191–3. *See also* letters

Xavier, Francis, xxi, 97, 99, 104, 117, 184, 248

Yi Sun, Admiral, 221

Zeami, 229, 230. *See also Nô*
Zebras, 170. *See also* horses